Two Eagles in the Sun

A Guide to U.S. Hispanic Culture

Richard C. Campbell

Revised Edition

Two Eagles in the Sun
A Guide to U.S. Hispanic Culture

Published by:
Two Eagles Press International®
1029 Hickory Drive
P.O. Box 208
Las Cruces, NM 88004 USA
505-523-7911
FAX 505-523-1953
TwoEaglesPress@AOL.com
www.twoeaglespress.com

Cover design, layout, and illustration by Paul E. Huntsberger, unless other-wise attributed. Drawings by Gabriel Sánchez, photos by Richard Campbell, and reproduced art by Hal Marcus and José Cisneros acknowledged in the text.

Printed and bound in the U.S.A.

Library of Congress Catalog Control Number 2002 141700

ISBN 1-884512-75-5 : $19.95

Table of Contents

Foreword 1st Edition
Joe Olvera—Freelance journalist, creative writer, columnist

The best part of Richard Campbell's book is that he doesn't miss a trick when it comes to writing about the cultural traditions of Mexicans in the United States. His book is concise, precise, and an invaluable addition in providing knowledge for those people who may want to know more about these people, otherwise known as Mexican Americans or Chicanos.

Campbell has an excellent grasp of Mexican, Mexican American, and Chicano culture and, more importantly, he understands the nuances among the three groups, who are supposed to be the same but who, in reality, are not.

Campbell says in his preface that he wrote his book for his fellow Anglos so that they can understand the "immense sociological changes across America." He wants Anglos to understand Mexican Hispanics in the Southwest and he writes with both detachment and with passion. But he does accept his limitations.

Told by a friend that he is more Mexican than Anglo, Campbell puts his philosophy in perspective: "It's not correct, of course, that I am Mexican. I am Anglo. I can never feel all that Hispanics feel. I do not understand subtle nuances of their culture."

What a trickster Campbell is. I beg to differ with him because he certainly understands more than he's letting on, or that he's willing to admit, perhaps out of modesty. Campbell's book is a potpourri of facts, observations and explanations. He covers the gamut of Mexican, Mexican American, and Chicano cultural realities.

Campbell's book will open some eyes, as it has opened mine. Some of the things Campbell writes about, even I didn't know. And I have done extensive research into my own people's history. But I guess it took someone like Campbell, who sees things in a different light, to write this book.

Richard Campbell has written and compiled a most valuable work, one in which even the most die-hard Chicano will take pleasure. Campbell's book teaches, it educates and it makes Mexican Hispanics understand themselves a little bit better. For the Anglo who wants to learn more about the Mexican Hispanics, Campbell's book will prove an invaluable resource.

Read this book, understand it, study it and, most important, have fun with it, because it's an accurate portrayal of the many cultural realities which color a Mexican Hispanic's life in the Southwest.

Foreword 2nd Edition

Adair Margo—Owner, Adair Margo Gallery; Chairman, President's Committee on the Arts and Humanities

My first introduction to *Two Eagles in the Sun* came after a presentation I made on El Paso's murals. While showing slides of vibrant outdoor paintings, the image of a mural entitled *Entelequía* flashed on the screen. The meaning of the word escaped me and I continued my remarks. Before leaving, an intelligent, unassuming man thanked me for sharing my appreciation of border art and he introduced himself as Richard Campbell. The next morning, a copy of his book was on my desk and, when I opened it to the page marked, there was the image of *Entelequía* with the derivation of the word going back to Aristotle! (See page 72)

In perusing the book, I was fascinated by the breadth of subjects covered in a distilled and easy format, a mini-encyclopedia on Hispanic culture. Not only did it respond to the question raised the day before, but it also answered other questions I had never thought to ask about my own border experience—the everyday details that, if we pay attention, enrich and deepen our lives.

Hispanics and Anglos have lived with mutual respect for many years along our border. The renowned El Paso artist Tom Lea wrote beautifully about our co-existence:

> It has always seemed to me that I was fortunate in being born on the border in a town where two nations and two people meet, where more than one mode of life and one mode of thought are in constant confrontation, to test and to broaden and to deepen one's view of the world. At El Paso del Norte I believe men are reminded daily that human beings do not all speak one tongue, all share in one fine set of aims and ideals, all conform to one established pattern of conduct, or all accept one definition of the good life or the bad or the purpose in it.

As a transplant from Michigan to the southwest, Richard Campbell shares his experiences with Hispanics "through Anglo eyes" in an entertaining and accessible way. This book demonstrates how Hispanic influences are contributing to the texture and strength of America.

Preface—
How It Began and Continued

How it began. It was a New World we looked upon in 1961 when we Michiganders stepped off the train at isolated Lamy, New Mexico. We were introduced to charming Santa Fe, then fascinating Española, Santa Cruz, and Chimayó. But were we still in the United States? We felt nothing repulsive, but the setting was so completely different from Michigan. The winding, narrow roads. Few street signs (in those days). Historic plaza and church. Sweet aromas from nighttime fireplace burnings (someone called it *piñon*). Irrigation ditches. Exotic place names. Red something-or-other hanging on adobe house walls. Well, we chose to live there for the next sixteen and a half years. Later, in 1978, El Paso became home.

How it continued. During these decades, I have become close to Spanish Americans, Costa Ricans, Mexicans, Mexican Americans, Latinos, and Chicanos. I have felt heart-to-heart with children, youth, and adults in church, school, and community center. I have done language study in Guadalajara, Mexico, and San José, Costa Rica, and acquired a bit of Spanish fluency. Travel has taken me to Mexico, El Salvador, Honduras, Costa Rica, Guatemala, Panama, Ecuador, Peru, Argentina, and Brazil. My son-in-law was born in Mexico, making four of my grandchildren half Mexican. A personal memory fits here. One day at school I was enjoying a chat with a returning student from Mexico. While discussing something that an Anglo person had said to him that morning, I reminded the youth that I was Anglo. He exclaimed with some humor but more seriousness, "Oh, you're Mexican!" I considered that a compliment.

Now decades after Lamy, New Mexico, and after so many experiences in other places, too, I have the temerity to write a book about Hispanic culture as seen through my Anglo eyes, even doing a second edition.

So why would an Anglo write about Hispanics? I have wanted to share these four decades of experience in and enjoyment of Hispanic culture and people and thus to contribute something to their deeper view of America—one nation under God, *diverse and* indivisible, with liberty and justice for all.

And what would an Anglo get from this book? They can use the book to relate more understandingly to Hispanic family members, neighbors, friends, co-workers, fellow church and club members, associates in community affairs, strangers on the street or in a restaurant, and, certainly, in travel.

But why would Hispanics have any interest in the book? Beyond what many know already, to learn even more about who they are, to affirm their heritage, and to give a tool for sharing that heritage with their children who often are disconnected from their roots.

A disclaimer. I do not write as an expert. Obviously, I am not Hispanic. I am a northern European-Anglo American. I cannot pretend to feel all that Hispanics feel from their history and in today's society, to catch subtle nuances of their culture and language. But neither am I the same Anglo who left Michigan in 1961. So maybe after all I am not totally Anglo, strange as that might sound. Some acculturation has taken place. My credentials, then, are those experiences and learnings. And after writing this book, I have felt affirmed and gratified by responses from Hispanics and Anglos alike.

Almost a new book. Although I am an unknown author, this book has gone through two printings since 1995. All copies have been sold, and a second edition has become necessary as orders continue to arrive. Many errors have been corrected, style polished, and some sections omitted. Most of all, dramatic changes in the Hispanic community over the past decade have been recorded. Considerable and fascinating new information has been added. Puerto Rico and Cuba are spotlighted. Consequently, this edition is no mere rehash of the first. In many ways, this is not the same book.

My deep thanks. Books do not drop out of the sky. Many people have assisted me, and to them I express my gratitude. I begin by thanking my wife Pat for her endless patience, helpful advice, and constant encouragement. There are so many other helpful persons, also, in ways large and small: Mary Ann Plaut, Dale Walker, Gabriel Sánchez, José Cisneros, Texas Western Press, Hal Marcus, Joe Olvera, Jeff Danziger, Mary Ann and Carlos Romero, Armijo Branch Library, El Paso Association for the Performing Arts, Dr. Charles Hawkins, Dr. M. Lawrence Ellzey Jr., Dr. Lorenzo LaFarelle, grandson Nicholas Ashby and his friend Nathaniel Morris, Alex Apostolides, Flora Sanford, Julie Gallegos, Gloria Estrada, Randy Limbird, José Luis García, Dr. Bill Martin, Bea Martin, Andrew Martin, Paul Ashby, Lucinda Ashby McEvilly, Dr. Perseu dos Santos, and Dr. Paul Huntsberger (my publisher).

My dedications. Finally, I dedicated the first edition to the following persons because they let me enter into their culture and lives: the many dear friends in New Mexico's Española Valley, my former students during fourteen years at Lydia Patterson Institute, and the boys since 1994 in *Los Duros* at Houchen Community Center. To all of them, *muchísimas gracias siempre.*

Now it is my honor to dedicate this second edition to the Santoscoy family in Guadalajara, Mexico, for their extra-mile hospitality during language study at Butler Institute in that summer month of 1969. I dedicate this edition also to the Cabezas family in Cartago, Costa Rica, for providing me a door into their language and culture and for making us a part of their *familia.*

Just in case I never publish another book, I want to make an additional dedication: to my wife, soul mate, and best friend Pat; to our six children and their spouses who make us so proud; and to the eleven beautiful grandchildren who are a special joy. They all make me an extremely rich person.

❙ Richard C. Campbell, El Paso, Texas, December 2002

Prologue—
Some Thoughts to Begin Our Journey

Several observations arise as we begin this look at cultures in modern America. The most obvious observation is the surprising growth rate of many different cultures. America is not homogenous. People from every place on the globe are changing the sights and sounds and smells of our land. Since the beginning of our history and long thereafter, most Americans have thought of themselves as one ethnic people. The image of "melting pot" is almost sacred. Actually, that term is rather modern, coined in 1908 and entering *Webster's Dictionary* only in 1934. From the beginning of our nation, statistically, fully three out of five Americans in 1790 were not of English origin. Nevertheless, a dominant culture did develop after 1790, often described as WASP (white, Anglo-Saxon, Protestant).

Not today! Western European Americans are observing in their own cities and even rural areas a flood of colors and customs from other nations. One of those growing cultures is Hispanic. Its growth was depicted by Isidro Lucas as "the browning of America." In this twenty-first century, Hispanics are the largest ethnic "minority" group in the country, and all minorities together are close to becoming a majority.

A further observation is that many Whites are often indifferent to or, in some cases, outright hostile to other cultures. For example, in contrast to multi-lingual proficiency in much of the world, Roger Axtell remarks that "most of the English-speaking world remains as cheerfully monolingual as Queen Victoria's parakeet." Often, in Letters to the Editor in a typical daily newspaper, one reads complaints about "too much Spanish" or "too many Mexicans." Fear is almost palpable. Dire warnings surface about tribalism, Balkanization, "Quebecization," and pollution of American culture. The sociological change, of course, does have its problems; but more on that later.

A third thought is that many non-Hispanics today *do* want to understand their Hispanic fellow citizens, neighbors, friends, and even family. Today's youth, who commonly accept diversity far better than some of their elders, are eager to understand the society in which they live. This book can be a tool to help in that understanding. Realize, though, that

Hispanic culture is in no way a monolithic structure. The varieties are endless. This book's material will focus on what is generic in American Hispanic life, then on the Mexican, Puerto Rican, and Cuban influences. Clearly, the material on Mexican influence predominates. That fact shows no narrow prejudice but only the limits of the author's experience. But adding something on Puerto Rico, Cuba, and a brief section on the Dominican Republic was an attempt to make the story more complete.

With this introduction behind us, let us now begin our journey, reminding ourselves that exploring other cultures can be one of life's most satisfying delights. Many will discover that this journey, once begun, never really ends.

Hispanics in the United States— Looking for a Name

What Name Should We Use?

Paul Engle wrote about "old names worn water-smooth under the tongue." That, to be sure, is not our problem in examining a variety of terms commonly used to refer to the fastest growing culture in our nation. What do we call these citizens? What do they call themselves? Hispanic, Hispano, Spanish American, Latino/a, Chicano/a, *la raza,* Mexican American, Puerto Rican American, or Cuban American? What about others from the Caribbean or Central and South America?

Why Is an Answer So Difficult?

On one hand, people in this culture descend from forebears in Spain as well as from pre-Colombian indigenous civilizations in the Americas. These two streams came together to flow into a new cultural current, a *mestizo* current, that is, a mixed race and culture. History and the Spanish language are common bonds.

On the other hand, the culture is not homogeneous. Rather, it is a mosaic composed of vividly different shapes and colors. Columnist Roger Hernandez, while extolling the Hispanic impact on America, goes on to show the diversity. Some Hispanics are white and "have no ethnic profile at all," like former rock star Jerry Garcia. Others in this culture have "some cultural distinctiveness," but no more so than a third-generation Italian or Greek. Others are assimilated, but they still treasure their cultural heritage and are both bicultural and bilingual. Hernandez himself belongs in this category; yet, he says, the children and grandchildren will likely become thoroughly assimilated.

Very visible are the recent immigrants "who are culturally and linguistically lost." Other immigrants have lived here for a generation or more and know just enough English to function in this society. Last of all, from a different angle, persons with dark black or brown skin in any of the above categories confront racial prejudices in this country and are often labeled as African Americans.

Beyond all of this multiplicity, we have immigrants from Mexico,

1

Puerto Rico, Cuba, the Caribbean, and Central or South America. Others trace their ancestry to settlers in what is now the U.S. as far back as the 16th century Spanish Conquest. Some speak only Spanish, English and Spanish, or only English. Some have just crossed the border, legally or illegally; others are American citizens or are acquiring citizenship. Some individuals have Spanish names, others do not.

Why Is the Term "Hispanic" More and More Accepted?

The umbrella term that gradually has gained general though not total acceptance is "Hispanic." According to Ellyn Ferguson, the term comes from *España* (Spain) or the Roman name *Hispania* given to the Spanish-Portuguese peninsula. The word Hispanic appeared in the '70s during the Nixon Administration, entered the 1980 Census as a test on five to ten percent of the forms, and incorporated on all forms in the 1990 Census. This designation, as with those of other ethnic and racial terms, provides statistics for study of social and economic conditions, for enforcing civil rights laws on job discrimination, and for shaping federal policies.

Mike Davis quotes Neil Foley who says that the term "is partially to acknowledge one's 'whiteness'…, whiteness with a twist of salsa…." Jeoffrey Fox, however, thinks the term emphasizes Spanish-language heritage with no racial connotations. The late world-renowned Mexican writer Octavio Paz put his blessing on the word by declaring that "…the most common term, Hispanics, covers all of them in their complex unity."

Hispanics sometimes feel offended when referred to as Hispanic. One such person is the author and poet Sandra Cisneros. She accepts Latina, *Chicana, Tejana,* or Mexican American, but she will not even allow her photograph on the cover of *Hispanic Magazine.* These persons resent the word's origins in government bureaucracy and the absence of indigenous roots. The term Indohispanic has been tried with little enthusiastic support. Cisneros calls Hispanic disrespectful, colonistic, imposed, and destructive of Latino identity—much like corralling all Anglos (Irish, Polish, Greek, Lithuanian, and English) and calling them Englishers. In any case, Hispanics in this country normally prefer to identify themselves as Mexican, Cuban, or Puerto Rican rather than Hispanic or Latino, or they are just American.

Anglos on the whole feel comfortable with Hispanic. They see the cultural unity in a people rather than the diversity. That is to say, they see that Hispanics are different but they definitely are not Asian, northern European, or continental African.

One poll in 2000 by *Hispanic Trends, Inc.,* discovered that 65 percent of Hispanics preferred Hispanic, and 30 percent favored Latino. Results showed the same outcome in Texas with 67 percent and 52 percent in California and New York. Raul Yzaguire, president of the National Council of La Raza, provides another point of view. He thinks that the use of the term Hispanic supports American unity among various Spanish-speaking groups. An immigrant senses that he/she is no longer Nicaraguan, Mexican, or Colombian but belongs to a new grouping, Hispanic. As quoted by Himilce Novas, that feeling encourages assimilation, "the first American word that applies to him or her." Perhaps this last poll indicates a gradual shift in the term Hispanics are using to refer to themselves.

Mike Davis summarizes the situation this way: "There is no current, consensual term that adequately reflects the fusion of Iberian, African and Indian origins shared by so many tens of millions." Since the debate will probably never be resolved, many Hispanics favor Carlos Guerra's advice to anyone who wants to label him: "Carlos Guerra is fine, thank you." As far as this book is concerned, in the absence of any true orthodoxy, for better or worse, Hispanic will be the choice of wording.

What Is the Next Most Common Term?

A very common alternative to "Hispanic" is "Latino/a." Etymologically, the word refers to the culture of Rome and its Latin language. Rome's expansion reached France, Portugal, and Spain and from there to Mexico, Puerto Rico, Cuba in the Caribbean, and Central and South America. Roger Hernandez suggests that the term embraces Brazil's Portuguese speakers and Haiti's French speakers.

According to Ilan Stavans, Hispanic is favored by conservatives. It seems to fit when used with demographics, education, urban development, drugs, or health. Latino seems to be the liberal term, used by intellectuals, artists, musicians, and movie stars. The term reflects the heritage of Roman law and Romance languages. Yet, some ask, "What is Latin about Latin America?" The media in large urban centers are favoring the term *hispano* (shortened form of the adjective *hispanico*).

Ilan Stavans contends that Latinos prefer the use of Latino by Anglos. Joe Olvera, however, sees Hispanic as a convenient umbrella word invented by Anglo government and used widely by the media; he seems fairly comfortable with it. The National Council of La Raza sees Latino more popular in California, New York, and Chicago, while Hispanic or Mexican American is favored in Texas and New Mexico (but it is important to use Spanish American in north central New Mexico). La Raza uses Hispanic and Latino interchangeably. Both Hispanic and Latino, however, fail to express indigenous roots.

Who Are Anglos?

The word "Anglo" in the U.S. Southwest refers to white, English-speaking Americans. The term, according to Nakayama and Martin (1999), can include a number of ethnically distinct groups. In Canada the word is used with some contempt by French-Canadians against the English-speaking population. Some Hispanics probably use the word "Anglo" similarly.

But non-Hispanics, referring to themselves, are not in agreement either. Many of European descent but not from Great Britain cannot possibly think of themselves as Anglos, or English. Maribeth Bandas, a Latina also with Irish blood, sputters that "Anglo is to Celtic what Cortés is to Moctezuma." In fact, Anglos themselves, in one poll, prefer terms like "White," "Caucasian," "White American," or "European American."

In this debate unanimity will never be achieved. Therefore, in the absence of any true orthodoxy, for better or worse, Anglo will be the choice of wording in this book.

Who Are Caucasians?

Although the word no longer has a scientific use, it still appears commonly in referring to people with white or light skin color and straight to wavy hair. The point here is that Spaniards are as Caucasian as the British or Dutch.

What Does *Gringo* Mean?

Carey McWilliams believes that *gringo* comes from the song, "Green Grow the Rushes, O!," sung in 1846 by American soldiers invading Mexico. Marcienne Rocard finds origins in *The New English Dictionary* of 1884, taking the word from the Greek *griego*, a Mexican nickname for foreigner, especially Americans. *Hablar en griego* is something like "It's all Greek." A third theory suggests that during the Mexican War the Yankee "green coats" became *gringos* in Mexican speech.

Among Hispanic and Anglo friends, *gringo* can be heard in harmless and playful banter. In general conversation or publications, the word can be relatively innocent. It can also be strongly negative. Chicano leader José Angel Gutiérrez years ago described the term as "an attitude," much as blacks use white or honky—defined by Rocard as "paternalistic, ethnocentric, xenophobic." So, what *gringo* means depends on the situation and the speaker.

What Is the Origin of the Word *Chicano*?

Some Mexican Hispanics—usually young activists or activist academics—and Mexican Americans who feel strongly about their Aztec and

Mexican roots and sense the disparity between the *barrio* and the larger non-Hispanic society use this important word.

Rafaela Castro presents three theories on the origins of *Chicano.*

1. In *Náhuatl* (the Spanish spelling of the language of the Aztecs), a *meshicano* was an inhabitant of Mexico (with *Náhuatl* pronunciation of the *x* as *sh,* as in *Méshico).* The Spanish changed the *sh* sound to *chi* (still with a soft *sh* sound), thus *meshicano,* which went from *mechicano* to *Chicano.*

2. With the word's origin in Chihuahua, the *chi* from the city's name was combined with the *cano* of *Mexicano* and eventually to *Chicano.*

3. When Anglo Americans moved into the Southwest, Mexicans were given the name *chico,* like "kid" for Americans, then added *ano* from *Mexicano* to form *Chicano.*

Whatever the linguistic root, *chicano* is seldom used in Mexico itself.

What Is the Modern History of the Word *Chicano?*

Marcienne Rocard explains that the word appeared originally in the early 1930s in writings of sociologist Manuel Gamio. The term was applied to new, unskilled immigrants who were called *cholos* or *chicanos.* During the "zoot suit" riots in the forties, the word surfaced again and appeared also in a short story by Mario Suárez as a synonym for *mexicano.* In the late 1960s, student groups in southern California and the Raza Unida Party started using *chicano.* The Mexican-American Law Students Association changed its name to Chicano Law Students Association. Most of all, **Rodolfo ("Corky") Gonzales** used the word for the Chicano Youth Liberation Conference in 1969 in Denver. He used the word particularly for young *barrio* activists. Pride in heritage centered on Mexican indigenous roots and on images of emotional or actual separation from American culture. The central image was the story of *Aztlán.*

How Did the Concept of *Aztlán* Become a *Chicano* Symbol?

In March of 1969, "Corky" Gonzales, Chicano activist in Denver, called a youth convention that drafted a manifesto, *el Plan Espiritual de Aztlán (The Spiritual Plan of Aztlán).* This name *Aztlán* was the mythical Aztec place of origin, northwest of present-day Mexico City. From there, around 1100 A.D./C.E., the ancestors migrated to Tenochtitlán on which site the present capital is built. This name *Aztlán* became a common symbol in the *chicano* literature. The manifesto called for expelling the Anglo and forming a *chicano* nation above the Río Grande. For some, *Aztlán* was a call to violence. Probably for most it was a spiritual vision of a new society of love and justice, a dream given form with that word from the mythical past.

What Does the Term *Chicano/a* Mean Today?

Today the stridency of the '60s and '70s is largely muted. Yet, the word *chicano* still serves as an emotional focus, observes Rocard, just as "soul" does for African Americans. According to Isidro Lucas, the word fuses pride in Spanish and indigenous heritage contained in the concept of *la raza* (the race), dissatisfaction with unresolved pain in the Hispanic community, and determination to work within the system to make things different. At the same time, many Mexican Americans dislike *chicano* because the word is too hostile and divisive. For them, the term Mexican American feels more comfortable.

Many Anglos would appreciate the statement in 1971 by Abelardo Delgado, who included in the concept of *chicanismo* even "a few Anglos whose *tequilic* hearts are in the right place," Anglos who might not have all the *chicano* feelings but who share "our dreams and our *causa*."

Are Other Terms Also Used?

Following the war with Mexico in the mid-1800s, the 100,000 Mexicans who chose to remain in former Mexican territory were called "Mexicans," though now they were American citizens. After the census of 1940 they became "Spanish-Speaking Whites." During the 1950s, '60s and '70s, usage favored Spanish-Surnamed Whites. All the while, both Anglos and Spanish-speaking people generally used Mexican for those poor and dark but used Spaniard or Hispanic-American for those of lighter skin, more affluent, and of direct descent from colonists and *conquistadores* from Spain. In the 1920s in New Mexico, long-established families, resenting new immigrants from Mexico, began using Spanish-American. Likewise in the '20s in Texas, New Mexico, and Colorado, "Latin-Americans" came into use. After 1960, militants in the *barrios* (Mexican neighborhoods) around the United States, especially in southern California, introduced "Mexican-American." Later the use of the hyphen was criticized as a symbol of inferior status.

Why Does the Term "Mexican" Bother Some Mexican Americans?

"Mexican" has long had a negative connotation among many Northern European Americans, and Mexican-origin people began to understand the feeling very quickly. So they searched for a label that could "whiten" and "Europeanize" them and thus raise their social status (in Oscar Martínez's phrase). "Spanish" and "Latin" and later "Hispanic" became popular. Furthermore, as thousands and thousands of poor and illiterate Mexicans poured into the country after 1910 and into the 1920s, European Americans began classifying all Mexicans alike, both citizens and immigrants, as "alien, ignorant, and downtrodden."

What Does the Term *la Raza* Signify?

In 1925 José Vasconcelos, Mexican educator and thinker, wrote his visionary tome, *La raza cósmica* (*The Cosmic Race*). His general theme was that Spanish America had the opportunity to become that rich blending of all the world's races, and to lead the entire world in achieving "the creation of a race (*una raza*) constructed with the treasure of all those before us, the final race, the universal race (*la raza cósmica*)." The term today coalesces the past with its pride of heritage and the future vision of a world more human. Thoughtful Hispanics feel an inward sense of a people being born, "a people marching toward the future that has already begun," in the words of Virgilio Elizondo. As such, he continues, the Mexican American could help eliminate the stereotypes that Anglos and Latin Americans have of each other and could be the bridge for bringing greater unity to the two Americas. Andrés Guerrero points out that in English the word race brings to mind color, but *la raza* has no such implication. Instead, *raza* judges on the basis of *corazón* (heart).

Rafael Castro says *la raza* is a vibrant term in Latin America. Instead of Columbus Day as in the U.S., the day is *Día de la Raza* (Day of the Race, or Hispanic people). That usage occurs in the U.S. among Chicanos, Puerto Ricans in New York City, and Cubans in Miami. But why *la raza?* Hispanic roots penetrate the soil of two cultures: (1) Spain with its own rich amalgamation of Iberian, Roman, Greek, Jewish, Celtic, Germanic, and Arab cultures, and (2) Amerindian civilizations like the Incas in Peru, other tribes throughout South America, tribes in Central America, and the Mayas, Olmecs, Zapotecs, Mixtecas, Toltecs and Aztecas in Guatemala and Mexico. Add to this mixture African and Asian influences, the profound impact of the French during their conquest in the mid-1800s, and the pervasive impact of American culture across the decades. One can begin to see the rich variety that goes into the concept of *la raza*. The coming together of three racial and cultural currents has produced a Latin American culture called *mestizo,* or a mixed culture.

Who Is a *Pachuco?*

In the '40s and '50s, Mexican American youth expressed their rebellion

against Anglo society by exhibiting a distinctive style of clothes, haircut, and walk.
The *pachuco* was showing his pride, violence, independence, and protest against
racial discrimination. Octavio Paz,
Mexico's famous writer, sees the
pachuco with this unconquerable
determination to be different, yet as a
victim gaining recognition and
becoming a part of the very society
being defied. In any case, these

Pachucos—Gabriel Sánchez

young *barrio* men could be identified by their long hair and a long
chain dangling down narrow cuffed pants, along with a distinctive kind
of swagger when they walked.

Rafael Castro adds that besides the *pachuco's* appearance, their lingo
(*chicano* slang, *pochismos*, *chicano* Spanglish) sets them apart. El Paso
and Cd. Juárez youth began this lifestyle in the 1920s and '30s. The word
pachuco is a possible slang reference to El Paso, from which El Paso's
nickname is derived, *El Chuko*. When some El Paso youth settled in Los
Angeles in the 1940s, they became known as a gang with a distinct subculture. When they settled elsewhere in the Southwest, they spread the
pachuco way.

What Are Some Other Terms That Are Helpful to Know?

- *Cholo*: A Mexican American term for some *barrio* youth who mimic
  yesterday's pachucos, persons whom John West calls "stompers."
- *Gabacho* (also spelled *gavacho*) or *gabardonos:* Americans. The
  word has a negative connotation.
- *Güero:* Like "whitey" or "blondie," often used for *gringo*.
- *Norteamericanos,* or *estadounidenses:* North Americans, United
  States-ers, Americans.
- *Pocho:* Rafael Castro defines the word *pocho* as culturally half
  Mexican. The person has Mexican background but was born and
  reared in the U.S., is culturally half American, and is less than fluent
  in Spanish. In other words, the person is partially anglicized. A web
  site named *Pocho Magazine* describes the Southwest as *Pocholandia*.
  In Mexico the word has a satirical tone. In the U.S., Chicanos sometimes use the word with a self-deprecating sense of survival in a prejudiced society. English words rendered in Spanish are called *pochismos* or *fronterazos* (see "Anglicisms" in Chapter Three).

■ *Wetback:* A Mexican citizen who entered the U.S. with no legal papers, also called *mojado.* In Spanish the word *mojado* means wet, the image of a water-soaked person who swims or wades across the Río Grande to come to this country. The politically correct term now is "undocumented" (*indocumentado).*

What Terms Are Used for
Chicanos Who Become More Like Anglos?
Some Chicanos will use the word *agringado* (anglicized), in teasing or even in criticism, for a family member or friend who changes a Spanish name to English (such as Carlos to Charlie), speaks mostly in English, and marries an Anglo woman. Other terms used are *inglesado* or *americanizado* (Englishized or Americanized) and *agavachado* (like *gavacho,* or an Anglo). But *agringado,* says Rafaela Castro, is particularly strong because of negative connotations with the word *gringo.*

What Are Two Identifying Names Used in Puerto Rico?
■ *Borinquén* is the name Puerto Ricans use for their island. The word means "land of the brave lord," from the word the original *Taínos* used. A *Puertorriqueño/a* (Puerto Rican) is called a *Boricua* or a *Boriqueño/ña.*
■ *Jíbaro* is a Puerto Rican name for a machete-wielding field worker who, in earlier years, was the backbone of the Puerto Rican agricultural economy. Today, the word is a synonym for "hick."

What Are Two Identifying Names Used in Cuba and the U.S.?
■ *Gusano,* meaning worm in Spanish, is the name Castro Cubans give Cuban exiles in the U.S. Himilce Novas informs us that some Latinos in the U.S. use the term for Cuban Americans, at times for fun.
■ *Yuca,* from *yuca* (yucca,) a fibrous tuber, a cassava, and a mainstay of Cuban meals, has an adapted, modern meaning. As *yuca* the word means a Cuban yuppie, i.e., a young, upwardly mobile Cuban American, usually very acculturated.
■ *Habanero,* a *cubano* (Cuban) from Havana, the capital.

Hispanic Roots—
Bloodstream & Footprints

What Does a Hispanic Person Look Like?

Although many Hispanics have brown skin and black hair, this cannot be assumed. Roger Hernandez remarks that the former president of Peru, Fujimori, was Japanese. A former Chilean president, Patricio Aylwin, had a Welsh name. Argentina's former President Menem had Arab blood. On the streets of a Latin American city or here in the United States, one can find Hispanics with dark complexions but also with light skin and even blond hair. Hispanics exhibit absolutely no one appearance, although a darker complexion is extremely common.

Are Hispanics a Separate Race?

This question is an academic minefield. Anthropologists are in complete disarray in deciding how many races exist, and what they are. Clyde Kluckhohn admits a valid concept of race but fears that clear distinctions are few and too complex for common understanding. Europe alone is an anthropological mishmash. Books and articles often continue to refer simplistically to versions of white, black, yellow, brown, and red races. Anthropologist Victor Barnouw allows Caucasoid (white but including brown Mediterranean types), Negroid (Africans and Melanesians), and Mongoloid (Japanese, Chinese, Eskimos, and American Indians) plus Bushmen of South Africa, Ainu of northern Japan, Australian aborigines, and Polynesians. S.L. Price claims more genetic variants in Africa than anywhere else in the world. Among black Americans, ninety percent have at least some white ancestry. The bottom line, however, is that race is determined by hereditary physical traits, not language, nationality, or religion. No Mexican or Jewish race can be in this definition.

It is true that *Census 2000* for the first time allowed respondents to classify themselves in multiple racial categories, with Tiger Woods as an example of someone Black, Hispanic, and Thai. In Census summaries and in magazine and newspaper articles, "Hispanics" stands equal to Whites, Blacks, Asians, and Native Americans—as if Hispanics were a separate race instead of an ethnic group.

But Hispanics are not a parallel race. Even before the events in the Americas, just through Spanish veins alone flows the blood of ancient Iberians, Phoenicians, Greeks, Carthaginians, Sephardic Jews, Romans, Visigoths, and the North African Moors (Arab-Berber). In other words, the Spanish bloodline is *una mezcla,* a mixture.

In the Americas, the Spanish, the Amerindians, and the Blacks forged a new culture and a physical binding. Edwin E. Sylvest speaks of *mestizaje* (a mixing), a process of cultural and biological blending. "In the flesh and cultures of Hispanic-Americans emerges a new humanity that ... is perfected, not by exclusion, by decrees of *limpieza de sangre* (purity of blood), but by inclusion." In Roger Hernandez's words, "Hispanic immigrants here are white, black, Indian, Asian, of mixed race." Beyond this point, scholars will have to carry on the debate.

What Are the Hispanic's Spanish Roots?
The early *conquistadores* bought to the New World the traditions of Spain's various regions. Himilce Novas credits Castile from the central plateau for the contribution of the official and literary form of the Spanish language. Andalucia on the southern coast produced a lively culture around dance and horses. The people also combined both a Jewish and a Moorish heritage into their own. This area, with the longest Moorish occupation, sent forty percent of the Spanish settlers to America. Galicia, in the northwest corner of Spain and north of Portugal, has a Celtic or Gaelic heritage (complete with bagpipes and kilt) and call themselves *Gallegos,* a common Spanish surname. Towns in the provinces of León, Aragón, and Navarre have names that can be found in the New World. Catalonia, on the northeast coast, bred a fresh and artistic culture; artists Picasso, Dalí, and Miró all came from this province. The Basque provinces have a language unrelated to any other in the world, and its people call themselves Iberians, not Spanish. Nevertheless, Basque names appear in the U.S. Some Basques came to the U.S. around 1900 and settled in Utah and Idaho. In the Spanish Colonial and Mexican periods, they entered California and became leaders in the western sheep industry.

How Was Colonial Mexican Society Organized?
Colonial Mexico's society had rigid divisions that could at the same time be remarkably flexible. The Spaniard from Spain (*peninsulares* and *gachupines*) and the New World Spaniard (*criollos*) were the two original dominant groups, but intermingling of these people with the indigenous population produced in time the fast-growing and eventually dom-

inant social group called *mestizos*. Modern Mexico is essentially a *mesti-zo* society, which holds true, then, for Mexican Americans as well. In any Mexican or Mexican American group, it is easy to see every degree of color from the dark skin of the Mesoamerican to the very light skin of the Spaniard. An explanation comes from the renowned Mexican scholar, writer, and educator, José Vasconcelos, who commented that "while your American grandfathers shot the Indians, ours married them."

Are Hispanics Cousins to the Irish?
Thomas Cahill says that "even the English do not consider the Irish as Anglos," quoting historian Charles Kinsley who called Irish "white chimpanzees." Thus, Ireland's never-ending "Troubles." Around 600 B.C./B.C.E. one branch of Celts settled in Iberia (in Spain's province of Galicia) where one can find bagpipes, ghosts, and goblins to this day. Other branches settled in France (the Gauls), Turkey (Galatians), and Britain (Britons). Britons were pushed by the Angles and Saxons into Wales (Welsh), while Iberians and British Celts reached Ireland by 350 B.C./B.C.E. Few realize how Irish culture served as "the leaven of medieval civilization" as it preserved scholarship during tumultuous centuries in the rest of Europe. Later, Vikings, Normans, and English conquerors crippled that vibrant Irish culture.

Roger Hernandez claims "a kinship between the Hispanic and Irish worlds." He points to Spanish immigration to Latin America by mostly those from Celtic Galicia, to Irish leaders in Latin America's struggle with Spain (O'Higgins in Chile), and to the music style of Galicia reflected in the music of Mexico and Cuba. So, maybe the shamrock and chile are connected.

What Was the Jewish Presence in Spanish History?
After the destruction of Jerusalem in 70 A.D./C.E., many Jews found their way to Spain. These Spanish Jews carry the name of Sephardim, while Jews from elsewhere in Europe are Ashkenazi Jews. In danger of genocide by Germanic tribes who conquered Spain, the Jews invited Muslim Moors from North Africa to rescue them. The Moors took over Spain in 711. Moors and Jews lived together in quiet tolerance. Great Jewish scholars such as Maimonides wrote literature, music, law, biblical studies, and philosophy in Arabic. In the twelfth century, however, fanatical Arabs known as the Almohads took over southern Spain and persecuted the Jews. Many Jews fled to the north where Christian rulers were preparing to reconquer the peninsula. But in time even the Christian rulers fanatically organized the Inquisition and massacred Jews unless

they converted to Christianity. By 1492, King Ferdinand and Queen Isabella had forced the Moors out of Spain. The royals then expelled the unconverted Jews as well. Those expelled Jews went largely to the New World and made an intellectual impact on the new culture that we today call Hispanic.

Where Are the African Roots in Hispanic Culture?
Often obscured in Mexican consciousness, Latin American history was forged out of three cultures, not just two: European, indigenous, and also African cultures. Roberto Rodríguez, Patrisia Gonzales, and Antonia Marta Borrero inform us that *Moor* (North Africa) was synonymous with dark in medieval times, and that Moorish culture impacted Spain for nearly eight centuries. In 1492, **Pedro Alonso Niño** ("The Negro") piloted one of Columbus's ships.

One free black, **Juan Garrido,** came with Cortés, the conqueror of Mexico, and became the first wheat farmer in New Spain and explored Michoacán and Lower California. Most blacks, however, came as slaves. Cortés started that horrible practice, a few hundred a year, until importation became a torrent and reached over 2,000,000 by the early seventeenth century, a record among all the colonies of New Spain. Most slaves in Mexico came from the Congo and Angola. Most were male. Blacks were classified as *bozales* (slaves direct from Africa), *ladinos* (slaves previously in Spain or the Caribbean and functional in Spanish), and *negros criollos* (blacks born in New Spain). *Zambos* (black-Indian) and *mulattos* (black-Spanish) then became the most numerous. Blacks labored in pearl fishing, on sugar plantations, and in mines. Some were artisans, others in charge of Indian laborers. Many were servants of the wealthy and outfitted in ostentatious finery. In some of the top convents in Mexico City, the women slaves outnumbered the nuns. Slave revolts were a constant fear and became reality in 1546, 1570, 1612 (29 blacks hanged), 1646, and 1665.

Miscegenation was common. Black men most often took indigenous women. Spaniards and *criollos* normally took *mulattas* (female mixed black and Spanish). By 1793 there were 369,790 *mulattos* (black Spanish and black Indian), most of whom were free and permitted to mingle in society, eventually intermarrying and mixing with the *mestizos*. By the end of the colonial period all such clear differences of classification had disappeared. If the truth were known, there is probably at least a drop of African blood in most Mexicans and Hispanics. The slaves brought their songs, food, dances, crafts, and religion and wove them permanently into the indigenous and Spanish cultures.

Further evidence can be found in Mexico's later history of famous *mulattos*. **José María Morelos y Pavón** was a leader in Mexico's independence movement. **Vicente Guerrero** became Mexico's second president. **Lázaro Cárdenas** served as President from 1934 to 1940. For the infusion of African bloodlines into Puerto Rico, Cuba and the Dominican Republic, read those sections in "Chapter X."

Are There Even Hispanic Asian Roots?

Of course. One theory sees migrations of Asiatics anytime between 14,000 to 50,000 years ago, across the Bering Strait to Alaska, then down North America to Mexico and South America. Homer Noley, however, claims that recent scholarship questions this long-held view and insists that research has not unearthed enough evidence for the Bering Strait crossing. Noley summarizes: "Nobody knows the origins of the Native Tribes on this continent." Another theory suggests Polynesian voyages. In colonial Mexico, Asians, like Blacks, came usually as slaves, about 600 a year in the seventeenth century. They came from the Philippines, China, Japan, and Portuguese India. Most took Spanish names and mixed with the rest of society.

Furthermore, serious two-way travel occurred with Japan in the sixteenth and seventeenth centuries. The Spanish viceroy in Mexico City sent diplomats to the Japanese shoguns. Franciscan missionaries traveled to win converts in Japan. St. **Felipe de Jesús**, the first Mexican canonized, died in Japan as a martyr in 1597. Likewise, Japanese emissaries visited Mexico City and saw the rich markets available for Japanese trade. But Japan's doors closed to the outside world in 1640, not to be opened again for 200 years. By then Mexico had turned north and east for political and economic relationships.

Will Someone Claim Arab Roots, Too!

Absolutely. Arabian Islam controlled Spain for 781 years and bequeathed its art, architecture, customs, and language. The first evidence is in the ten percent of Spanish vocabulary that has Arabic roots. Here are some examples of Spanish words with Arab roots:

- *acequia:* irrigation ditch.
- *albanil: alwazir*, constructor, builder.
- *alcohol: al-kuhl*, alcohol.
- *álgebra: al-yabra, reducción*, reduction.
- *barrio: barri, afuera*, outside.
- *cifra: zifr, cero*, zero.
- *Guadalajara: wadi-al-hiyara, valle de fortalezas*, valley of forts.

- *jarra: yarra, vasija,* jar.
- *ojalá: wash-Allah, quiera Dios,* God willing.
- *tarifa: ta'rif, lista de precios,* price list.

Beyond language, Emiliano Paz quotes writer Louis Bertrand, who finds three benefits from Arab culture: the idea of the university, art and architecture, and poetry. Lorenzo Lafarelle adds here a zealous protection of women. Bertrand states, however, some negative cultural attitudes: excessive individualism, *machismo,* a tendency toward anarchy (James Michener's term is "tribal fragmentation"), and fatalism.

We do know that the Moor gave Spain a civilization richer and deeper than any other in feudal Europe at that time. Consider Arab mathematics (decimal system, algebra), architecture (inner courtyards, Moorish arch, tile roofs), decorative arts (designed wall and floor tiles), music (guitar, castanet, tambourine), dance *(fandango, flamenco, bolero),* food *(paella),* and medicinal herbs.

Other possible influences can be seen in glasswork, irrigation systems, and coin-giving to beggars. The common Spanish expression, *si Dios quiere* (God willing), could reflect Muslim theology about Allah and determinism. And the phrase *Que será será,* with its patient acceptance of life's hardships as well as joys, could also come from Islamic theology.

Lawrence Roen suggests still more examples of possible Arabic influence in Hispanic life. A salesman in Amman serves coffee and sweet breads and engages in long conversation before talking business. He even defers until the next morning the real business at hand. This pattern is also totally Latin American. Make an appointment in Tunis, and you can count on waiting. In Latin America, too, schedules succumb to the conversation of the moment. The clock is just not relevant. Again, Islamic law is based on common sense and individual circumstances, not inflexible codes and legislation as in the Anglo world. Likewise, Latin American courts can operate where relationships trump rules. In addition, Rosen sees a parallel both in Arabic and Latin American dependence on *mordidas* (bribes) to influence government officials. Or is that just a universal pattern?

Where Can We See Spanish Influence in the United States?

Agriculture. Spanish farmers planted wheat, oats, barley, grapevines, olives, and many fruits. Sheep, cattle, horses, hogs, and fowl came with Oñate's expedition to New Mexico in 1598, from Spanish ranches in northern Mexico, and from Father Kino's work in Arizona. The Spanish taught the use of donkeys and oxen for pulling loads and plowing fields and of horses to carry warriors into battle. Cowboys are direct descendants of Moorish and Spanish cattlemen. Alfalfa was planted in New Mexico and cotton throughout the South via New Orleans. New Orleans was important also for sugar cane imports and the first sugar refinery. The mission gardens in California became the base for that state's agriculture. And one more contribution: the cat!

Architecture. Much of the Southwest was a territory of scarce timber, and the climate offered both hot summers and cold winters. So, a practical building style was developed: *adobe* bricks, earth roofs, and *viga* supports. This has become the Pueblo style for twentieth-century houses, especially in New Mexico. California style reflects Spanish features of patio, projecting balconies, red tile roofs, iron grillwork, carved door panels, tile floors, and stucco walls.

Art. Some of America's best artists, while studying in Paris with French teachers, were influenced by Spanish painters. Some of these were Trumbell, Dannat, Chase, Eakins, Whistler, Henri, Cassatt, and Sargent. In 1989 a nationwide exhibition featured 160 paintings, sculptures, and drawings by over 118 artists from 14 Spanish and Portuguese-speaking countries in Latin America. The exhibit showed the influence of Spain on these artists and also the impact of Latin American art on this country.

Food. Whether in Santa Fe or Chicago, restaurants routinely serve *enchiladas* and *tacos*. *Tortillas* and spicy sauces are commonly found in grocery stores around the country. It should not be a surprise to know that this delectable cuisine is now enjoyed throughout the world. In a store window in "The Shambles," a shopping district in York, England, sit very proudly some cans of OLD EL PASO™ refries. A Mexican restaurant can be found beside the docks in Copenhagen, Denmark, on the Left Bank in Paris, and in Old Town in Geneva, Switzerland.

Geography. At one time Spain ruled over a huge area of the continental United States. As a result, over 2,000 American cities have Spanish names: 400 in California, 250 in New Mexico, and 250 in Texas. The graphic at the right shows figures for all the states:

Number of American Cities with Spanish Names

Language. Spanish is our nation's dominant second language and was taught for the first time in a course in Philadelphia in 1776. Cotton Mather was a scholar in the language. Benjamin Franklin, John Adams, and Thomas Jefferson all studied and read Spanish. So did Methodism's John Wesley. A long list of Spanish words has become an everyday part of English usage:

alfalfa	canary	Eldorado	indigo	paragon	sherry
alligator	cannibal	embargo	maize	parasol	soda
armada	canoe	fandango	maroon	potato	sombrero
barbecue	cargo	flotilla	mosquito	quinine	stampede
barricade	chocolate	gala	mulatto	sarsaparilla	tobacco
bravado	cigar	grandee	mustang	savanna	tomato
buffalo	cocoa	guerrilla	Negro	sierra	tornado
cacao	desperado	hurricane	palaver	siesta	vanilla

Literature. In Puritan library lists from the seventeenth century, Shakespeare is not found, but *Don Quixote* is there. Cervantes's novel was a favorite of John Adams, who often read it for sheer pleasure on his travels. It was the only novel Thomas Jefferson selected from his collection of books for the University of Virginia. Washington Irving, Nathaniel Hawthorne, and Edgar Allen Poe referred to *Don Quixote*. Herman Melville had marginal notes in his copy and from its inspiration wrote *Moby Dick*. Walt Whitman refers to the novel. So does Mark Twain. In fact, Huck Finn and Tom Sawyer actually reflect Sancho Panza and Don Quixote. Some of the expressions in this Spanish classic are known by all of us: "a bird in the hand is worth two in the bush," "murder will out," or "tilting at windmills."

Religion. The Spanish erected the first Christian church building in the United States. One source assigns this distinction to Fray **Juan de Padilla** near Wichita, Kansas, during Coronado's expedition in 1540. Santa Fe, New Mexico insists that its San Miguel Mission is the oldest church in the United States. Just as insistently, St. Augustine, Florida, makes that claim for one of its old churches.

Technology. Spaniards taught Indians how to use the wheel on carts and introduced them to water and pottery wheels.

How Is Hispanic Culture Celebrated in the U.S.?
The answer is Hispanic Heritage Month. President Lyndon B. Johnson signed the first proclamation on September 17, 1968, creating Hispanic Heritage Week. In 1988 Congress extended the celebration to a month.

The dates fall each year between September 15 and October 15. On September 15 Mexico's church bells ring, celebrating the memory of Father Hidalgo's *el Grito de Dolores* in 1810 (the Cry of Dolores, the Mexican town where Hidalgo called for independence from Spain). This day is observed also in Costa Rica, El Salvador, Honduras, Guatemala, and Nicaragua. On September 16 parades, ceremonies, and programs fill schedules held throughout Mexico and among some Hispanics in many cities in the United States. Actually, 1821 is the date eleven years after Hidalgo when Mexico officially proclaimed its independence after defeating the Spanish armies.

American Hispanics use this time to affirm their past and future goals. They also try to make all Americans aware of that heritage and hope that these Americans will respect what Hispanics have given this country and what they continue to offer in so many ways. Hispanics also hope that other Americans will focus on the needs and concerns of Hispanic communities across the land. Hispanic Heritage Month features art exhibits, theater and film productions, music and dance festivals, displays and food booths, fund raising balls, banquets, conventions, luncheons, conferences, trade shows, soccer games and races, fiestas, and *mariachi* Masses. One Hispanic criticism, in the opinion of José Burciaga, is that this observance does not include the Indo-American heritage. Even if this be so, the many celebrations still remind the nation not just of an ethnic presence but also of a strong force in our rapidly changing society.

How Does Hispanic Heritage Month Reflect Hispanic Social Struggle?

Yolanda Chávez Leyva points out how this special month looks back to Latino political activism. The year 1968 was one of Latino restlessness. Thousands marched the streets to demand equal education, employment, and political access. East Los Angeles rioted. New Mexican Hispanics struggled for ancient land-grant rights. César Chávez in California mobilized the grape boycott to demand decent working conditions and fair pay.

In 1970, Chicanos in Crystal City, Texas, created the Raza Unida Party. Over 20,000 attended a national moratorium rally in Los Angeles to protest the Vietnam War. By 1971 the first Chicana conference assembled in Houston, and the next year Chicana seamstresses organized and won a strike against Farah Manufacturing Co. in El Paso. Puerto Rican youth formed the Young Lord's Party and the Puerto Rican Students' Union. Hispanic voices began to get a hearing.

Consequently, every September 15 when the National Hispanic Heritage Month begins, we should be reminded of Latino struggles in the '60s and '70s over poverty, health care, police brutality, and political exclusion that led finally to national recognition of a culture so important to American life.

How Do American Hispanics Feel About Latin America?

For many decades, American Hispanics have felt somewhat ignored by Latin American countries, including Mexico. José Armas thought that Latin Americans really had no idea what it was like "to live within the belly of the giant, facing the same obstacles for visibility and acceptance." Mexico's recently-elected President, Vicente Fox, has made it crystal clear that both American Hispanics and also the entire American people are important to Mexico, that Mexico is important to the United States, and that concrete political and social realities need to be changed. Likewise, official visits and talks between the two Presidents have become more substantive. We will await more action.

How Do American Hispanics Feel About Spain?

Most American Hispanics generally seem to feel indifferent toward Spain, a feeling reciprocated by Spaniards, but yet not totally. In Spain the Institute of Iberoamerican Cooperation tries formally to encourage communication and eventually trade between Spain and U.S. Hispanics. In the fall of 2000, the crown prince of Spain gave the keynote address at the grand opening of Albuquerque's Hispanic Cultural Center, and the prince himself is honorary president of the Center's board of trustees.

Where feelings do exist toward Spain, those feelings for some are outrage over the barbarism of the Conquest. Others admire the Spanish culture and even at times sense an unarticulated desire for some kind of relationship with the other third of the major cultural roots that make Latin America what it is.

Spanish—
Language of the Angels

What Is the Connection between Culture and Language?

Why do most tourists or casual visitors never learn about another country or culture at a deeper level? The reason is the connection between culture and language. Sabine Ulibarri presents this eloquent explanation:

The language...carries within it the history, the culture, the traditions, the very life of a people.... Language is people. We cannot even conceive of a people without a language, or a language without a people.... To know one is to know the other.

Victor Villanueva Jr. shares this quote: "to speak a language is to take on a world, a culture." Miguel de Unamuno finds within a language "an implicit philosophy, a way of looking at the world, hence a world-view."

Why Is Spanish Called "the Language of the Angels"?

Tomás Navarro states that "every language is pleasing, sweet, and harmonious to those who speak it as their native tongue." True, but Hispanics and non-Hispanics alike have described Spanish as "sonorous, harmonious, elegant, and expressive," as Navarro quotes Swedish philologist F. Wullf. Dorothy Pillsbury in her colorful descriptions of life in old Santa Fe observed that the city telephone directory could be sung without too much effort—with names like Candelario, Aragón, Desederio, and Luján.

E. Stanley Jones, the Methodist missionary and writer, records in his autobiography how he once appeared on a speaking tour in South America. He suddenly became aware that English is direct, while Spanish is more indirect. He recalled how he would make a blunt Anglo statement, only to sense that his interpreter "would curve my straight lines so beautifully that they would fall upon their souls like dew. They loved it that way."

Technically speaking, the Spanish language is called *castellano*, which some see as one of the richest and most expressive languages of the world. A common explanation is that one learns English to conduct business, French to make love, but Spanish to pray.

Where in the World Is Spanish Spoken?
Among the world's leading language groups, Chinese ranks first in number of speakers, English is second, Spanish is third (the rankings vary). Spanish is spoken by 297 million persons in the following places:

- Spain.
- Andorra.
- Latin America (but not Brazil), including parts of the Caribbean such as Puerto Rico, Cuba, and the Dominican Republic.
- United States (Spanish is the number two language here).
- Parts of Canada.
- Parts of the Philippine Islands.
- Equatorial Guinea.

One man complained that he had studied Castilian Spanish in high school, then went to South America with confident expectations of conversing with the people, only to discover that communication was simply impossible. When asked where he had visited, he replied, "Brazil." What he hadn't known before was that Portuguese is a linguistic cousin to Spanish, but that doesn't mean that cousins necessarily can understand each other.

What Are the Linguistic Sources for Spanish Vocabulary?
Spanish may be spoken in heaven, but its historical development took place right here on earth. Any language in touch with other cultures, nations and civilizations will adopt and adapt words from other languages. Thus a language evolves and develops, just as with English. Spanish evolved from these basic sources:

Indigenous Iberian: *gorra, mogote, zorro, pizarra, izquierda,* and words terminating in *az, ez, iz, oz* and *uz.*

Portuguese: If it is perhaps "archaic Spanish" that never evolved, the language has given words behind common Spanish words, e.g., *cueva, blanco, hoja.* Also, *macho, clavel, dibujo, flamenco, jonje, viaje.*

Latin (from Roman conquerors, 75%): *planta, ánimo, libro, aurora, ardor, vigor, honor, mundo, tribunal, amigo, ejemplo, bueno, señor, águila, agua, corona, culpa, lengua, luna, justo, libre.*

Greek: (8%) *teología, ídolo, limosna, biblia, apóstol, mártir, ángel, atmósfera, análisis, periscopio, filatelia, filosofía, biblioteca, drama, teatro, poesía, gramática.*

Hebrew: *fariseo, pascua, rabino, Satanás, Adán, Eva, Abel, David, Ester, Judit, María, Gabriel, aleluya, amén, jubileo, sábado.*

Celtic (from northwestern Spanish province of Galicia): *gaita* (bagpipe), and some Spanish surnames like O'Connell, O'Gorman, O'Higgins, and O'Donoju.

Arabic (from 800 years of Moorish occupation of Spain, 10%): *algodón, azúcar, alcohol, cifra, álgebra, barrio, almacén, alcalde, alquiler, tambor, aduana, naranja, azul, almuerzo, alfombra, albaricoque, ojalá, Guadalajara*. The cry *olé*, states Himilce Novas, is the Spanish adaptation of the Arabic *Allah* (God), or Praise Allah!, even if the occasion is a bullfight.

American indigenous (especially Aztec *Náhuatl* in pre-Conquest Mexico): *aguacate, atole, huarache, hule, cacao, camote, chicle, chocolate, coyote, ejote, guacamole, jícama, mecate, mescal, mezquite, milpa, mole, papalote, petaca, peyote, quetzal, tamal, tecolote, tilma, tiza, zacate, zapote*. African root words carried to the Caribbean islands entered the vocabulary, like *fulano* and *mengana* (Mr. and Ms. So and So).

French (especially in Mexico during French conquest in the mid-1800s): *blusa, bufete, camión, ficha, hotel, jardín, parque, pupitre, silueta, sargento, bolsa, debate, detalle, galante, personal, servilleta*.

Italian: *alerta, bravo, brújula, charlar, fachada, follete, piano, piloto, serenata, sonata, tercero, banca, estancia, novela, romanza*.

German: *banda, bandera, guerra, banco, rico, sala, votar*.

English: *bote, club, comité, cheque, dólar, turista, rosbif, túnel, fútbol, revolver, tanque*.

Is Spanish Related to Other Languages?

Spanish is a Romance language and thus related to Portuguese, French, Italian, Romanian, and dialects in western Austria and eastern Switzerland, Dalmatia in former Yugoslavia, and parts of Albania. Lorenzo LaFarelle gives examples of similarities with sister languages:

- *Cueva* (cave) in Spanish, *cova* in Portuguese, *cava* in Italian.
- *Blanco* (white) in Spanish, *branco* in Portuguese.
- *Hoja* (sheet, page) in Spanish, *foja* in Portuguese.

Is Latin American Spanish All the Same?

That question is like asking if there are variations in food, music, or weather! In Spain itself we find Castilian, Catalan, Basque and Provençal. Some would even ask if all of these can be called Spanish. Still, the Royal Spanish Language Academy (*Real Academia de la Lengua Española*) in Madrid tries heroically to standardize the language. It was Castilian Spanish that came to the Americas, but then this form was strongly affected by indigenous languages, for example Mexican Spanish by Aztec *Náhuatl*.

Variations among the 350 million Spanish-speakers in the nineteen nations of Latin America contribute still another challenge. One dictionary can scarcely do justice to this variety. In fact, two scholars at Augsburg University in Germany are issuing, slowly, a dictionary for each Latin American country. So far they have prepared volumes on Argentina and Cuba; next will be Bolivia, Uruguay, Chile, Costa Rica, Peru, and others.

Daniel Woolis gives examples of this Spanish variety.

- *Tinto* and *bocadillo* in Spain (red wine and sandwich) will get black coffee and candied *guayaba* in Colombia.
- *Cremallera* in Spain (zipper) comes out *cierre* in Argentina and *zíper* in Cuba.
- *Piruleta* in Spain (lollipop) becomes *chupetón* in Argentina and *chicharo* in Cuba.
- *Coger* in Spain (to take a bus or trip), is a four-letter word in Argentina.

Carlos Conde adds some more examples:

- In Mexico peanuts are *cacahuates* but *maní* in Colombia.
- In Mexico a turkey is *guajolote* but *pavo* in Lima.
- In Mexico a suit is *traje* but is *terno* in Quito.
- In Mexico gasoline is **gasolina** and tires are *llantas,* but in Montevideo one hears *nafta* and *neumáticos.*

One more illustration. The word for courage, *coraje,* can also mean anger. Its use for courage in northern New Mexico and in places along the border would be a mistake. *Valor* is much safer.

Why Does the Spanish "Lisp" Not Appear in the Americas?

The Spanish spoken in the Spanish province of Castile (*Castellano*) is the official language form of the country and the foundation of Spanish everywhere. Castilian Spanish has some different vocabulary, but the main difference is in pronunciation, particularly in the lisp sound. To illustrate, *sincero* (sincere, seen-**seh**-roh) in Latin American and American Spanish would become theen-**theh**-roh in Castilian Spanish. In Castilian, the consonants *c* and *z* before *e* or *i* get the *th* sound, as in thin. Latin America did not adopt this pronunciation and went on to develop its own extensive varieties of the language throughout the hemisphere.

Nevertheless, whatever regional or national form of Spanish is spoken anywhere, Himilce Novas assures us, that Spanish is basically Castilian. To put things another way, the Queen's English in London, New England's dropped r, the Texas drawl, the TV-radio's Midwestern standard English—it's all English.

Why Is Spanish Spoken Uniquely
in Northern New Mexico and Southern Colorado?

New Mexican and southern Colorado Spanish is a study all in itself. One scholarly view describes New Mexico Spanish as pure Castillian, possibly even from the form of Spain's Golden Age of the 17th century, reflecting Cervantes in *Don Quixote.* Another view finds a mixture of several Spanish dialects blended with some *Náhuatl* after the Conquest. Differences from Castillian surface in vulgarisms, rusticisms, provincialisms, colloquialisms, and pronunciation. Rafaela Castro quotes Aurelio Espinosa about that form of Spanish: It "is not a vulgar dialect, as many misinformed persons believe, but a rich archaic Spanish dialect."

Is Spanglish a Legitimate Language?

Spanglish is a way to describe the hybrid combination of Spanish and English spoken commonly among Hispanic Americans. A speaker switches back and forth effortlessly, much to the horrified consternation of other Hispanics who consider this mixing to be a pollution of their pure language. But language is always in transition from outside influences. Even in Costa Rica's capital, San José, a country very proud of its correct Spanish, parking signs will sometimes read *parqueo* instead of the correct *estacionamiento.*

Changing from one language to another is common anywhere and is called code switching, something very complex that involves sound, vocabulary, syntax, and meaning. This process is not careless, degenerate, or inferior, explains Arnulfo Ramírez. It is the natural result of different language groups that come into intimate contact with each other. In other words, Spanglish is legitimate if it communicates. Enjoy this comical illustration of Spanglish in action, from Mary Ann and Carlos Romero of Santa Fe ©1978:

> *Mira,* Honey.... *¡Pronto!* shouts Papá from in front of the television set.... *Qúe* funny commercial they showed. *Era un* commercial *de* some kind of deodorant for *los pies. Estaba* this guy *en el* bowling alley and he took off *sus* shoes, *y todos* around him were overcome.... *Se desmayaron... hasta el* dog.... You know, *Vieja...,* speaking of deodorants, *ese* new one *en el* red can you bought *el otro día* is no good. It makes me feel sticky *todo el día.* En *el* red can? *Viejo, yo no sé porque* you don't read labels. The stuff en *el* red can *no es* deodorant.... *Es* hair spray!

Certain Hispanics do not think Spanglish is funny at all. Roger Hernandez quotes Yale Spanish literature professor Roberto González Echevarría:

Spanglish is an invasion of Spanish by English. Spanglish is street Spanish as if the language of Cervantes, Lorca, García Márquez, Borges and Paz does not have an essence and dignity of its own.

Hernandez concludes that "When Hispanic-Americans use Spanglish because they don't know 'real' Spanish, the survival of the language of Cervantes and Borges in the United States is in grave danger."

Another viewpoint, though, is that Spanglish expresses the coming together of two languages and cultures. Now, if language, to use David del Valle's expression, "...is the window through which we look at the world," Spanglish shows the attempt of many Hispanics to look at life through two different lenses, at times a commingling, at times a clash. We can assume this argument will go on forever, so let's enjoy one more example so at least everyone can laugh. You'll love this one!

'Twas the night before Christmas and all through the *casa.*
Not a creature was stirring—*¡Caramba! ¿Qué pasa?*
Los niños were tucked away in their *camas,*
Some in long underwear, some in *pijamas,*
While hanging the stockings with *mucho cuidado*
In hopes that old Santa would feel *obligado.*
To bring all children, both *buenos* and *malos,*
A nice batch of *dulces* and other *regalos.*
Outside in the yard there arose such a *grito*
That I jumped to my feet like a frightened *cabrito.*
I ran to the window and looked out *afuera,*
And who in the world do you think that it *era?*
Saint Nick in a sleigh and a big red *sombrero*
Came dashing along like a crazy *bombero.*
And pulling his sleigh instead of *venados*
Were eight little *burros* approaching *volados.*
I watched as they came, and this quaint little *hombre*
Was shouting and whistling and calling by *nombre:*
"¡Ay Pancho, ay Pepe, ay Cuco, ay Beto,
Ay Chato, ay Chopo, Macuco, y Nieto!"
Then standing erect with his hands on his *pecho*
He flew to the top of our very own *techo.*
With his round little belly like a bowl of *jalea,*
He struggled to squeeze down our old *chiminea,*
Then huffing and puffing at last in our *sala,*
With soot smeared all over his red suit *de gala,*
He filled all the stockings with lovely *regalos—*
For none of the *niños* had been very *malos.*

Then chuckling aloud, seeming very *contento,*
He turned like a flash and was gone like the *viento.*
And I heard him exclaim, and this is *verdad,*
Merry Christmas to all, and *¡Feliz Navidad!*

What Are Some Anglicisms in Spanish?

This is an intriguing feature of common Spanish usage. English words are given a Spanish form. Look at some examples:

Basic Spanish	English Translation	Anglicisms
almuerzo	lunch	*lonche*
camión	truck	*troca*
diez centavos	ten cents (dime)	*daime* (**da**ee-may)
escribir a máquina	to type	*taipear*
estacionar	to park (a car)	*parquear*
lavandería	laundry	*londri*
pantalla	screen	*escrín*
paseo	ride	*raite* (**rah**ee-tay)
alquiler	to rent	*rentar*

What Is *Caló?*

Jacob Ornstein-Galicia sees *caló* as a linguistic pattern spoken in *barrios* on both sides of the U.S.-Mexico border, mostly by working-class people. Like black English, this is not mere slang. In the U.S. Southwest the form is an actual language variant spoken by millions of people of all ages. Chicano activists in the '60s and '70s used *caló* for cultural identity (see Chapter One, "*Pachuco*").

Linguistic historians consider the form a very old argot with traces of French, English, Italian, Greek, and Hebrew. It was used by gypsies of Spain in the fifteenth century. It came to Mexico with the Spanish conquerors and moved into the language of the poor and often the criminal. Similar patterns are found throughout Latin America. Anglos struggling to learn Spanish will find *caló* completely mystifying and think it is another language.

One form of *caló* is to give new meanings to Spanish words.

Caló	Normal Meaning	New Meaning
arriba	high	on drugs
bote	boat	jail
cantón	region, district	house
carnal	sensual, worldly	brother, friend
chamba	lucky break	work
chota	heifer calf	police

gacho	bent down, slouching	bad
huevos	eggs	guts, "balls"
jefe	chief (masc.)	father
jefa	chief (fem.)	mother, wife
¡órale!	ask, demand	let's go!
lira	lyre, harp	guitar
pedo	fart	drunk, trouble
tirar la vuelta	to throw a turn (lit.)	to die
trompa	trumpet	mouth
tronado	blasted	on drugs
volar	to fly	to go away

A second form of *caló* is to create new Spanish words to replace standard words.

Spanish Word	**Standard Meaning**	**Caló Word**
novia	girl friend	*chavalona, ruca, vieja*
compañero	close friend	*compa, compita, bro*
sí	yes	*simón (sí + -món)*
no	no	*nombre*
muy bien	very good	*a toda madre, chido*
ausentarse	to skip school	*zorrear* (to fox)
¡no lo creo!	Unbelievable!	*¡Ah, cañón!*
chavalo, chamaco	guy, dude	*vato/bato*
número uno	number one	*chingón*
hola	hello	*ése, ésele, órale*

A third form of *caló* is the use of literal Spanish rendering of the English words, like *carrucha caliente* (hot car, or stolen automobile) or *dame una quebrada* (give me a break).

How Is Standard Spanish Determined?

Spanish variations are obvious throughout Latin America and within Spain, too. Costa Ricans think the Mexican accent is amusing. Argentine Spanish sounds like Italian. But to guard vocabulary and grammar in Latin America, national academies seek to preserve a pure Spanish. The North American Academy was founded in 1973 with the intention to correct and maintain Spanish in the style of the Southwest. But probably the most effective standardization of the language, states Sally Said, comes from journalistic Spanish in Spanish language newspapers in urban centers in the U.S.

How Does a Person Ever Pronounce Those Spanish Words?

Spanish is completely phonetic. Learn and practice these rules, and there will be no sweat, unlike English or German.

1. **a** is always **ah** (father).
2. **e** is always **eh** (met).
3. **i** is always **ee** (meet).
4. **o** is always **oh** (boat).
5. **u** is always **oo** (mood, food).
6. **b** and **v** are practically the same, pronounced as a soft **v** with lips together.
7. **c** is like **k** (cat) but like **s** (city) before **e** or **i.**
8. **ch** is like English or can become a soft **sh** (sure).
9. **d** gets a **th** sound, with tongue against teeth, as does **t.**
10. **g** is hard (go) but like **h** before **e** or **i** (hen).
11. **h** is always silent.
12. **j** is rough, like a guttural **h.**
13. **ll** has a **y** sound, like *yo.*
14. **ñ** sounds like canyon.
15. **r** has a slight trill with tongue.
16. **rr** has a strong trill.
17. **z** has the **s** sound.
18. The other consonants sound the same as in English.
19. An accent mark over a syllable means to emphasize.

Now, then, you are ready for a practice exercise. Cover the words in parentheses, then check your answers:

1.	*Padre*	(**pah**-dreh).
2.	*Centro*	(**cehn**-troh).
3.	*Mio*	(**mee**-oh).
4.	*Poco*	(**poh**-coh).
5.	*Uno*	(**oo**-noh), *una* (**oo**-nah).
6.	*Baca, vámonos*	(**bvah**-cah), **bva**-moh-nohs).
7.	*Ciudad, cama*	(see-oo-**dahd, cah**-mah).
8.	*Nada*	(**nah**-dah).
9.	*Grande, gente*	(**grahn**-deh, **hehn**-teh).
10.	*Hacha*	(**ah**-chah).
11.	*Hija*	(**ee**-hah).
12.	*Valle*	(**vah**-yeh).
13.	*Niño*	(**neen**-yoh).
14.	*Rojo, perro*	(**roh**-ho, **peh**-roh).
15.	*Tarde*	(**tar**-deh).
16.	*Plaza*	(**plah**-sah).

17. *Limón, página*   (lee-**mohn**, **pah**-hee-nah).

How Does Spanish Differ from English in Its Rhythm?
Language is measured by stress groups or syllable clusters within the sentence. Spanish rhythm moves in groupings of five to ten syllables, preferably seven to eight. By contrast, English commonly uses four to eight syllables, mostly six to seven. It is this difference that makes Anglos think that Spanish speakers talk so rapidly.

Are Those Accents on Spanish Words Just Decoration?
No, no. They are guides to pronunciation. For example, understanding that Martínez is pronounced Mar-**tee**-nez would prevent the use of Mar-tee-**nez**. The rules can seem tricky, but here they are:
1. Words ending in a vowel, n, or s are accented on the next to the last syllable.
2. All other consonant endings have accents on the last syllable.
3. Any exceptions use an accent mark to show where to place the stress, e.g., Aztlán, Juárez, árbol.

What Are Those Other Mysterious Marks?
The letter n sometimes has a mark over it, ~ or tilde, to form a different letter, the *eñe* (**éh**-nyeh). Also, a question begins with an upside down ¿, and an exclamation begins with an upside down ¡.

How Is Capitalization Different?
In Spanish, proper names of people and places are capitalized, just as in English, but not days of the week or months of the year. Thus, it is *septiembre* (September) or *domingo* (Sunday). In book titles, only the first word is capitalized.

Why the Strange Seven?
The number seven gets an added little line, like 7̵. The purpose is clarity, distinguishing the number 7 from a careless 1 or number 7 like a careless z. This form of seven is used throughout continental Europe. Some Anglo teachers in American schools become very upset over this strange deviation from New England practice. Children have been called unpatriotic for using this form! Oddly enough, computers put a line through the zero, like Ø, and no one gets excited about that. To add insult to injury, the z gets a line also, like ƶ, so that no one thinks the letter is a 2.

What Are Some Basic Spanish Phrases and Words?

- *Buenos días* (**bweh**-nohs **dee**-ahs): good morning.
- *Buenas tardes* (**bweh**-nahs **tar**-dehs): good afternoon.
- *Buenas noches* (**bweh**-nahs **no**-chehs): good evening, good night.
- *Hola* (**oh**-lah): hello.
- *¿Cómo está usted?* or, *¿cómo está?* (**coh**-moh eh-**stah** oo-**stehd**): how are you? Similar phrases are *¿Cómo le ha ido? ¿Cómo le va? ¿Qúe húbole?*
- *Muy bien, gracias, ¿y Ud.?* (**moo**-ee bee-**yen**, **grah**-see-ahs, ee oo-**stedh**?): very fine, thank you, and you?
- *Adiós* (ah-dee-**ohs**): good bye.
- *De nada* (deh **nah**-dah): you're welcome.
- *Muchas gracias* (**moo**-chahs **grah**-see-ahs): thank you very much.
- *Perdóname* (pehr-**doh**-nah-meh): excuse me, pardon me.
- *Por favor* (por fah-**vor**): please.
- *Hable más despacio por favor* (**ah**-bleh mahs dehs-**pah**-see-o por-fah-**vor**): speak more slowly, please.
- *¿Cuánto?* (**kwahn**-toh): how much?
- *¿Donde?* (**dohn**-deh): where?
- *¿Cuándo?* (**kwahn**-doh): when?
- *¿Dónde está?* (**dohn**-deh ehs-**tah**)? where is _____?
- *¿Cómo se llama usted?* (**coh**-moh seh **yah**-mah oos-**tehd**): what is your name?
- *Me llamo* (meh **yah**-moh): my name is _____.
- *No entiendo* (no ehn-tee-**ehn**-doh): I don't understand.
- *Lo siento* (loh see-**ehn**-toh): I'm sorry.
- *No le hace* (no leh **ah**-seh): it doesn't matter.
- *Tengo que irme* (**ten**-goh keh **eer**-meh): I have to go.
- *Me gusta* (meh **goos**-tah): I like _____.
- *Me alegro* (meh ah-**leh**-groh): I'm glad.
- *Tengo hambre* (**ten**-goh **ahm**-breh): I'm hungry.
- *Tengo sed* (**ten**-goh **sehd**): I'm thirsty.
- *Tengo frío* (**ten**-goh **free**-oh): I'm cold.
- *Tengo calor* (**ten**-goh cah-**lor**): I'm hot.
- *Estoy cansado* (ehs-**toy** cahn-**sah**-doh): I'm tired.
- *¿Qúe hora es?* (**keh oh**-rah **ehs**): what time is it?
- *Yo* (yoh): I.
- *Ud.* (oo-**stehd**): you. Familiar (intimate) form of you is *tú* (too).
- *El* (el): he. *Ella* (**eh**-yah): she.
- *Nosotros* (noh-**soh**-trohs): we.
- *Ellos* (**eh**-yohs), *ellas* (**eh**-yahs): they (masc., fem.).

How Is the Word Mexico Correctly Pronounced?
Although it is perfectly proper to say **Mek**-see-koh here in the United States, in Spanish the pronunciation has a sound not found in English. The x (or j, as in *Méjico*) gets a soft, throaty sound.

What Are Some Choice Examples of "Strong Language"?
Sometimes it is helpful to know if you are being cursed by a student, customer, salesperson, coworker, or even a boss. In northern New Mexico, an Anglo teacher in a church-related school knew little Spanish, but the legend goes that she understood Spanish profanity enough to scare the living daylights out of some unsuspecting little rascal who might shout some strong language on the playground, or at her. Of course, if there is no desire to learn this vocabulary, or if its inclusion here is offensive, the easiest remedy would be to turn the page quickly and to think "expletive deleted."

- *a la ve* (short form for *a la verga,* or penis).
- *cabrón* or *cabrones* (goat, but meaning bastard).
- *cabrones ojetes* (dumb a—hole).
- *mierda* (sh—t).
- *culo* (a—).
- *jodido* (f—ed up).
- *huevones* (literally eggs or balls).
- *maldito* (damned).
- *pendejo* (fool, literally pubic hair).
- *pinche maricón* (lousy fairy).
- *puta* (whore, harlot).

Octavio Paz and Alan Riding describe the most automatic Mexican curse word, meaning literally "to rape," none other than the strong Mexican favorite from the root *chingar.*

- *hijo de la chingada* (S.O.B., Mexican form of *hijo de puta*). In fact, *¡Viva México, hijos de la chingada!* is a national "battle cry...of challenge and affirmation."
- *chinga tu madre* (rape your mother, or f—k).
- *vete a la chingada* (go to hell).
- *ahora te chingas* (you're f—ed now).
- *que se chinguen* (f—k them).

But derivatives of this volatile word can be also very innocent:

- *chingón* (a person who is the best, excellent, admirable. Used only with family or close friends).
- *se chingó* (something broke).
- *chingaquedito* (silently deceptive, then violence).

▪ *hizo una chingadera* (someone rashly defies the rules).
▪ *chingadazo* (heavy blow).
▪ *chingadera* (dirty trick).
▪ *no chingues* (don't annoy me).
▪ *me chingaron* (I lost out).

Should Some Spanish Words Be Used Carefully?

Alan Riding explains how *madre* (mother) is used for formally addressing one's mother, but *mamá* is more common, and the Virgin Mary is *nuestra Madre*. But *chinga tu madre* or *tu madre* is a strong insult. *Una madre* is something unimportant. *Un desmadre* is a chaos. *Madreador* is a bouncer or hired tough guy. *Partir la madre* is to shatter someone. *Poca madre* means no shame, *a toda madre* means something wonderful, but *me vale madre* declares something is completely unimportant. *Madrecita* is a son's loving word for his mother, while *mamacita* is used for a mistress or by a vulgar youth passing a girl on the street.

In much the same way, *padre* is the formal word for father but with *papá* or *papito* or *papi* the more common usages. Yet a mother can call her son those same names. But be careful here: *padrote* (big father) means a pimp!

What Is the Most Popular Name for Baby Boys in California?

According to Mike Davis, that name is José.

Why Do Hispanics Use So Many Personal Names?

As an example, an Hispanic might identify himself as José Alberto Sánchez Rodríguez. The first and second names are like saying Joseph Albert. The third name is the family name from the father. The last name is the mother's family name. Hispanics moving in Anglo society will usually use that third name as the last name, José Sánchez. In Hispanic circles the fourth name is sometimes indicated simply by the first letter, thus José Alberto Sánchez R. Married women, unless anglicized, will identify themselves as Josefina García de Sánchez; García is her own family name, while Sánchez is the family name of her husband. Increasingly, such traditional forms are disappearing in normal American Hispanic social life.

What Are the Most Common Spanish Family Names?

A study by Vigil of names in Albuquerque, New Mexico, comes up with this list, in order of frequency:

1. García (Gahr-**see**-ah)   2. Martínez (Mar-**tee**-ness)

3. Chávez (**Chah**-vess)   4. Sánchez (**Sahn**-chess)
5. González (Gohn-**sah**-less)   6. Montoya (Mon-**toh**-ya)
7. Romero (Roh-**meh**-roh)   8. Baca (**Bah**-kah)
9. Gallegos (Gah-**yeh**-gohs)   10. Trujillo (True-**hee**-yoh)

Nationally, the top surnames among Hispanics are García, Martínez and Rodríguez. They are also among the 25 most common surnames in the United States—out of 88,000 other possibilities.

One name has an unusual variation. Enrique Gonzales (ending with **s** instead of **z,** and no accent) explains a spelling that comes perhaps from the county and city of Gonzales east of San Antonio and south of Austin, Texas. Rafael Gonzales was governor of Coahuila, Texas, when Texas was part of Mexico. The spelling can be found also in Louisiana and California.

What Are Popular Customs with Names?
Hispanics love nicknames (*apodos* or *seudónimos*). Common ones are:

Abelardo to Lalo	Alicia to Licha
Alfonso to Poncho	Cecilia to Ceci
Antonio to Toño	Concepción to Concha
Armando to Mando	Consuelo to Chelo
Eduardo, Everado to Lalo	Cristina to Cristi
Enrique to Kiki or Kike	Enriqueta to Queta or Kiki
Ernesto to Neto	Fabiola to Fabi
Francisco to Paco, Pancho	Graciela to Chila
Guillermo to Memo	Guadalupe to Lupe
Horacio to Nacho	Josefina to Chepa
Javier to Javi	Liliana to Lili
Jesús to Chucho, Chuy	Lourdes to Lula
José to Pepe	María to Mari
Manuel to Mani	Minerva to Mini
Rafael to Rafa	Natalia to Nati
Raymundo to Mundo	Otilia to Tila
Roberto to Beto	Rosario to Chayo
Vicente to Chente	Socorro to Soco
	Teresa to Tere

Another custom is to change a name to diminutive form to express affection, such as Josué to Josuecito, Juan to Juanito, Juana to Juanita, Lupe to Lupita, and Oscar to Oscarito. A third custom is reversals. English speakers sometimes are startled to hear Spanish-speaking husbands call their wives *vieja* (literally, old woman) or wives call their husbands *viejo* (old man), but everything is very tender and loving in those words. Or the husband may call his wife *gorda* (fat woman), or the wife may call the husband *gordo* (fat man), again with all respect and affection. An older man might be called *joven,* which literally means young man, while a young man might be called *viejo,* which literally means old man. A thin person might become *gordo* or *gorda* (fat). A fat person might be referred to as *flaco* or *flaca* (skinny). A fourth custom concerns institutions. A school, for example, gets the article put in front of its name, and thus Bowie High School becomes *la Bowie.* Lydia Patterson Institute becomes *la Lydia.* Cathedral High School becomes *la Cate.* José Burciaga assures us that all such naming means affection.

Why Are Biblical Names So Common among Hispanics?

According to Arthur Tenorio, such a custom reflects an old tradition emerging from the religious faith within the culture. Although this custom is waning, yet very common names today are Abel, Anna, Abram, Adam, Benjamín, Daniel, David, Esther, Eva, Gabriel, Isaac, Isabel, Jesse, Jesús, Joaquín (Jacob), José (Joseph), Juan (John), Magdalena, Manuel (from Immanuel, Messiah), María, Martha, Miguel (Michael), Moisés (Moses), Noé (Noah), Rebecca, Raquel (Rachel), Rubén (Reuben), and Tomás (Thomas).

Just a word about the name *Jesús.* The biblical connection and the religious significance are obvious. To name someone Jesus is meant to be an honor, but Anglo/northern European parents never call their child Jesus. Nor is an Anglo/northern European child ever named Angel. But thousands of Hispanics do not seem to mind carrying such an imposing role model. And, if *Jesús* becomes a burden, *Chuy* lies close at hand.

Why Is Someone Called *Vato?*

Vato or *bato,* Rafaela Castro tells us, means dude or guy. It entered Chicano vocabulary in the 1940s and goes well with the environment of the *barrio cholo.* A *vato loco* (crazy dude) could be a gang member or just a colorful personality. But the term is used proudly for ethnic identity. In rural New Mexico, some people use the regular Spanish meaning of simpleton.

Why Is It Helpful to Know Some Spanish?

First of all, knowing the language is helpful in communication. People understand on a deeper level when their native tongue is used. Next, knowing the language is helpful in establishing relationships. Hispanics appreciate any efforts to learn their beautiful language and even faulty efforts to speak it. Again, the language is a vehicle for understanding Hispanic culture. Culture is transmitted best through language.

Anthropologist Clyde Kluckholn explains that language is more than a vehicle for exchanging ideas and information. "Every language," he says, "is also a special way of looking at the world and interpreting experience. Concealed in the structure of each different language are a whole set of unconscious assumptions about the world and life in it."

One more advantage in knowing some Spanish is the ability to pronounce names correctly. A respected anchorman on a major TV network regularly mispronounces the name of a Hispanic correspondent in Latin America. On El Paso TV and radio one can hear San Djah-**sin**-toh **Pla**-zuh instead of San Hah-**seen**-toh **Pla**-sah. The home field of the Los Angeles Dodgers has been called Shah-**vez** Ravine instead of **Cháh**-ves Ravine. The *Río Grande* comes out as Rio Grand. A TV news report on Haiti referred to the junta, pronounced **djuhn**-tah instead of **hoon**-tah.

Many Anglos fall into these inaccurate pronunciation habits in any language. Into a church mission among Native Americans in British Columbia there entered one day a formidable-looking English anthropologist who informed Mark, the pastor, that since her youth she had been interested in the culture of the Quackadoodles. Mark corrected her and carefully pronounced the word *Kwacutals*. Her retort? "Young man, for the past century in England this band has been known as the Quackadoodles and as the Quackadoodles, it will be known forever." So much for cultural sensitivity with the language!

What Typical Problems Do English Speakers Have with Spanish?

As with any language, there are vocabulary traps. Although *papá* is father and *papas* are potatoes, *Papa* is the Pope! Another trap is the verb *embarazar* which means "to be confused or upset" or "to be pregnant." So, when a woman is pregnant, she is *embarazada* (feminine form). A smart man, however, will not even get close to the technically correct masculine form *embarazado* (I am embarrassed)—unless he welcomes hysterical laughter from his friends. Instead, he will choose *tengo vergüenza* (literally, I have embarrassment).

In grammar, the pronouns, prepositions, word order, irregular verbs and the subjunctive mood are the worst of the linguistic jungles. In pronunciation, problems often occur with the "d" and "t" sound but more commonly with the single and double "r". English speakers sometimes forget to give the broad "ah" sound to "a" or the "eh" sound to "e." An easy error by native English speakers is to give the English "uh" sound to the Spanish final "a" instead of the sound "ah." Thus, *mesa* (**meh**-sah) so often becomes **meh**-suh. A common grammatical problem is the double negative. In Spanish, *no tengo nada que hacer* (I don't have nothing to do) is acceptable. In English this form is incorrect, but often the lesson is difficult to learn by English speakers with Spanish-language background. And when some Anglos try to pronounce Spanish with English pronunciation, the resulting sound is not exactly musical, e.g., when *animalitos* turns into *a-nih-muh-lee-tayoz*.

Of course, strange idioms are peculiar to each Spanish-speaking country. Beyond vocabulary, grammar and idioms, a very common trap is literal translation. Carlos Conde relates how former U.S. House Speaker Newt Gingrich once sent greetings to Mexican Americans for the *Cinco de Mayo* celebration. His office issued a Spanish-language press release that identified Gingrich as the *"Hablador de la Casa."* Using a standard dictionary, some staff worker came out with a literal translation that made Gingrich "Big Mouth of the House," or "Loudmouth," or even "Liar."

The most common complaint, however, among Anglos is that Spanish speakers frequently fail to enunciate their words clearly and speak too rapidly. Strange that Spanish speakers say the same thing about those speaking English.

What Typical Problems Do Spanish Speakers Have with English?
Words beginning with "ch" or "sh" are particularly troublesome. Thus, "church" often becomes "shursh." The "i" sound is another trap. The most embarrassing example occurs when a Hispanic talks about the "sheet" on the bed, but the word comes out "sh-t." Or "ship" becomes "sheep." Someone heading for the "beach" makes it sound like "bitch." One of the values for Anglos in studying Spanish (or any other language) is the memory of their own pronunciation, vocabulary, or grammatical blunders. That's a quick cure for laughing at another's mistakes in English.

How Does the Spanish Language Express the Hispanic Soul?
All languages reveal how their speakers see their world. Spanish is no exception. In English the same word is used for a human or an animal body part (leg); Spanish sometimes uses one word for a person *(pierna)* but another for an animal *(pata)*. In other words, humans are special.

Other illustrations abound. In English we use the subjunctive mood very rarely (e.g., if I were you), but in Spanish this construction is an intricate system expressing life's uncertainty and variety. It has been suggested that the subjunctive's richness represents a revolt against the rigidity of Latin grammar and allows great individual variation. That's culture.

In English, the consonants are important, stressing the precision of Anglo culture. In Spanish, the vowels are important, expressing the emotion and variety of persons. English has one form for you, but Spanish has the formal *usted* and the informal *tú*, plus in some Latin American countries, such as Costa Rica, the very intimate *vos*. In other words, persons are stressed over things in Hispanic culture, and the language itself shows this.

Do All Hispanics Speak Spanish?

No invariable pattern of Spanish usage exists among Hispanics in the U.S. Spanish often is dominant at home, in church, in the neighborhood, or in recreation. At school English is used in class, but a mixture of Spanish, and at times English, is used outside of class. At work the language will depend on the work force, the kind of work, and the location. At church the usage will be determined by the usage in the congregation. On the other hand, many Hispanics speak English all the time except when conversing with Spanish-speaking relatives or the elderly.

In a study a decade ago, Eldín Villafañe, quoting Justo González, found that about 13 percent of Hispanics speak only English at home, 19 percent speak only Spanish, but nearly 81 percent will understand an English speaker. Speak Spanish and the percentage rises to 88 percent. The *Census 2000 Supplementary Survey* found 8 million Hispanics use English predominantly at home. But 72 percent of Hispanics who speak Spanish at home also speak English well or adequately.

For Hispanics who speak only English, Justo González points out that such a person who does not handle Spanish or is English-language dominant is still a genuine Hispanic. "Let us not," González writes, "so idolize our culture that we oppress another Hispanic who does not speak as we do, or even one who has never learned how to speak Spanish because the pressures of society were too great."

Is Learning Spanish as Popular as Some Say It Is?

Here are the percentages of preferred choices among Americans in learning a second language.

1. Spanish: 44%	2. French: 23%	3. German: 9%	
4. Italian: 7%	8. Chinese: 3%	9. Russian: 2%	

The preferred choice among Hispanics for a foreign language other than English is French at 46 percent.

Why Is Learning Spanish Popular Now?

In past history, a few famous persons here and there learned Spanish. In 16th century England, the founder of Methodism, John Wesley, studied Spanish (John Wesley, *Journal*, 1:237). Benjamin Franklin began studying French and Italian before moving to Spanish (*Benjamin Franklin's Autobiography*, p.101) and learned it in nineteen days while sailing the Atlantic to France and in France "improved his Spanish by reading *Don Quixote* in the original...." (Fawn M. Brodie, *Thomas Jefferson: An Ultimate History*, p.235).

But in our time of history, with the Hispanic population increasing rapidly in the United States, learning Spanish is a necessity or at least a tremendous advantage. Deborah Sharp describes this development.

> From feed lot managers in Nebraska to New York City stockbrokers, Americans are scrambling to learn a language now spoken by many of the 35.3 million Hispanics in the United States.... Americans are finding that not knowing Spanish can be a handicap, whether dealing with immigrants or schmoozing at a business lunch in the boss's native tongue.

Across the country, Sharp writes, staff training in Spanish becomes more and more common: a few examples are a bank in Oregon, a teachers union in Washington, and law enforcement officials in Detroit. And President George W. Bush delivers at least parts of some speeches in Spanish. This development is not just a fad; it's just a contemporary fact of life.

What Is the Goal for Most Second-Language Learners?

The most realistic goal for many is basic language competency, that is, being able to hear and speak enough to communicate, ideally with pronunciation as correct as possible. Beyond that stage would come the facility to read in Spanish and then to write. Many resources are available to reach this goal—in self-study, in small groups, or in formal classes.

The very best method, of course, and one not realistic for the average person, is an immersion experience in a language program in another country. Classes will be important, but even more helpful is to live with a local family and to absorb the language and the culture together. Lira and Gordenstein write about speaking, thinking, emoting, dreaming, loving, and disliking others in the language.

The final word on Spanish language learning is this. Spanish speakers are extremely proud of their language, and they respect others who speak the language correctly (as do English speakers). But equally they respect those who, despite errors, make the effort to use the language.

Hispanic Cultural Values— What's Most Important?

CULTURE AND VALUES

What Is a Culture?

Edward B. Tylor states that culture is the same as civilization, "...that complex whole which includes knowledge, belief, art, morals, law, custom, and any other capabilities and habits acquired by man (sic) as a member of society." Culture includes language, dance, habits, and patterns of relationships. Culture comes from collective human groups "... and continues in time through the customs, rituals, and practices of groups and institutions."

Are There Cultures within Cultures?

Eric Hyman explains how cultures usually get connected with a nation, an ethnic group, a geographic area, or a language. But each of these cultures has smaller cultures. For example, everyone knows that in the U.S. the differences between New England and the Deep South, between the Midwest and the Southwest, are obvious in language, arts, food, religion, dress, customs, values and history. Furthermore, subcultures exist within economic classes and occupations. And look at religions of any kind. Culture is complex.

Do Cultures Change?

Eric Hyman details how cultures change. Western civilization in the days of Homer, Julius Caesar, Louis XVI, or Charles Dickens were all different, and are even more different today. Christianity in the days of Constantine was different than the faith today. The United States for Washington was not what it was for Lincoln, nor for Theodore Roosevelt, nor even for us in our own time.

How Do Cultures Express Values?

Personal values are those ideas, beliefs, commitments, and focuses that are most important and that drive one's life. But how do values and culture relate? Clifford Geertz defines culture as "a web of meaning." The many facets of a group's life express that network of meaning, or values. In all cultures, the meaning comes through history, language, art, music, customs, literature, even food. In other words, values—the central life focus—directly express what a culture believes, what a culture feels to be most important.

One caution fits here. The transfer of values from countries of origin often results in changes during acculturation in the U.S., and everyone adapts differently. Therefore, not every Hispanic will express equally the values listed in the following descriptions.

How Is *la Raza* a Basic Value?

The concept of *la raza* (see Chapter One, "What Does the Term *la Raza* Signify?" and Chapter Two, "Are Hispanics a Separate Race?") refers more to a general culture than racial inheritance, or a "web of meaning." The confluence of Spanish, Arab, Amerindian, African, Asian, French, and American cultures has resulted in a rich source of pride and belonging, a sense of uniqueness.

What Are the Strong Values in *la Raza?*

Virgilio Elizondo will be our guide in much of the value descriptions that follow.

Acceptance. Life is accepted as it is, with its hard blows, and is faced sometimes with a fatalism.

Courtesy. Lovely expressions exist for moments of greeting or farewell. In fact, courtesy often demands that one says what the other wants to hear. "Yes" may mean "I hear you" rather than offending with a "no."

Family. Coming from pre-Columbian culture, the family is the basis for society and gives meaning to one's life. Children are a special pride and joy. When a family member is in the hospital, the whole family will crowd into the room.

Friendship. Relationships come before things and are higher than rules or laws.

Life and Death. Mexicans, more than any other Latin Americans, have a unique view of life and death. John Condon states that understanding the Mexican view of death is essential in understanding Mexico. Anglos, on the other hand, seem to be afraid even to speak about death. Persons "pass away," not "die." But the Mexican relaxes with the topic, jokes about it, mocks it, even celebrates it. John Condon gives these examples: *Día de los Muertos* (Day of the Dead), the bloody crucifixes of a dying Jesus (both described in Chapter VII), devils displayed in some Christmas creches, and bull fights. These items and events are more than symbols; they are experiences with a definite reality.

Passion. Emotion appears to be stronger than cold logic. Thus, the day's greeting does not give a mere "good morning" but a generous *buenos días*, not one day but many. Consider also the difference in style in a soccer game. Roger Hernandez portrays northern European players in carefully-planned strategic formations; players from southern Europe and Latin America "tend to be inventive." This is passion.

Persons. Each person has his/her personal, individual dignity. Being comes before doing. Persons are not audiences but actors, and must be approached as individuals more than as groups. Spanish individualism, the *Yo*, is the engine of the culture. It is persons and friendships, not organizations, universal principles, or laws.

Religion. The Hispanic is deeply religious. Sacred shrines, pictures, statues, candles, ceremonies, traditions, and beliefs fill daily life. Women tend to be more devout and more faithful to the church than men. Saying goodbye is expressed with a benediction, *vaya con Dios* (go with God). Any fortunate circumstance becomes a thanksgiving with a *gracias a Dios* (thank God), frequently worded "thanks God." Angel Flores explains that *Adios*, goodbye, is actually a prayer: *a Dios le encomiendo* (I commend you to God).

Space. Roger Axtell speaks of "bubbles of personal space," of "personal buffer zones." Americans need 12-15 inches; add the other person's space and there may be 24-30 inches between. Asians stand even farther apart. Latin Americans (and people from the Middle East), however, stand close to each other when talking. Friends like to do more touching in conversation than in Anglo culture, like grasping forearm or elbow or at least one's lapel. One can observe, also, that pedestrians get closer to a passing car in the street while trying to cross to the other side.

Time. The focus is on the now, the present moment or the immediate person. *Mañana* doesn't always mean tomorrow but may mean simply "later."

Work and *Fiesta*. Work well done is important, but fun and fiesta are important, too.

Do All Hispanics Share These Values?

In a broad way these descriptions are easily observed by anyone living among Hispanics, and so in general they can be considered valid. On the other hand, Javier Quiñones-Ortiz offers a word of caution. He lists the usual values of respect for others' dignity, family, community celebration through fiesta, appreciation for life and time as God's gift, and devotion to the Virgin—from the Pastoral Letter on Hispanic Ministry of the North American Bishops of the Roman Catholic Church. Then he admits, "as much as I would like to believe this..., I find that many of these claims are either inflated or simply not true." He goes on to claim only that "we are who we are period."

Probably both viewpoints have truth. Courtesy can be forgotten. Life's blows can turn anyone to bitterness. Fiesta can become drunken excess. Families can feud and fight. Faith can become dead ritual. In fact, other cultures around the world often hold to many of these same values, and can depart from them in the same way.

BEAUTY

How Do Hispanic Values on Beauty Affect Modern Advertising?

Patricia Duarte looks at Hispanic beauty standards. Spanish-language television does try to perpetuate the typical American female model among Hispanas. As a result, some analysts feel that many Latino women are too focused on facial and body beauty. One survey showed that Hispanas "spend 43 percent more on fragrances, 42 percent more on clothes, 20 percent more on shoes, and 27 percent more on personal care items than non-Latinas do." In one office, 80 percent of the women get manicures and pedicures.

But because a Latina might not always measure up to the American advertising industry's tall, thin, and white super model, the women are very prone to depression, according to Duarte, more so than non-Hispanic whites or African Americans. Olive–skinned women are labeled "black" in some agencies.

Latinas do cope with obesity. Duarte bluntly asserts that Hispanic women do not exercise enough and eat too much sweet bread and fried meat. Mexican American women are the most overweight at 67.8 percent (only 34 percent of Cubans and 37.3 percent of Puerto Ricans). Predictably, cosmetic surgery is increasing in popularity for more affluent Hispanas: face-lifts, liposuction, breast augmentation, and nose adjustments.

In general, Hispanas want to feel comfortable about who they are (wherever they are on the modeling scale), affirming the traditional belief that beauty is more than in the face but even more so in "attitude and confidence." Then they adopt American beauty standards and try to find a balance. Duarte urges Hispanic mothers to teach their daughters that they are beautiful with their brown skin and dark hair. Outer beauty is only part of a person, and inner beauty is far more essential. No one, however, is overlooking those many gorgeous Hispanas blessed with both inner and outer beauty.

CELEBRATION/ENJOYMENT
Why Is Everyone So Excited about *Fiestas?*
Mexico's great writer, Octavio Paz, gives a perspective here. Whereas Americans believe in "hygiene, health, work and contentment," they might not know the "pure joy" in the night of a *fiesta* when "...our voices explode into brilliant lights, and life and death mingle together...." The Mexican has known suffering. The *fiesta* declares that history cannot stifle laughter and friendship, music and love. *Fiesta* is celebration, the proclamation, in Elizondo's words, that "life is a gift and is worth living."

COURTESY
What Are Some Typical Hispanic Courtesies?
Courtesy is a definite Latino value. When entering a room, everyone is greeted with a handshake and *abrazo*. When beginning conversation, one first inquires about the other's family. When leaving a conversation, one always says *"permiso"* (your permission, please). If someone is eating snacks or enjoying a soft drink and another person comes along, one always offers to share. After someone sneezes, the automatic words are *salud* (health), to which the sneezer says *gracias*. One more example is the way one passes an object to another. The object is handed directly to a person, never tossed. Change is placed in the hand, not on the counter.

In San José, Costa Rica, a sign at a bus stop reads, *"Sr. pasajero, por favor aborde aquí"* (Mr. passenger, please board here). In English we do with "Bus stop."

Perhaps the Spanish word *sí* needs explaining. Dorothy Pillsbury illustrates how the little word is not always used according to English-speaking expectations. She describes how she would ask Roberto, the neighborhood handyman, to go to her house on a particular day to fix a broken window. Roberto would give her a straight-in-the eye *"Sí, sí,"* only Roberto would not necessarily show up on that day. She finally realized that *"sí"* meant that Roberto would truly like to help her but was busy that day. Courtesy would not allow him to say no.

Avoidance is another example of expressing courtesy, explain Martin and Nakayama. Whereas Anglo Americans prefer direct speech, such as "getting to the point," other cultures, such as Hispanic, Japanese, and Arab, prefer a more indirect style. Not giving offense and preserving harmony is more important than detailed honesty. Hispanics answer with what they think the other person wants to hear. "Yes" can simply mean that the other person has been heard, not that anyone will show up the next morning at eight o'clock. A Tunisian international student in this country took several months to learn that if someone asked directions and the student didn't know what to say, an honest "I don't know" is better than an extended, polite conversation and a vague, unspecific response.

FAMILY

What Is the Most Basic of All These Values?

Many would insist, along with Roger Hernandez, that "the family is the most sacrosanct value of Hispanic life..., above careers, above personal convenience, above having fun." This value is emphasized, for example, by three dramatic religious events that express the centrality of this value; *quinceañeras, Día de los Muertos* and *las Posadas*. The same value occurs in *Día de las Madres*.

How Does Social Class Impact Family Life?

Guadalupe Silva finds some cultural similarities between Hispanic and Anglo cultures. For example, wealthy families have advantages that money provides, such as better education, luxuries beyond necessities, travel, leisure, hired help, comfortable house, better diet, health care, cultural enrichment, and more congenial neighborhoods.

On the other hand, families in poverty—definitely not all of them, but, sadly, very frequently—are more apt to experience illegitimacy, abandonment, alcoholism, physical abuse, and drug use that profoundly affect healthy family life. Often beyond such chaos are cramped quarters, inadequate diet, dangerous neighborhoods, little enrichment from music and books, limited understanding of rearing and disciplining children and youth, and weak skills at communication. In these ways, therefore, economics affects families similarly on both social levels in both cultures.

Nevertheless, beyond generalities, affluent families can also be scenes of interpersonal poverty; and families in poverty can be relationally, intellectually, culturally, and spiritually rich.

What Does Extended Family Mean?

Extended family is the extensive relationships among parents and children, grandparents, uncles, aunts, cousins, and parents-in-law. This includes godparents *(padrinos)*, close friends *(cuate* is someone much-liked by the family), *tocayos* (persons with the same first name), and respected couples. Michael Erard explains that the traditional Hispanic family has "an egalitarianism in which everybody cares for everybody."

How Is Male Authority in the Family Changing?

A feature of traditional Hispanic family life is the strong male authority figure. This feature undergoes change, however, in the movement for healthy female individuality. Another example of change occurs when Latino fathers face difficult adjustments when their children become teenagers. Older Latin American tradition gives the father strong family authority. Strictness is expected. Parents assume that unmarried youth will live at home. Dating means chaperones. Firm curfews demand a return home at earlier hours. Americanized youth caught between two cultures often rebel. Second generation fathers commonly adapt and are less strict. More dialogue goes on. But Hispanic fathers walk on this tightrope between Latino concern for security and American urge for freedom. The inner struggle, admits Roger Hernandez, is not easy.

What Is the Custom of *Compadrazgo?*

This custom within Hispanic culture contributes strength to family life by using a tradition that is also a spiritual commitment. Two adults chosen to become *compadres* (co-parents) to another family's child at baptism become the child's godparents (*padrinos*). The godfather is called a *padrino,* the godmother a *madrina.* These two persons also become *compadres* to the child's parents. Sometimes the *padrinos* assist in naming the child, and perhaps the child receives the first or middle name of a godparent. At confirmation, and later at the time of a wedding, the parents of the bride become *compadres* to the parents of the groom. The arrangement is something serious, too. The godparents have a parental responsibility for the child, just as the parents do. They are part of the family. They give gifts at Christmas, birthdays, and graduation. If the parents die, the *compadres* are committed, if able, to assume full parental care.

The custom has a background in medieval Europe that was transferred to Colonial Mexico, although no one knows exactly how the early priests incorporated this arrangement among the indigenous people. Across the centuries, godparents frequently were chosen from a higher economic class as economic security for the child, even employers or political figures. Normally, modern godparents are chosen from close friends or relatives. Godsons are *ahijados* and goddaughters are *ahijadas.* Certainly in a small town, this network eventually would connect nearly the entire community. Interestingly, the church today seems to have no need to offer education on godparent duties. An innate realization prevails.

Sandoval points out that el *compadrazgo* "enlarges and strengthens the tapestry of the Hispano community." It unites the family with the ancient culture. And it can resolve some complications in foster care, guardianship, and adoption.

What Are the Attitudes Toward Rearing Children?

Traditionally the chain of command has the eldest male receiving strong respect and obedience. Boys are commonly given more liberty and are allowed louder and more aggressive behavior. Girls commonly are expected to be more feminine. Sisters may take charge of other sisters inside the home, but outside it is the older brothers who feel responsible for girls and boys alike.

How Are the Elderly Shown Honor?

First, *los ancianos* (the elderly) are not seen as a burden but as persons of worth to be honored, respected, and given their rightful place in the family. Elizondo mentions two Hispanic customs that connect here. First, families do not allow the *viejitos* (old people) to sit around without meaning for their lives. Instead, they are given some household task to perform, no matter how old the person might be. Second, traditional Hispanics will not normally send their elderly to rest homes. That would mean deserting them and dehumanizing the family.

HAPPINESS

How Do Many Hispanics Measure Success and Happiness?

An AARP study on "Money and the American Family" discovered that strong family ties, a long life, and religious faith are three basic Hispanic values. Money is not the main goal in life. Financial advancement and professional climbing in the big cities, however, often bring more conformity to the more materialistic American mindset.

PERSONHOOD

What Is Individualism?

Hispanic individualism, the *Yo*, is the pulse of the culture. It is persons and friendships, not organizations, universal principles, or laws. In Dr. John Mackay's words, the Hispanic does not try to subvert law but to transcend it by "the grace of personal privilege." On one hand, this inner force can mean anarchy, violence, following a leader blindly, or resistance to collective action. On the other hand, this personalism promotes devotion to friends and to defense of human dignity. Thus, *el personalismo* encapsulates far more than the English word "personalism." Its influence touches personal and community relationships, education, politics, technology, employment, courtesies, and even Spanish grammar.

John Condon compares the North American and Mexican individualism. North Americans see all persons as the same but evaluated in terms of character and accomplishments. Mexican individualism centers on innate, individual uniqueness. This inner quality (soul or spirit, *alma* or *espíritu*) cannot be measured by behavior or achievements. This basic dignity is easily offended. It can rise above rules or abstract principles. It does not necessarily compete, either, because each person is the better person, no matter the outcome.

What Is the Significance of *Macho* or *Machismo?*

Lorenzo LaFarelle finds the background of *machismo* among the Arab Moors in old Spain. Their influence developed Spanish upper class men who were "he-men" with family pride and long tradition. Such men were extremely jealous of their wives, defended their honor, and allowed their female roles only within the home. Conversely, to have mistresses meant a man was *muy hombre* (a real man). While it is true that this attitude exists in many cultures, the Spanish language has such a vivid word for the phenomenon.

The terms *macho* and *machismo* today exist in common speech. Actually, though, the words have two meanings. Negatively, they refer to male *chauvinism*—domineering, totalitarian, stern, and aggressive behavior, sometimes exhibited in abusive treatment of wife and children, show of physical and sexual strength, out-drinking and out-fighting all competitors, and displaying no fear of death.

Ricardo Sandoval reports that, in a recent poll, 92 percent of Mexican men believed that a woman's main role should be in the home. Also most traditional male Hispanics do not help out in the home (even though the woman has worked all week and likewise would like free time on weekends).

Positively, *machismo,* in Rafaela Castro's description, means manliness, personal pride, and responsibility: *un hombre macho* "is a man who symbolizes dignity, takes care of his family, has respect for all women, especially his mother and wife, and possesses a strong sense of self-identify and character." Therefore, before we carelessly throw around *macho* as some kind of epithet, we would be wise to remember this positive meaning.

There is even a third meaning. In the early 1970s Ricardo Sánchez first mentioned a "new *machismo,*" not male aggressiveness and virility but rather Hispanic life-strength and energy for men and women alike.

What Are Some Changes among Modern Hispanic Women?

Welcome or not to males, changes are taking place among Hispanics. In Mexico, Sandoval points out that women hold leading positions in two political parties and nearly a fifth of the seats in Congress. They make up 56 percent of the nation's voters (a right won only in 1955) and have power in all but one Mexican state. After all, women are more apt to vote than men. Women also comprise 55 percent of students at the National Autonomous University of Mexico.

In the U.S., especially in the upper and middle classes, Hispanic women have taken important positions in the professions, business and politics. In the mid-'90s, Dr. Carmen Inoa Vázquez and R. Rosa María Gil, two Hispanic therapists, co-authored a book with the provocative title *The Maria Paradox: How Latinas Can Merge Old World Traditions with New World Self-Esteem*. They began with the blockbuster concept of *marianismo*. After centuries of a belief system in which the Virgin Mary is a role model of submission, self sacrifice and sexual abstinence, the authors see the concept binding modern Latinas in a losing life style. This gender role where men see women as unequals and resist any female assertiveness speaks of a bygone day. Whether or not men accept the theology of that concept, Hispanic men are wise to see that "The times they are a-changin'."

TIME

Is the *Mañana* Syndrome Really Laziness?

In John Grisham's *The Testament*, Nate takes a taxi into a little Brazilian town and gets caught in a traffic jam. He thought it strange that the driver kept so calm as he imagined the eruption of temper in New York or Washington. He reminded himself that this was South America. "The clocks run slower. Nothing was urgent. Time was not as crucial. Take off your watch, Nate told himself."

John Condon's helpful perspective reminds us that five world continents have the same Latin American sense of time. Northern Europeans, British, and North Americans are in the minority on this one.

Anglos seldom realize that they have a totally different awareness of time. The Hispanic lives in the now, the Anglo in the future. For the Hispanic, what goes on in the present moment will not be tarnished by worrying over an appointment to be somewhere else, and thus someone can be late without the guilt that Anglos feel. Elizondo adds another theory about *mañana*. The Hispanic, he says, accepts the reality of life's limitations, that not everything will be accomplished by five o'clock or even in a lifetime. So, some things can wait until tomorrow. The moment is to be enjoyed. By contrast, the Anglo lives often with frenetic effort in the hope of enjoying tomorrow's achievement or retirement. The Hispanic value we see here is simply the present moment, the now.

WORK
What Is the Hispanic Work Ethic?

Forget the stereotype of the lazy Latino languidly lounging in the shade, sipping his *tequila*. To be sure, such can be found, as in any ethnic group. But as an example, the ethnic group in Chicago with the least education is found in the Mexican *barrio*. The people speak little English, but they are most likely to be employed. Only 33 percent of Mexican fathers believe that the government should give financial aid if one is unemployed, in contrast to 75 percent of black fathers, and no doubt high also among Anglo men. Hispanics of all origins have been known as "demons for work," men who often hold two jobs. And no one needs evidence for the hard-working Hispanic woman in home, field, factory, or office.

In the contemporary global economy, however, Hispanics are facing the challenge of cultural change in the workplace. Eva Kras, in her work on modernizing Mexican management style, emphasizes the need for Latinos to fit into today's nearly universal work standards of time and punctuality, personal accountability, verbal integrity, and reduction of "gray areas of ethics." Especially important to learn is teamwork that stresses group planning and decision making. And none other than José de la Cerda Gastelum from Guadalajara is quoted with these words: After so many years with "an outmoded management style," "mediocrity," and ignorance "of the imperatives of quality and efficiency..., we have to insist on ever greater quality."

At the very same time, Anglo managers who arrive to head departments will need to be sensitive to Hispanic values of family, religion, interpersonal relationships, and individual personhood versus total emphasis on tasks. A manager needs to be aware of Hispanic emotional sensitivity to criticism, also the importance of etiquette and courtesy, work and recreation, and a harmonious work environment. Healthy for Anglo workers too!

THREE VALUES IN ONE
How Does Speechmaking Illustrate Several Cultural Values?

Courtesy is a strong Hispanic value, and one example is speechmaking. Speeches are common at receptions, family or church or community gatherings, and whenever someone receives a plaque or certificate or any kind of public honor. The master of ceremonies or leader of a program presents the honoree. The honoree responds with more than just a smile and a brief thank you. People feel the need to express something significant about the occasion, to share warm appreciation about someone present, or to remind why everyone is together. These speeches rise to heights of eloquence or use simple words. One does not just receive an honor but also honors those who give the honor. This is courtesy.

Individualism gets expressed in the need to stand alone and address the world, even if the address is very similar to what someone else has already said. Individuality does not get lost in a crowd.

Expressiveness needs to be verbalized. This is the Latino temperament. The same passionate temperament is apparent in Italy, Greece, and throughout the Mediterranean world. The cultures of northern Europe and Great Britain, by contrast, are more reserved and less verbal.

An impressive interpretation of Hispanic speechmaking comes from Victor Villanueva Jr. He suggests that the style of Hispanic discourse is an inheritance from fifth-century Greece (B.C., or B.C.E.). This Greek rhetorical style was called sophistry. The style was absorbed by Arabs in the Byzantine Empire and by Rome. Byzantium Rome for a time ruled Spain. Islamic Moors ruled there for nearly 800 years. Now observe a similarity between Arab discourse and writing and the Spanish style: repetition of words, metaphor, poetry, a florid touch.

VALUES PROBLEMS
Do Hispanic Values Ever Cause Some Problems?
Fr. Virgilio Elizondo enumerates four problems that Hispanics frequently have in their relationships.

Individualism: Individuals pull in many directions and make teamwork more difficult.

Vagueness: Perhaps from ancient indigenous backgrounds, everyone tries so hard to be courteous that often no one knows what needs to be done or who should do it. Also, the courtesy that "beats around the bush" (such as the inability to give detailed answers that are requested) instead of open responses can confuse North Americans.

Extremism: When individual dignity and family pride get offended, revenge can get out of hand.

Unconcern: Unconcern for material things can be noble among the poor. But, laments Fr. Elizondo, many Latinos with excessive wealth often apathetically avoid any responsibility toward the less fortunate. Something universal is obvious here, too.

COMPARISONS AND POSSIBILITIES
How Can We Compare Values between Hispanic and Anglo Cultures?

Octavio Paz, one of Mexico's great writers and poets, recently deceased, discerned a sharp contrast between Mexico and the U.S. Actually, he saw two civilizations. His analysis is extremely thought-provoking.

The United States: North Americans are children of the Protestant Reformation and of the modern world (like the Enlightenment and the scientific method). They place value on the future and change, yet at the same time some search for ancestral roots.

Mexico: Mexicans are children of the Spanish Empire and the Catholic Counter-Reformation that opposed modernity. They focus on pyramids, cathedrals, and the Virgin—symbols of permanence. Concurrently, since 1800, Mexico has searched for ways to modernize and enter the future.

Which Hispanic Values Could Enrich American Life?

No culture is perfect, but many Hispanics feel that their culture offers much to balance American values. Pat Mora wants to see Hispanics "warm the cool emotional climate of this automated nation." Hispanics value fiesta, celebration, music, and *abrazos.* Their homes stress courtesy, warm interpersonal relationships, family, education, respect for authority, care for the elderly and newborns, and expression of feelings.

> If we stop merely tolerating one another, though, and learn from our diversity, we can perhaps create work places that value people as well as computers, work places touched and warmed by the growing Hispanic population.

Fr. Virgilio Elizondo suggests these values that could enrich American life: (1) Appreciation of one's own culture and language. (2) Contentment with what we need rather than compulsive desire for what we want. (3) Time for leisure and persons, for relaxation and *fiesta,* for friendships and families, rather than the constant drive to achieve and succeed.

Mike Davis comments provocatively: "Latinos are already deeply American..., and they are thoroughly engaged in the project of further defining what Americanness means." That is a powerful contribution.

Fabulous Food—
Full Stomach, Contented Heart

Does Latin American Food Live up to Its Reputation?

A common Spanish *dicho* (saying) is *panza llena, corazón contento* (full stomach, contented heart). Latin American food comes in a spectacular variety of distinctive dishes from Mexico, Puerto Rico, Cuba, the Caribbean, Central and South America, and Spain. After a typical meal, the Spanish saying is, *Estoy muy satisfecho* (I am very satisfied), but one really means, less elegantly, "I'm stuffed!"

In this book, the overwhelming preponderance of food described will be Mexican, a fact that simply reflects the author's need for future gastronomical experiences.

What Are the Many Varieties of Mexican Food?

Mexican food is not homogeneous. Food in Veracruz and Yucatán is different from food in Guadalajara and Chihuahua and along the U.S.–Mexico border. The following list, however, gives the most general items that fill a Mexican plate.

- *Arroz con pollo:* white rice, chicken pieces, green peas, tomato sauce, chopped onions, chopped bell pepper, pimiento strips, garlic, salt, pepper, oregano, saffron, dry sherry—a meal in itself.
- *Atole:* thick corn gruel.
- *Bizcochitos:* sugar cookies flavored with anise.
- *Bolillos:* like tiny French bread loaves, light and fluffy on the inside, with crisp crust, sometimes called *francesitos.*
- *Buñuelos:* a pastry made from flour and egg, butter and milk, then rolled into a tortilla, fried in hot oil, and sprinkled with cinnamon and sugar. A Christmas holiday specialty.
- *Burrito:* flour *tortilla* wrapped around almost anything available: meat, cheese, beans, stew, potatoes, onion, and chile.
- *Caldillo* or *caldo:* soup with large chunks of meat or fish, carrots, potatoes, onions—like a stew.
- *Carne adovada:* pork strips marinated and cooked in red chile, garlic, and oregano.

- *Carne asada:* roasted or barbecued beef or pork, cut in strips.
- *Carne al carbón:* meat cooked on grill.
- *Carnitas:* strips of beef or pork marinated in green chile and spices.
- *Chalupas:* corn tortillas fried and layered with beef or chicken, beans, shredded lettuce, *guacamole* and *salsa.*
- *Chilaquiles:* dried corn *tortillas* baked in sauce of chile and cheese.
- *Chile con queso:* melted cheese and green chile dip.
- *Chile rellenos:* green chiles filled with cheese, dipped in some beaten egg, then fried.
- *Chimichanga:* originating at El Charro restaurant in Tucson in the 1950s, this is a large, deep-fried *burrito.*
- *Chorizo:* a spicy pork sausage.
- *Empanaditas:* little pies stuffed with meat or fruit.
- *Enchiladas:* corn tortillas laid flat and topped with green or red chile sauce, chopped onions, and cheese—or also with meat. Many choose a fried egg on top. The other *enchilada* type is rolled.
- *Fajitas:* really from South Texas, these are small strips of beef or chicken marinated in a special sauce, fried, and put into a folded flour tortilla, along with fried onions, guacamole, lettuce, tomato pieces, green chiles, and sour cream.
- *Flan:* custard with caramel sauce.
- *Flautas:* fried corn *tortillas* rolled tight like a flute *(flauta),* filled with meat and topped with *guacamole* (avocado), sour cream, and hot sauce.
- *Frijoles refritos:* pinto beans fried and mashed.
- *Guacamole:* mashed avocados used as dip or garnish. Popular in northern New Mexico since the mid-twentieth century. Recipe includes chopped green chile, onion, garlic, and tomato, then a bit of Worcestershire sauce with salt and pepper.
- *Huevos rancheros:* fried eggs on a corn tortilla and covered with chile and cheese.
- *Jícama:* pronounced **hee**-kah-mah, this vegetable looks like a turnip. Blessed with low calories and a sweet, crunchy taste, the tuber (90 percent water and high in fiber) spruces up a tossed salad or serves as a snack for scooping up guacamole, salsa, or dips. *Jícama* is useful in stews or with stir-fried beef, chicken, or pork.
- *Menudo:* tripe chopped and cooked with *posole* (hominy, pork, and chile). Alicia López claims the best preparation is to simmer the soup overnight. Absolutely necessary are *francesitos* or *bolillos.*
- *Mole* (**móh**-leh): chicken or beef pieces in a luscious chocolate sauce containing, naturally, some chile, on a tortilla.
- *Nachos: tostadas* under beans, melted cheese, and *jalapeños.*

- *Natillas:* dessert composed of flour, milk, sugar, cinnamon, nutmeg, and egg mixture boiled until thickened. Served warm or cold.
- *Pico de gallo:* salsa with tomatoes, onions, and fresh chiles, all finely chopped, and cilantro.
- *Posole: posole* corn (hominy) stew cooked with pork or beef cubes and red chile.
- *Quesadilla:* flour tortillas holding shredded cheese and perhaps meat.
- *Refritos:* refried pinto beans.
- *Sopa:* thin noodles with tomato sauce.
- *Sopaipillas:* biscuit dough rolled thin, cut into squares, then deep-fat fried until they puff into golden-brown little "pillows," served with honey. Sticky but scrumptious!
- *Taco:* fried, crisp corn *tortilla* in a "u" fold containing ground beef or brisket shreds, chopped lettuce, tomatoes, salsa, *guacamole* and sour cream.
- *Tamales:* corn meal mush mixed with pork or chicken and hot sauce, then wrapped in corn husks and boiled. Another delectable version adds green chile and cheese with the meat.
- *Tortilla:* flat cornmeal or flour pancake with no leavening, eggs, or milk. Corn *tortillas* contain only ground corn and water, thus fat-free. Most flour tortillas have vegetable shortening but not the traditional lard. Calories? About 115 in flour, 60 in corn. New twist: use *tortillas* as a peanut butter sandwich or as a bun for hot dogs.
- *Tostadas/Tostaditas:* fried (or baked) corn *tortillas* cut into small pieces (another term is "tortilla chips"), eaten plain or dipped into *salsa,* sour cream or *guacamole.* Also used in *tortilla* soup and *chilaquiles. Tostadas* can refer also to large flour tortillas fried until crispy and topped with *guacamole* or *frijoles con queso* (avocado or beans with cheese).
- *Tres leches:* a sponge cake soaked in three kinds of milk (regular, evaporated and condensed) topped with whipped cream and maraschino cherries.

What Common Flavors Are Used in Mexican Cooking?

Comino (cumin), *cilantro* (coriander), cinnamon, cloves, and oregano are the general favorites. Above all, of course, garlic, onions, and chile help give that distinctive taste to this marvelous cuisine.

Are *Chili con Carne* and Caesar Salad Mexican?

Not the first item. A Mexican dictionary defines it as a "detestable dish with a false Mexican title." *Chili con carne* was created around 1880 by German residents in San Antonio, Texas, in 1908, after the development of chile powder. The dish was produced in cans by a German from New Braunfels, Texas. And please note the spelling. In New Mexico, at least, *chile* (with e) refers to the real biting pods that make mouth and throat burn. U.S. Senator Pete Dominici (R-NM) entered the official spelling of *chili* (with i) into the *Congressional Record* to refer **only** to Texas *chili con carne.*

But Caesar Salad? Mexican? Yes. During the Prohibition Era, César Cardini, owner of a hotel in Tijuana, Mexico, assembled this new salad for his customers. A Californian sneaked the recipe across the border, and now everybody knows about Caesar Salad.

What Is the Hottest Topic in Mexican Cuisine?
The obvious answer is chile, called "vegetable dynamite" and "the wine of the Mexican poor." Chile is found all over the world and throughout Latin America, but Mexico certainly makes chile a specialty. As many as 3,500 to 7,000 varieties come in sizes like a pea to New Mexico's BIG JIM at twelve inches in length. Chile comes sweet and mild to tart and hot. By the way, in Spanish, "hot" food is not *caliente* (hot like temperature) but *picante* (hot like a bite or sting).

Is Chile Really as Popular as Some Claim?
Chile is big business, using 28,700 acres in New Mexico, California, Arizona, and Texas. New Mexico alone produces nearly 100,000 tons annually. Chile lovers can get nearly lyrical over this topic, like Kathleen Rafael:
> From fork to mouth—the moment of truth is on the tip of the tongue. Restless taste buds stand at attention as the assault comes full force. The mouth burns, the eyes water, and the nose drips. Gasping, before the thrill is gone, the fork retrieves another mouthful. This is outrageous! This is delicious! This is heaven! Yes, this is eating green chile.

In Albuquerque there is an annual National Fiery Foods Show. A hundred exhibits are visited by thousands who pay three dollars admission to sample hot food from twenty states, Mexico, and Jamaica. One company markets "a scientifically engineered *jalapeño* for gringos." Would you believe even green *jalapeño* lollipops?

Almost unbelievable is one more example of chile-mania: ED'S ORIGINAL CAVE CREEK CHILI BEER™ (beer with a chili pepper floating in the bottle) from Black Mountain Brewing Co., Cave Creek, Arizona.

Why Is Chile So Popular?
E.A. "Tony" Mares testifies as a true chile witness. He confesses that
> ...even when I am at my troglodytic and misanthropic worst, isolated and wanting no human company, a bowl of steamy hot green or red

chile...will bring me back to a psychological condition of identification with my fellow human beings.

Why this compulsion? Nicolle Carroll gives four reasons for the popularity of chile:

1. Increasing immigration from Latin America.
2. Addiction: "eating a hot chile is like culinary bungee jumping. The first plunge is scary, but once you're over the shock you can't wait to try it again."
3. Fitness craze: no fat and inexpensive.
4. Chile spices up food, and that's exotic.

Alice Merriott gives three other answers:

1. People value the Vitamin C.
2. People like the stimulation, "comparable to...the lightest wines."
3. "Chile-lovers don't need a reason. They like chile, and the pain of eating it only tickles their masochistic palates."

What Is the History of Chile?

Some evidence points to indigenous Amerindian use of chile in Bolivia and Peru as far back as 7500 B.C./B.C.E. (Before the Common Era) as the *piquín* pepper. The Incas apparently cultivated chile by 2300 B.C.E. and even worshiped the plant as something holy (like divine fire?), naming it Ucha, the name of a chief character in their creation myth.

Before 1500 B.C.E. these chiles had reached Mexico and had become a part of spicy native food. By 500 C.E. (Common Era) the Mayas used chile in a hot breakfast cereal and for evening stews. Around 120 C.E. the Aztecs ate red and green *chilies* (in *Náhuatl*) of many sizes. Moctezuma, we are told, enjoyed a light breakfast of chile and nothing else. Obviously, he overlooked a clever military strategy against Cortés—simply blowing scorching chile breath on the helpless Spanish invaders! Much of Mexican food comes from this chile-rich Aztec culture. Pueblo Indians learned about the food from trade with Mayas and Aztecs.

Columbus found chile in the West Indies, saw a resemblance to black pepper, and called them peppers. He took samples back to Spain, and by 1600 Spain was transporting New World silver, spices, and fiery Mexican chile peppers as far as Africa, the Philippines, China, and Japan—thus spicier Szechuan Chinese and Thai cuisines. In a reflex motion, the Spaniards gave the word to a country in their empire: Chile. Mexicans, of course, wasted no time in cauterizing their throats and stomachs. An early Spanish settler and priest, Fray **Bartolomé de las Casa**, in the 16th century exclaimed: "*Sin el chile los mexicanos no creen que están comiendo*" (without chile, Mexicans don't believe they're eating).

Although the first scientific treatise on the subject came from botanist John Gerhard in England in 1597 *(The Herbals or General Historie of Plantes)*, nothing too dramatic happened over the next four hundred years until in modern times New Mexico State University researchers began developing new types of chile for the popular market. Fabian Garcia was the first researcher. He devoted thirty years at the Agricultural Experiment Station there. He developed the first scientifically produced chile, NEW MEXICO NO. 9, that was popular until the 1950s. His successor was Dr. Roy Nakayama who grew up picking chiles in the Mesilla Valley. In 1955 he turned out NEW MEXICO NO. 6 which was milder and therefore easier to market outside New Mexico. Subsequently, after ten years of more research, NUMEX BIG JIM appeared in 1974. Pollen had been borrowed from a Peruvian type, crossed with ANAHEIM, native CHIMAYO, and other New Mexican varieties to produce BIG JIM. It was named in honor of Las Cruces farmer Jim Lytle. BIG JIM is a foot long, costs less to pick than smaller chiles, is hotter than some, and pleases the canning industry. Dr. Nakayama produced also the NEW MEXICO NAKY which provided extractable color for paprika.

Taking over after Nakayama's retirement in 1984, Dr. Paul Bosland has produced NU MEX SUNRISE, SUNSET, and ECLIPSE, also the NU MEX SUNGLOW, SUNFLARE, and SUNBURST, all of them for use in ornamental *ristras* (string of chiles hanging on the wall). The NU MEX CONQUISTADOR has flavor "but with no heat." The NU MEX BAILEY PIQUIN not only has heat but can be harvested by machine. Who knows now what lies ahead in this hot field.

An event in the 1965 session of the New Mexico legislature should not be a surprise. In that session Rep. Arencio Gonzales (D-San Miguel) sponsored an earthshaking bill to make chile the state vegetable. Predictably, the pinto bean enthusiasts, represented by Rep. John Bigbee (R-Torrance), proposed an amendment to make *frijoles* (beans) the co-official vegetable. With commendable political maturity, that legislature passed the amended bill unanimously.

What Railroad Was Named after Chiles?

In the late 1800s the old Denver & Rio Grande narrow gauge railroad line was built between Santa Fe and Alamosa, Colorado. The trains carried mail and passengers and was called the "Chile Line" because the cars were painted red. Its climb from Santa Fe through the Río Grande Gorge to Embudo and then up to Alamosa presented a rigorous challenge to the engines. Chile growers in northern New Mexico exchanged their chile and orchard fruit for Colorado's beans, wheat, and potatoes. Gradually, improved roads and transportation made the little line obsolete. In the fall of 1941, the nation needed iron for the war effort and tore up the tracks, bringing an end to a bit of chile history.

Is Chile a Vegetable or a Fruit?
Despite the New Mexico legislature's recognition of chile as the state vegetable, we must refine the issue more precisely. In the words of Michelle Jacquez-Ortiz, in the pod, chile is a fruit. When eaten as a main course dish, it is a vegetable. When dehydrated and ground into a powder, it is a spice. In this life everything is complex!

Why Are Chiles So Hot?
The tongue-burning ingredient in chile is capsaicin (cap-**say**-ih-sin), a colorless, biting, transparent compound ($C18H27NO3$). The oily, orange-colored acid is found alongside the seeds and veins of the chile pod. The heat is measured in Scoville units: 10,000 units in mild chile, 15,000 in Caribe chile, and 40,000 in a *pequín quebrado*—which is considered beyond what most ordinary human beings can tolerate.

By the way, the heat in chile is literal. The capsaicin (from the Greek *kaptos*, meaning "to bite") gives an adrenaline rush by stimulating sensitive nerve cells in the mouth and grabbing protein receptors on the cell surfaces. Those receptors are the same ones activated by the touch of a hot iron on the skin.

Which Is the Hottest Chile?
TIME magazine's Guy García, after interviews with chefs, reading, and personal experiment, ranks the *habanero* at the top. He doesn't recommend it unless you have "an asbestos tongue and a fireproof stomach."

Which Is Hotter: Green or Red Chile?
Neither one, according to Griggs Restaurant in El Paso. When a green chile matures to red, the capsaicin does not change, but the fructose does. Thus, red chiles with more fructose seem sweeter. Also, the general rule tells us that the smaller a chile, the hotter. Incidentally, our experts inform us that the most effective fire prevention in chile eating is milk or ice cream; "the oil in dairy products buffers the capsaicin."

Won't Hot Mexican Food Damage the Stomach?
Modern research has demolished this fear of what hot chile might do to the lining of the stomach. Chile will not by itself cause stomach ulcers. In fact, capsaicin often protects the stomach from aspirin damage.

Neither will chile cause stomach cancer, a disease, by the way, with a very low incidence in Mexico City.

What Are the Benefits of Chile Besides Sinus Clearance and Taste Thrill?
The Pueblos and early Spanish used chile to improve digestion, preserve food, and disinfect wounds. Mayas used chile to treat coughs and sore throats. Note: the American Medical Association now recommends a sore throat gargle with 10 drops of Tabasco sauce in a half-glass of warm water. That's one cheap prescription. Today we know about a much wider range of alleged benefits of chile.

- Offers a rich source of vitamins A and C. One green pod has six times as much Vitamin C as an orange; when it turns red it has twice the amount of Vitamin A as a carrot. Now add amounts of Vitamin E, B1 (thiamin), B2 (riboflavin), B3 (niacin) and dietary fiber thrown in for free.
- Lowers cholesterol. Dr.Andrew Weil thinks future research will show other benefits for the heart.
- Fights cluster headaches and possibly colon cancer (chile's beta-carotene) and perhaps sinusitis and even depression.
- Produces a natural high as the capsaicin stirs up endorphins.
- Speeds up metabolism for weight reduction.
- Reduces heartburn and chronic indigestion. An Italian study found that capsaicin capsules taken before meals can reduce ordinary digestive problems by 60 percent.
- Fights diabetic pain caused by damage to the nerves.
- Aids relief of psoriasis and itching from dialysis treatments.
- Creates a natural decongestant by making body fluids flow.
- Improves digestion by stimulating production of saliva which in turn fights flatulence, dry mouth, stomach cramps, and indigestion.
- In small doses, chile can make one more alert by increasing activity of the nervous system.
- Relieves toothache by numbing tooth pain.
- Might fight cancer with its high levels of antioxidants and vitamins to slow or prevent the development of cancer cells.

And that's not all. Look now at an amazing range of extremely practical chile uses available for happy daily living: chile is the sting in ginger ale, the zing in mace-like sprays, the anti-inflammatory in creams for arthritis and muscle aches, the spice in ABSOULT PEPPAR VODKA™ and in BUMBLE BEE JALAPEÑO TUNA,™ a coating applied to nails to discourage nail biting, and a coloring used in food in zoos to increase the pink color of flamingos and in aquariums to keep goldfish looking golden. Chile is a coloring used in paints, cosmetics, clothing dyes, lipstick, and candles. It goes into cookies, breads, cheesecakes, and ice cream.

In Alaska, chile is put on electric cables to stop rodents from chewing them and on boat hulls to prevent barnacles. But get this: In some South American tribes, mothers rub chiles on their breasts to wean their little ones; in Panama fishermen dangle chiles behind their boats to avoid sharks; and, naturally, some folks use chiles as an aphrodisiac!

By now, a person might be visualizing old-time peddlers selling their mysterious nostrums that were guaranteed to cure everything from headaches to hives and hemorrhoids. Whatever any "practical" uses, the main role of chile is to enhance the joy of eating.

Is There Any Other Chile Factoid One Needs to Know?

What is paprika? The word means chile in Hungarian and refers to any ground powder of red chile that lacks pungency.

How can a person reduce "the chile burn"? In the mouth, use milk, butter or sugar. On the hands, gloves are smart, but otherwise a good scrub with soap and water followed by a menthol cream or PREPARATION H™ will help.

Where did the *ristra* custom originate? Ristras are those lovely red garlands of chiles drying in the sunshine on walls of houses in New Mexico. In Spanish colonial times these garlands were not decorations but a practical method to dry and store red chiles. After winter plucking, the peppers were ground into powder for food. In northern New Mexico the ristras also served as cash (in the 1700s, one ristra could buy a pound of chocolate, two pounds of sugar, or a deerskin). Texas humorist John Kelso laughingly calls New Mexico the only state "where they eat the decor." As a footnote, every ristra needs 180 chiles woven into clusters of three and a central wire or cord about six feet long.

Chile Ristra

Where can one find the best chile? Some aficionados swear by chile from the Española Valley in northern New Mexico; others prefer chile from Hatch in the south that calls itself "Chile Town, U.S.A."

What Is a Food, a Package, and a Spoon All in One?

This riddle's answer is a *tortilla*. Corn *tortillas* were the common bread of pre-Columbian Indians and in *Náhuatl* they were called *tlasxcalli*. The uses of the *tortilla* are varied. They are eaten as bread. They are used as a spoon to eat other food. They are used as *tacos, enchiladas, flautas, tostadas,* and *nachos.* More recently they have been used with *fajitas. Tortillas* filled with beans, meat, or potatoes become *burritos. Burritos* fried become *chimichangas.* In the words of food expert Diana Kennedy, we have here "perhaps the most versatile piece of foodstuff the world has ever known." *Tortilla* sales reached $3.5 billion in 1999, not including chips, and has climbed even higher since then, up from only $300 million in 1980. These sales figures surpass bagels, pita bread, and croissants combined.

What Ancient Mexican Food Is Served for Breakfast, Lunch, or Dinner?

Dating to pre-Conquest *Náhuatl* speaking Indians of Mexico and Central America and named *tamalli* in Aztec *Náhuatl,* the *tamal* (often called *tamale* in singular form) is pork or chicken mixed in cornmeal (*masa* or corn flour), with red or green chile, and wrapped into a cornhusk for steaming. Served with this dish could be *posole, empanaditas* (little pies similar to a turnover) and *bizcochitos.* Denise Kusel coined the phrase "tamale madness."

Are Little *Burros* Animals or Food?

Burros are donkeys or asses, but *burritos* (little *burros*) that people eat are flour *tortillas.* Fillings usually include beans, potatoes, and chile with meat. Chicanos in Texas came up with this item in the 1920s. Commercial marketing of *burritos* began in San Francisco in 1961 and now *burritos* appear on all Mexican restaurant menus. As a historical tidbit, one theory traces the *burrito* to the Spanish who brought flour *tortillas* to Mexico. Bean *burritos* in larger flour *tortillas* were more filling than those with corn *tortillas.* This handy cowboy ration became useful when riding on the trail.

How Could *Guacamole* Be a Terrorist Threat?

The ingredients of *guacamole* are mashed avocado, tomato, green chile, garlic, salt, and drops of lemon juice. *Guacamole* is served as dip with *tostadas* or chips; as a salad; or as garnish with *enchiladas, flautas,* or other dishes. Have you heard, though, of a momentary panic? Mayor Richard Daly of Chicago received a fearful report from a restaurant customer about some green globs that looked like a bio-terrorist attack. The Mayor answered, "Guacamole is not dangerous. It's good for you."

Recent research seems to agree with the mayor. Fear of the avocado's fat and calorie content has made many people avoid this food. But the fat is only 5 grams, and 3 grams are monounsaturated fat that helps the heart. Some studies claim that avocados can reduce inflammation and pain, lower cholesterol and triglycerides, prevent or lower high blood pressure and heart attacks, fight cancer, benefit pregnant women, help diabetics, and enhance health in general.

What Are Some Factoids about *Menudo?*

A Hispanic invites an Anglo friend to have *menudo* with him for breakfast at a Mexican restaurant. The friend trusts his friend and dutifully places his order, only to find out after a few mouthfuls that he is eating the stomach lining of a cow, maybe with pig's or calf's feet, as well as less threatening ingredients like *posole* or hominy, onions, garlic, and chile. There is a moment of mild shock. The Hispanic beams as he imagines how the gastronomic delight of his friend matches his own. Rafaela Castro mentions that in certain areas of Mexico the honest name for this delicacy is *panza* (stomach). Humor aside, now, many Anglos and practically all Mexican Americans consider this dish to be the ultimate way to begin Saturday or Sunday morning, or Christmas Day, New Year's Day, Super Bowl Sunday or, let's admit it, any ordinary day. Now, beyond the joy of eating, some persons even use *menudo* to cure Asian flu and hangovers.

What Is the Story of Beans in the Mexican Diet?

Frijoles can be pinto or black beans, a key part of Mexican food. They can be cooked fresh along with onions, spices, cheese, and chiles— even beer. *Refritos* (refries) are actually once-fried, traditionally in cholesterol-clogging lard, but they are now available fried in safer vegetable oil. *Refritos* go well in *burritos* or with scrambled eggs, also as a side dish with almost anything. Rafaela Castro gives us a bit of bean history. Beans show up in Peruvian mountain caves dating back 8,000 years. From Peru the beans seem to have moved (no pun intended) as far as Mexico, appearing in the Valley of Mexico around 6,000 to 7,000 years ago and in New Mexico around 2,300 years ago. American Indians raised fifty different species of beans. From this bean background we can see why a derogatory word for Mexicans has been "beaners." Children reared in poverty have been known to eat cooked dried beans as if they were chocolate fudge!

What Is Replacing Ketchup in the U.S.?

A decade ago Regina Schrambling described how *salsa* had become the winner over ketchup. Coming from the Aztecs, low in calories, high in Vitamin C and fiber, free of fat or cholesterol or sugar, *salsa* has multiple uses: straight with chips or mixed with sour cream, flavored with *burritos* or *tacos* or even with potatoes and pasta, as salad dressing, as a fish sauce, a meat marinade, or something to spice up any vegetable, even appropriate with desserts like papaya, strawberries, and bananas.

The usual ingredients in *salsa* are tomatoes, chopped onions, minced clove garlic, chopped jalapeño or serrano chiles, cilantro, salt, and pepper.

What Mexican Food Came from Egypt by Way of Spain?

It's bread. Guadalupe Silva presents the vocabulary of Mexican bread: *bolillos, birotes* (in Guadalajara), *tortas* (in Puebla), *pan de agua* (in Torreón), and *francesitos* (in El Paso). The ancient Egyptian recipe came with the Spanish conquistadors and was refined during the French occupation under Emperor Maximilian and Empress Carlota in the mid-1800s. *Bolillos* are a bread with crispy crust but soft inside. Calories are low. There are no fats or additives, only natural flour, salt, leavening, water, and sometimes a bit of sugar. Increasingly, American bakeries try to produce a similar product using a frozen base, but this commercial product is noticeably different from bread prepared with fresh ingredients and baked in traditional ovens.

Bolillos— Gabriel Sánchez

What Mexican Drink Matches the Fire of the *Jalapeño?*

Tequila has been called "part of the soul of Mexico." It is produced in the town of Tequila, near Guadalajara, in the state of Jalisco, and is distilled from the juice of the large, spiny, blue maguey plant. TEQUILA SAUZA™ is the largest company.

Pre-Columbian Aztecs drank a primitive, foamy brew, although drunkenness brought the death penalty. The elderly and nursing mothers used the drink for nutrition. In rural Mexico today the brew is thought to cure syphilis, purify the blood, and provide an aphrodisiac. It is used as antiseptic for wounds, aftershave lotion, insect repellent, charcoal lighter, cholesterol antidote, digestive aid, diuretic, and laxative. Apparently, the only limits are the imagination of the user. Not all Hispanics drink liquor, but most of those who do will know about *tequila.*

What Is a Popular Mild Mexican Beverage?

Agua de horchata can send Mexican Hispanics into ecstasy. The ingredients are melon or cantaloupe seeds mixed with milk, sugar, cinnamon, and perhaps a drop of vanilla. An easier method is to avoid the seeds and use cooked rice instead.

What Is a Favorite Mexican Lenten Dessert?

A Mexican dish named *capirotada* (a little bit of everything) is a bread pudding mixing *piloncillo* cones or dark-brown sugar, French bread, crumbled or shredded Mexican or jack cheese, cinnamon, water, vanilla, dark raisins, and chopped walnuts or pecans. According to Melissa Martínez, this was originally a Lenten dessert that now appears at Christmas and other special times of the year.

Why Can Traditional Mexican Cooking Lead to Health Problems?

No one can criticize the flavor, quantity, or nutrition. Corn and beans together form a complete protein. When vegetables and fruits are added—like chile, tomatoes, avocados, and squash—the nutritional level is high. Besides, beans alone might counteract heart disease and circulatory problems.

But when beans are cooked in lard and loaded with cheese on a daily basis, and when a person does not get sufficient exercise, people can put on weight, notably among lower socio-economic groups. To this base, add soft drinks, candies, white flour instead of corn tortillas, hamburgers and pizza. Zarela Martínez understands why 48 percent of Mexican Americans are overweight and 42 percent are clinically obese. Worse yet, 25 percent between ages 45 and 74 will become diabetic. Others will develop cancer, hypertension, and heart diseases. Martínez emphasizes this obesity will have an increasingly "devastating impact on the nation's health care system."

Here are some tips for solving this problem and encouraging better health for Hispanics and non-Hispanics alike.

1. Eat less red meat and avoid poultry skins.
2. Stop frying food in lard. Soften and heat *tortillas* in vegetable or olive oil. Baseball's legendary pitcher, Satchel Paige, used to say that he avoided fried meats because they angry up the blood. Ditto for *chimichangas* and its cousins.
3. Use less cheese with *enchiladas* or use low-fat or *soya* cheese.
4. Buy vegetarian refries and whole wheat *tortillas* (no cholesterol, low saturated fat).
5. Go easy on those chips, *guacamole,* and sour cream.

What Is Moctezuma's Chief Legacy to Mexican Cuisine?

Chocolate! Mexico's Aztec ruler gave Cortés, the Spanish conqueror, a foamy chocolate drink in a golden goblet; and nearly five centuries later we Americans savor fourteen pounds of that dark delight per person every year. Moctezuma himself downed fifty cups a day. Columbus first discovered the Aztec *xocoatl* (bitter juice) on his second voyage in 1502, but it was Cortés who wrote King Carlos I of Spain about this "divine drink." Kept a Spanish secret until the mid-1600s, chocolate inevitably spread to Italy, France, and England. Today it is a world industry that delights our palates with chocolate ice cream, candy bars, brownies, cakes, mousses, and elegant individual candies with all sorts of designs and fillings.

In Mexico this "divine" delicacy has its place mainly in a hot beverage with cinnamon or in the exquisite seasoning for *mole* (**móh**-leh) sauce with chicken or turkey. We are told that women in the state of Chiapas years ago were excommunicated by their bishop for refusing to give up their chocolate drinks during Mass. That is genuine chocoholism.

What Is the National Dish of Mexico?

We have looked quite thoroughly at Mexican food, but we must mention one dish in particular. That dish is *mole*, a delectable mixture of chicken with cocoa powder, tomato sauce, onions, peanut butter, garlic, chile, and spices covering a flour *tortilla*.

Mole poblano is the full name of this dish, because somewhere in the dish's origins the dish was served in the Mexican city of Puebla, and its citizens are called *poblanos*. *Mole poblano* (with turkey) is the most common form of at least fifteen kinds altogether. One story relates how Moctezuma prepared *mole* at a banquet for Cortés and his soldiers, thinking that they were gods. Another legend tells about sixteenth century nuns at Puebla who heard that their archbishop was arriving for a visit. Desperately, they prayed for a menu idea. An angel directed them to chop everything in sight and edible, including all the available chiles, spices, herbs, cinnamon, and even chocolate. The nuns killed their only turkey, put everything together, and served the delicious meal from a huge pot to a very impressed archbishop. The national dish of Mexico was born.

What Are Examples of Puerto Rican Cuisine?

Puerto Rican food reflects original *Taíno* tribes (corn, tropical fruit, seafood, *achiote* seeds), Spanish conquerors (beef, pork, rice, wheat, olive oil), and imports by African slaves (okra and *yautia)*. The blend is called *cocina criolla* (creole kitchen). Here is a list of typical Puerto Rican food today.

Appetizers/snacks. *Bacalaitos* (fried codfish fritters), *empanadillas* (small turnovers with fish or beef), *pasteles* (deep-fried meat and vegetable patties), *alcapurrías* (banana croquettes stuffed with beef or pork), *pirulis* (sugar sticks), *granizados* (tropical fruit ice), *churros* (deep-fried sugary donut sticks), and *piraguas* (shaved ice cone covered with fruity syrup).

Soups. Look for black bean soup; vegetable soup (also with plantains and meats); okra soup; chicken soup (with rice, often with pieces of pumpkin, diced potatoes or *yautias)*; fish soup (with both head and tail, flavored with garlic, spices, onions, tomatoes, vinegar, and sherry); and chick peas soup (with pig's feet, pumpkin, *chorizos,* salt pork, tomatoes, cilantro leaves, chile peppers, cabbage, or potatoes).

Puerto Rico's most traditional dish, and common at Christmas and other special occasions, is a gumbo called *asopao*. It features rice with chicken or shellfish, spiced with all kinds of seasonings, along with vegetables like tomatoes, onions, green peas or asparagus, olives, and chile peppers.

Seasonings. Distinctive Puerto Rican flavors emerge by using *adobo* (a mix of peppers, oregano, garlic, salt, olive oil, lime juice or vinegar—all rubbed into meat before roasting. *Sofrito* is another mix of onions, garlic, coriander, peppers, oregano, olive oil, and *achiote* seeds (giving a bright yellow color).

Main dishes. Stews are cooked in a *caldero* (heavy kettle), such as *guisada puertorriqueña* (beef stew), with chunks of beef, the usual flavorings, and perhaps raisins. Meat pies *(pastelón de carne)* have salt pork or ham fillings with a pastry topping. Roasted meat of all kinds is rubbed with the *adobo* mix. Chicken is a major dish: *arroz con pollo* (chicken with rice), sweet and sour chicken *(apollo agridulce)*, and broiled chicken *(pollitos asados a la parrilla)*. Fish and shellfish are sprinkled with lime juice and the usual seasonings, then fried or grilled and served with vegetables. Shrimp cooked in beer, also boiled crab, are other choices. Egg omelets are prepared with onions, cubed potatoes, and olive oil.

Also a favorite at Christmas and other special times is roasted, barbecued pig, or *lechón asada*. The pig is roasted for several hours in an open pit, then basted with sour orange juice and *anchiote* coloring. The marinade will have garlic, sweet chile peppers, vinegar, lime juice, salt, and olive oil. *Adobo* marinade goes with pig or goat meat.

Side dishes. Vegetables can be *chayote* (like squash) or breadfruit (a tropical fruit), also yucca. These are marinated in *mojo* (hot olive oil, lemon juice, sliced raw onions, garlic, cumin, and water). *Plátanos* (green plantains, a banana variety that cannot be eaten raw) is the most popular side dish, baked, fried, or boiled. *Tostones* are sliced, lightly fried, crushed, and refried plantains served with meat and poultry dishes.

Desserts. *Flan* is caramel custard. Other desserts are *queso blanco* (white cheese with guava jelly); coconut in many forms (with sweet potatoes, as *flan,* as squares with meringue, or as bread pudding); *arroz con dulce* is cooked rice and coconut cream, often with raisins; orange layer cake, banana cupcakes, guava cake, and pumpkin cocktail

Beverages. Coffee is strong, usually *con leche* (with warm milk). Even stronger drinks are *Cuba Libre* (rum and coke), *piña colada* (rum, coconut cream, and pineapple juice), and beer. Fruit juices are made from pineapple, coconut, papaya, lime, tamarind, or mangos.

What Are Features of Cuban Cuisine?

Cuban cuisine, like Puerto Rico's, has many sources: Spanish (*paella,* rice, seafood, and chicken), and a rice and bean dish named *Moros y Cristianos* (black Moors and white Christians); African (slaves brought black beans); and French (pastries and chicken fricassee). Cuban food does not at all resemble Mexican food with its fiery chiles. Cuban spices and techniques reflect Spain with additional Caribbean touches and the peasant cuisine that cares little for exact measurement and timing. As elsewhere, Cuban Americans consume hamburgers, hot dogs, pizza, and soft drinks as compulsively as other Americans. But here is a typical Cuban menu.

Breakfast. *Tostada* (buttered Cuban bread toasted on a grill) with *café con leche* (coffee with warm milk). The coffee is strong espresso. Pieces of the *tostada* get dunked into the coffee as some people soak donuts.

Lunch. Cuban sandwiches are slices of pork or ham with Swiss cheese, pickles, and mustard on sweet egg bread. Another item is beefsteak slices with lettuce and tomatoes on bread. Fried potato sticks or fried plantain chips complete the meal.

Snacks. Favorites are finger foods (*bocaditos* or small sandwiches with ham spread), *batidos* (tropical milk shakes), or *empenadas* (flaky turnovers filled with meat, cheese, or guava).

Dinner. Meat dishes are fish of all kinds, *lechón asado* (roast pig), *ropa vieja* (shredded beef dish with guava paste and cream cheese), *picadillo* (hash), and *arroz con pollo* (rice and chicken). Vegetables and side dishes commonly are *plátanos verdes o maduros* (fried green or ripe plantain), *plátonos dulces fritos* (fried sweet plantain), *moros* (black beans and rice), and *yuca* (casava).

Desserts. Desserts, with *café con leche,* of course, include *flan* and *pudín de pan* (bread and rice puddings).

Drinks. *Daquiri* and *mojito* are popular choices, both made from lime juice and pure cane rum.

Hispanic Folk Culture—
From Adobe to Weaving

FOLK OR POPULAR CULTURE

Folk culture means the ways in which a people and a culture express its traditional arts, celebrations, customs, dances, gestures, idioms, legends, health and healing, music, proverbs, religion, and sports. For clarification, Martin and Nakayama define **high culture** as elite activities (symphony, ballet, opera, great literature, art). **Low culture** is activities of common folk (music, videos, game shows, wrestling, stock car races, TV talk shows). "Low" is a poor word choice here; "common" would be better. The emphasis is on **common tradition.**

FOLK ARCHITECTURE
What Is the Most Typical Example of Folk Architecture?

Adobe (mud-straw mixture) originated in ancient Egypt and Babylonia. Some writers claim that *adobe* came to the Americas with the Spanish conquerors and was immediately adopted by Native Americans in Mexico and in today's Southwest. The other viewpoint claims the Spanish were familiar with *adobe,* found *adobe* also among the Aztecs, then added the forming of mud-straw into bricks. Since Spanish colonial days, *adobe* houses have been the typical style of construction.

The contemporary craze for *adobe* may come from aesthetic and nostalgic feelings, but originally and still today the reasons are also practical. *Adobe* is the finest insulation in existence. It keeps a house warm in winter and cool in summer. What a pity that this simple, functional product is more expensive today than conventional materials. Most modern construction uses cinder block with brown plaster to make the surface of a wall look like *adobe.*

How Is *Adobe* Made?

Alice Merriot in *The Valley Below* gives a vivid description of *adobe*-in-the-making in the old days. She depicts Manuel as he mixed clay with water and finely-chopped straw, one part straw to twenty parts mud. The mixing was done with a long-handled hoe. Then by wheelbarrow the paste was trundled to a spot where the load was emptied into a mold constructed with 1 x 5 boards with a partition down the middle. Punching the mud down with his hands, then smoothing with a shovel, Manuel carefully lifted the form. Before him lay two 5 x 12 x 14 inch bricks. After drying in the sun, the bricks shrink to 4 x 10 x 12 inches. Manuel turned out twelve hundred bricks during six workdays.

Today, *adobe* is made by a machine that produces up to 15,000 bricks daily. Dirt, water, and shredded straw are poured into a huge concrete pit and then into a mold machine.

What Was *Jacal* Construction?

In addition to stone masonry, logs, and *adobe,* another style was *jacal* (hah-**cahl**). Using material and craftsmen immediately available, the early settlers put together vertical rows of six-foot-high wood poles (*varillas*) sunk into the ground and frequently with tree bark left in place. Horizontal logs were laid on top. The entire structure was given a mud plastering inside and out, and a flat roof supported by *vigas* fitted into the horizontal logs. In this case, the mud-straw is not called *adobe*. Actually, Native Americans in New Mexico made use of this *jacal* style before they ever saw Spaniards. Spanish colonists borrowed the concept for homes, storage rooms, and pens for domesticated animals. Their metal tools allowed a stronger and more permanent structure. With usage carried into the early 1900s, a few remain to this day.

FOLK ART
What Are Some Examples of Folk Art?

Rafaela Castro refers to the purposes of folk art: to express ethnic identity, to attempt village economic self sufficiency in the earlier twentieth century, and to provide symbols of religious faith.

> *Bultos* are *santos,* three-dimensional figures of saints or of Christ and carved in wood. Peter López finds *retablos* and *bultos* as far back as the 9th century A.D./C.E. and common throughout Europe. They were brought by Spain to Mexico and into New Mexico. After Mexico became independent from Spain in 1821, priests left the territory and took most church art. Northern New Mexico villagers took up this craft to help keep Catholic faith alive and to hold the church together when clergy were so scarce. Perhaps the *penitentes* also became some of the artisans. The craft died out by 1870, a fact encouraged by Archbishop Lamy's objection to laity-based religion. But in the 1960s, the Spanish market developed, with a powerful resurgence in the 1970s. The finest collection of this religious folk art can be seen at the International Folk Art Museum in Santa Fe, New Mexico.

Colcha **embroidery art** (*colcha* means bedspread) uses geometric, floral or scenic designs, and religious or secular images, employing the colcha stitch. Such work serves as wall hangings, table or bed covers, and altar covers.

Filigree is a jewelry craft with origins in ancient Egypt and Greece. It entered Spanish culture from the Moors. A very thin gold or silver wire gets twists and curls until patterns emerge for earrings and necklaces.

Murals (see below).

Ojos de Dios are ritual symbols made by the Huichol tribe in Mexico's western Sierra Madre mountains and replicated in souvenir shops everywhere in the Southwest. Constructed of yarn and bamboo sticks and forming a square at an angle, the center represents the eye of God looking at the one praying for health and good life.

Paintings of *la Virgen de Guadalupe*.

Paper work such as *papel picado* is tissue paper cut into intricate designs and strung on long strings. The occasion will be special days and holidays. These are commonly strung in restaurants.

Reredos are *santos* painted on screens and placed behind church altars.

Retablos were created in the 1700s in New Mexico to honor the saints (including the Virgin and Jesus) or to give thanks (for a successful operation or healing, release from prison, or any answer to prayer), according to Rafaela Castro. Another purpose was to document a vow made to a saint and to give thanks for a miracle or answer, thus the name *retablos ex-voto* (from a vow). These works were quite artistic and usually were placed in a church or shrine. According to S. Derrickson Moore, New Mexico State University's Art Gallery has the largest public collection of *retablos* in the U.S., with over 1,700 objects.

Straw applique made into figures.

Tin art features metal work for wall decorations, niches, crucifixes, frames, jewelry boxes and mirrors. The skill is a New Mexican speciality and is still alive.

Weaving (see below).

Do Directions Exist for Making These Crafts?

Angel Vigil's *Una Linda Raza* includes details for making the following items: *santos, colcha* embroidery, *colcha* blanket, tin lantern and frame, *piñata, papel picado,* and *ojos de Dios*.

Why Are Murals More Profound Than Most Anglos Realize?

Murals are not graffiti as some Anglos insist but rather a colorful form of folk art. In *barrios* across America, murals become art-on-the-street, a popular art form that sings and shouts and cries. Their themes range from religious faith to Aztec heritage, personal identity, and social political concerns. In John West's expression, murals express "...the aims and pains of a subculture long deprived of a voice."

The origin of murals in the U.S. began in 1932 in Los Angeles when the Mexican muralist David Alfaro Siqueiros painted a mural on Olvera Street, the oldest section of the city. The theme was Mexican exploitation, showing a crucified figure and immigrant labor. The work was partly, and later completely, whitewashed. This censorship was undercut when the painting began reappearing through the whitewash. The murals developed further themes, like police brutality, border crossings, drug addiction, gang warfare, poverty, and exclusion. Murals now speak their themes from *barrio* walls across the nation.

A vivid mural adorns the west wall of the Boys' Club in El Paso's *El Segundo Barrio*. Juan Contreras and Joe Olivas provide the following interpretation. The title of the mural, *Entelequía/Entelechy,* is taken from Aristotle and Tillich to mean perfection of being or self-actualization. Carlos Rosas painted the mural in 1976 and slightly changed it in 1989. The design begins on the right with a redbrick tenement and an ugly black cockroach. To the left is a pulsating sun (perhaps Tonatiuh, the Fifth Sun in Aztec mythology), representing a new historical era. Next appear three faces of a Chicano youth. His first face has lines that segment the face into white, turquoise and other colors. The second face is brown with an enormous eagle over his shoulders and hair. The third face is brown with black hair and looks out upon American society with dignity and self respect. The lad belongs to both cultures. All three faces look north, but the *barrio* forms the background.

"Entelequía" by Carlos Rosas and Felipe Gallegos, 1976, restored 1989, El Paso's Boy's Club—Photo by Richard Campbell

What Makes New Mexico Weaving So Popular?

Weaving is a universal art. The Navajo tribe made it a speciality; the Middle East has done the same. But for over two centuries, around 100 weavers in north central New Mexico have produced on their horizontal treadle loom an array of rugs, blankets, and tapestries that now are familiar to shoppers and tourists around the world. Among the small villages in the northern New Mexico mountains, different styles have developed. Angel Vigil lists the JERGA style (hand-spun wool and natural colors); RIO GRANDE (a series of color bands); SALTILLO (a center design laid over a bordered, figured background, from the *serapes* of Mexico); and CHIMAYÓ (a central geometrical design with end borders. a style now dominant).

Chimayó is a little village nestled in the mountains eight miles east of Española, New Mexico. The village is famous for its old church (*el Santuario*) with its healing mud, the restaurant close by, Rancho de Chimayó, and Santa Cruz Lake a few miles distant. The village has several weaving shops that turn out the traditional blankets that increasingly are being used for wall hangings, couch covers, bed spreads, curtains, chair and table covers and even floor rugs. In addition, the traditional weaving now turns out products like vests, pillow cases, and place mats that are purchased by customers as far away as Japan. One of the best-known family shops is the Ortega Weaving Shop begun in the early 1900s by Nicacio Ortega, himself a fifth generation weaver from Spanish settlers who arrived in the early 1700s. David Ortega and his sons represent the sixth and seventh generations still running this business. An Ortega shop can be found also in Albuquerque's "Old Town." Another well-known shop is Trujillo's Weaving House, opened after World War II but with over 70 years of weaving experience in the family. Cintenela is the third shop with active weaving. Contract workers in their homes supply much of the current production. Individual weavers work in Hernández, Truchas, Cundiyó, Española, Córdova, Mendenales, and Los Ojos as well as in the San Luis Valley of southern Colorado. The entire guild continues to use traditional forms but also explores innovative ideas.

FOLK CELEBRATIONS

What Are Three Kinds of Traditional Latino Celebrations?

Latin America generally has three kinds of traditional celebrations, or *fiestas*. Religious celebrations are treated in the chapter on religion. Two other kinds of celebrations express the centrality of family and country.

Familial. *Día de la Madre* (Mother's Day, May 10 in Mexico) and also days of baptisms, confirmations, and quinceañeras.

Patriotic. Many Latin American nations, including Mexico, celebrate their independence on September 16. Mexico dramatizes Fr. Hidalgo's shout for freedom *(el Grito de Independencia)* at 11:00 P.M. on September 15. Mexico adds *Cinco de Mayo* (victory over the French at Puebla in 1863) among a few others. Puerto Rico's cry for freedom, *el Grito de Lares* (the Cry from Lares), falls on September 23, its Constitution Day on July 25. Cuba honors an early cry for independence *(el Grito de Yara,* or Cry from Yara) on October 10.

On the East coast, fiesta fun came to the mainland from Puerto Rico. In New York City, the Puerto Rican Day Parade gathers more crowds than the Saint Patrick's Day Parade. On that day in June, carnival dancing groups and marching bands follow the floats, with vote-seeking politicians bringing up the rear. At other times in warm months, Himilce Novas refers to parties of all kinds in homes and clubs (called a *pabry,* Puerto Rican for party), street fairs, and *santo* processions alive with drums, traditional island costumes, and African-style *bombas* music.

How Do Some Hispanics Celebrate New Year's Eve?
Probably "the same way anyone else does" would be one answer; some go to parties, blow horns, set off fire crackers, dance into the wee hours of the morning, invite family and friends for a night at home, or go to bed early. But Holly Ocasio Rizzo portrays certain old customs that sometimes might still take place. In southern Colorado and northern New Mexico, people traditionally carried out *los días,* going from house to house with their guitars and singing to their neighbors. Beginning late at night, the singers got little sleep as hour after hour they sang impromptu verses that wished a joyful New Year. Those visited might then sing back, and everyone gathered inside for *posole, chile, bizcochitos,* and drinks. Those with Mexican, Puerto Rican, and Cuban roots have an old custom of swallowing whole grapes. At midnight, each person eats twelve grapes. Mexican custom dictates one for each month, with good luck in each. Puerto Ricans eat one for each chime at the midnight hour. Cubans insist on red grapes and put them into a glass of *sidra* or apple cider from Spain. Older Cubans sometimes dump a bucket of water outside the house to get rid of bad spirits.

What Is the Famous Poem for New Year's Eve?
In a tavern in South El Paso, Guillermo Aguirre y Fierro composed a poem that is repeated on New Year's Day by Hispanics from Mexico to Spain to Argentina to *barrios* in the United States. In the poem six happy bohemians are celebrating New Year's Eve with lots of rum, whiskey, and Scotch. At the stroke of midnight it is time for *Feliz Año Nuevo*

(Happy New Year), and the toasts begin: to the new year, to hope, to yesterday, to an unresponsive woman much-loved. Then, Arturo toasts his mother, the woman who embraced and kissed him, who taught him, who gave him her heart, who became the light of his soul. He concludes: "To my Mother, bohemians, who is melted sweetness and the star in the bitterness of my black nights." The poem is even more dramatic in Spanish and is known as *el Brindis del Bohemio* (the toast of the Bohemian). Sometimes the poem is read over the radio as a New Year's Eve ritual.

What Is a Common Custom among People after New Year's Day?

Whenever a person sees a friend after New Year's Day, the custom is to say "*Próspero* (or *feliz*) *Año Nuevo*" (a Prosperous or Happy New Year) and to give friends *un abrazo* (an embrace).

What Is a *Piñata?*

A *piñata* is a papier-mâché form covered with crepe paper and decorated to look like an animal or person. The center is a clay pot filled with candies, nuts, fruits, or perhaps small toys. The *piñata* is hung high on a rope that can be raised or lowered. Blindfolded children try to hit the moving target with a long stick. The assembled party crowd sings:

Dale, dale, dale,	Hit it, hit it, hit it,
No pierdas el tiene,	Don't lose your grip,
Porque si lo pierdes,	Because if you lose it,
Pierdes el camino.	You lose the way.

This happy custom has been traditional on Christmas Eve and for birthdays but now is popular also for other holidays and all kinds of parties.

The origins of this festive object are not known. Theresa Walker finds versions dating to Aztec days. Some think Marco Polo brought the *piñata* from China to Italy. Others think Italian nobility invented it in the 16th century for their amusement. In any case, 16th century Spaniards borrowed it from Italy and developed the *Dance of the Piñata* for the first Sunday of Lent and added painted designs on the surface. Missionaries in Mexico used the object to teach Christianity. The original clay pot had the horns of the devil. The stick represented God, the rope was human temptations, the rope movement was sin's complexity, the blindfold was the human problem in recognizing sin, and breaking the pot was conquest of good over evil. The spilled treats were God's graces in the lives of people who defeat evil. In later years, the *piñata* became Judas on Good Friday. Later, *piñata* became part of the *posadas* celebration.

Tourist demand has made *piñatas* into a hot sales item that comes in shapes of burros, cartoon heroes, Halloween witches, Thanksgiving turkeys, Christmas Santas, and Easter bunnies. The U.S. annually imports close to a million *piñatas* from Mexico. Would you believe that in the last ten years *piñatas*, after balloons, have become the second most popular decoration at parties in the U.S.? Even "Made in Taiwan" can be found. A thriving industry booms on the American side of the border too. Predictably, HALLMARK™ in 1998 added *piñatas* to its offerings, featuring circular, square and pentagonal shapes and images of TWEETY BIRD,™ MINNIE MOUSE,™ WINNIE THE POOH™ and BARBIE™ This Hispanic tradition has crossed over into American life

Piñata—
Gabriel Sánchez

Why Do Mexican Hispanics Celebrate *Cinco de Mayo?*

By 1862, Mexico had stopped paying its foreign debts. While the U.S. was fighting its Civil War, France's Emperor Napoleon III received an invitation from some misguided upper-class Mexicans and Catholic bishops to intervene. Not only would debts be paid, but also **Benito Juárez's** liberal reforms would be cancelled. Napoleon decided to invade Mexico, not just to regain loaned money, but also to extend French power in this hemisphere. French forces advanced along the same tortuous, uphill route that Cortés took 300 years earlier. When they reached the town of Puebla, a bloody battle took place. The date was *Cinco de Mayo* (May 5), 1862. The scene was 90 miles southeast of Mexico City.

Lorenzo LaFarelle describes how 5,000 ragged, ill-equipped Mexican troops under Gen. **Ignacio Zaragoza** waited patiently. The advancing 6,000 well-trained Imperial Army soldiers of Napoleon III were commanded by Gen. Lorencez. The French army's goal was to install Archduke Fernando Maximilian of Austria and his wife, Princess Carlota of Belgium, as rulers in Mexico City.

Early that morning, in the heights outside the city, the two armies collided with unrelenting hand-to-hand and bayonet combat and furious cavalry charges. Four French assaults lasted into late afternoon. Over 500 casualties lay on the field before Gen. Lorencez ordered a retreat. The number one army in the world had been repulsed by a ragged Mexican force with 50-year-old weapons.

Mexican chests still puff out proudly over one of Mexico's finest hours. Unfortunately, a year later the French returned and put Emperor Maximilian and Empress Carlota on the throne. In 1867, with strong hints from the U.S. now no longer embroiled in its Civil War, and Napoleon's need for troops in Europe, the French withdrew. Maximilian stayed and faced a firing squad. Carlota fled to Europe to plead for help only to succumb to decades of insanity. Benito Juárez returned to power and his program of reform.

Surprisingly, *Cinco de Mayo* is celebrated more in the U.S. than in Mexico, largely the result of American commercialism. Victor Landa refers to the event as a "sell-abration." Still, the annual celebration becomes exciting for many Mexican Americans.

Why Do Hispanics Celebrate Other National Independence Days?

Many non-Hispanics raise eyebrows here, but Hispanic Americans do celebrate July 4, America's Independence Day. At the same time, these citizens also treasure their national origins. To celebrate that reality, they enthusiastically celebrate along with those in Mexico, Puerto Rico, Cuba, or wherever.

Mexico: *Diez y Seis de Septiembre* (September 16). On the night before, from each government building across the nation and on TV from Mexico City, the bell rings to commemorate Fr. **Hidalgo**'s *grito* or cry for independence at the town of Dolores—although independence did not arrive for another decade.

Puerto Rico: Commonwealth Day and Constitution Day are July 25. *El Grito de Lares* (the Cry of Lares) is celebrated on September 23.

Cuba: Independence Day is May 20. *El Grito de Yara* (the Cry of Yara) is October 10.

FOLK CLOTHING
What Are *Guayaberas?*

The *guayabera* (pronounced gwhy-yah-**bare**-ah) has become a popular shirt in the United States, mostly as short-sleeve summer attire, although now it is available also with long sleeves. The shirt comes in different colors and elegant embroidery. Its loose fit keeps the wearer cool. One can find *guayaberas* in the Philippines, Indonesia, Cuba, Nicaragua, the Middle East, Mexico, and now the United States. Most are manufactured in Korea or Hong Kong with a cotton-polyester blend. Though originally the purpose of the shirt was comfort, designer names of Givenchy, de la Renta, and Dior have begun to display a new trendy commercialism.

In El Paso, former Mayor Jonathan Rogers wore *guayaberas* to city meetings in summer. Former Mexican President Luis Echeverría enthusiastically promoted their use to replace the formal tuxedo. He and his staff once attended a diplomatic dinner in Japan. They all wore *guayaberas* and were promptly told by their hosts to return to their rooms and dress in tuxedos or risk insulting the Japanese government.

Closer to home, José Antonio Burciaga tells of his days in third grade in El Paso where the Anglo nuns ordered his friend Memo to tuck his shirt inside his trousers. The shirt was a *guayabera!* Memo obeyed but was furious as his friends laughed at his funny appearance.

The origins of the *guayabera* are obscure. Perhaps the item comes from eighteenth-century Cuba. In Cuba's War of Independence, José Martí's followers wore the shirt as a political statement. Guayabera Day is actually celebrated among Cubans in Miami. Some believe *guayaberas* originated in Mexico in the Vera Cruz and Yucatán regions.

FOLK COURTESIES
What Are Some Common Expressions of Courtesy?

In the morning one greets another with *¿cómo amaneció?* (how are you this morning?). During the day, leaving the room or the table, one says *permiso* (permission), the answer being *es propio* (it is proper). If introduced to a person, one uses the formal manner of giving one's name and then adding *para servirle* (I am here to serve you), or *a sus órdenes* (I am at your command). If introduced to someone, a good reply is *mucho gusto* (much pleasure), or *gusto en conocerlo/la* (a pleasure to know you).

Here are some other expressions:

- Leaving or entering a room where others are eating: *buen provecho* (may you benefit from it).
- Host/hostess greeting visitors: *mi casa es su casa* (my house is your house).
- Leaving the room to go to bed: *que sueñe con los angelitos* (may you dream about the little angels) or even *que sueñe conmigo* (may you dream about me).

The use of these expressions, common throughout Latin America, may get dimmer the closer one lives to the U.S. border. A common and beautiful phrase used to say farewell is *vaya con Dios* (go with God). Whereas in English we use "God be with you," the Spanish phrase could picture a God who not only is with us but also One who goes ahead of us so we can follow. We are not just together; we are moving forward together.

What Is a Typical Act of Courtesy?

If someone raves about something a Hispanic person owns (a book, tape, or CD, or some other attractive item), that item will often be presented as a gift. Embarrassing or not, it would be discourteous to refuse it. This gesture, of course, is not automatic or constant.

When Should One Use the Familiar Form of "You"?

Spanish has a formal and an intimate form of the word "you": *Ud.* (*usted*) and *tú*. The intimate form is used with friends and family. Until there is a clear relationship established, someone using the language should stick to the formal *usted*. Just to complicate things, in Spain, Costa Rica and a few other countries—not Mexico—a very familiar form reserved for family and the closest friends is not *Ud.*, not even *tú*, but *vos*.

FOLK DRAMA

What Are Examples of Hispanic Folk Drama?

A very old art form of religious folk drama is called the *pastorela*, or pastoral. The most popular was *los Pastores* (The Shepherds). Other presentations were *Adán y Eva* (Adam and Eve), *los Tres Reyes* (The Three Kings), *el Niño Perdido* (The Lost Child), *las Cuatro Apariciones de Nuestra Señora de Guadalupe* (The Four Appearances of Our Lady of Guadalupe), and *los Moros y Cristianos* (The Moors and the Christians). These folk plays, presented during the Christmas season, go back 400 years to 1598 in New Mexico. Philip Ortego attributes their survival to the fervor of the Spanish soldiers and missionaries to express the piety of Spain and to instruct the Native Americans in the Christian faith.

Across these many years, the presentations have been held in churches. In villages too poor or small to afford a priest, *los Pastores* would take the place of Christmas Eve midnight Mass. Inevitably, in some locations, the nativity play developed from religious instruction to theatrical entertainment and received an added touch of comedy. These productions are still scheduled in churches and schools. In the small northern New Mexico village of Chimayó many years ago, and perhaps still the tradition, one of the folk plays was held outdoors on a cold December night with both actors and shivering spectators warmed a bit by a blazing bonfire.

FOLK GESTURES

How Do Non-Verbal Gestures Reflect World Cultures?

Different cultures have different gestures for easy communication. Sometimes knowing the differences are essential to function in those societies. To illustrate, according to Roger Axtell, in our American culture the head signals for no and yes are the exact opposite in Bulgaria. A former U.S president was embarrassed after giving a backwards peace sign in Australia; that's obscene. Also in Australia the thumbs-up gesture is considered vulgar; in Bangladesh it's obscene. Standing with hands in pockets is impolite in Japan, France, and Belgium. Showing one's shoe sole in Egypt is an insult. Whistling in public is impolite in India. The closed fist is obscene in Pakistan. Pounding fist into cupped hand is vulgar in Brazil. In Spain women don't cross legs, and men don't use the obscene O.K. sign with thumb and forefinger. The A.O.K. sign means worthless in France, money in Spain, but can signal "Screw you!" in parts of Latin America, especially Brazil. A "V" over the nose with forefinger and middle finger with palm toward face is obscene in Mexico and Saudi Arabia.

Perhaps these examples will emphasize the importance now of looking at some Hispanic gestures.

Do Hispanics Have Their Own Gestures?

In Hispanic culture some gestures are considered quite benign:

- Touching an elbow (codo) with the other hand is calling someone tight, stingy, or cheap. The person is called codo. But be careful here; this sign can also mean "Up yours."
- Holding thumb and index finger about an inch apart means "Wait a moment."
- Holding thumb and index finger farther apart means "There's more to come."
- Holding fingers together and curled and moving them rapidly toward and away from the mouth means "I'm hungry."
- Calling someone to come to you is done not by moving the hand repeatedly toward the face and fingers curled up but with palm down and fingers moving like scratching inward or moving the whole hand.
- Raising an index finger indicates the height of a person. Arm out and palm down is used only for animals.
- Putting an object or money into the other person's hand is proper, not laying it on a table or a counter.

Raúl Yzaguirre points out that a Hispanic juror who lowers his/her eyes during court proceedings is not revealing guilt or innocence but submission. Naturally, such a gesture from indigenous origins after the Conquest could also show respect. The same expression could occur at school, work, or home.

Other gestures are not as innocent. Here are some rough expressions presented for practical completeness, not for personal use! Please turn the page if this material is too offensive. The purpose here is not to shock or to be cute, but to introduce complete reality.

- Holding up a fist can mean, "F— you!"
- Putting the thumb in back of the top frontal teeth and thrusting it vigorously outside speaks of dislike and anger.
- Making a fist and throwing the arm hard behind the back of the head is like using the finger, or to say "Go to h—."
- Putting the left hand over the right biceps while doing the above motion, well, it's the above meaning but very strong.
- Pointing the index finger across the other hand is another strong expression, like "S.O.B.!" or "To h— with you!"
- Shaking the fist rapidly up and down says "I can beat you," or "I'm better than you!"
- Holding hands with palms up, raised and lowered as if holding something heavy means that someone is considered lazy.
- Standing with hands on hips can express hostility or challenge.
- Standing with hands in pockets is impolite.

FOLK MEDICINE
What Is *el Curandismo?*
The traditional practice of folk medicine is called *curandismo*. The healer is a *curandero* or *curandera*. With historical roots in Moorish, Christian, and Aztec theories and practices, *curandismo* remains a potent reality even today among many Hispanics. Practitioners have specialties. There is the *yerbero* or herbalist, the *partera* or midwife, the *sobador* or *sobadora* who uses massage, the *señora* who reads cards to foretell the future, and the *espiritista* or parapsychologist. In Mexico the name *bruja* or "witch" is common but still means a folk doctor-psychologist. Among the procedures are: lighting candles, saying prayers, rubbing, applying eggs (an animal sacrifice) or lemons, burning incense, anointing with oils, prescribing herbal teas, applying purple onion and garlic for protection, calling on spirits—but also giving antibiotics, which are available without prescription in Mexico.

The basic belief is that all healing power is a gift from God. For that reason most practitioners do not charge, or charge what the client offers. Traditionally, this folk medicine has included also the belief in outside, supernatural forces that cause maladies but can be removed by hex or black magic.

Many people think of this folk medicine as simple witchcraft, but there is another side. The voodoo and occult need not lie at the heart of the system. A *sobador* in a *barrio* manipulates the nerve points along the spine, arms, and legs. The pain relief is not magic but rather medical artistry belonging in today's category of alternative medicine. Even many health care professionals are seeing in *el curandismo* a holistic kind of health care that legitimately can supplement modern medicine in Hispanic *barrios*. Treatment is free or inexpensive, uses Spanish, needs no appointment, and exists in the neighborhood. Dr. Raymond Gardea, an El Paso physician, fears some excesses in these treatments but admits their value in many cases of mental illness. Roberto Ramírez, who directs a mental health clinic in Las Cruces, New Mexico, runs his program with healers as co-workers where needed, especially among immigrants. Let it be remembered that Peru's Incas treated malaria with a tea made from the ground bark of the Chinchona tree, or Peruvian Bark. The synthetic version in our time became quinine. During the Vietnam War, a strain of malaria appeared that was resistant to synthetics. Guess what was brought in. Yes, Peruvian Bark.

What Are Some Ailments Treated by *Curanderos/as?*

- *Mal de ojo* (evil eye): Symptoms are irritability, drooping eyes, fever, headache, vomiting, all from the effect of someone else's eye. The remedy is wearing a deer's eye charm or maybe a simple touch.
- *Susto* (fright): Symptoms are weakness, chills, headache, indigestion, depression, nausea, or irritability. Causes are bad news or sudden scare.
- *Desasombro:* More than *susto,* this is like the shock of stepping on a poisonous snake.
- *Caída de mollera:* Baby dehydration.
- *Empacho:* Symptoms are diarrhea and indigestion, mostly in children.
- *Mal aire* (bad air): Symptoms are upper respiratory infection, stiff neck, chills, dizziness, headache, i.e., a bad cold.
- *Bilis:* Symptoms are too much bile, gas, constipation, or sour taste in the mouth, maybe from suppressed anger or liver problems.

What Herbs Are Used by *Curanderos?*
The following pharmacopoeia comes from Elisea Torres and his work in *Green Medicine* and also Angel Vigil in *Una Linda Raza.*
- Alfalfa *(alfalfa):* For stomach pains.
- Aloe Vera *(zabila, sabila):* For healing wounds and burns.
- Anise *(anís estrellado):* As tea with milk for colic but with water for cough or eyewash.

- Antelope horns *(inmortal):* For asthma.
- Basil *(albahaca, laurel):* As tea for sedative, or for sore throat, mouth sores, and insect stings.
- Blackberry *(zarzamora):* As tea for inflamed gums, mouth ulcers, or diarrhea.
- Bougainvillea *(buganvilla):* As tea for sore throat or cough.
- Cactus *(nopal):* For rash.
- Camphor *(alcanfor):* For earache, rheumatism, or headache.
- Chamomile *(manzanilla):* As tea for sedative, indigestion, fever, or head congestion. Chamomile flowers are used to break cigarette addiction.
- Cinnamon *(canela):* As oil for rheumatism, tea for indigestion.
- Cloves *(clavo):* For toothache or headache.
- Coriander *(cilantro):* As tea for nausea or diarrhea.
- Corn silk *(barba de maíz):* For urinary tract infections.
- Cumin *(comino):* As tea for teething babies.
- Dandelion *(diente de león):* As tea for diuretic, also to dissolve kidney and bladder stones. Ground roots serve as a laxative, the juice for warts.
- Delphinium or Larkspur *(espuela de caballero, delfinio):* As a poultice to help remove body lice. Flowers and seeds are ground and soaked in alcohol or vinegar.
- Eucalyptus *(eucalipto):* As tea for indigestion, congestion, or cough. Dried leaves are smoked to treat asthma.
- Garlic *(ajo):* As tea for stomach ulcers or liver or kidney problems, or crushed and mixed with brown sugar to make a cough syrup. Also crushed and mixed with oil for burns and peeled and wrapped in gauze to insert in the ear for earache. Garlic is another healthy ingredient in Mexican cooking. Dr. Andrew Weil claims that garlic lowers cholesterol, reduces blood clotting, helps lower blood pressure, works well as an antibiotic against fungal infections, and has antibacterial and antiviral effects as well. The antibiotic, antibacterial, and antiviral benefits are lost when the garlic is cooked or dried.
- Ginger *(jenibre):* As tea for flu.
- Indian paintbrush *(flor de Santa Rita):* For water retention.
- Jimson reed *(toloache):* As an external analgesic.
- Lavender *(alhucema):* For colic, gas, and indigestion.
- Lemon *(limón):* As juice for antiseptic, with honey for colds.
- Lettuce *(lechuga):* As tea for constipation and nerves.
- Marijuana *(marijuana):* As tincture for rheumatism.
- Milkweed *(lecheros):* For skin infections.

- Mint *(hierba buena)*: As tea for stomach-ache and nausea, also as a mild stimulant.
- Mustard *(mostaza):* As a plaster for chest colds, or taken internally for stomach trouble.
- Nutmeg *(nuez moscado):* For indigestion.
- Onion *(cebolla):* For anemia, exhaustion, bronchial problems, and gas when eaten raw. As tea, with honey, for cough or sore throat. As poultice for burns, bites, arthritis, or rheumatic pains.
- Oregano *(orégano):* As tea to regulate menstruation and to relieve cramps. Also for sore throat and bronchitis.
- Papaya *(papaya):* For external application to infected wounds, or taken internally for stomach ulcers.
- Parsley *(perejil):* As tea for alcoholism, gallstones, indigestion, and menstrual cramps.
- Root of wild celery *(oshá):* As an antiseptic.
- Root of wild cherry *(capulín):* For viral infections.
- Rosemary *(romero):* For indigestion and baldness.
- Rue *(ruda):* For earache.
- Sage *(salvia):* As tea for diarrhea, weaning babies, depression, gum disease, and general wounds.
- Thyme *(tomillo):* As cold tea for headache, as hot tea for sedative and for diarrhea, used externally for sores and insect repellent.
- Yucca root *(amole):* As hair shampoo.

Just one humorous addition. *Espazote* does not show up in ordinary Spanish dictionaries, but Kathleen Raphael lists it as one of the three most popular herbs in New Mexico, after *yerba buena* and *manzanilla.* The herb is not only a seasoning but also an antiflatulent when put in beans. Katia LeMone, who lives near Las Cruces, phrases the benefit somewhat more graphically: "It takes the farts out of beans."

What's the Information on Catclaw, or *Uña de Gato*?
This herb's scientific name is *Uncaria tomentosa.* Many Hispanics take this herb daily and claim to feel better for it. The plant is found in a small area of Peru's Amazon rain forest. In fact, some effort has been made to induce impoverished farmers in the Amazon to substitute *uña de gato* for coca as one prong of a strategy against the drug trade. The plant's reputation for relieving arthritis goes back centuries among the Peruvian tribes. Jorge Béjar reports that these people claim also that the herb is good for tumors, as a contraceptive, and as an aphrodisiac. Actor Andy García claims that *uña de gato* saved him from prostate cancer. Even in Europe the remedy is popular. Numerous studies have focused

on *uña de gato,* and some evidence seems to support the belief that the plant acts as an anti-inflammatory, boasts the immune system, and relieves depression. Some Peruvian hospitals use the plant to help cancer and AIDS patients. One can purchase *uña de gato* wood bark or capsule and tablet forms of the herb.

Would a Person Go to a *Botánica* for a Prescription?

A *botánica* in Puerto Rico, Cuba or the U.S. is a store that sells "natural" medications, mostly herbs. An extra service offers *santería* (see under "Religion") paraphernalia such as statues, candles and beads. A customer can also have a consultation with a *santera* (priestess) who is often the owner. But for VALIUM,™ VASOTEC,™ or VIAGRA,™ the place to go would be a *farmacia* or *botica.*

What's the Cure for Evil Eye?

Mal de ojo (bad or evil eye) is a "folk illness," using Rafaela Castro's phrase. This folk belief exists around the world, particularly in the Mediterranean region, eastern Europe, North Africa, Central America, Mexico, and southwestern U.S. Some believe that certain individuals or even witches can spread *mal de ojo,* either accidentally or intentionally. *Mal de ojo* usually can be transferred from a stronger person to someone weaker, just by a glance. The cause is a suspicion or jealousy about another individual's conduct. Symptoms of the disease, supposedly, are vomiting, diarrhea, weight loss, maybe death. But what an imaginative cure! The healer takes an unbroken, raw egg, sweeps it over but does not touch the ill person, reciting prayers like the Hail Mary or the Our Father. Theoretically, the egg absorbs the fever from the victim, is broken into a bowl of water, and is put under the victim's bed. All night the egg continues to pull the fever. In the morning, if the egg looks cooked, that indicates the person had *mal de ojo.* The egg water then is thrown over the shoulder toward the sun.

FOLK MISCELLANY

Why Are Flowers Important to Hispanics?

As the Spaniards approached the Aztec capital of Tenochtitlán in 1519, they observed the dazzling beauty of the city, its temples and canals, its gardens and orchards, its trees of oak, sycamore, and cedar. And flowers, flowers everywhere, both for daily delight among the people and also for lavish use in temple ceremonies. To this day, flowers are important in the culture. They are grown in gardens, sold on street corners, placed on graves, given as gifts, and displayed in homes and churches.

Natural or artificial, it doesn't matter. A flower is more than a flower; to use the poet's line, A thing of beauty is a joy forever.

What Is a *Fogón?*

No one ever forgets the smell of *piñon* wood gently floating through the crisp, cold air of a New Mexico night. That smoke usually emanates from a unique fireplace called a *fogón*, built into a corner of a room. No andirons are used. Logs are placed on end and leaned together toward the center, visualized by Dorothy Pillsbury as "...an outdoor campfire, moved into a corner of the home."

Fogón—Gabriel Sánchez

Why All the Graffiti on Buildings?

Graffiti exists everywhere: in the ruins of Pompeii, on walls in Lima and Paris, in New York City's subway tunnels, and, yes, in *barrios* of the Southwest. Sometimes the expressions are personal, about individuals and lovers and gangs. At other times there are words about Aztec or Mexican roots or political allegiances or social protest.

Ordinary graffiti appears on public walls and buildings all over the world. Most of the time such work is considered illegal and brings forth public graffiti removal crews and legal problems if the vandals are caught. But in many *barrios*, there is such a thing as "barrio calligraphy." Rafaela Castro traces this phenomenon to the 1930s and '40s. This form of graffiti uses Gothic lettering. Another feature is block lettering with shadowed edging giving a three dimensional appearance. Looped lettering has an S-loop around every straight line of a letter. Interesting footnote: The Gothic-lettered graffiti is omnipresent on the walls along train tracks in Paris, too.

"Typical Graffiti in El Paso, Texas"—Photo by Richard Campbell

What Is the Strange Lettering in the Corner on Many Graffiti Walls?
Those words are *con safos*, meaning, in Rafaela Castro's free translation, "Don't mess with this," written as *c/s* or *C.S.* This signing acts as a protection against defacement and includes a warning of retaliation. At times *c/s* will appear after a person's name on a letter, essay or Internet message.

What Are Lowriders?
This colorful phenomenon among some Hispanic youth and young adults is almost a cult. The decorating of and adding equipment to cars has become a part of folk culture. The custom originated in Mexican American *barrios* in the late 1930s and later became a twin of the zoot suit to protest discrimination and to assert cultural identity through bizarre clothing and cars. At first, heavy stones or sacks of cement were loaded into car trunks or springs, and suspensions received some crude tinkering to make the cars ride close to the ground. In the 1960s someone thought of installing hydraulic pumps from helicopters or airplanes to lift and lower the vehicles. Today a large industry supplies equipment that not only lifts and lowers the car but also raises it up on two wheels or even bounces the car off the ground. In addition, the cars might get chrome wheels, bumpers, and plush upholstering. Above all, they will be painted and striped using vivid fluorescent colors and customized with mural-like designs in front and back. From the car-decorating developed the custom of "cruising," driving slowly through towns in much the same way Mexican youth used to stroll or ride their horses around the town plaza.

In the early days of this custom, lowriders would buy an old car and begin to add basic adornment. Today the sport has become expensive enough for some to spend $25,000 to $50,000 to customize a good car or pickup truck. Still, among poorer young men, the traditional and cheaper lowrider still flourishes.

So, in Los Angeles where the custom began, in Dallas/Fort Worth, San Antonio, El Paso, and in New Mexico's Española Valley (which claims to be the lowriding capital of the world), individuals and clubs carry on their customizing and cruising. One of those lowriders explained why he followed the sport. He felt that lowriding reflected his Chicano identity, his *machismo*; the bright paint outside and the crushed velour inside allowed the whole world to see who he really is.

What Are *Luminarias* or *Farolitos*?
Luminarias have become popular all over the country, and that is what they are invariably called. But in New Mexico a lively debate goes on

and never seems to end. Northerners insist on using *farolitos*, southerners prefer *luminarias*. Peter Ortega presents the case for differentiating between *luminarias* and *farolitos*.

Luminaria technically refers to the small bonfires on *la Nochebuena* (Christmas Eve). In fact, we may have here a throwback to pre-Christian customs in ancient Spain where large bonfires were lit on hilltops to celebrate feasts of gods or goddesses. It is possible that the early Christians adopted and Christianized this custom for their own Christmas festivities. So, across the centuries the faithful would light these bonfires in a plaza or along a road to beautify the holy night and to symbolize guidance for the shepherds in their search for the manger.

Farolitos are something else. In the far-off Philippines, people learned from the Chinese how to make colorful lanterns. These came to Mexico through normal commerce and became common at *fiestas* in churches and homes. These lanterns were brought north from Mexico in the colonial period, especially to Santa Fe. A problem soon arose. The delicate and expensive Chinese paper lanterns could not survive more than one season in that northern climate. At about this same time Yankee traders were traveling the Santa Fe Trail to Santa Fe. Among all their wares, they had brown paper bags. These along with flickering candles became the *farolito* whose gentle glow adorns Christmas Eve so beautifully.

How are *luminarias/farolitos* made? Nothing could be simpler, although some people have electrified the bags! The genuine *luminaria/farolito* begins with a number ten paper sack (6 x 3/5 x 11 1/6), the top folded down about an inch all around. Pour an inch or so of dirt or the equivalent (gravel, even cat litter) in the bottom of the sack. Insert a small votive candle. Light with match. *Es todo* (that's all).

What Folk Tradition Uses Empty Eggshells?

Cascarones are decorated eggshells (from *cáscara* or shell). Rafaela Castro traces this tradition to the early 1800s in Mexico and now popular in Texas, Arizona, and California. The process can be time-consuming. Someone makes a small hole in the eggshell and blows out the contents. The empty shell then gets painted and finally filled with confetti or cologne. The real fun begins when a person takes a *cascarón* and

breaks it on someone's head. The occasions for this folk item are weddings, *fiestas,* dances, any holiday, especially Easter in the spring.

Do Latinos Drive Differently?

With similarities elsewhere in the world, Latin American driving has a
common pattern. In Guadalajara, Mexico, after a traffic light turns green,
a smart driver waits to let four to six cars go through on the red light. El
Paso, Texas, is rapidly imitating this pattern. In Lima, Peru, the advice is
"offensive driving" to avoid becoming dead meat. In Rio de Janeiro, a
taxi ride from a theater to the hotel late at night can resemble the
Indianapolis 500. In Costa Rica, the huge potholes are not avoided but
hit calmly at full speed. John Grisham in *The Testament* depicts a roaring
ride on the streets of Corumbá, Brazil, "...slowing only slightly at red
lights, completely ignoring stop signs, and in general bullying cars and
motorcycles..., a traffic system where the rules of the road, if any, were
ignored." Some such patterns can appear at times in the U.S.

Why Do Hispanics Frequently Answer the Telephone with *Bueno?*

Anglos often feel nonplused when hearing on the other end of the
phone, "*¡Bueno!*" Why this usage? The meaning is obviously "hello." But
why *bueno?* Explanations are not available. Is the word possibly a terse-
ly-abbreviated *buenos días?* Just a theory.

Why Do Hispanics Say *Salud* after Someone Sneezes?

After someone sneezes, inevitably another person utters *salud* (health),
as in English when people say "God bless you" or when Germans use
Gesundheit (health). No one knows for certain how this custom originated. Even the ancient Greeks and Romans had it. It is possible that
during the Middle Ages, with plagues decimating the people, a sneeze
could be an alarming sign of infection that needed divine protection.
Centuries later, all such expressions have become a mere ritual or courtesy, although some may still feel that the word offers some safety from
various kinds of trouble.

Why Is Tattooing So Popular?

Rafaela Castro describes the popularity of *tatuaje* (tattooing) as something very common among Chicano youth and especially among prisoners and gangs. The tattoo was apparently common in Aztec, Maya, and
Inca cultures. Capt. John Cook coined the word from Tahitian *ta–tu,*
meaning "to mark." Among Chicanos, religious symbolism seems the
most popular. Tattoos are symbols of Chicano identity and pride, both

by presenting oneself with a unique design and also by connecting one-self with friends in the *barrio*. Many youth, however, with tattoos small and large, are neither gang members nor in trouble with the law. The skin art is *macho* and more and more a trend to imitate.

Why Is the *Abrazo* Preferred to the Handshake?

Hispanic culture expresses closeness and touching, passion and warmth. The handshake alone is simply too cold and impersonal for close friends and family. Although when used alone, a Hispanic handshake might easily last longer and include the left hand's grasp of the other's arm. But if there is any warm relationship at all, there is an *abrazo*.

The *abrazo* has a clear ritual. There can be an initial handshake, then the *abrazo* with two strong slaps on the back, concluding often with another handshake. It would be perilous, however, to extend this *abrazo* to just anybody, and certainly not to someone in a rank or position above. In normal casual and business relations, the handshake is best.

Ross Buck, professor at the University of Connecticut, observes that "the closer you get to the equator, the more hugging people do." Not only do Hispanics and Italians hug more than northern Europeans, but Mexicans and Central Americans hug more than Chileans, for example. There seems to be a touch factor in culture. An international study scrutinized couples in restaurants to find out how many times per hour they touched each other. In England, they averaged zero; in Florida two; in Paris 110; in Puerto Rico 180. To illustrate the range of cultural differences here, Japanese stand enough apart so that they do not collide heads when bowing. When saying goodbye, Hispanics always shake hands with or without an *abrazo*. Anglos often say goodbye, turn and leave.

Marc Simmons relates the experience of William Carr Lane, New Mexico's second territorial governor in 1852. In a letter to his wife in far-away St. Louis, he wrote: "I get fifty *abrazos* (embraces) daily. The custom does not suit my taste."

FOLK MUSIC

What Are Some Well-Known Mexican Folk Songs?

These folk songs are "songs of the people" and with unknown specific origins, explains Rafaela Castro. In general, though, the songs originated in Spain before the emigration to the New World and came with the Spanish conquerors. Although some music has been written, most of these songs exist only orally. We know only a fraction of what used to exist. Different versions remain because the singers often improvised. The earliest examples were romances, then the *corridos* and the *décimas* (poetic narratives), the *alabados* (*penitente* hymns) and the *canciones* (nineteenth century free-form songs on human emotions). An outstanding modern collection, found in Linda Ronstadt's celebration of her Hispanic roots, is expressed in her ground-breaking album *Canciones de Mi Padre*. Here are some better known examples of some folksongs:

- *Aguinaldo* is a Puerto Rican children's song.
- *Cielito lindo* is an all-time favorite.
- *Las mañanitas* is popular in Mexican *mariachi* serenading.
- *La paloma* and *la golondrina.*
- *La cucaracha,* explains John West, was sung during the Mexican Revolution by Pancho Villa's male and female soldiers as they marched to battle. The singers were like underdogs, like the lowly cockroach, but something indestructible!
- *De colores* is a song embedded deeply in Mexican tradition, maybe with Caribbean origins, and increasingly popular with non-Hispanics. It is the song that closes the film, *The Milagro Beanfield War,* and is a favorite in the Protestant spiritual renewal program "Walk to Emmaus."
- *La bamba,* made famous by **Richie Valens,** came from a Spanish colonial song around 1790. It was a dance tune in Veracruz in the 1800s and early 1900s. It became a popular Mexican dance by 1830. The song is *son jarocho* (country dance music) from Veracruz, with African influences, and accompanied by a small harp, a small eight-string guitar and a small four-string guitar. The dance step is a foot-stomping *zapateado*. Valens mixed in a rock beat, and that's what one hears so often on the radio.

FOLK NEIGHBORHOODS
What Is the Significance of a *Barrio?*

A *barrio* is a city neighborhood with Hispanic residents. By the way, the word is not pronounced **bay**-ree-oh but rather **bah**-ree-oh. For decades, a Hispanic *barrio* has meant the poorer section of a city, always vibrant with life but full of problems. In modern America, Hispanics in their *barrios* are doing more than creating their own neighborhoods. They are adding warmth and color to urban life, "[enriching] public space" and "[preserving] our urban commons" in Mike Davis's wording. We are referring to rich painted colors on houses (yellow, rose, purple, blue—"sheer visual terrorism" to non-Hispanics); family festivals with loud, late-at-night radio music; weed-filled lots replaced by gardens; strong color and figures on community murals; soccer frenzy; Chicano art dealers and booksellers; outdoor restaurants; even Latino *bohemias* rivaling Greenwich Village.

True to form, city bureaucracies frustrate this enthusiasm with zoning codes, encouraging "instant-slum" apartment complexes, passing laws that prevent Hispanic homeowners to add legal additions for relatives or renters, restricting weekend garage or lawn sales, outlawing street vendors and street-corner labor markets, building "junk retail space" instead of parks, and creating toxic dump sites from industry and construction. But Hispanics in their *barrios* keep trying to turn on the lights "in the dead spaces of North American cities,... to tropicalize the national vision of 'the city on the hill.'"

FOLK ORAL LITERATURE
What Are the Features of Border Folklore?
Philip Ortego succinctly depicts the development of Southwest border folklore. We must remember that Spanish invaders and later immigrants brought their European literary culture from the beginning. For example, they established a printing press in Mexico City in 1529, over a century earlier than the British did in their colonies. After the Anglo American victory over Mexico in 1848, Mexican American literature evolved over the next half-century as writers faced the gradual change from Spanish style, themes, and language to English language and American literary patterns. Mexican immigrants brought also the drama, poetry, and folktales from the Old World to Mexico that had been passed on for generations. Immediately apparent are legends about the devil, strange events among the saints, and common mistakes and problems of ordinary people and even animals.

Beyond those themes, Mexican Americans created new tales reflecting their new political environment, in particular, their marginalization in American society. These many folk tales still survive in South Texas, New Mexico, and Mexico itself.

Why Is Witchcraft Prominent in Mexican Folk Culture?
Witches and witchcraft (*brujería*) are commonly accepted in the American Southwest and in Mexico. Lorenzo LaFarelle tells of witchcraft practiced among many of the Mexican tribes and certainly before and after the Aztecs. Rafaela Castro describes witches and potions causing disease; witches taking the form of a cat, pig, or, in New Mexico, witches as balls of fire in the sky; and *curanderas* called in to undo the work of witches. The worst of all curses is to be changed into an owl. An owl's hoot is pure evil. For example, a woman who sells her soul to the devil might be changed into an owl at night; she then is called a *lechuza*. Also commonly believed was the existence of elves and gob-

lins (*duendes, pichilingis*). They carried out invisible, mischievous pranks and tricks.

What Is *la Llorona?*

La llorona (the weeping woman) is an example of a universal folk tale. The tale is similar to Lilith in Jewish folklore and Lamia among the Greeks. In the female *llorona* version, compare Dracula and Frankenstein. Similar tales appear in Scandinavian, French, Gaelic, African and American Indian mythology. Lorenzo LaFarelle finds the story's appearance in the Americas in the years 1509-1519 among the Aztecs.

In the story, a grieving lady eternally searches for her little boy. She is seen on city streets, in woods, along rivers, at night, in daylight. In some versions she herself killed the child and is forced to wander forever as penance. Often she is dangerous, luring young men to their deaths. Or she may be only a ghostly presence whose wailing is heard in the night but whose form remains invisible. Supposedly, this woman's wailing could be heard in the middle of the night throughout Mexico's Central Valley and on the streets of Tenochtitlán, the soon-to-be-conquered Aztec capital, according to the *Aztec Crónicas* (Chronicles). So terrified were the people that the emperor Moctezuma summoned his priest-astrologers for an explanation. To his consternation, they told him the wailing represented a mother crying for the terrible fate ahead for the Aztec nation. The nation would be conquered by white people from the East and would bring death, enslavement, and destruction to the Old Order.

Then along came Captain **Hernán Cortés**, the seeming fulfillment of this omen and a turning point in the history of this continent and of Europe as well. After the Conquest, Spanish soldiers reported hearing the eerie sound and gave it the name *la Llorona*. This story no doubt came with the Spanish explorers into New Mexico and persists to this day in its general story-form among people in the United States, Mexico, Latin America and Spain. The story is the most persistent legend in New Mexico. But the variations are endless. Some versions have the woman murdering her children. Or she is looking for bad or mischievous children (a form very handy for some parents coping with unruly little ones). Or one will die of a heart attack if anyone sees her. Or she can change herself at will into a dog. Even adults will admit to belief in this story. Years ago in an article in *The New Mexican* in Santa Fe, Emily Drabanski described this story as "a legend that will not die."

Clarissa Pinkola Estés finds more modern versions of *la Llorona* portrayed as "the female protagonist" in union-busting wars, in forced return of Mexicans from the U.S. in the '50s, in the Spanish Land Grant struggles in New Mexico, and in tensions over a factory-polluted river in Colorado. The tale seems to evolve as it "builds on the psychic issues of each generation." Here are some other *cuentos* (stories) from the Southwest and New Mexico, from Angel Vigil and Rafaela Castro:

- *Duendes:* God and the devil had an argument when time began. Some angels stayed with God; others went to the devil. A number of them caught between the two realms when the doors closed became *duendes* (dwarfs) and went to Earth to cause mischief among humans.

- *Bailando con el diablo:* The devil appears at community dances, all handsome in a suit, and skilled at dancing. He asks the prettiest girl to dance. The girl agrees without the permission of her parents or against their warnings. They dance all night, whereupon the girl notices the man's feet have turned to animal feet. He disappears. The girl faints, suffers a burn, or even dies. This story was another not-so-subtle tale used to teach young girls about obedience to parents.

- *La mano negra:* If children were misbehaving or didn't help at home, they were warned about a Black Hand that would appear at night, take them from their bed, kidnap them—and they would never return home. More gentle child psychology.

- *María de Jesús Cornel de Agreda:* The Blue Lady with blue veil or garments would frequently visit the sick and poor children to help and heal. A story exists about such a woman, perhaps true in part, in 17th century Spain. She lived in a convent, wrote books, and claimed that she made flights to New Mexico to help the Indians.

- *El abuelo:* The grandfather is the bogeyman in Hispanic folk literature. Also called *el coco,* who wanders in northern New Mexico, this figure supposedly appeared at Christmastime to test and discipline children who hadn't learned their catechism and prayers. With scary black cape, large horns and whip, he would knock on doors days before Christmas, make a bloodcurdling outcry, crack his whip, ask if the children have been good, hear the parents defend their children's good behavior, form children and parents in a circle while holding hands, and dance and sing. Throughout the year, expectedly, parents would solve misbehavior by warning, "If you don't behave, I will call the bogeyman, *¡el abuelo!*"

- *Los comanches:* This heroic folk tale made into drama in northern New Mexico was done in the open air in daylight. It re-enacted the battle between Spanish soldiers and the Comanches. The drama reflected the constant fear of Indian raids where horses and food were stolen and women and children kidnapped. The battle was fought in 1774, in which the Indians were defeated, and the story was written in 1789.

- *El diablo:* The Spanish missionaries often used this story. Children were taught not to fear *el diablo* (the devil) because he could be defeated by the sign of the cross and by saying, *"¡Jesús, María y José!"* (Jesus, Mary and Joseph).
- *Don Cacahuate:* Mr. Peanut *(cacahuate)* represented the simpleton or fool, *Señor Tonto* (dimwit). He was always in trouble and barely survived.

FOLK RELIGION
How Do We Explain Mexican Catholic Folk Religion?

Rafaela Castro pictures this fascinating development. The frequent lack of priests, discrimination by Anglo Catholic churches, and a shortage of priests who spoke Spanish caused many Mexican Catholics to depend less on the institutional church and the clergy. In public they developed processions, *fiestas,* and other community celebrations. At home they placed family shrines, pictures, statues, carvings, and candles. But in areas with a heavy Mexican American population, the Catholic Church vigorously tried to form a parish in every Chicano community. Such churches allowed religious life in Spanish, celebrated Mexican Independence Day with a *fiesta,* ate traditional foods, wore traditional clothing, and prayed in traditional forms. The church was an oasis in an often-hostile desert. Religious celebrations of the saints brought the community together and created excitement for the Masses, processions, picnics, horse races, games, and dances that filled an entire day. Religion and culture stood together by following the church's calendar, particularly the period of *Cuaresma* (Lent) and *Pascua* (Easter). Equally powerful were the celebrations of the *Fiesta de la Virgen de Guadalupe,* Advent, Christmas, and *el Día de los Santos Reyes.* In a few words, the church with its culturally-expressive ceremonies and customs brought together family, community, culture, politics, and spiritual experience that affected the total life of the people.

What Is the Day of the Dead *(el Día de los Muertos)*?

On November 2, after All Saints Day on November 1, while non-Hispanics are recovering from Halloween, Mexican Catholics observe a unique ritual called *el Día de los Muertos* (Day of the Dead, or All Souls Day). The tradition goes back to ancient and complex Aztec and Mayan ceremonies and ritual altar offerings to honor their dead. The tradition was blended into Catholic faith to celebrate the Christian belief that death is a part of life and that life follows death. Mexicans put their own touch on the form and made a mockery, a joke, of death with dramatic humor and warm remembrance of loved ones with God. The event became a spiritual holiday.

Guadalupe Silva and Bernard Ruiz explain some of the customs used. Since this is a holy day of obligation, most devout Catholics will attend Mass first. Then, traditionally, whole families go to the cemeteries to clean the graves and paint the tombstones. Sometimes offerings are presented. Some sing, pray, share remembrances, then enjoy the favorite foods and drinks of the deceased. Some believe that the spirits of the loved ones return and enjoy the smell of those foods. Special altars are erected at home or at the cemetery and decorated with a picture of a loved one, paper or seasonal flowers (mostly mums or marigolds), lighted candles, skull candies, and Day of the Dead bread. It's time for a loved one's favorite music. On occasion, *mariachis* or *marimbas* are hired. In Mexico, traditionally on the day itself, deceased children are remembered; the next day focuses on deceased adults.

Except in central and southern Mexico, this colorful tradition has been either diluted to mere grave-cleaning and placing of artificial flowers or has disappeared entirely in *americanización*. Even in Mexico, concern arises when the day gets shoved out by Halloween. At times the observance is confused with Halloween, which is a complete error. But, wherever and in whatever form this event is maintained, the Day of the Dead lifts up Catholic faith, Hispanic tradition, and family love.

How Are *Quinceañeras* a Form of Folk Religion?

Every Hispanic girl dreams about her *quinceañera* (from *quince*, fifteen, and *años*, years) in her fifteenth year. These celebrations are very common in Texas, definitely in El Paso and San Antonio, also in other large urban areas such as Los Angeles, Miami, and Chicago, according to Rafaela Castro.

María Cortés González and José Armas describe what happens. This event is an affirmation of Christian faith and a rite of passage, a "coming out," dating back to Toltec, Aztec, and Mayan rites which the Spaniards blended into their own Catholic rituals. The *quinceañera* is both family *fiesta* (sometimes costing $5-8000) and a religious event in which a girl renews her love to God and enters womanhood. The young girls take classes for preparation. They arrange for the invitations, the white limousine, 14 escorts and attendants, godparents (who hopefully help pay the bill), flower girl, the priest, church and hall, band, cake, ring, and dinner—the complexity resembles a full wedding. Some priests feel the growing expense is becoming excessive.

Family and friends gather at the church. The ceremony begins with Mass. Special symbolic gifts are presented that could include a doll (goodbye to childhood), a diamond ring (teenage responsibilities), a Bible, a rosary, a necklace, or a bracelet. The priest's sermon will challenge the girl to be faithful to the Lord and might move to warnings about teenage temptations.

The event then moves from sanctuary to hall for dinner and a formal procession. Slippers are exchanged for adult shoes. The father has the honor of the first dance with his daughter. Into the wee hours the assembled guests revel in happiness, conversation, flowers, balloons, music, and dancing. This is more than a fifteenth-year observance; it is church ritual and recommitment, family *fiesta,* and cultural tradition.

What Is So Distinctive about Traditional Cemeteries?

In New Mexico, cemeteries are called *camposantos* (holy fields; the standard word for cemetery is *cementerio*) and have a distinct personality. Visit Hernández, Alcalde, Chimayó, Truchas, Peñasco, Ranchos de Taos, or Mora for proof. Dorothy Benrimo, Rebecca Salsbury James, and E. Boyd have illustrated these sites with stark photos. Found on hills, in fields near the villages, or usually on dry, unusable soil, each cemetery gives the feeling of quiet simplicity, more of life than of death. These cemeteries have no imposing temple-like mausoleums, no neat lawns (only grasses, flowers, weeds, cactus, and stones), no orderly rows with graves facing east (they extend in all directions); no granite tombstones (often just a rough stone, iron marker, or crosses). Wooden crosses in all shapes stand or lean as they try to peer above the grass and weeds. The wood is gray from sun, rain, and snow. Sometimes a wooden picket or iron fence surrounds a grave site. Around the *camposanto* stands a wire fence with a gate. What can seem incongruous are the plastic flowers and wreaths sometimes leaning against the crosses. Graves often have a cement marker with a *nicho* (niche) to hold a statue of the Virgin or a picture of the deceased. Rafaela Castro shares a quote from Terry Jordan: "Hispanic graveyards...combine to comfort the bereaved and startle the gringo."

Why Are Rocks, Flowers, and Lone Crosses Piled along a Highway?

Those sites are called *descansos* (resting places) and are found from California to New Mexico. They mark the spot of a fatal highway accident. Grieving families maintain the memorial site with new plastic flowers. Some Hispanics believe that the soul of the victim needs the site to keep from wandering endlessly and pestering the family until a cross is erected. Often a victim's photo is placed at the cross to make the soul's resting place easier to find.

Who Are the Important Saints in the Folk Culture?

Joe Montoya relates the importance of the saints. For centuries children have received the names of saints. The name José is extremely common among males and María among females.

Since the saints are said to intercede with God with petitions for help, countless *cuentos* (stories) relate miraculous deeds of saints in individual lives. Popular saints among Chicanos are *la Virgen de Guadalupe, San Antonio de Padua, San José* and *Santiago*. Individuals born on a particular saint's day claim that saint as their own. Towns and villages often have their special saint and hold annual festivals in that saint's honor. December 12, of course, is the day when the Virgin of Guadalupe is honored. Other Madonnas around the world have their own days and feasts.

Santo Niño de Atocha was a very popular Mexican frontier saint. Some reported that he ran so many errands of mercy at night that he kept wearing out his shoes. He became the patron saint of pilgrims and travelers and in later tradition gave power to old *el Santuario* (name of the church) at Chimayó, New Mexico, where one sees the hole with the sacred mud and a room with crutches and other body aids left behind by those professing healing.

Some saints, not recognized by the church, squeeze into the pantheon quite mysteriously. These figures have become real because so many people feel that the institutional church does not understand or relate to them. In New Mexico, one *cuento* refers to *San Amagón* and *San Amaviche* who allegedly promote *maldad y travesura* (like the devil's helpers who instigate bad and mischievous behavior).

Juan Soldado (Soldier John), as described by Julie Watson, has a tomb visited daily in Tijuana, Mexico. Among the flood of those trying to enter the U.S., Juan is the unofficial patron saint of Mexicans sneaking across the border. Still another example is *Don Pedrito Jaramillo*, a liquor supplier known for his herbal medicine and faith healing. His shrine stands in South Texas.

What Role Do Saints Play among Hispanic Catholics?

Roman Catholicism emphasizes the role of the church's saints in the lives of the faithful. The church teaches that the saints intercede with God on their behalf. The saints are considered alive, can hear prayers, and can make little miracles happen in daily life. In the Southwest and in Mexico, reports Rafaela Castro, some believers who do not receive what they requested from a saint will turn the saint's statue to face the wall, put it in a drawer, or bury it in the ground until the request is received. Castro reports that, in California, some Hispanic home sellers whose house is not moving fast enough on the market will bury a statue of St. James upside down to encourage more sales action.

Who Is the First Puerto Rican Saint?

No one yet. But in 1999, Pope John Paul II beatified **Carlos Rodríguez,** a layman in Puerto Rico. He was an office clerk, gave his time to the work of the church, and has one healing miracle reported. One more miracle and sainthood will likely follow.

Are the *Penitentes* Still Active in Northern New Mexico?

Who are the *penitentes?* This is a secret, sacred Spanish American brotherhood in the mountain villages of northern New Mexico and southern Colorado. The men celebrate a secret liturgy of prayers, songs, and processions. Their main event comes during Lent, especially in Holy Week from Wednesday through Saturday morning. Members re-enact Christ's crucifixion and burial like a Greek tragic drama. For decades rumors have circulated about actual crucifixions, but these reports are impossible to document adequately. That's Bill Tate's conclusion after studying the subject. Reports of extreme flagellations also have been a part of the *penitente* image.

Tate goes on to describe how the *penitentes* go back to the days following Oñate's expedition in 1598 when Spanish colonists penetrated into the remote valleys of the area. First as part of colonial government and later under independent Mexico, these people lived in general isolation. Mexico City was preoccupied with its many problems. Federal financial support, military presence and public programs were nil. No legal system existed. Franciscan priests had fled and were not replaced. In Jacqueline Meketa's summary, "The consequence of such neglect was a populace dependent upon its own [meager] resources" in dealing with "misery, danger and poverty," a "subsistence level" life with debt peonage and Indian raids.

Churches also were neglected from far-off centers of administration, and priests were few. In a movement of spiritual preservation, men began to erect buildings called *moradas* to hold meetings. Some think the roots of this movement go back to the flagellant sect of the Third Order of St. Francis. Franciscans came with the early expeditions into

New Mexico and brought with them the literature of St. Teresa of Avila and St. John of the Cross. On the other hand, Alberto López Pulido explains how some recent scholarship dismisses this theory and instead emphasizes the movement as "practical Catholicism" unjustly misrepresented in many church and secular writings and in reality expressing a fresh creativity-in-isolation that could teach all churches today.

When Archbishop Lamy arrived in the mid-1800s, reforms were instituted to control such independent ecclesiastical life, such as insisting on the use of traditional liturgy. The independence movement continued anyway. In time, however, both church and government forced the *penitentes* underground until Archbishop Edwin Byrne in 1947 allowed the groups to function again in their *moradas* on condition that they followed certain rules of the church. Nearly seven hundred members in 40 New Mexican communities still function, such as in Santa Cruz and Alcalde.

The significance of the movement? The *penitentes* represented a depth of religious faith in the soul of northern New Mexicans that was there with or without the clergy. At the altars in the homes the faithful experienced God at times far more deeply than at the church, avers Andrés Guerrero. The *penitentes* illustrated also the conflict between independent, creative movements and centralized institutional authority. The solution years later was a compromise.

What Are Some Other Colorful Religious Customs?
Shrines. In the front or back yard, the small *gruta* (grotto) or shrine is a common sight. The construction normally is made of cement or wood. In a cemetery, the *gruta* often honors the saint of the deceased person and can be large enough to have an iron gate to prevent vandalism. In a house, the shrine might be a *nicho* (niche), a small nook in a wall. The contents of a *gruta* will be a statue of the Virgin, another Madonna or a saint, plus flowers and a photo. This practice provides a tangible reminder of God, faith, and prayer.

Family Chapels. In northern New Mexico, priests were rare in this colony with few settlers, long distances between settlements, and dismal roads. Faithful Catholics often set aside a special room or a corner of a room with a small altar and flickering candles. In the 1700s, those with some land and money began erecting tiny family chapels. Even today, this custom continues as an expression of family-oriented faith. Driving through the northern New Mexico villages, atop a hill or behind an adobe house, the traveler notices small, immaculate *capillitas* (little chapels). Good examples exist at Chimayó, eloquently described by Gussie Fauntleroy. Sometimes as tiny as 10 by 12 feet, these private, family chapels are often painted white with a white cross and even a bell on the roof. Such structures very often fulfill a promise made after God's blessings or a miracle are received.

Altars (or *altarcitos*, little altars) are common in devout families. Again, in those long periods without priests, the wealthier people could build chapels; the poor settled for home altars. Such altars still are built. They can be a small table, a shelf, or just a niche in the wall. Accoutrements can be votive candles, statue of a saint, a statue or picture of *la Virgen*, a personal item, or flowers. Women are the traditional creators of these centers of devotion.

Hymns *(Alabados)* come from ancient praises to the Virgin Mary, Jesus Christ, or a patron saint. The music fuses medieval chants with indigenous tunes. Starting with *alabado sea* (praised be), the stanzas can go on indefinitely. New Mexican *penitentes* sing them during Lent and Holy Week activities. People voice them in private prayers at home and at funerals. The early Catholic missionaries introduced these songs to teach the Christian faith.

Miracles. This is a major feature of Southwest religion among Hispanic Catholics. At Socorro, Texas, legend tells of a wooden statue of San Miguel (Saint Michael) that reposes in a chapel there. In 1838 the cart carrying the statue suddenly could not be moved. The problem was interpreted as a miracle, with the statute placed in a shrine. From Santa Fe, New Mexico, comes the legend of the Miraculous Stairway in the Chapel of Our Lady of Light. Legend attributes the stairway to St. Joseph the carpenter. In 1878 the chapel had been built with no staircase to the balcony. The nuns prayed to St. Joseph. On the ninth day an old man offered to build a stairway. Three months later he disappeared, but the thirty-three step, double-circle stairway was in place—without center support or nails!

Mt. Cristo Rey
Pilgrimage—
Gabriel Sánchez

Pilgrimages. In 1933 Pope Pius XI called the Catholic Church to create special 900th-year celebrations of Christ's crucifixion and resurrection. In El Paso, at a high point where Texas, New Mexico and Mexico meet, a landmark mountain became a local project, launched in 1934 with a metal cross on the mountaintop. In 1938, Spanish sculptor Urbici Soler received a commission from the Catholic Diocese of El Paso to erect a thirty-two-foot cement statue of Christ. The statue would measure forty feet by counting the rock base and would cost over $60,000, a hefty sum at that time. Since the erection of the statue, an annual climb up *Mt. Cristo Rey* (Mountain of Christ the King) takes place in October or November. Some pilgrims do the final mile on their knees. Mass is then celebrated at the top with one or more bishops as celebrants. The 4.5-mile hike attracts as many as 40,000 persons from the entire area—to present requests to God, to express thanks, to fulfill promises, to set an example for the young, or to seek God's presence in their lives. A United Methodist group makes the climb on Easter Sunday afternoon. The trek is not for the frail. But for those who climb, the view alone is worth it.

Is *Santería* Practiced in the U.S.?

Santería (a religion about the saints) is a practice popular in Cuba, Puerto Rico, the Dominican Republic, and the U.S. It is a fusion of African Yoruba religions (present day Nigeria and Benin) and was brought by slaves to sugar plantations in Cuba as early as the 16th century. Blended with Roman Catholic forms by the Spanish, African gods get changed to Christian saints. Both male and female priests lead in worship of a variety of deities, regularly accompanied by animal sacrifice (but not human). Himilce Novas remarks that any American city with Spanish-Caribbean people will have places of *santería* worship. Similar to Haitian voodoo and Brazilian Macumba, *santería* believes in one supreme being, in saints or spirits (*orishas*) who can enter someone's life and become part of that person's personality. Priests (*santeros*) have the magical powers of the *orishas*. Rituals employ musical rhythms with drums and dancing, offerings of food and animal sacrifices, divination with bone fetishes, and trance-like seizures.

FOLK SPORTS AND GAMES
What Are the Most Popular Sports among Hispanics?

American Hispanics delight in all the sports that everyone enjoys, but certain sports appeal to Hispanics. *Número uno* is baseball (see "Baseball" under "Hispanics Who Enrich America Today"). The second most popular sport is soccer, that universal sport played around the globe. (See "Soccer" below). A third popular sport is boxing, not only among *barrio* youth in gyms and community centers across the country but also by youth and adults attending community boxing exhibitions.

Why Is Soccer a Passion among Hispanics?

Antecedents of this sport reach back to ancient history and go around the world. In the mid- and late-1800s, the game's rules were formalized and tournaments began. With the most recent origins in England, British sailors, businessmen, engineers, and artisans promoted soccer as they touched world ports.

Latin Americans are passionate about soccer. Stadiums are packed and fans nearly go into orbit when a goal is made. Notice also that barbed wire fences keep fans from storming the field or attacking the referees. The one lonely spot in the world where soccer passion has been weaker is the United States, but youth leagues have sprouted up everywhere, with more than 3 million children engaged. Hispanic immigrants have brought their soccer skills to this country and play on high school, college, and professional teams. Go to Washington, D.C. at RFK Stadium. Watch the Hispanic home team play and observe the whistle blowing, the drum banging, and the singing and cheering, mostly by Latinos. That is soccer passion.

How Did Cuban Baseball Influence American Baseball?

Baseball began in the U.S. with Abner Doubleday in 1846. Milton Jamail narrates how **Nemesio Guilló** took the first bat and ball from the U.S. to Cuba in 1864. Today, baseball is a Cuban national passion, not soccer. In the 1800s, Cuba was constantly torn by fierce civil strife in struggling for independence from Spain, particularly in 1868-1878. Many Cubans fled to the Dominican Republic, Puerto Rico, Venezuela, and Mexico, taking baseball with them.

Then in the early 1900s, Cuban players entered the American major leagues. After World War II, 39 had reached that level. Roger Hernandez brings up the role of Cuban **Roberto Estalella** who signed with the Washington Senators in 1935 (although a mulatto and not too dark, he was "safe"); a few other light-skinned Cubans followed. Hernandez sees Estalella as a forerunner who made possible Jackie Robinson's entry into racist baseball in 1947 to break baseball's color wall. When Castro came to power, he de-professionalized baseball. Aside from some who escape Cuba, Cuban players are considered amateurs in the world baseball scene. But in post-Castro years ahead, expect an infusion of Cuban athletes who could inject enormous quality and spirit into America's game.

Orlando "El Duque" Hernández has a thrilling story to tell, related by Vincent Cinisomo. Hernandez was a star pitcher on the Cuban national team. In 1996, after his baseball-playing brother defected to play in the U.S., the Cuban government kicked El Duque off the team; he found work as a janitor at $8 a month. Totally disillusioned, Hernández and seven others in December 1997 boarded an unsafe raft and floated to an uninhabited island in the Bahamas. After a rescue, El Duque eventually got a deal from the New York Yankees at $6.6 million dollars. What a change in fortune! But most of all, he relishes the freedom he has in his new country.

What Are the *Charreadas?*

In Mexico and along the border one finds a form of Mexican rodeo called *charreada*. Whereas the American rodeo speaks of the strength and speed of the western cowboy of past and present, the *charreada* stresses also elegance and style. The performers are called *charros* or *charras*. The program is a complicated social affair that involves parades, competitions, costumes, music, dancing, and food. John West comments that it is difficult to know whether to describe *charreada* as "custom, festival, or sport."

The custom came from Salamanca, Spain, in the 16th century and after the Conquest entered popular Mexican culture. *Charros* referred to the rural mounted police organized by President Benito Juárez to maintain law and order. The sport became the national urban sport after the 1910 Revolution. *Charros* came to symbolize Mexican *machismo* (masculinity). *Mariachis* adopted the costume, and films and TV stereotyped it. In more recent times, some Hispanics have criticized the tradition of lassoing the legs of a galloping horse and throwing the animal to the ground. Some states, such as California, have outlawed the practice. Others are considering doing so. But traditionalists complain that something essential to Mexican culture would be lost by banning cockfighting.

Is Cockfighting Still Allowed?

Cockfighting, recently banned in Oklahoma and illegal in Texas, is legal in New Mexico, Arizona, Louisiana, and Mexico (there a national sport, no less). It is legal to breed fighting roosters, however, in Texas. The birds are fed with scientific exactness and trained for physical endurance, but the killer instinct comes naturally. Carefully matched by weight and age and outfitted with gaff (like an ice pick) or knife, the birds might battle for two hours or more, until one rooster is dead. The fight occurs in a fenced, small arena or pit (*palenque)* with chairs for spectators, and gambling is heavy. Rejected by many for its cruelty, cockfighting is common along the border.

What Is the Hispanic Game *Huachas?*

You can find them in El Paso, Las Cruces, even Austin. Both wealthy and not-so-wealthy engage in a game called *huachas* (**wah**-shahs). The word comes from the Spanish pronunciation of the English word "washer," used instead of the Spanish *arandela*, according to Ann and Albert Manchester. "No one plays *arandelas*," they point out. Another Spanish word for washer is *rondana* and used at HOME DEPOT™.

The game is played with 2½-inch machine washers (*huachas*) painted different colors, tossed into 1-inch holes 30 feet apart with 3-inch PVC pipe pieces in the holes. Two players on a team with 4 washers oppose an equal team at the opposite hole. If a tossed washer lands in the hole, the team gets 4 points. If a washer lands on the edge of the hole, but not in it, there are 1 or 2 points (rules are not absolutely rigid). A washer nearer the hole than the opponent's gets 1 point. Twenty-one points make a winner.

This simple pastime may well have originated in some form in Aztec times. A similar game was played in Mexico with silver pesos. And perhaps railroad workers brought the game from Mexico and played *huachas* to fill their free time. El Paso, which claims to be the *huachas* capital of the world, has weekend and annual tournaments. The same scene exists in Las Cruces, New Mexico. But why this game rather than horseshoes that it resembles so closely? Players answer that some can't afford horseshoes, these rules are simple, the playing field can be almost anywhere, equipment is minimal, and *huachas* are about as cheap as anything one can think of.

FOLK WISDOM

What Are Some Examples of Folk Wisdom, or Proverbs?

Proverbs, or folk wisdom, are found in every nation and culture. The Spanish word for proverbs is *dichos* (sayings) or *refranes*. Margarita Mondrus-Ferrer Engle finds origins in "biblical proverbs, church doctrine, ancient and classical authors, fables, history, experience, superstition, humor and gossip." Categories are symbolism, observations on life, universal sayings, warnings, laments, humor, acceptance, tradition, advice, stoicism, true wisdom, satire, community problems, and society.

Out of hundreds of possibilities, let these selections illustrate this rich folk wisdom.

- *En boca cerrada no entra mosca:* In a closed mouth no fly enters.
- *Más vale prevenir que curar:* Better to prevent than to cure.
- *Los lunes ni las gallinas ponen:* On Mondays not even the hens lay.
- *Al que madruga, Dios le ayuda:* Early risers have God's help.

- *Más vale un hecho que cien palabras:* Better one deed than a hundred words.
- *Algo es algo, dijo el calvo:* Something is something, said the bald man.
- *Palabra sin obra, guitarra sin cuerda:* Word without deed is like guitar without string.
- *Poco a poco se llega lejos:* Little by little gets you far.
- *Hombre precavido vale por dos:* One prepared is worth two unprepared.
- *Un asno viejo sabe más que un potro:* An old ass knows more than a young colt.
- *Quien adelante no mira, atrás se queda:* One who doesn't look ahead stays behind.
- *Para todo hay remedio, menos la muerte:* Everything has a remedy except death.
- *Cada panadero alaba su pan:* Every baker praises his own bread.
- *Vamos a ver, dijo un ciego:* Let's see, said a blind man.
- *Barriga llena, corazón contento:* Full belly, happy heart.

Víctor Martínez tells us about a new "invention," modeled on the Chinese restaurant's ubiquitous fortune cookie. Now it's *Takitos*, the brain child of Sid Martínez. The taco-shaped cookies have Spanish *dichos* written inside. *Takitos* are sold now in 40 states, and the business is growing.

What Are Some Examples of Hispanic Riddles?
Adivinanzas (riddles) are brainteasers for entertainment, simple children's ditties, or real challenges to a person's cultural knowledge. These examples are from Angel Vigil:

Cajita de Dios bendita que se abre y se cierra y no se marchita. ¿Qué es?
A little box, blessed by God, that opens and shuts but never wears out. What is it? An eye.

En el agua no me mojo, en brazos y no me abrazo, en el aire y no me caigo. ¿Qué es?
I am in water but I am not wet. I am in arms but I do not hug. I am in the air, but I do not fall. What is it? The letter A.

¿Qué tiene boca y no puede comer?
What has a mouth but cannot eat? What is it? A river.

Me acuesto blanca, me levanto pinta. ¿Qué es?
I lie down white, I get up spotted. What is it? A tortilla.

Hispanics & Religion— Tradition & Change

CATHOLICS AND PROTESTANTS
Is There a Typical Hispanic Catholic?

Through the center of Hispanic culture runs a deep current of spirituality. Even when shouting ¡olé! at a bull fight, Latinos are using a Spanish adaptation of the Arabic name for God, meaning "Praise Allah!" Commonly, *gracias a Dios* (thank God) expresses all kinds of gratitude. *Si Dios quiere* (if God wills) expresses submission to God's will. These expressions are spoken constantly.

For most Hispanics (though not all), this spirituality is Roman Catholic. In the future, over half of the 60 million American Roman Catholics will be Hispanic. Hispanics offer unique qualities to the Catholic Church, says William V. D'Antonio, who presents this picture of a typical Hispanic Catholic.

- Younger and less formally educated.
- Generally with lower income.
- Less likely than Anglos to be a registered parish member.
- Less likely to attend weekly Mass (30 percent to 39 percent).
- Stronger commitment to Our Lady of Guadalupe.
- In contrast to most Anglos, more likely to emphasize being a Catholic than living a certain way.
- More likely to stress individual conscience above church leaders, even on topics like abortion, non-marital sex, and women priests.
- More likely to support a more democratic voice in church decision-making rather than by diocesan or Vatican mandates.

Luis G. Pedraja suggests one other contribution of Hispanics to both the Catholic and the Protestant Churches: *mestizaje*, the mixture of races and cultures. Hispanics contain a diversity of Spanish, Native American, African, Asian, and Arab roots and thus can enable the churches to reflect "the human face of a God incarnate in the concrete images of many people...."

Finally, a nationwide survey by the National Conference of Catholic Bishops, presented by Guadalupe Silva, adds the contributions of family strength and values, emotional faith, love of celebration in ritual, popular ethnic religious practices, and the value of persons over things.

How Do Hispanics View Catholic Church Changes?

Tom Roberts describes a "seismic shift" taking place within the entire American Catholic Church. The impetus for this change comes from the pedophilia scandals among the priests. Beneath this scandal, though, is the deeper issue of church authority, openness, and responsibility. Where local priests are open and sensitive to the laity, parishes continue to feel more confident about their church, despite the failure of their upper leadership. Even before the scandals, younger Catholics no longer displayed unquestioning loyalty to the hierarchy and Rome. The real action today, where laity are expressing themselves, is in the local parish, not in hierarchical offices.

Many Hispanic Catholics with such open priests deal with the fire storm better than Anglos. Jesuit Fr. Alan Figueroa Dick, in an editorial, says:

Hispanic culture is perhaps more anchored in earthy reality. Mediterranean peoples separate the ideal from the reality..., and they can live with that ambiguity. Northern Europeans have a harder time with gray.

To be sure, when this honest openness does not exist, Hispanics are as angry as anyone else as they deal with their feelings of betrayal.

How Do Some Hispanics Criticize the Catholic Church?

Hispanics today comprise over a third of 65.3 million U.S. Catholics. Despite the constant increase of Hispanics in the Catholic Church, many Hispanics in this country feel that the institutional church fails to take this Hispanic constituency seriously. Pastor and theologian, Msgr. Arturo Bañuelas, wishes the Catholic church would answer his question: "Are we Latinos to be seen as a blessing or as a pastoral problem?" Raymond Rodríguez states that the 45,000 Catholic priests include less than 1 percent Latino clergy. Seminary training does not always equip men for Hispanic ministry in a new day. Nor are recruitment and ordination of Latino priests sufficient to serve the growing number of Hispanic parishioners.

The previously mentioned survey by the Catholic bishops discovered that 63 percent of respondents think that diocesan programs do not encourage Hispanic leadership. Sixty-three percent of diocesan administration have no Hispanics in central office management, and 73 percent have no Hispanics managing Catholic charities. English-dominant younger Hispanics in the Southwest ask for Masses in English and a more celebratory worship style with more community connection. Furthermore, although concerned about loss of membership to sectarian proselytism, many are equally concerned about the lack of aggressive Catholic evangelizing among immigrant newcomers, most of them Hispanic.

Is the Catholic Church Facing a Hispanic Exodus?

The main worry is the loss of thousands of members. In some places as many as one-fifth to one-fourth of Hispanics no longer consider themselves to be Catholics, according to Demetria Martínez in the *National Catholic Reporter*. This exodus has been estimated at one million over the past fifteen years at a rate now of 60,000-100,000 a year. More Puerto Ricans than Mexicans leave, and more in the East than in the West. In a Catholic survey, 56 percent of Hispanic Catholics had received an invitation to another church, 51 percent more than once.

The flow of Hispanics from Roman Catholic churches in the last quarter century has been astounding, says Leslie Wirpsa. Fr. Andrew Greeley calls this exodus a "hemorrhage." Segundo Pantoja refers to a 1992 survey that counted American Latino Catholics at 66 percent and 23 percent among other Christian denominations and groups.

In the U.S. as a whole, says Leslie Wirpsa, American Catholicism is middle-class, while so many Hispanics are not. Many Hispanics feel segregated and even homeless in their own church. Cultural flash points between Hispanics and Anglos can be observed in different details like time, registration for Holy Communion, and use of offering envelopes. Also, so many middle-class Anglo parishioners do not comprehend or appreciate cultural differences. Anglos resist sharing power, and they commonly are reluctant to dialogue on what Hispanics really need.

How Strong Are the Pentecostals among Hispanics?

The significant exodus of Hispanics from Catholicism to non-Catholic faiths is most evident among the Pentecostal churches. Such groups, including Assembly of God and others, are sometimes referred to as the "Aleluyas." Often meeting in storefront buildings but increasingly in larger structures, Pentecostal worship features loud and emotional expression, such as singing with guitar and other instrumental accompaniment, speaking in tongues, healings, revelations, and baptisms in the Holy Spirit. Sermons consist of biblical commentary and exhortation. Shouts of "aleluya," "*alabado sea Dios*," and prayers to the Holy Spirit punctuate the meetings. Sociologists find a strong correlation between lower-economic status and this preference for emotional expression in worship. Women make up the largest number of participants.

Besides emotional worship that commonly makes God more personal and real, Pentecostal churches offer Latino pastors; the almost exclusive use of Spanish in worship and church life; belief in healing miracles; a strict adherence to a lifestyle that abhors alcohol and drugs; a concern for daily problems of housing, health, and immigration; practical concern for families in need; and through-the-week services and meetings that become the social center of a family's life. Segundo Pantoja, in his analysis of this phenomenon, says that "there is a well-established trend for Latinos to affiliate with expressions of the Protestant faith that are different from the Mainline or Historical churches."

In more middle-class Pentecostal congregations, the emotional tendency is lower and services are quieter, more ritualistic, and more likely to feature bilingual preaching and singing. This quieter worship expression is even more evident in mainline Protestant denominational churches. At the same time, the atmosphere of emotion and fervor is witnessed similarly in the charismatic groups within the Roman Catholic Church.

Are Many Hispanics in Mainline Protestant Churches?

David Maldonado says that historic Protestantism is not a mere footnote to the Hispanic church's story but instead plays a significant though much smaller role. For example, 50,000 Hispanics are United Methodists, mostly in the Southwest. The work of Presbyterians in northern New Mexico has been significant. The various denominations are now routinely producing Christian education and worship resources in Spanish.

But significant changes are occurring within those same denominations.

Language and culture. In congregations that continue to receive new immigrants, Spanish is spoken and Hispanic culture remains strong. But in congregations with growing numbers of second, third, and fourth generation Hispanics, English is used more and more. Especially is this so with youth whose world is English, pizza, and rock music. A tension exists in those churches between maintaining cultural roots and adapting to acculturated younger generations.

Youth. Paradoxically, many Hispanic Protestant youth reveal a deepening desire to express their faith as Hispanics.

Society. From historic tendencies to exist withdrawn from society and community, a minority of Hispanic Protestants, along with their sisters and brothers among all churches, including the Catholic Church, struggle to extend faith and worship to concern for community and social justice.

Ecumenism. From historic patterns (still very common in the U.S. and in Latin America) where Hispanic Protestants attack Catholicism, here and there one can see an openness to a broader, more tolerant theological base, that is, for Christian relationships through a common faith that still allows differences. Vatican II remains powerful.

Social Struggle. Hispanic Protestants have occasionally linked arms with Hispanic Catholics to work among farm workers in California and in the Lower Valley of Texas, to join in community struggles and even in political participation in the *barrios* of our large cities. Justo González calls this "a new ecumenism."

How Did Hispanic Protestant and Catholic Conflict Develop?

Protestant denominations moved into the former Mexican Southwest immediately after the Treaty of Guadalupe Hidalgo in 1848. They invested funds for literature, personnel, and property. This investment accompanied the Anglo cultural, economic, and political impact on the former Mexican society, as described by David Maldonado. The Protestant agenda was to convert Catholics to Protestantism and to "Americanize" them. Protestant piety insisted that converts withdraw from Mexican and Catholic customs. Hispanic Protestant churches avoided accoutrements like candles, stained glass windows, and incense. The attitude was clearly anti-Catholic and anti-Papist. In a natural response, in their efforts to protect their parishioners, Catholic clergy often encouraged fear and mistrust toward Hispanic Protestants.

How Do Protestant Hispanics Handle the Catholic Tradition?

Most Hispanic Protestants, certainly members of Pentecostal and independent churches, reject anything faintly resembling Catholicism. The worship services are informal, with emotional singing, praying, and preaching. Guitar complements organ or piano as do folksy choruses along with the hymns. Holy Communion will be occasional. Some churches have weekday services nearly every night and twice on Sunday. Hispanics in mainline Protestant denominations generally follow much of the Anglo Protestant models in their search for their identity. Theologically, evangelicals reject doctrines about the Virgin Mary, the Pope, and the seven Sacraments. But Robert Gómez of the United Methodist Church admits how ignoring the "deep cultural images on the conscious level" ignores also the "collective unconscious of the *mestizo* mother-figure in the faith." This buried awareness comes out, he states, in the emotional observance of Mother's Day in both churches. Tomás Atencio, professor at the University of New Mexico, despite his deep Protestant roots, admits "the deep tug of symbol and myth in many Protestant Hispanics, tugs they seldom dare to share in public."

HIDDEN JUDAISM
Does Hidden Judaism Appear among Hispanics?

This question is a most intriguing theme, which explains this long discourse. The year 1492 is an important date. Columbus sailed on his first voyage, but that is not all. In that same year the Spanish conquered the Muslim Moors after nearly 800 years of domination that had profoundly affected the Spanish world outlook. In that year also the king and queen issued the Edict of Expulsion. Muslims had to convert to Catholicism or face prison or death. Jews faced expulsion, too.

Before 1492, Spanish Jews were affluent and influential. Youth were even permitted to intermarry. Suddenly, Jews were vulnerable; all non-Catholics were perceived as national threats. Under the pressure of imprisonment, torture, or death, or all three, many Jews and Muslims became *conversos,* or converted Christians. Crypto-Jews is another term. They were called *marranos* (swine) by fellow Jews, or New Christians. In *Don Quixote,* Sancho Panza boasts of being one of those having "...four fingers' depth of honest old Christian fat on their souls," that is, no Jewish or Moorish blood at all.

The Catholic Church's cruel Inquisition made conversion a tempting option to avoid terrible punishment and death. Thousands of those Sephardic Jews chose exile; no one knows how many—maybe 200,000 or a half-million. Around half fled to other European countries like Portugal, others to North Africa. When the Inquisition also reached Portugal, many Jews fled to the Americas, to today's New England, Canada, and Latin America. A sizeable group settled on the Central Plateau of Costa Rica. Gonzalo Chacón Trejos discovers the quality of Costa Rican culture today—sophisticated, progressive, anti-militaristic, education-focused, tolerant, peaceful—as evidence of that Jewish influx. Another large group reached Mexico where outwardly they lived as Catholics but secretly clung to their Jewish traditions, like use of Sabbath candles, Hebrew prayers in Spanish, circumcision, and unleavened bread.

Hernando Alonso, for instance, arrived with **Cortés,** engaged in the Conquest, and as a reward received a large land grant. Alonso was one of the first cowboys. Eighty miles north of Mexico City, at Actopán, he ran a cattle ranch and bred the first foals born in America. Other ranchers and horse breeders also were Jewish. Monclava, a Jewish ranching settlement south of the Río Grande, bred long-horned cattle and mustangs. For the most part, hidden Jews mingled with the general population and became peddlers, merchants, craftsmen, soldiers, priests, and scholars. Some Jews were international traders and estate owners. One was a governor, another a member of the Mexico City Council.

Slowly, these persons and their offspring lost their Jewish identity and became completely assimilated by the close of the colonial period. But eventually the Inquisition reached Mexico. If Jews were found out, their crime of heresy brought severe punishment. Alonso himself was arrested, charged with secret Judaism, and burned at the stake. In 1596, nine Jews were burned at the stake, including five from the prominent family of **Luis Carvajal,** governor, no less, of Nuevo León. A later outburst against Jews erupted in 1642-1649; twelve died at the stake after being garroted, and one was burned alive.

It takes no imagination to understand the flight of many Mexican Jews into the isolated mountain areas of modern-day northern New Mexico. Today, as many as 1,500 families with Jewish heritage may live there. Some are only dimly aware of those roots, others not at all, some very aware. A few have turned to Judaism. Scholars at the University of New Mexico, among them Stanley M. Hordes and Tomás Atencio, have searched in the past for further traces of Spanish Jews.

Here are some clues they pay attention to.

Surnames of persons condemned by the Inquisition, such as Rodríguez, Nieto, Carvajal, Díaz, Hernández, Pérez. Interestingly, Rodríguez and Hernández are among four possibly Jewish names of persons with Oñate in 1598.

Other Sephardic (Spanish Jewish) surnames, listed in Jewish encyclopedias: Arias, Avia, Acefeco, Atencio, Bargas, Barrios, Bravo, Cáceres, Carillo, Carrasco, Castro, Chaves, Delgado, Escudero, Medina, Mendes, Olgúin, Peres, Paz, Romero, Rosales, Rubín, Safrán, Sanches, Sosa, Silva, Súarez, Tamuz, Torres, Treviño, Vaez, Villanueva.

Dislike for pork or shellfish.

Certain foods such as *pan de España* or *de León* (a sweet bread), *dulces* or candy like *leche quemado* (wrapped in paper squares with a dim Star of David inscribed).

Meat dishes on Fridays.

Candles on Friday nights.

Reluctance to light a fire on Saturday.

Food preparation before Friday sunset.

Attention to body cleanliness, like taking a bath before Friday night's meal, or changing clothes for Saturday's trip from ranch to town.

Separation from the husband for three months after childbirth, or being extremely modest during menstruation.

Silver amulets that are generations old and supposedly prevent sickness.

A synagogue in El Paso, Texas, welcomes back to the fold those whose families long ago might have been Jewish in faith. Look, too, at some famous Hispanics who have acknowledged their Jewish ancestry: actress **Rita Moreno,** dictator **Fidel Castro,** artist **Diego Rivera,** and photographer **Guillermo Kahlo,** father of **Frida Kahlo.** And one theory suggests that **Christopher Columbus** himself was a Spanish Jew whose family had moved to Italy and taken the Spanish form of the name. He always wrote his brother in Spanish, states Gary MacEoin, and spoke defective Italian.

Arlynn Nellhaus of the *Jerusalem Post* relates a story found in the *San Francisco Chronicle* about a boy named **Antonio López** in a mountain village in northern New Mexico. One day his grandfather began pouring water on the boy's head. After the little fellow yelled, "Why, Grandpa?," the old man finally took him for a walk to explain that they were really Jews. "But why the water splashed on my head?" the boy kept asking. The grandfather finally replied, "To remove the baptism!" Today, Antonio López, after abandoning both Catholicism and Judaism, is a Russian Orthodox priest.

One more tantalizing story comes from Alex Apostolides. Near the base of Hidden Mountain, about 15 miles south of Los Lunas, New Mexico, a town south of Albuquerque, a 100-ton basalt rock known as the Los Lunas Stone has something unique on one surface. Nine lines with 216 letters are similar to the Ten Commandments in Hebrew in Exodus 20. Scholars such as Robert Pfeiffer and Cyrus Gordon and members of the Western Epigraphic Society have agreed that the script is ancient Canaanite-Hebrew, found also on the Moabite Stone from the 9th century B.C./B.C.E. Multiple theories try to explain this phenomenon. Dan E. Rohrer of the Western Epigraphic Society and Apostolides suggest that the letters were chiseled by a Spanish Jew, a *converso* (secret Jew) who might have been an unknown member of **Don Juan de Oñate's** expedition in 1598 en route northward to establish San Gabriel, the temporary capital of New Mexico. Since we know that some Jews traveled with Oñate on that journey, this explanation carries some weight in solving this intriguing mystery.

For further reading on this topic, you may consult Henry J. Tobias, *A History of the Jews in New Mexico* (1990), and *Deep in the Heart: The Lives and Legends of Texas Jews,* by the Texas Jewish Historical Society.

AZTEC RELIGION
What Are Parallels Between Aztec Religion and Christianity?
With William H. Prescott as our source, we are told that the goddess Cioacóatl was depicted with a serpent nearby, and the Aztec goddess

gave women pain in childbirth as a result of the coming of sin and death into the world.

A story about a great flood is similar to stories from around the world and in biblical Genesis. A boat floats on water at the foot of a mountain. A dove appears, and the man and wife survive.

At Cholula stands a 180-foot brick pyramid where, tradition says, the natives attempted to construct a building to the clouds, but the offended gods sent fire from heaven and interrupted the project. This sounds like the Tower of Babel.

Quetzalcóatl, the white god with beard, had strangely disappeared and was expected to return soon from the East. Some of the Spaniards saw in this figure the likeness of Jesus.

The cross was a symbol in ancient Egypt and Syria, too, but its form amazed the early Spaniards as they viewed it in Aztec temples. Its image can be seen today on a wall of a building in Palenque, showing a child apparently in adoration.

Mural "Aztec 'Xochitl,' Ixtalaccihuatl, and Popocatepetl," by Felipe Adame and others, 1987, restored 1991, 600 block Campbell Street, El Paso, Texas—Photo by Richard Campbell.

The Spanish also found an Aztec baptism wherein water was placed on the head and lips of an infant, a name was conferred, and a prayer was offered to the goddess Cioacóatl, the goddess of childbirth, that the child be cleansed of sin and be born anew.

One ceremony reminded the Spaniards of Holy Communion. The image of an Aztec deity was created of corn flour, mixed with blood, consecrated by priests, distributed among the people, and eaten together. Worshippers felt sorrow for their misdeeds and claimed that the eaten mixture "was the flesh of the deity."

The early conquerors were both amazed and disturbed by all of this resemblance. Some found comparisons and considered them mere imagination. Others saw a trick of Satan to confuse by counterfeit parallels and thus to destroy those who believed. In later centuries some scholars saw a common source in eastern Asia or Egypt. Kingsborough thought that Mexico was colonized by the ten lost tribes of Israel!

VIRGIN OF GUADALUPE
Why Is the Virgin of Guadalupe Important to Hispanics?

The First Lady of Mexico is not really the wife of the President. She is instead the **la Virgin de Guadalupe.** Except for liberals, agnostics, and nearly all Protestants, the Virgin is a vital part of the lives of most Mexicans.

The story of the Virgin goes back to the Spanish Conquest. Fray **Juan de Zumárraga,** first archbishop of Mexico, decreed that eleven pagan shrines be destroyed. The most important of those shrines was that of the virgin Aztec goddess of earth and corn, **Tonantzín.** The shrine stood upon the hill of Tepeyac, northeast of Tenochtitlán, today's Mexico City.

Early on the morning of December 9, 1531, a poor Indian, **Juan Diego,** was crossing Tepeyac Hill from his village on the way to Mass at the Franciscan church at Tlatelolco. Suddenly, he heard music and a soft voice calling his name. Speaking in *Náhuatl* and addressing him as "my son," the voice of a dark-skinned Virgin asked him to tell the bishop to build a church on that site so that she could be near her people. She said, "I am the Mother of all of you who dwell in this land."

Not surprisingly, Juan had trouble convincing the bishop of this story, and when he returned to the hill the Virgin appeared again and urged Juan to try once more. On the next day the bishop heard the man more kindly and asked for some evidence. Reporting again to the Virgin, Juan was told to return the next day. On Monday, Juan's uncle was sick, so Juan stayed at home and forgot about his appointment at Tepeyac. But on Tuesday he returned. The Virgin appeared and instructed him to pick up some roses as the bishop's evidence.

Sure enough, among the rocks, instead of cactus plants he saw lovely Castilian roses. The Virgin told Juan to hide the roses in his *tilma* (cape) and to go to the bishop. When the cape fell to the floor in front of the bishop, both men stared at an image on the cloth. The image was the Virgin of Guadalupe. On his knees now, the bishop begged Juan for forgiveness and placed the cloth over the chapel altar. Later, a chapel was built on the site of the appearance. Thousands of Indians became converts. In 1754 Pope Benedict XIV proclaimed the Virgin to be the Patroness and Protectress of New Spain. Ironically, Father Hidalgo launched the revolt against Spain in 1810 with a banner of the Virgin leading his forces.

Today the basilica on Tepeyac Hill is the holiest shrine in Mexico. December 12 celebrates the Virgin's appearance to Diego and brings out huge crowds. Elizondo calls this celebration "the Easter service of the people..., that takes the place of the Easter lilies of western Christianity."

One theory traces the origin of the Virgin's name to the appearance of the Virgin to terminally-ill **Juan Bernardino,** Juan Diego's uncle. He asked her name. She called herself Holy Mary of Guadalupe. But in *Náhuatl* which she used, Juan Bernardino could have heard not Guadalupe but *Coatlaxopeuh,* pronounced *Cuatlashupe. Cóatl* means serpent, *tla* is a particle, and *xopeuh* means crushed or stepped on. Thus, the reading would be "Holy Virgin Mary who crushed the serpent." The serpent symbolized the old Aztec religion, now crushed by this new faith. This is how Andrés Guerrero explains the name.

Before Juan Diego died in 1548, he dictated the story to **Antonio Valeriano,** which was then written in the *Nicán Mopohua* in *Náhuatl.* It was placed also in the *Codex Tetlapalco,* the oldest surviving book in the Americas. Begun before 1454, the book relates Aztec history from their arrival in the Valley of Mexico to the Spanish Conquest.

Virgin de Guadalupe— Gabriel Sánchez

Apart from faith, then, how do some explain the power of Guadalupe? Octavio Paz states that the cult of the Virgin of Guadalupe is the center of Mexican Catholicism. No surprise. The hill of Tepeyac had been a sanctuary for Tonantzín, the Aztec goddess of fertility, representing manifestations of Coátlicue (Mother of the Gods) and Tlazolteótl (the Devourer of Filth and the Goddess of Carnal Things). Two of the masculine gods, Quetzalcóatl and Huitzilopochtli, had plummeted to defeat. People began returning with desperation to the goddess of the fertility of the earth, of seed, and of harvest.

Another possibility was described in the exhibition of Guadalupe in the gallery of Perkins School of Theology at Southern Methodist University in Dallas in 1992. The statue of *Nuestra Señora de Guadalupe* in the choir loft of the monastery in Estremadura, Spain, dating from 1449, is dark-skinned and very similar in appearance to the image on the *tilma* of Juan Diego. It could be significant that a Marian devotion was centered at Estremadura.

Here is one example. **Miguel de Cervantes Saavedra,** who wrote *Don Quixote,* lost his left hand at the Battle of Lepanto (1571). After release from prison in Algeria, he made a pilgrimage to Estremadura to express his gratitude for protection. Another example is **Columbus,** a devotee of the saint. Following his first voyage, he and his crew visited Guadalupe's shrine to express thanks for protection during a storm. The indigenous men he had brought from the New World were baptized there. Still another example is **Cortés** who was born and reared in Medellín, a few miles from Estremadura. Often he sent gifts to the shrine. **Bernal Díaz del Castillo,** who was in Cortés's army and wrote the chronicle of events, reported in chapter 52 that Cortés wanted to leave with the native chiefs of Cempola an image of "a great Lady, who is Mother of Our Lord Jesus Christ, in whom we believe, and whom we adore, so that they also have her as patroness and advocate." Even more, twelve Franciscan missionaries in Mexico were led by **Martín de Valencia** who was influenced by **Juan de Puebla,** one deeply devoted to Guadalupe. Therefore, the meanings at the shrine in Spain could by some means have been transferred to Tepeyac and thus have become a central symbol for Mexican identity in the following centuries.

Is the Juan Diego Story History or Legend?

A professional poll of Catholics would be helpful, but no doubt many Catholics do take the story as literal history. The belief is an emotional part of their faith. Defenders today insist on solid evidence for **Juan Diego's** existence and refer to his house located under a 17th century church in a sprawling suburb of Mexico City. John Allen adds other arguments that are used: the literary evidence in the Aztec narrative called *El Nican Mopohua,* 25 other documents dated 1550-1590, Juan Diego's death certificate, and the enduring power of the story in the life of the Catholic Church.

Many Catholic scholars, though, do not think the story itself is literally true. The evidence above, they say, is not that trustworthy. In 1999, in the midst of efforts to canonize Juan Diego, an uproar temporarily upset the Vatican when the former abbot of the Basilica of Guadalupe in Mexico City, Guillermo Schulenburg, in a letter to the Vatican, questioned the historical authenticity of the Diego story. According to John Rice, clergy at the time of the Conquest saw the apparition story as "...a device cooked up by local Indians to continue worshipping their Aztec goddess—Tonantzín—'Our Mother'—whose shrine was at Tepeyac." Moreover, church officials apparently ignored the story for over a hundred years. In addition, the Marian cult had existed in Spain long before the Mexican story. Do we see a simple transfer?

Fr. Virgilio Elizondo insists carefully that the story we have is probably not scientifically documented history. The literary genre is folklore, a genre of the poor. Still, he (and others) would acknowledge the possibility of a kernel of fact imbedded within the legend. Even if the story were legend, it nevertheless could hold truths from God. Elizondo laments that Guadalupe's concern for the poor and oppressed has disturbed the comfortable, and they find it easier to concentrate on pomp and ritual.

Elizondo, despite his historical disclaimer, does go on to present the Virgin as the Mother of Jesus, one of his first disciples, a model for mothers and women everywhere, the one who inspires people to follow Jesus as she did, and especially one whom Christians follow in the struggle for social justice. Elizondo points to the Virgin's dark skin, her appearance to an oppressed Indian, her speaking in *Náhuatl.* In other words, this Virgin identified with Juan Diego's conquered people. Elizondo's words are poetic: The Virgin is "...the temple in whom and through whom Christ's saving presence is continually incarnated into the soil of the Americas." Andrés Guerrero sees her as a symbol of liberation against oppression.

Monsignor Arturo Bañuelas, pastor of St. Pius X Catholic Church in El Paso, refers to "...a *mestiza* virgin,...the symbol of a call for a new temple in America,...committed to respect our differences as gifts from God and not as weapons or excuses for divisions." Elsewhere he commented that "Guadalupe is the most powerful and significant symbol of *mestizaje* or cultural mixture." Hispanic life "values the sacred, the mystical," so December 12 is a time for Hispanic Catholics to renew their faith through honor and love of the Virgin, and in addition to renew their pride in their culture and heritage. Sr. Teresa Maya refers to British historian David A. Brading who offers this thesis. He pushes beyond historical evidence and past theological debates to concentrate on what is essentially a symbol. The symbol has moved in an evolutionary pattern within Mexican history with "a charm and presence that exerts a power over the faithful." Since no one can deny that reality, Brading writes, why cannot one believe that the Holy Spirit worked through a humble Indian and a painter? Why could not the Holy Spirit have developed that evolution within the Mexican soul that placed Mexican identity on a warm religious base? But the real question, he says, is how the Holy Spirit will work now in an age of globalization and secularization to bring Guadalupe into this new generation of Mexicans and Hispanics.

In March, 2002, the Archdiocese of Mexico City officially presented a revised image of Juan Diego. As a preparation for planned canonization by the Pope in the summer of that year, church leaders in the Mexico City diocese changed the drawing of Juan Diego. He was no longer a dark-skinned, conquered Aztec but rather a lighter-skinned European with long hair and full beard. Critics called it "modern marketing," reported David Sedeno and Laurence Iliff. Some felt the move was "to de-indigenize Juan Diego and make him look more like an urban Catholic." Indians from southern Mexico, descendants of those from Juan Diego's time, feel the church and government have abandoned the indigenous Mexican people by making Juan Diego "a little less Indian."

How Do Mexican Hispanics Show Their Fervor for the Virgin?

The symbolic presence of *la Virgen de Guadalupe* (the Virgin of Guadalupe), says Rubén Martínez, is "ubiquitous." Pictures can be found on home and office walls, sweatshirts, baseball caps, murals, prayer cards, medals, and T-shirts. Other objects are in cars, living rooms, backyard shrines, and "in every barrio church from East Los Angeles to El Paso." Perhaps more prayers are offered to the Virgin than to Jesus. Martínez puts *La Virgen* "at the center of the Mexican soul." December 12 is the big day of celebration in all Catholic churches to honor the Virgin, the same day in Juan Diego's account of the image on the sacred cloth. Sometimes choral groups gather in the church at daybreak for *mariachi* serenades.

Santa Fe, New Mexico, shows its own distinctive honor to the Virgin. Rafaela Castro relates the story of a 28-inch statue of the Virgin Mary that was brought to New Spain in 1625 by a Fray **Benavides** and given the name *la Conquistadora*, named for the Spanish conquerors. In New Mexico, during the Pueblo Revolt of 1680, the statue was taken to a town in Mexico for safety where it stayed for thirteen years. When Don **Diego de Vargas** led Spanish soldiers to reconquer Santa Fe in 1692, he had the statue with him and installed it in a tower of the cathedral.

Now fast forward. In 1954, Francis Cardinal Spellman crowned *la Conquistadora*, and in 1960 a representative of Pope John XXIII did the same. This Mary is today the guardian and patron saint of Santa Fe and a reminder of that bloodless Spanish reconquest. A footnote comment belongs here. In no way do Hispanics have a total monopoly on reverence for the Virgin Mary. Browse through any volume of great art from Europe or anywhere in the world. Or listen to any collection of great music (like the classical renditions of *Ave Maria*). The figure of Mary has captured the imagination of all humankind.

Why Does All of Latin America Honor the Mexican Virgin?
Pope Benedict XIV in 1754 proclaimed the Virgin to be the Patroness and Protectress of New Spain. On October 12, 1945, she was crowned Queen of the Americas. In 1999 Pope John Paul II exalted her to be Patroness of the Americas. For the first time, all of Latin America— North, South, and Central—now honors the Lady of Guadalupe.

When Has the Virgin Played a Role in Hispanic History?
In 1810, Father **Hidalgo** launched the Mexican Revolt against Spain with a banner of the Virgin leading his forces. In the 1960s, César Chávez led the farm worker movement in California with a banner of *la Virgen Morena* in marches of protest against the grape growers and on behalf of the migrant workers. Out of that struggle emerged the United Farm Workers union.

Why Does the Virgin of Guadalupe Have a Website?
For the December 12, 2001, celebration when Diego was beatified (the step before canonization), Pope John Paul II himself launched a website so anyone unable to visit the basilica in Mexico City could send their petitions to the Virgin by e-mail. The Pope was the first visitor to the site filled with Masses, souvenir shop, the story of 1531, and the Virgin at Tepeyac. The website address is *www.virgendeguadalupe.org.mx.*

HISPANICS AND ISLAM
Are Some Hispanics Actually Turning to Islam?
Talk about a cultural/religious shift! Still a small movement but gaining strength, some Hispanics in New York, Puerto Rico, Mexico, Spain, and Central and South America are turning to a faith with roots in the history of Spain and the Conquest. From 40,000 such converts in 1997, the estimate now is 60,000 or more. Deborah Kong explains some reasons for the turn: disenchantment with Roman Catholicism, a religious simplicity in Islam for faith and life, and intermarriage. This development is something to watch in the future.

SEASONS OF THE CHURCH YEAR
Are Poinsettias a Gift from Mexico?
Well, sort of. The flower grew in Mexico. Joel Roberts Poinsett, first U.S. ambassador to the newly-independent Republic of Mexico in 1825-1829, became quite unpopular for interfering in Mexican politics and was recalled to the U.S. He had long admired a gorgeous red flower, called the Nativity flower, seen at Christmastime in many Mexican churches

(because that was the season when the plant flowered). So, when he returned, he brought home cuttings of the red flower which botanists later named *Poinsettia pulcherrima* in his honor. A century later, a Southern California farmer developed a version of the flower that could be grown indoors as a potted plant. Today the dramatic splash of poinsettian red in homes, churches, offices, and stores has become as much a part of Christmas as the Christmas tree. The flower's other name is *Flor de la Noche Buena* (Flower of the Holy Night, or Christmas Eve).

When Is the Traditional Christmas Observed?
The season traditionally starts on December 12, the Feast of the Virgin of Guadalupe, continues with *las Posadas, la Nochebuena,* Christmas Day, and ends on January 6, *el Día de los Reyes Magos* (the Day of the Three Kings).

What Happens in *las Posadas?*
This lovely custom is one of Mexico's unique contributions to the celebration of *la Navidad.* Origins are traced to Aztec customs. The early Spanish priests by 1540, concerned about teaching Christianity to the Indians, took the Aztec celebration of the birth of the god Huitzilopochtli and transferred the imagery to the birth of Jesus. Rafaela Castro pinpoints the Christian beginnings of the observance to the town of Acolmán that sits near the pyramids of Teotihuacán.

The traditional observance takes place on the nine nights of December 16 to 24. Pilgrimage participants, sometimes in two groups, carry the images of St. Joseph and the Virgin Mary. They sing the *villancicos* (carols) and in song ask for shelter. If there are two groups, the other group chants the refusal. On the last night, the home opens and the figures are placed in the *nacimiento* (creche). A party always follows, complete with *piñata,* music, dancing, food, and candy.

Perhaps this is where to sound a sad note on a happy theme. Guadalupe Silva laments the slow but steady decline in observing many of the old traditions, replaced by the American Santa Claus, his reindeer, and the Christmas tree. *Posada* processions today are done mostly by churches and schools.

Puerto Rico has had a lovely tradition, somewhat similar to *las posadas.* Nine days before Christmas, people go from house to house singing the carols. The singers are invited inside to enjoy food, drink, and gifts. The family in that house then joins the procession which proceeds to another house.

What Is a Traditional Christmas Eve (*la Nochebuena*)?

Christmas Eve is called *la Nochebuena* (the Good Night). Outside, *luminarias* (really *farolitos*) are lit. These are small, brown paper sacks with a votive candle resting on sand at the bottom. In one traditional version, these candles light the path for the Holy Family on their journey to Bethlehem. In another version the shepherds are searching for the Christ Child. The soft glow of these simple lights adds the perfect touch to the mood of this special night. At midnight there is *la Misa del Gallo* (Mass of the Rooster), recalling the legend of the rooster on the first *Nochebuena* who flew above the manger and announced, *"Cristo nació"* (Christ has been born), whereupon a second rooster crowed, *"¡En Belén!"* (in Bethlehem).

Either before or after Mass, everyone joins in a festive meal with tasty dishes that vary from region to region. In northern New Mexico, a table groans with *tamales, posole,* and *enchiladas.* Around the edges one would find *empanaditas* (small fried pies), *bizcochitos* (cookies), and *capirotada* (bread pudding), all washed down with coffee, Mexican chocolate, and, in many cases, some *vino* (wine). That's about all a Christmas Eve could handle! These various Christmas customs are lovingly portrayed by Peter Ortega in his *Christmas in Old Santa Fe* .

Do Hispanics and Anglos Sing Common Christmas Carols?

Christmas carols are called *villancicos.* In Puerto Rico, nine days before Christmas, people traditionally go from house to house singing the carols. The singers are invited inside to enjoy food, drink, and gifts. The family in that house then joins the procession and proceeds to another house.

Silent Night is sung in Spanish (in which form Hispanics feel a romantic beauty like a prayer, says Burciaga). Anglicized Hispanics, of course, sing the other common carols. But distinctive *villancicos* in Spanish lend a new beauty to this lovely season. Here are the Spanish words for *Silent Night,* the carol which Joseph Mohr in long-ago Austria composed in German.

Noche de paz, noche de amor!	Night of Peace, night of love,
Todo duerme en derredor,	Everything everywhere is sleeping.
Entre los astros que esparcen su luz,	Among the stars that scatter their light,
Bella, anunciando al niñito Jesús,	One beautiful star proclaims the Baby Jesus,
Brilla la estrella de paz,	The star of peace is shining.
Brilla la estrella de paz.	The star of peace is shining.

Many distinctive *villancicos* in Spanish expand the Christmas repertoire. One popular carol in northern New Mexico stands out: *Vamos todos a Belén.*

Coro	**Chorus:**
Vamos todos a Belén con amor y gozo;	Let's all go to Bethlehem with love and joy;
Adoremos al Señor nuestro Redentor.	Let's adore the Lord our Redeemer.
1. *Derrama una estrella, divino dulzor;*	1.A star radiates divine sweetness
hermosa doncella nos da al Salvador.	A beautiful maiden gives us the Savior.
2. *La noche fue día;*	2.The night became like day;
un angel bajó, nadando entre luces,	An angel descended, floating amid the lights,
que así nos habló.	And spoke thus to us.
3. *Felices pastores, la dicha triunfó*	3.Blessed shepherds, happiness has triumphed.
el cielo es rasga, la vida nació.	Heaven is opened. Life is born.
4. *Felices suspiros, mi pecho dará;*	4.Happy sighs will fill my breast
y ardiente mi lengua, tu amor cantará.	And my ardent tongue will sing your love.

When Does the Christmas Season End?

It's not Christmas Eve or Christmas Day; it's the Feast of Epiphany on January 6, *el Día de los Santos Reyes* (or *el Día de los Tres Reyes, el Día de Reyes, el Día de los Reyes Magos)*, that is, the Day of the Holy Kings (or the Day of the Three Kings, the Day of the Kings, the Day of the Wise Kings). This is the twelfth day after Christmas. Technically existing on liturgical calendars of mainline Protestant denominations but seldom given attention, the day gets far more emphasis by Anglicans, Eastern Orthodox, and Roman Catholics. The focus is on Matthew's story in the *New Testament* of the arrival of *Magi* (Wise Men, probably astrologers from Persia) to see the Baby Jesus in Bethlehem (Matthew 2:11). Their visit symbolizes the universality of the event as Gentiles (persons out-side Judaism) came to bring their gifts to the Christ Child. Of course, no one knows that the travelers numbered three, and the names of Melchior, Caspar, and Balthasar are just a literary creation from Henry van Dyke's *The Other Wise Man.*

Traditionally, in Puerto Rico and Mexico, on the night of January 5, the children put out their shoes. Food is left for the Kings on their rapid nighttime journey. Puerto Ricans might even put out some grass for the camels. The next morning, excited youngsters open their gifts. By the way, in past times gifts have been more common on this morning than on Christmas Eve or Day. The day for some is a time also for charitable giving. But today, along with the Santa Claus tale, the American customs become increasingly more common as old traditions decline.

In El Paso, the cathedral and *barrio* churches are full at evening Mass. In El Segundo Barrio in El Paso, the gifts on the following morning are typically candy, peanuts, and fruit. One tradition, however, that survives the changing times is the *Rosca de Reyes* (the Bread of Kings). The bread is dough prepared and mixed with cinnamon and eggs, twisted into swirling shapes, and topped with sugar and pieces of dried fruit. Or the shape could be round, with raisins, grated orange and lemon rind in the dough, all topped with candied cherries and pineapple slivers. Inside the bread are a tiny plastic or porcelain Baby Jesus, almonds, and coins. Whoever bites into a coin or almond gets good luck during the year. Whoever finds the Baby Jesus must give a party for the same group, preferably on *el Día de la Calendaria*, February 2 (Candlemass or Feast of Presentation). The focus changes to Mary's purification and the Baby's dedication in the Temple forty days after the birth (Luke 2). The party will feature hot toddies *(calientitos)* made with Jamaica leaves, sugar cane, cinnamon, guavas, other fresh fruits, and maybe some rum.

How Do Catholic Hispanics Celebrate Lent and Holy Week?

Ash Wednesday is "the day of all days," *Miércoles de Ceniza*. Coming from indigenous traditions, the ashes symbolize not only the church's message of repentance but also the unity of people with Mother Earth, explains Virgilio Elizondo. Churches are crowded. Often people write their faults on pieces of paper and burn them in a special container. They visit the sad Stations of the Cross. Then, Palm Sunday has its entry pageant, sometimes with *mariachi* bands and palm branches. On Holy Thursday the priest ceremonially washes the people's feet and then celebrates the Eucharist. Families sometimes gather for prayer during the night. On Good Friday afternoon the faithful attend the three-hour service with the Seven Words. As people remember the Virgin's sadness, they receive strength to carry their own sorrows. On Saturday the worshippers remember the Lord's burial, or *Vigilia Pascual*. In this service, attendants light candles (symbols of the risen Christ). Worshippers take these home to light in their family gatherings. Priests bless water for persons scheduled for baptism. Sunday morning is *Domingo de Pascua* (Sunday of the Resurrection) with procession, baptisms, renewal of baptismal vows, and Mass.

How Does Eating Change During Lent?

For Catholics everywhere, Lent is a time to fast and to forego meat on Fridays. Even if this tradition has softened among some of the faithful, many Hispanics frequently continue to carry on the custom. One special Lenten dish, meatless, of course, is described by Rafaela Castro. The dish is *capirotada*. It is made of layers of toasted bread slices, cheese, peanuts, and raisins, soaked in a sauce of cinnamon and brown sugar. At times almonds, bananas, and small candies are thrown in as well.

The original recipe might come from the recipe collection of the chef for King Felipe IV of Spain in 1667. Today the dish is considered a dessert, very much like English bread pudding.

Why Do Hispanic Churches Have a Bleeding Jesus on His Cross?

Many Latin Americans and American Hispanics have known poverty, suffering, and death. Their forms of the crucified Jesus reflect the experiences they know, writes William Conway: "Jesus suffers with these people." The resurrection is the goal of the Church's mission, but the dying Jesus is the image of daily experience.

Paul Theroux, describing reactions of appalled tourists when they gazed on the crucifixes of the suffering Christ in Latin America's churches, answered and silenced them with these words:

Bleeding Jesus— Gabriel Sánchez

In order to believe that Christ suffered you have to know that he suffered more than you. In the United States, the Christ statue looks a bit bruised, a few teardrops, some mild abrasions. But here? How is it possible to suffer more than these Indians? Burned alive, clubbed to death, staked out on the ground and ritually trampled or tortured.... They had to be persuaded that his suffering was worse than theirs....

Spanish philosopher Miguel de Unamuno acknowledges the "triumphant, heavenly, glorious Christ...of the Transfiguration..., of the Ascension..., for when we shall have triumphed..., transfigured...," ascended." But for Hispanics in their daily lives, "...in this bull-ring of the world, in this life which is nothing but tragic bull fighting, [it is] the other Christ, the livid, the purple, the bleeding and exsanguinous."

OTHER RELIGIOUS OBSERVANCES
What Is the Most Revered Holy Day?

Roberto L. Gómez sees a connection between the place of the Virgin of Guadalupe and "the most holy day for all the mestizo churches, Roman Catholic or Protestant," *el Día de las Madres* (Mother's Day). This occasion is given highest honor. One traditional observance among Hispanics is to honor mothers by hiring *mariachis* for an early morning serenade outside the residence. The musicians will probably be singing, "*Las mañanitas.*"

Qúe linda está la mañana,   How beautiful is the morning,
En que vengo a saludarte,   When I come to greet you;
Venimos todos con gusto,   We all come with delight
Y placer a felicitarte.   And pleasure to congratulate you.

What Is a Major Family Religious Event for Young Children?

As Virgilio Elizondo describes it, baptism *(el bautismo)* expresses both family love and Christian community. Spiritual ties are forged in that event among parents, godparents, child, and church. A new life is incorporated into the family of faith. Adults are reminded of their own baptismal vows. Photographs record the event, and another time for food and celebration is at hand.

What Religious Feast Day Is Most Fun for Youngsters?

On June 24 young Mexicans and Hispanic Americans have a marvelous time throwing buckets of water on family and friends—and even cars at intersections—to honor the Day of John the Baptist who baptized Jesus in the River Jordan.

What Are Some Distinctive Wedding Customs?

In wedding customs, Mexican Hispanics deliberately maintain their culture and heritage. The wedding takes place at the church, usually in the morning. The large wedding group of *padrinos* (sponsors) will include *padrinos de ramo* (*ramo* is the bride's bouquet), *padrinos de lazo* (the ornamental cord), *padrinos de arras* (small box with 13 silver or gold coins), and the *cojines* (kneeling cushions) or the *pajes* carried by children or adults—as well as bridesmaids, escorts, flower girl, and ring bearer *(pajecitos)*. *Las arras* (coins) symbolize the sharing of worldly goods, the groom's first gift to his bride, and placed in her hands during the ceremony. *El lazo* (double-looped cord placed around the shoulders of the couple as they kneel, a picture of the rosary) symbolizes unity in marriage that will be enhanced by praying the rosary and worshiping together. The rings symbolize marital unity and enduring love. Toward the end of the service, a bouquet of flowers is presented to the Virgin. At some point the priest preaches a short sermon. The reception will follow, usually at a hall.

The newlyweds enter to much applause and then lead *la Marcha de los Novios* (The March of the Sweethearts). Led by the musicians, the couple, followed by couples of *padrinos*, families, and guests march around the room. Eventually, everyone forms an arch of outstretched arms for the bride and groom to pass through. This exercise is normally followed by a dinner, in many cases truly sumptuous. Another traditional event is the dollar dance where each dancer pins a dollar bill to the groom's or bride's clothing—an indirect way to give a financial boost to the new household. Cake is cut, champagne toasts are drunk, cake and *bizcochitos* are passed around, and dancing and mariachi music fill the night and the wee morning hours.

What Are Some Funeral Customs?

After the death of a loved one, evenings are spent in the chapel of a funeral home, or in a home in smaller communities. These gatherings are called *velorios.* Mourners pray the rosary (meaning roses, signifying the flowering of new life from the seed of the dead life). Among Hispanic Protestants, families and friends gather in the funeral home chapel for one or more evenings and have a worship service with music, scripture reading, poems, prayers, and a brief sermon.

The funeral is held in the church and includes the Mass. Afterwards, the tradition is to have nine days of prayer in the family home to pray for the dead one's soul. On each anniversary, the newspaper carries an invitation to people to worship together at a commemorative Mass.

Creative Spirit— The Soul of a Culture

Where Is the Hispanic Creative Spirit Expressed?

The creative spirit within the Hispanic soul can be seen, heard, and felt in the creative arts—music, dance, art, architecture, theater, film, comedy, and literature. Contemporary artistic expressions build on the rich legacy from Spain and the equally rich legacy from the indigenous civilizations. Here in the Americas, a stunningly creative development has evolved, which Juan González helpfully interprets. So often denied access to the cultural scene in the United States, Latinos began creating their own "parallel subterranean storehouse of music, dance, theater, journalism, literature, and folklore—in English as well as Spanish." In time a fusion began as each Hispanic cultural group borrowed from the others; reshaped African and European music, dance, and theater; and unwittingly created "a dazzling array of hybrid forms that are today uniquely American." Indeed, this cultural evolution has been brilliant.

ARCHITECTURE

What Is Hispanic Architecture?

Hispanic architecture incorporates three styles today. The first is wide use of classic Spanish style with Moorish arches, walled courtyards, and water fountains. A second popular style is Santa Fe, which uses corner fireplaces, whitewashed walls, ceiling beams *(vigas)*, hand-carved doors, woven rugs, designed ceramic tiles, and adobe with stucco. A third contemporary style uses warm colors on modernistic forms surrounding open, sunny patios and plazas. Modern Hispanic architecture does not slavishly imitate seventeenth century Spain. Today, a number of architectural companies stand in the top ranks of contemporary design. Among them are Fort-Brescia and his company Architectónica who have designed buildings in Washington, Miami, and Los Angeles.

ART

How Strong Is the Hispanic Presence in Art?

An art lover can look at many art treasures of classical and modern

Spain without traveling across the Atlantic. In northeast Manhattan, the building of the Hispanic Society of America sits in Washington Heights. Besides its outstanding library of rare books (second only to *la Biblioteca Nacional de Madrid,* the National Library of Madrid, in Spain), its collection of paintings holds works by **Greco, Velásquez** and **Goya** and modern artists like **Casas, Rusiñol, Nonell,** and **Zuluoaga.** Another important site is the Meadows Museum on the campus of Southern Methodist University in Dallas, Texas. Its building houses the finest collection of Spanish art outside of the Prado in Spain. Note the famous names of artists exhibited: **Gallego, Yañez de la Almedina, Juanes, Miranda, Montañes, Ribera, Velásquez, Pereda. Murillo, Cabezalero, Goya, Coello, López, Sánchez Perrier, Aranda, Regoyos, Gris, Fortuny,** and **Miró**—representing the late fifteenth century to the twentieth.

American art exhibits. Since the late 1990s, exhibitions of Hispanic art have become a regular event. Here are some of those events:

1989

The Latin American Spirit: Art and Artists in the United States, 1920-1970, by the Bronx Museum of the Arts in New York City, was a traveling exhibit of great Mexican artists like **Rivera, Orozco, Fernando Botero,** and **Jesús Rafael Soto,** plus many previously unknown Hispanic artists.

1990

Mexico: Splendor of Thirty Centuries by the Metropolitan Museum of Art in New York City featured 365 objects including a five-ton stone Olmec head from 300-900 C.E.; Mayan, Toltec, and Aztec works; Spanish palace and mission art from the sixteenth century; baroque and Mexican art in the seventeenth century; early twentieth century murals and paintings by **Diego Rivera, José Clemente Orozco, David Alfaro Siqueiros,** and **Rufino Tamayo** (Mexico's four great ones); and **Frida Kahlo**'s works from 1949. TIME gave the exhibit the highest acclaim.

1992

Chicano Art: Resistance and Affirmation featuring nearly 200 works of Chicano creative expression in the 1960s, with the names of **Paul Sierra, Christina Fernández, Rubert García, Gronk, Patricia Rodríguez, John Valadez** and **Patsi Valdez** as well as many folk muralists.

2000

Arte Latino: Treasures from the Smithsonian American Art Museum in Washington, DC, was a stunning display of paintings, weavings, wood carvings, embroidery, crosses, a metal and glass chandelier, *santeros,* an abstract of bent nails, and at the entrance a dramatic molded fiberglass figure of Cuatémoc in gleaming red that spoke both of Spanish conquest and the fires of Vietnam.

Some women artists deserving mention are **Charlotta Espinoza, Margo Oroña, Santa Barraza, Thelma Ortiz Muriada,** and **Carmen Garza.** One more name belongs here: **Frida Kahlo,** whom Himilce Novas honors as "the only woman artist of Mexican descent who has achieved superstar status in the United States." The wife of Mexican muralist **Diego Rivera** (who had physical handicaps and died young), Kahlo became an inspiration to *chicanas* who saw her as a symbol of liberated women everywhere. Kahlo's work and life are presented in a 2001 collection with essays, *Frida,* by a 2001 stamp issue with one of her famous self portraits (the stamp has received criticism because of the leftist political beliefs that the artist espoused), and a movie.

Can Hispanic Art Be Generalized?

Robert Hughes, in a special issue of TIME in 1988, insisted that Latino art is diverse in subject matter and details of style. But what distinguishes Mexican art in particular is the splash of brilliant color, its realism, and sometimes surrealism. It is art that grabs attention, stirs the soul, celebrates ethnic daily life, and engages often in political and social protest, all the while expressing an ethnic art form that keeps on winning wider and deeper respect.

COMEDY
Who Ranks As the Premier Hispanic Comedian?

The most renowned and revered comic actor in the Spanish-speaking world is undoubtedly **Cantínflas,** "the Latin Charlie Chaplin." His films are the top money makers throughout Latin America and are seen in constant reruns on television. In American films, he appeared in 1956 as Passepartout, Phineas Fogg's valet, in David Niven's *Around the World in Eighty Days,* and in *Pepe.* A half-block Diego Rivera mural in Mexico City honors Mexico's cultural heroes, and Mario Moreno, a.k.a. Cantínflas, stands in the center. Moreover, he received two thousand write-in votes in one of Mexico's presidential elections. Even a Spanish verb honors him: *cantinflear,* to talk much but to say little that's important. The name came from a

Cantínflas—
Gabriel Sánchez

heckler's call, "*En la cantina tú inflas*" (in the barroom you talk big"). His death in 1993 from lung cancer at eighty-one brought out long lines of citizens to pay their respects to the man who had made them laugh for so many years.

Like Charlie Chaplin, he portrayed a sad little street bum with sagging pants, battered hat, and a tattered vest. The painted, miniature mustache at each end of his upper lip completed his costume which remained the same for sixty years. A phenomenally successful millionaire business-man as well, he made Mexico and all the world laugh at politicians, the famous, and themselves. His death has left a void in the comedy of Latin America. Current Latino comedians are presented in Appendix B, "Hispanics in American Life Today."

DANCE
What Are the Origins of Mexican Dance?
Those origins go back directly to Aztec and Spanish cultures. The Aztecs enjoyed a regular series of religious ceremonies full of singing, music, and dance. Schools for song and dance were located near the temples. Youth began their studies at age 12. Other dances had military flavor as well as celebration of natural beauty. Angel Vigil explains how song and dance were deeply ingrained in the Aztec soul. So, the Spanish wisely encouraged this custom and promoted *fiestas,* but substituted Christian names and symbols. Rosa Guerrero finds Egyptian, Arab, Jewish, and African influences in Mexican dance. The Spanish themselves brought guitars, waltzes, and polkas.

How Has Mexican *Folklórico* Developed?
The most colorful dances are called *folklórico*, or folk dances. These dramatic dances are presented from time to time for American audiences by *Ballet Folklórico de México* and other groups from Mexico. With bril-liant costuming and colorful stage settings, ancient Mayan, Olmec, and Aztec myths come alive and mingle with dances from Europe and Africa. A ticket to witness "the myth, the magic, and the spectacle that is Mexico" is worth every penny spent.

In El Paso, Rosa Guerrero, educator, dance historian, and founder of Rosa Guerrero International Ballet Folklórico, has achieved national recognition with her youth performers who have been trained in these classic folk dances. Four typical dances are performed by *folklórico* groups, as described by Angel Vigil:

   ▪ *Los Concheros:* Colorful, sacred Aztec dances from Querétaro and
     after the Conquest, the dance features circular movement around a

central fire, large feathered headdresses, rhythm-sounding bells around ankles and knees, and constant drum-beating.

- *La Danza del Venado* (Deer Dance): Sacred ritual from the Yaqui tribe of northern Mexico, the movements illustrate the chase and capture of a wild animal. The dancer in loincloth has gourd rattles in hand, shells around legs and ankles, and a stuffed deer head with antlers. He does his graceful movements and vigorous leaps accompanied by a flute and small drum.

- *Los Viejitos* (The Little Old Men): A comical dance from Michoacán, its use of *zapateado* (foot-stamping) rhythms reveal Spanish as well as indigenous origins. The dancers, dressed as old men with canes and wearing rough-toothed grins, gradually become athletic young men before returning to old age and hobbling off the stage.

- *El Jarabe Tapatío* (The Mexican Hat Dance): The national dance of Mexico that originated in Guadalajara, Jalisco, *jarabe* is a generic name for over 70 dance steps from southern Spain. *Tapatío* is the adjective referring to the state of Jalisco. Using *zapateado* steps, the movements represent the flirting courtship of a gallant young man dressed like a *charro* horseman and a maiden dressed with shawl and hair braids. She teases him, so the youth throws his hat on the floor between them and dances with his hands behind his back. After both dance around the hat, the maiden stoops down, picks up the hat and puts it on her head, thus accepting his love. The dance ends as both dance joyously and face the audience.

One ancient dance drama is *los Matachines* (meaning masked sword dancers). The origins of *los Matachines* are foggy. Some scholars find beginnings in pagan Europe's sword dances. Others favor Arabic Moors in North Africa. Most, however, see origins from the Moorish-Christian conflicts after the Moorish conquest in the 700s. Spanish *conquistadores* brought the dance form to Mexico, and the priests used the dance to teach Catholic beliefs and to convert native people to Christianity. The tradition came later to New Mexico and continues into these modern times.

Angel Vigil depicts how the drama begins with the entrance of *los Matachines*. They represent the arrival of the Spaniards in the New World. *Monarca* (the monarch), who is Moctezuma, appears, and also *Malinche* (the first convert) representing the arrival of Christianity to these shores. Afterwards comes the sword fight between *el Abuelo* (the grandfather) who protects *Malinche* and *el Toro* (the bull) who tempts people to do evil. All the while the characters act comically and play pranks on the audience. *El Toro* tries to tempt *Malinche* but is killed by *el Abuelo*, who in turn gets converted to Christianity by *Malinche*. The entire drama entertains with masks, tall headdresses with long feathers, rattle shaking, bells on ankles, and music of drum and violin.

This dance presentation occurs usually for the feast of the Virgin of Guadalupe on December 12, then later in the Christmas season. The Pueblos at Picurís, Taos, Nambé, and other northern New Mexican villages perform the dance on Christmas Eve. San Juan and Santa Clara Pueblos do so on Christmas Day. The village of El Rancho dances on New Year's Day, and for Alcalde the dates are December 26 and 27. By contrast, Bernalillo dances on San Lorenzo feast days, August 9-11. In Tijeras Canyon the occasion takes place between May and October.

Where Did the *Tango* Come from?

The *tango* from Argentina continues strong worldwide. Joe Vidueira claims that the style is one of the most enduring of all dances and is even now entering a new resurgence. He points to movies in the later '90s where the *tango* appears—with actors as divergent as Arnold Schwarzeneggar, Al Pucino, and Madonna, also with **Julio Iglesias** and other singers such as **Luis Miguel, Roberto Carlos,** and **Placido Domingo.**

What Are the Characteristics of the Mexican Community Dance?

El baile (the dance) has been a valued part of Hispanic entertainment life. In Texas, New Mexico, and California, explains Rafaela Castro, the isolation of Hispanic communities created a need for community gatherings. Dancing provided otherwise scarce entertainment and gave an outlet for limited social life for women. Courtships were formed, families communicated, and, yes, more than one dispute was settled by a fight. Major holiday celebrations, professional meetings, *quinceañeras,* and weddings commonly conclude with *un baile.*

Various styles of folk dancing developed over the years.

- Waltzes were learned by the common folk from the rich and the Viennese waltz became popular in the Porfirio Díaz period.
- Ballroom is common in California.
- Polkas, common in northern Mexico and danced with *conjunto norteño* music, entered Mexico after the U.S.-Mexican War or in the mid-1860s during Maximilian's time.
- *Varsoviana* and the *schottische* are from European immigrants.

Is *Flamenco* Still Alive?

Definitely. *Flamenco* has roots in Gypsy culture in East India along with mixtures from Turkey and Egypt. It came to full birth in Andalusia in southern Spain, explains Anthony Della Flora. The dance style combines Gypsy-style *cante* (song), graceful *baile* (dance) with *taconeros* (footwork), *toque* (guitar), *palmas* (rhythmic hand-clapping), and *castañuelas* (castanets). *Flamenco* dancers speak of the dance as something more than an art form; it is a way of life. The dance is very emotional and passionate, yet subtle. Two world-famous specialists are **Amaya** and **Joaquín Encinías.**

Whereas *flamenco* has a lower profile in its Spanish homeland, Albuquerque and Santa Fe have become American centers for this art form. Albuquerque has its National Institute of Flamenco and an internationally-acclaimed dance program at the University of New Mexico. **Eva Eninías Sandoval** puts together an annual Festival Flamenco in Albuquerque that brings international superstars to appreciative audiences each summer. Santa Fe is home for **Maria Benítez** and her Institute for Spanish Arts (which sponsors annual 10 to 12-week summer workshops) and the *Teatro Flamenco* touring company. Both Benítez and Sandoval, incidentally, credit **Vicente Romero** for introducing *flamenco* to northern New Mexico in the early '70s.

FILM
Are Hispanics Creating Films?
In the world of film, Joseph Tovares admits that "Chicano cinema is still in its infancy." In the recent past, excellent films have appeared with Hispanic acting and directing, such as *El Norte, The Ballad of Gregorio Cortez, Stand and Deliver, El Mariachi, Like Water for Chocolate, The Old Gringo,* and *Down for the Barrio.* More recently, **Gregory Nava** has directed *Mi Familia/My Family* (with **Jimmy Smits** and **Edward James Olmos**). Jimmy Smits made *Price of Glory* (with **Jon Seda** and **Paul Rodriguez**). On television, **Gregory Navas** has created and directs *American Family* on PBS (with **Edward James Olmos, Raquel Welch, Esai Morales,** and a totally Hispanic cast). Other shows with Hispanic casts or major actors are *Resurrection Blvd., Dora the Explorer, Dark Angel, The Sopranos, Taína,* and *The Brothers García.*

LITERATURE
What Is One of the Earliest Spanish Epic Poems?
Rodrigo de Vivar lived in the Spanish province of Castilla and died in 1090. Lorenzo LaFarelle depicts him as a great leader who bravely fought the Moors. For that reason he was called *El Cid Campeador. Cid* in old Spanish meant *señor, jefe,* leader. In 1140, a collection of epic poems was written in his honor to describe his deeds, exile, and return

to favor. Called *Cantar de mío Cid* (Song of My Lord), this Spanish classic comes from Spain's Moorish period.

Who Are Older Latino Writers?

Juan González reminds us to go back far enough, to **Gaspar Pérez de Villagrá,** who in 1610 wrote the first epic poem in U.S. history, *Historia de la Nueva México.* Villagrá was a member of the Oñate expedition in 1598. He wrote in the style of Spain's Golden Age (metrical lines of eleven syllables each). González claims that some of the passages are the equal of the *Iliad* or *Paradise Lost.*

Two centuries later, Padre **Félix Varela** made his mark. This Cuban priest published Cuba's first pro-independence newspaper and translated major English books into Spanish (such as Thomas Jefferson's *A Manual of Parliamentary Practice* and Sir Humphry Davy's *Elements of Agricultural Chemistry*). Exiled from Cuba, in New York City he took over a parish church, worked among the poor, became the father of the Catholic press in America, and founded the nation's first ecclesiastical review (the weekly *Catholic Observer)* and two Catholic literary and theological journals.

Who Are Some Hispanic Poets?

From a rather unlikely source like Friedrich Nietzsche comes a lovely phrase about dancing with a pen. Hispanic writers have certainly danced with a pen and have given us a large body of literature that enriches all human culture. Until recently, poetry was the main genre. In the ancient Aztec culture, the *Náhuatl* word for poetry was *in xochitl, in cuicatl,* meaning "flower and song." Virgilio Elizondo thinks the reason is that poetry is more expansive, more profoundly communicating. One significant type of Hispanic writing is Chicano poetry, a feature of which is its use of Spanish and English in alternating combination, expressive of that new *mestizo* culture that is becoming more and more aware of itself. Bryce Milligan points out that most literary movements begin with poetry simply because that art form stands closest to oral literature and also because it is natural for political expression.

In the 1960s, during the early days of the Chicano Movement, **Rodolfo "Corky" Gonzales,** the articulate activist in Denver, Colorado, composed the powerful poem, *I Am Joaquín.* The poem is still a classic expression of Chicano pride, indignation, protest, and affirmation in the struggle for civil rights and basic dignity.

Ricardo Sánchez, an El Pasoan who died in 1995, wrote both in English and Spanish and became a voice for Chicano empowerment. As

Maya Angelou described him, he was a great poet, preacher, teacher, priest, rabbi, guru, master, rebel, and maverick.

In 2000, **Luis Alberto Urrea,** with 64 vivid photographs by **José Gálvez,** published *Vatos* (street slang for dude, guy, pal, brother), a poetic depiction of Chicano men in their *barrios*. A partial list of other poets would include **Tomás Rivera, Tino Villanueva, Abelardo Delgado, José Antonio Villarreal, Oscar Acosta, Alurista,** and **Gary Soto.**

Who Are Some More Recent Latino Novelists/Writers?

Fray **Angélico Chávez,** New Mexico's literary hero, from 1939 to 1992 wrote 22 books that encompassed poetry, a novel, history, and biographies. *My Penitente Land* is a favorite of many readers. **Sabine Ulibarri,** retired professor at the University of New Mexico, was author of more than 15 books about New Mexican Hispanic culture and folklore. His best-known work was *My Grandma Smoked Cigars* with stories and idioms from his origins in Tierra Amarilla, New Mexico. **Américo Paredes** (d. 1999) in the '50s and '60s stood nearly alone in presenting a true picture of Mexican/Chicano history and culture. His landmark work was *With a Pistol in His Hand,* the account of Gregorio Cortez. In 1971 he founded the Center for Mexican American Studies at U.T.-Austin and still later the Folklore Center there. For an impressive survey of other Mexican American and Chicano literature from 1848 to 1974, read Marcienne Rocard's *The Children of the Sun.*

In 1971 **Rudolfo A. Anaya** produced his well-known work, *Bless Me, Última,* for which he received the Quinto Sol literary award. The setting is a small village in northern New Mexico. The story weaves threads of ancestors, the moon goddess, the Virgin of Guadalupe, *Última* the *curandera*, medicinal herbs, the myth of *la Llorona*, the devil's powers, the Golden Carp, and Antonio's boyhood friends and family. This novel richly rewards anyone who reads it, attested by the 300,000 copies sold.

Thirteen other creations came from his pen in the '80s and '90s. Considered the "dean of Chicano literature," Anaya recently wrote *An Elegy on the Death of César Chávez*. Furthermore, Abelardo Baeza has written an excellent biography of Anaya, with photos, bibliography and other helps. The title is *Man of Aztlán: A Biography of Rudolfo Anaya.*

In the 1980s an explosion of all kinds of Hispanic literature took place, and they make up a vital part of the literary scene in the United States today. We can list only some names and works: **Tomás Rivera, Rolando Hinojosa, Aristeo Brito,** and **Nicholás Mohr.** Oscar Hijuelos wrote *The Mambo Kings Play Songs of Love* which won the 1990 Pulitzer Prize for Fiction, the first for a U.S.-born Latino. **Dagoberto Gilb,** from El

Paso, in 1994 was nominated for a top U.S. fiction award. **Víctor Villaseñor's** *Rain of Gold* has been called "a full-blooded American classic," a Hispanic *Roots*. Albuquerque's **Jimmy Santiago Baca** has produced a novel, essays, poems and scripts for three screen plays. **Richard Rodríguez** reflects on Mexico and the United States and his own struggle to reconcile his Hispanic past and present. **Abelardo Delgado** was born in Chihuahua and grew up in El Paso's El Segundo Barrio. He has been called by Salvador Balcorta "the poet's poet" and "one of the grandfathers of Chicano poetry." **Sandra Cisneros's** *The House on Mango Street* has sold over 220,000 copies. **Julia Álvarez** wrote the popular *How the García Girls Lost Their Accents*. Other recognized names are **Pat Mora, Sandra Benítez, Ana Castillo, Judith Ortiz Kofer, Esmeralda Santiago, Denise Chávez, Carolina García-Aguilera,** and Mexico's **Laura Esquivel,** whose *Like Water for Chocolate* became a movie. Just recently, the publishing house Rayo has begun publishing books "by Latinos and for Latinos." Rayo wants to become the major publisher of Hispanic writers in English and Spanish.

What Is *Literatura Chicanesca?*

This is writing about Chicanos by non-Chicanos. Carl and Paula Shirley tell us that the term appeared first in 1976 with Francisco A. Lomelí and Donaldo W. Urioste. Cecil Robinson claims that such writers have an objectivity and detachment that give a view both from outside and also from within. Others insist that this genre cannot be honest or realistic. Examples of those who have tried are Paul Horgan, Oliver LaFarge, Frank Waters, John Nichols *(The Milagro Beanfield War)*, and Jim Sagel *(Tunoma's Honey)*. Some Hispanics concede that good *literatura chicanesca* is possible, but the demands for knowledge, honesty, and sensitivity are heavy.

Still other examples of *chicanesca* are from Chester Seltzer who wrote under the pseudonym of **Amado Muro** in *The Collected Stories of Amado Muro*. But the most intriguing writer is **B. Traven** and his *Treasure of the Sierra Madre, The General from the Jungle,* and *Rebellion of the Hanged* (the latter used to be required reading in many Mexican schools). A complicated mixture is the legend of Zorro. According to *Hispanic* magazine, Irishman William Lamport, exiled for radical views, left London for Spain and changed his name to **Guillén Lombardo.** Joining the Spanish army and shipped to Mexico, he had his life described by Mexican General **Vicente Rica Palacios** and portrayed as Zorro in *Memoirs of an Imposter.* In 1929, Johnston McCaulley made *Zorro* into a masked hero located in Spanish California.

Who Are Outstanding Writers from Latin America?

Probably the best-known novelist is Colombian by birth but Mexican and European by residence, **Gabriel García Márquez.** In 1982 he won the Nobel Prize for Literature. English translations are available for reading *One Hundred Years of Solitude, Chronicle of a Death Foretold, Love in a Time of Cholera,* and *The General in His Labyrinth.* His novels utilize a modern writing style termed magical realism.

Another Mexican novelist is world-renowned **Carlos Fuentes.** Readers can enjoy *The Death of Artemio Cruz, The Old Gringo* (also made into a movie), and *The Years with Laura Díaz.*

Mexican writer **Octavio Paz** created poetry and essays and in 1990 became another Mexican writer honored with the Nobel Prize for Literature. His analyzes of Mexican history and society are widely-known in the U.S., especially his celebrated *Labyrinth of Solitude.*

Going farther into Latin America, American readers can find Argentina's **Jorge Luis Borge** and Peru's **Mario Vargas Llosa.** Chile has given the world the poets **Pablo Neruda** and **Gabriela Mistral,** also the novelist **Isabel Allende.** Now it would be a crime not to add one more example, from 16th century Spain, **Miguel de Cervantes** and *Don Quixote.* Lorenzo LaFarelle calls this writing "the world's first and greatest novel," "next to the Bible ...the [world's] most widely read work," and "Spain's greatest contribution to the literature of the Western world."

How Popular Are Comic Strips among *Latinos/as?*

Perhaps as a surprise to some, comic strips are a form of literature and are extremely popular throughout Latin America and among Hispanics in the U.S. Each week Mexican comic strips run nearly 9 million copies in Mexico alone, besides shipments to Central and South America and the U.S.

Out of the Mexican Revolution and its mural art, **José Guadalupe Posada,** an engraver, began comic pop art. He reflected the historical events taking place. He made *Calavera* (skull), a Mexican pop character, into a Mexican icon or symbol, like Uncle Sam in the U.S. Today, a popular strip throughout Latin America is named *Mafalda* drawn by the Argentine cartoonist **Abel Quesada.**

Ilan Stavans traces Latino comic strips even to Aztec times in explaining the popularity of these drawings. In the *El Paso Times,* a strip named *Baldo* runs regularly and reflects details of Hispanic family life and adolescence. In the popular cartoon strip *Zits,* Jeremy's best friend is Héctor, a Chicano lad. The same Ilan Stavans has published a cartoon history, *Latino USA,* with illustrations by **Lalo Alcáraz** of the Chicano magazine *Pocho.*

MUSIC
How Has Latino Music Influenced American Music?

Juan González sees music as the preeminent area where Latin America has influenced American culture. South Texas produced the *corridos* (folk ballads) that described wars, crimes, love affairs, cattle drives, and railroads. In New Orleans, **Louis Moreau Gottschalk** (1829-1869) introduced Cuban music. Mexican, Cuban, and Spanish residents of the city produced ragtime in the city's Latin Quarter. Latino ragtime influenced black American music and evolved into American jazz. Eventually, a combination of Mexican, Cuban, and even Brazilian elements came together. In 1913 a *tango* performance ignited a craze that lasted for years. That was followed by *marimba* bands and *habanera* songs. In the late 1920s Caribbean and especially Puerto Rican musicians worked with ragtime and jazz masters in New York City to reshape that city's musical world. Puerto Rican **Rafael Hernández** was one of those musicians; he later became Puerto Rico's greatest composer, singer, and bandleader.

In 1929, Cuban **Mario Bauza** moved to New York City and performed with masters like Duke Ellington. Carlos Ortega credited the arrival of the *rumba* (an Afro-Cuban form, later a popular dance) in 1930 with **Don Azpiaz** and the Havana Casino Orchestra. Big-band leaders like **Xavier Cugat** and **Desi Arnaz** also pushed the *rumba* with *maracas, claves, bongos, congas,* and *timbales.*

Tito Guizar was a Mexican singer/guitarist in the '20s who settled in Los Angeles. His guitar and *mariachi* sound helped popularize Mexican music in concerts around the country. He also appeared in movies and on radio. He has been called "the Father of Chicano music" (but see **Eduardo "Lalo" Guerrero** below). In the 1940s, in Harlem and Manhattan jazz clubs, Cubans and Puerto Ricans experimented with fusions of big band American music sounds and island instrumentation. All the American musical greats felt that influence: Glenn Miller, Cab Calloway, Charlie Parker, Woody Herman, and Nat "King" Cole. **Tito Puente** was most influential in developing Latin jazz. Juilliard-trained, he began in the 1940s and led his band for fifty years. He was nicknamed *el rey*, the king of *mambo* and of Latin jazz. Over the years he won five Grammies and turned out 119 albums.

For more than a half century, Cuban-born bandleader, composer, and arranger, **"Chico" O'Farrill,** blended Latin American and African rhythms with bebop jazz. Over the decades he worked with Benny Goodman, Dizzy Gillespie, Manchito, and Charlie "Bird" Parker. His *Afro-Cuban Jazz Suite* in 1950 firmly established Latin jazz.

Eduardo "Lalo" Guerrero created the Mexican Chipmunks *(Las Ardilitas de Lalo Guerro)*, later recorded in English. His music blended big band tunes with Spanish rhythms and English lyrics. He has been called the first great Chicano musical artist and honored for his social conscience and Chicano involvement. Identified as "the Father of Chicano music" and of Tejano music (but see **Tito Guizar** above), he has been received into the Tejano Music Hall of Fame, awarded the National Endowment for the Arts Heritage Fellowship, and presented the National Medal of the Arts by President Clinton.

Band leader **Desi Arnaz** made Cuban *conga* music familiar, beginning in 1951 through TV's *I Love Lucy* show. The 1950s heard *mambo* by **Tito Puente** and **Pérez Prado,** and Afro-Cuban jazz by Stan Kenton, Dizzy Gillespie, and many others. Latin and American music were fused in South Texas to develop *conjunto* or Tex-Mex music. Ranchera music gained popularity in the 1950s in Mexico by **José Alfredo Jiménez** but quickly became extremely popular in the American Southwest. Another style, *conjunto/norteño*, originated in South Texas in the 1950s. Early artists were **Naraciso Martínez** from San Benito, Texas, and **Santiago "El Flaco" Jiménez Sr.** from San Antonio.

In 1959, **Ritchie Valens** used a traditional Mexican wedding song and became famous with *La Bamba*. In 1959, at age 17, along with Buddy Holly, he died in a tragic plane crash. In 1969, **Carlos Santana** stirred Woodstock with *Evil Ways,* jumped to the top of mainstream rock, then began developing Latin rock, like *Oye Como Va.*

Trini López in the '60s became a leader in Latin pop. In his 40-year career, he recorded 50 albums, one of which in 1965 was a gold record that sold 500,000 copies and reached No. 2 on the weekly charts.

Likewise in the '60s, **Tony de la Rosa** claims to be the "Father of Tejano music" (but read about **Guerrero** above), followed by **Isidro López, Agustine Ramírez, Freddie Martínez, Sunny Ozuna, Carlos Guzmán,** *Little Joe and the Latineers,* and later *La Familia,* **Cha-Cha Jiménez, Laura Canales,** *Rene y Rene,* and others.

Linda Ronstadt promoted country rock. But her collection of traditional Mexican songs in *Canciones de mis Padres* helped prepare for the current acceptance of Latina music across the country. **Freddy Fender** produced wild Tex-Mex rock, while **"Little Joe" Hernández** worked on a musical mixture. Crooner **Julio Iglesias** sang concerts and sold the most albums in the most languages over all his fellow Latino singers. Then, in 1985, Cuban-born **Gloria Estefan** and her husband **Emilio** put together the *Miami Sound Machine's* blend of *salsa*, pop and jazz. She became the first Latina crossover star in 1985 and permanently impacted the

Hispanic music market. Also in 1985 **Selena,** Queen of Tejano music, sang *Dreaming of You.* Her murder, though, created an unpredicted consequence: Her songs immediately sold by the millions. Actually, her death was the turning point for the U.S. Latino music market for many reasons, as analyzed by David Borunda and Héctor Cantú. She convinced young Latinas that they, too, could have brown skin and have a future. She paved the way for a number of young Latino/a artists. And she opened the way for Latino business ventures, such as *People en Español, Telemundo, Univisión,* and Latin music sales in the U.S. market.

But why this huge audience for Hispanic music? Hispanics listen to radio more than other ethnic groups, but the death of Selena ignited what followed. If Selena's work could sell millions after her death, what could a live Latino/a pop star on tour accomplish? So the recording companies unleashed a deluge on America that enticed Latin music lovers from teens to adults. Suddenly, she became popular among Anglos, too.

Latino artists have changed the American music scene and non-Latino artists have influenced Latino music throughout the Americas. Carlos Ortega sees the Latino sound in Latin America sounding like their American peers. Wherever Latino music is heard, the music sells. In 1999 the total revenue was $291.6 million dollars. This long story about Latino music undoubtedly represents a dynamic record of musical evolution.

What Are Some Traditional Styles of Latino Music?

José Luis García is one of our guides through this complex subject.

- *Ranchera* (from *rancho,* ranch) is music from rural Mexico, like American country music. Rafaela Castro describes how Spanish words and *mariachi*-style music lift up the themes of love won and lost, nostalgia, Mexicanness, and life among the common people and the poor. Examples are *Las mañanitas, Guadalajara, El rancho grande, Cielito lindo,* and *La cucaracha. De colores* is possibly Caribbean but later became definitely Mexican. It closes the film *The Milagro Beanfield War,* and was the theme song of **César Chávez** and his protest marches in California. It has also become the theme song in the Protestant spiritual renewal program called Walk to Emmaus. **Vicente Fernández** and **Nydia** are two popular *ranchera* artists.

- American Southwest is a three- or four-man combo belting out polkas, *rancheras,* and *corridos* (ballads) with the accordion, the 12-string guitar (*bajo sexto*), and a bass. *Conjunto Norteño* is a type of *música ranchera.* It is a blend of European music introduced in the early 1800s, *ranchera,* blues, jazz, rock, and country with traditional

Mexican and Latin American styles. Popular examples are **Flaco Jiménez** and his band, also *Los Tigres del Norte*. A footnote question concerns the origin of the accordion in Texas and Mexico. Rafaela Castro presents two theories. One theory favors Europeans in San Antonio from where the style spread to the rest of Texas and into Mexico. A second theory picks German immigrants in Mexico in the 1860s. By the 1890s, the instrument was combined with the polka dance and became popular among the rural poor. In time, the music spread to the U.S.

- *Tejano* is urban music that combines *conjunto* in Spanish with jazz, country, rock, *mariachi,* and polka sounds with guitar, enlivened by glitzy clothes and dramatic lighting. *Los Palominos* and *Solido* are Grammy-winning groups.
- *Baladas* are love songs, such as *Con que manera te olvido, Somos novios* and *Adoro.*
- *Bolero* is pop romantic music. *Solamente una vez* is typical, also *Amigo.* **Agustín Lara,** the famous Mexican composer, strongly influenced *bolero* music, yet his best known work, *Granada,* is more like classic Spanish *flamenco*. **Luis Miguel** is a popular artist.
- *Nortec,* originating in Tijuana, is a mixture of traditional *Norteño* with accordion, *bajo sexto,* and electronic chording.
- *Banda* or *Tamborazo,* originating in Sinaloa, Mazatlán, and other nearby cities, uses tuba, trumpets, clarinets, saxophones, trombones, and a huge base drum called a *tambora.* The band with 15-18 members usually uses no lyrics.
- Classical is a repertoire unknown to many. In Mexico, **Manuel Ponce** composed *La estrellita,* salon music, romantic melodies, symphonies and concertos. **Carlos Chávez,** a student of Ponce, is Mexico's best-known conductor and composer of symphonies, ballet, and sonatas for piano and violin.
- Christian Pop is a soft jazz and rock idiom with biblical themes.
- *Habanera* came from Spain to Cuba around 1825, and by 1850 mixed Afro-Cuban rhythms at a slow tempo. Example: *La paloma.*
- *Tango* is a ballroom dance, perhaps from Nigerian origins.
- *Merengue* is a fast, folkloric dance common in Cuba, Puerto Rico, and the Dominican Republic. Today it is considered the national dance of the Dominicans.
- *Salsa* is dance music that uses trumpet, trombone, and saxophone with African-Cuban rhythms and a high-energy mix of jazz and rock. **Celia Cruz** has been crowned "The Queen of Salsa." A Grammy winner is **Robert Blades.**

- *Conga* is a Latin American rhythm with dancers in a long, twisting line. It uses a rhythmic mix of trombone, trumpet, saxophone, and *bongas* (hand-played drums). **Gloria Estefan** and others helped introduce this type of music.
- *Rumba* is a Cuban dance with intricate footwork and hip movements.
- *Samba,* from African origins, is a Brazilian ballroom dance.
- *Calypso* is music from Trinidad and elsewhere in the West Indies with spontaneous lyrics and often salted with humor.
- Tropical is Cuban and other Caribbean, Colombian, Costa Rican, and southern Mexican rhythmic styles (especially from Veracruz and elsewhere in southern Mexico)—a great style for dancing at beach parties. **Carlos Vives** is a Grammy winner in this style, also **Juan Luis Guerra.**
- *Ballenato* is rhythms of Colombia mixed with accordion.
- Latin Pop is Latin rhythms with themes of love and life. Examples are **Christina Aguilera, Paulina Rubio, Shakira, Celia Cruz, Thalia** and **Rosario Durcal, Ricky Martin** *(Livin' the Vida Loca),* **Luis Miguel, Chayanne, Juan Gabriel, Marco Antonio Solis, Marc Anthony, Freddy Fender** and **Baldema Huerta. Nelly Furtado** is a Grammy winner in regular pop.
- Latin Jazz is American jazz with Latin sounds and rhythms. **Tito Puente** and **Arturo O'Farrill** stand out as legends. Some current artists are **Ray Vega, Víctor Mendoza, Papo Vásquez, Willima Cepeda, Tony Martínez, Miguel Romero, Bobby Sanabria, Ralph Irizarry,** and **Hilario Durán. Antonio Sandoval** is a recognized artist in non-Latin jazz.
- Latin Rock, Latin rhythms made familiar to the American public by **Carlos Santana,** who blended a new sound of blues, rock, and Afro-Cuban sounds over a 30-year career. He has been inducted into Hollywood's Rock Walk and the Rock and Roll Hall of Fame. He sees his career as a mission to spread love, joy, and peace. *Los Lobos* from East Los Angeles began its group career in 1973 and received Billboard's Lifetime Achievement Award. The late **Jerry García** *(The Grateful Dead)* belongs in this group. Popular are the Colombian alternative rock band, *Aterciopelados,* and the Miami band, *Bacilos,* with its rock and tropical blend. The Internet lists 45 different Latin rock bands. Individuals worth mentioning are **Shakira, Juanes, Paulina Rubio, Ozomatli,** and **Fito Páez.** The genre has spread to Mexico with *Mana* and *Califanes.*
- Rap, from New York City's Puerto Rican youth in the '70s, is the genre that became popular in the '90s across the nation and then spread inter-

nationally. Juan Flores lists artists like *Mellow Man Ace, Kid Frost, Gerardo,* and *El General.* This *Nuyorikan* (New York) music fuses Puerto Rican *plena* and *bomba* with Black rap, Cuban *salsa,* ghetto protest in Spanglish, doo wop, boogaloo, Latin jazz, hip-hop, and reggae.

What Is the Story of the *Mariachis?*

Nobody is certain about the origin of *mariachis.* One theory thinks that *mariachis* began near Guadalajara and Chapala, in the town of Cocula, perhaps before the Conquest. Musical groups eventually were called *mariachis* (a *Náhuatl* word), which meant originally a tree and later a wooden floor for dancing. The instrumentation combined drums, bone flutes, guitar, and violin. In the late 1500s under Spanish influence other instruments were added: the *guitarrón* (six-string base guitar) and the *vihuela* (five-string guitar). Mexico's national dance, *jarabe tapitío,* was a Coca dance.

A simpler theory finds the origin in the days of Emperor Maximilian and the French occupation. He arranged for folk orchestras to play for parties and weddings. In French, *C'est un mariage* (it is a wedding) described not the ceremony but the musical groups who sang and played popular love songs afterwards. The French phrase went into Spanish as *es un mariachi.*

Jesús Alvarado and Katharine Díaz note that *mariachis* played for the Porfirio Díaz and Lázaro Cárdenas presidential inaugurations. This musical style slowly gained more stature but still remained relatively unknown.

Mariachi musical style changed in the 1930s, influenced by radio station XEW in Mexico City when the director added the trumpet. In the 1940s the musicians started to wear the waist-length *charro* jacket and white shirt, ruffled tie, tight-fitting pants with embroidery or silver buttons, wide *sombrero,* and boots. They also began standing rather than sitting. Today this music is common also in the U.S., with over 30 annual *mariachi* festivals all over the country.

Interested in a web site? Try *www.mariachi.org.* Strange as it sounds, some feel that the future of *mariachi* music lies here in the U.S. Many *mariachi* musicians cannot read music. They learn arrangements by ear and pass along this skill to younger musicians. Nevertheless, their performances represent true musicianship. And for wedding receptions, birthdays, Mothers' Day serenades, political meetings, conventions, and even funerals, *mariachis* always give added *chispa* (spark) to any event.

Where Is Latino Music within the New Globalization?

In the fall of 2001, TIME magazine issued a special edition entitled "Music

Goes Global." The article explained the "New Era" in world music. With Internet, TV, and omnipresent CDs, we now have a "vast electronic bazaar." Sounds of one culture borrow from other cultures, and the result is a musical hybrid that goes on evolving in this never-ending blending process. Brazil's Max de Castro mixes *samba* with rock, drum, and bass, hip-hop, and soul. The world's best bands (no longer from the U.S.) hail from Britain, Colombia, Ireland, Japan, Iceland, Madagascar, Brazil, Jamaica, Cuba, and Senegal. Christopher Farley declares, "Today, music is the universal language." So, Hispanic music, too, moves within this ongoing blending and mixing of cultures. **Shakira** said it best: "We Latinos are a race of fusion, and that is the music we make."

Are Guitars a Mexican Invention?

Hardly. The Moors were in Spain from 711 to 1492 when Ferdinand and Isabella finally expelled them. In those almost eight centuries, through science, philosophy, literature, and music, Spain became a center of Islamic culture. The Court of Abd al-Rahman (822-852) at Córdova boasted one of the greatest Islamic poet-musicians, Ziryab of Baghdad, who brought from India a musical system of enharmonic intervals and a repetitive and ornamental style. Perhaps the guitar came, then, from these Moors.

At the same time, gypsies were flourishing. Their music, blended with Andalusian (southern Spain) folk music, developed the *fandango* accompanied by guitar. At another level, Europe's Renaissance encouraged employment of musicians by princes to play sacred music in chapels and secular music for entertainment. Again, the guitar figured in this development. By the end of the sixteenth century, the five-string guitar was known throughout western Europe and was used to accompany popular songs and dances—in public theatres, at parties, in roadside booths, and by strolling actors. As a matter of fact, the guitar is mentioned in *Don Quixote* (young Basilio in Book Two, chapter five), and the two parts of that novel are dated 1605 and 1615. The wealthy increasingly ordered expensive and elaborate guitars during the early seventeenth century. In the other countries, interest in the instrument declined, but Spain was the one country where it remained popular and even became the national instrument. Of course, all of this musical development was brought to New Spain. Many folk songs and dances evolved around the guitar, in part because it was often the only readily available instrument. In the early nineteenth century, the guitar was frequently used for classical music in concerts for guitar with piano and for guitar with orchestra.

Why Does Cuban Music Have Such an African Style?

Eugene Holley Jr., in a review of Alejo Carpentier's classic *Music in Cuba*, chronicles a creative "melding" or "creolization" of the island's native *Taíno areíto* ceremonial dances and instruments [to] Spanish *tiranas, zapateos,* and *flamenco* [to] West African Yoruban and Congolese religious music. All of these types coalesced in Cuba as the *mambo, conga, cha-cha-cha, clave, rumba, guaracha,* and *habanera.*"

African musical forms came with the Spanish slave trade. Then the French brought their slaves in 1804 from neighboring Haiti as the owners fled the constant slave uprisings. From that influence came the *contradanza, danzón,* and the carnival *comparsa.* The *habanera* originated in Spain, then came to Cuba around 1825. This music added Afro-Cuban rhythms around 1850. An example is *La paloma.* Catholic churches and art salons preserved European classical and folk songs on the island, extending from *zarzuelas* to light operas and comic *bufo.* Cuban hip-hop and rap are produced today by *Orisha,* and *Grandes Ligas* uses biting social jabs on issues from racism to ecology. The *Buena Vista Social Club* has been popularizing pre-Revolutionary ballads from old dance hall days.

What Are Features of Puerto Rican Music?

When a person listens to Puerto Rican *salsa,* the ear will hear the influences from many diverse directions.

- Indigenous *Areyto: Güiro*—with *maracas.*
- Spanish: Church music and *zarzuelas* with guitar.
- African: *Mambo.*
- Cuban: *Habanera, guaracha, son*—with bongo drums
- Mexican: *Ranchera, bolera veracruzano.*
- Dominican: *Merengue.*
- Trinidian: *Calypso.*
- Argentinian: *Tango.*
- North American: Ragtime, rhythm and blues, rock, jazz, rap, *pleno,* hip-hop.
- EUROPEAN: Waltzes, marches, mazurkas—with harmony and counterpoint, piano and violin
- Venezuelan: *Criolla.*
- Brazilian: *Sambas.*

Many names belong to the development of Puerto Rican music: **Pedro Flores, Ladislao Martínez, Juan Morel Campos, Simón Madera, Ángel Mislan, Manuel Fernández Juncos, Rafael Hernández, Pedro Flores, Manuel Jiménes, Bobby Capo, Noel Estrada, Plácido Acevedo, Puch Valceiro, Sylvia Rexach,** and **Mirta Silva.** Classical composers are **José**

Campos Parsi, Antonio Ramires, and **Aponte Lede.** Jazz composers are **Tito Puente** and **Eddie Palmierei.**

What Non-Hispanic Singers Have Used Spanish in Their Songs?

There are four categories. One, the song is sung in Spanish, like Michael Jackson's *Todo Mi Amor Eres Tú.* Another type has a Spanish title and English and Spanish lyrics, from *Bésame Mucho* in 1944 to *Guantanamera* in 1966 to *La Isla Bonita* by Madonna in 1987. A third category, common in the decades of the '30s through the '70s, was orchestral music like **Herb Alpert's** *Tijuana Brass* in *Spanish Flea.* Alpert opened the way for Latin rock and foreign artists like **Sergio Mendes** from Brazil. Last of all, non-Hispanic singers present songs in English with a Latin American mood, like Gene Autrey's *South of the Border* (1939), Frank Sinatra in *Granada* (1960), Johnny Mathis in *María* (1960), and Simon and Garfunkel in *El Condor Pasa* (1970).

THEATER

What Is Hispanic Theater and Cinema?

Mexican theater has a long history. From Juan González we learn that the first Latino-owned theater in the U.S. was in Los Angeles. Professional performances had begun as early as the 1820s. Later some top-ranked Mexican and Latin American companies relocated there.

From these beginnings, Mexican theater truly began flourishing in the 1920s. Impetus came from artistic movements in the Mexican Revolution, migrants working in American factories during World War I, and returning Hispanic veterans who had seen the world and had money to enjoy sophisticated entertainment. Important playwrights were **Esteban Escalante, Gabriel Navarro, Adalberto Elías González,** and **Brigido Caro.** Their scenes came from Mexico, not Spain. Meanwhile, Spanish and Puerto Rican actors and playwrights started a strong theater movement in New York City and Tampa, among them Cuban actor **Alberto O'Farrill,** Puerto Rican actor **Erasmo Vando,** and Puerto Rican playwright **Gonzalo O'Neill.**

Today, however, perhaps Hispanic theater and film are the least-developed components of Hispanic artistic culture. But Philip Ortego describes the volatile 1965 grape workers' strike in Delano, California, out of which **Luis Valdez** developed *Teatro Campesino* (migrant theater) as he used Aztec myths translated into Chicano reality. From that work Valdez created *Zoot Suit,* the first Chicano production on Broadway. Still later, as writer-director, he produced *La Bamba,* the story of rock star **Ritchie Valens.**

Current important Hispanic playwrights are **Anthony J. García** and **Carlos Morton**. A recognized professional in El Paso, Texas, is **Héctor Serrano**. Now its former director, his annual production of *Viva El Paso!,* staged outdoors in McKelligon Canyon Amphitheater, has flourished since the mid-1970s. Summer evenings entertain large audiences with the history of El Paso through stellar performances of song, drama, and dance, highlighted with colorful costumes, backdrops, and theater lighting. Chicago has its own *Viva Chicago!* in September.

Overall, as Joseph Tovares comments, "Chicano cinema is still in its infancy." There seems to be a lack of clear ethnic identity in the minds of the larger population, unlike that of the African American. So, while an exciting challenge, Chicano film-making finds extreme difficulty in penetrating American culture.

Can Old Spanish Drama Still Be Found?

Yes, and one example comes from El Paso, Texas, where, since 1976, the *Siglo de Oro* (Century of Gold) celebration presents classic Spanish theater over more than a week of evenings. The cultural event's reputation is high throughout the entire Western Hemisphere. Each March groups arrive from Spain, Portugal, Mexico, Puerto Rico, and the Caribbean to participate. Playwrights from Spain's Golden Age are heard again: **Tirso de Molina, Lope de Vega, Fernando de Rojas, Miguel de Cervantes,** and **Calderón de la Barca.** Spain's literary achievements in that period are considered by some to be equal in quality to the work of Shakespeare and others in England during that same time.

What Is *Zarzuela?*

Zarzuela is Spanish operetta, dating to the 1600s when King Philip IV would have guests at his hunting lodge and would use common folk to entertain them. In the background was the European blackberry bush called *zarba*, with *zarzuela* becoming the word to describe the event. This form of theater mixes music, dance, and dialogue similar to light opera. In the 1700s, the French occupied Spain and tried to impose French theater. The elite accepted that, but commoners stayed with their own art form. El Paso has its annual *Festival de la Zarzuela* and hopes to become the *zarzuela* capital of the United States.

Modern Society—
Seeking an Identity in America

COMMONALITIES & STEREOTYPES
What Do Hispanic Americans Have in Common?

Mike Davis asserts that "if there is no reducible essence to *latinidad* (Latino identity), it does not necessarily follow that there is no substance." No one can put Hispanic identity into one word. Yet, we can find some commonalities and linkages within the immense variety of the culture. Here are some of those general features.

1. **A common language.** Spanish language links the vast majority of Hispanics, but with considerable variations from one country to another or even within a country. Of course, many American Hispanics cannot speak Spanish.

2. **A common religious background.** For the vast majority of Hispanics the Roman Catholic faith is a strong bond. But we see also a growing exodus of Hispanics *(los evangelicos)* to Pentecostal, independent, and mainline Protestant denominations. And now some Hispanics are turning to Islam.

3. **A divergent societal situation.** Some enjoy a dramatically growing affluence, career entry, and political strength. Many others face stubborn poverty and a discouraging sense of powerlessness. Hispanics have the least amount of health insurance, the highest poverty, and the lowest educational level of all minority groups.

4. **A common history.** The history begins with Spain and the indigenous civilizations, followed by four centuries of conquest, annexation, or exile. The history continues now as a major part of American society. Octavio Paz declared that Latino is "not an essence but a history."

5. **A dual identity.** American Hispanics find their primary identity as Americans, but many also have a strong identity in their cultural and national origins, whether Mexican, Cuban, Puerto Rican, Dominican, Guatemalan, Venezuelan, Peruvian, or any other kind of Hispanic American. Other American Hispanics feel little about their Latin American cultural roots.

6. **An increasing interrelatedness.** Through intermingling of styles in music and dance, through globalization and business interchange, by the dramatic entry of Hispanics into the life of American society (and especially in business and government), and by the recognition of powerful political clout in all future elections, Hispanics are more and more aware of a unity that connects all Hispanics, as well as the distinct and strong differences among them.

What Are the Usual Stereotypes about Hispanics?

Ramon Renteria's list comes from the Tomás Rivera Policy Institute in Austin and Perkins School of Theology at Southern Methodist University.

1. **All Hispanics like the name Hispanic.** Some accept it, while others prefer Latino or another term. No name has yet been found that encompasses both the Spanish and the indigenous ancestry. Some Hispanics hate the term Hispanic.

2. **All Hispanics speak Spanish.** In the 1950s and '60s, Hispanic schoolchildren were often punished for speaking Spanish. Many parents still avoid Spanish at home because they want the children to grow up knowing perfect English, or because one of the spouses does not know Spanish.

3. **All Hispanics are Catholic.** Around 70 percent of American Hispanics are Catholic. The others are distributed among mainline Protestant, Pentecostal, and independent churches. Small percentages are found among Mormons, Seventh Day Adventists, and Jehovah's Witnesses.

4. **All Hispanic food is spicy.** That is true along the Mexico-U.S. border, but not universally true throughout Latin America. Spicy is not at all a description of Cuban or Costa Rican food.

5. **All Hispanics have dark skin.** Though brown skin and black hair are common enough to contribute to this stereotype, the description cannot be assumed. On the streets of any Latin American city or here in the United States, one can find Hispanics from dark complexions to light skin and blond hair. General tendencies, yes, but no universal appearance.

DEMOGRAPHICS
How Are the Times 'A-changin'?

Bob Dylan's words fit today better than in his own time. *Census 2000* showed an incredible growth among the people called Hispanic. That growth means changing times for everybody. José Armas describes the following three important demographic, economic, and political developments.

NUMERICAL EXPLOSION

1. Hispanics are the **fastest growing** ethnic entity in the nation. Only 2 million Hispanics lived in the U.S. in 1948. Hispanics now number 35.3 million, or 12.6 percent of the total population, with most growth since 1970. But the 2000 count showed a 60 percent increase. Cynthia Orozco suggests counting Puerto Rico (nearly 4 million), plus a million uncounted in the Census, and the total has reached 40.3 million and growing. Fed by high birth rate and steady immigration, the growth rate was 58 percent during the 1990s, about 3 million more than originally predicted. Hispanics have become the largest ethnic minority, with 98.2 million predicted by 2050, or 24 percent of the U.S. population. That's one out of every four Americans.

2. This is true in **every state of the Union:** California had the largest surge, then Texas and Florida. Most Hispanics live in California and Texas. One-third of Texans are Hispanics. Guillermo X. García quotes Robert Stein who states that "Texas is no longer an Anglo-Saxon state." In fact, Mark Babineck declares that Texas will be over 50 percent Hispanic by 2030. Tammerlin Drummond gives other examples. In Muscatine, Iowa, Mexican grocers compete for Hispanic customers, and the *El Cabrito* restaurant dishes up *taquitos*. In Michigan, 276,000 Latinos celebrate a month-long *Grito de Dolores* to remember Fr. Hidalgo's shout for Mexico's independence in 1810. In Grand Rapids, Michigan, with a population of nearly 200,000, Hispanics grew from 9,394 in 1990 to 25,818 in 2000; the city is one of the ten top cities in the country for Hispanics to settle and start a business. And Utah with its 151,000 Hispanics holds an annual Utah Hispanic American Festival.

3. Hispanics in the U.S. make up the **fourth largest** Latino "nation" in the Western Hemisphere, after Mexico, Argentina, and Colombia. They will eventually be the second-largest Spanish language "nation."

4. **Mexicans make up the largest** U.S. Hispanic population (58.5 percent); then Central Americans (Salvadorans the largest), South Americans and others (28 percent); Puerto Ricans (9.6 percent); and Cubans (3.5 percent).

5. **States with the largest Hispanic populations** are California, Texas, New York, Florida, and Illinois. In California and Texas, 1 in 4 persons is Hispanic. The four states account for 60 percent of American Hispanics. Ten other states with the most rapid Hispanic growth since 1990 are North Carolina, Arkansas, Georgia,

Tennessee, Nevada, South Carolina, Alabama, Kentucky, Minnesota, and Nebraska.

6. **Cities with the largest Hispanic populations** are New York, Los Angeles, Houston, San Diego, Phoenix, and San Antonio. Latinos are growing rapidly in Dallas/Fort Worth, Chicago, Philadelphia, Boston suburbs, Anchorage, Portland, Salt Lake City, and Milwaukee. Although Los Angeles is the second-largest Mexican city in the world, it also has more Salvadorans than the capital of El Salvador. New York City has as many Puerto Ricans as San Juan, and New York State has as many Dominicans as Santo Domingo. In fact, "'Latinos in New York' no longer rhymes with Puerto Rico," Juan Flores comments. The city has more Mexicans from Puebla than residents from the Dominican Republic. The "new New Yorkers" combine people from all over Latin America and the Caribbean. We have "pan-Latinization" developed in one generation. And with tongue in cheek, Flores muses about the day when the city will inaugurate a "Festival Americano" to meet minority Anglo/White needs!

7. **Cities with the largest percentage of Hispanics** are El Paso (about 80 percent), Miami (62 percent), San Antonio (52 percent), and New York City's Bronx (49 percent). Counties with the largest number of Hispanics are Los Angeles, Dade (Fla.), Cook (Ill.), Harris (Tx.), and Orange (Cal.). East L.A. is the largest Hispanic/Chicano/Mexican community in the U.S.

8. **Median age** of all Hispanics is 25.9 years, the youngest of all the minority ethnic groups. Half are under 26, one-third under 18.

   ▪ Mexicans . . . . . . 25.9   ▪ South Americans .33.1
   ▪ Puerto Ricans .27.3   ▪ Spaniards 36.4
   ▪ Dominicans . . .29.5   ▪ Cubans 40.7

9. **Hispanics under age 18:** nearly 35 percent. Mexicans have the youngest average.

10. **Ten best cities** for Hispanics (among 354 cities, based on having a Latino population of over 10 percent, and considering diversity, cost of living, transportation, jobs, education, climate, crime, arts, health care and recreation).

   1. San Diego   2. Austin   3. Miami
   4. San Antonio   5. El Paso-Las Cruces   6. Albuquerque
   7. Tucson   8. Los Angeles   9. New York
   10. Raleigh-Durham-Chapel Hill

To put it mildly, this Hispanic growth will continue to affect America dramatically. Roger Hernandez tells us how: in political leaders whom we elect, in the food we eat, the music we listen to, the people who live next door, the language we hear at the mall, and how America sees itself as a nation.

Economic Surge.

1. **Median household income:** Annually $30,447 (2000), up from $28,330 (1998).
2. **American business** is placing increasing focus on the Hispanic market, now at $500 billion, $1 trillion by 2010, and $3 trillion by 2020.
3. Hispanics are #1 in seeking **new mortgages,** an investment leading to purchases of hundreds of items that go into furnishing a new home.
4. The Hispanic **middle class** grew 70.1 percent since 1979. Thus the Tomás Rivera Policy Institute claims that Hispanics are more middle class than anyone had realized, including Hispanics themselves. Around 2.5 million Hispanic households earn $40,000 to $140,000 annually.
5. Cuban Hispanics have the **highest median family income,** followed by Central and South Americans. Cynthia Orosco explains the Cuban achievement: U.S. government assistance, family encouragement for higher education, and high career goals from Cuban family tradition.
6. With more and more Hispanics graduating from college, Latinos generally reach **economic parity** with the general population by the end of the third or fourth generation. This matches the usual immigration patterns since the early 1900s.
7. Yet, according to William Plasencia, among 10,597 board seats in **Fortune 1000 companies,** Hispanics held only 14 and Latinos only 181 seats on those boards (1.7 percent).
8. Of all **U.S. executive, administrative, and managerial positions,** Hispanics hold less than 7 percent.
9. Hispanic **radio stations** broadcasting in Spanish grew from 67 in 1980 to more than 559 in the year 2000 (out of 12,800 stations in the country). This broadcasting now reaches 44 states. Add also 3 Spanish language TV networks and 350 Spanish-language newspapers.
10. Hispanic **public housing renters:** 19 percent of Hispanics.
11. **Home ownership:** 46 percent (46 percent Blacks, 52 percent Asians, 72 percent Anglos).
12. Hispanic **families in poverty:** 6.3 million or 21.7 percent (against 6.8 million and 24.3 percent in '98), the highest of all minority groups.
13. Hispanic **unemployment:** 9.2 percent (only 5.2 percent for non-Hispanics), though a constantly changing figure.

14. Hispanics **without college education:** 71 percent.
15. **High school graduation:** 60 percent.
16. **Dropout rate:** 40 percent.
17. **Intermarriage:** One-third of American Hispanics are married to non-Hispanic Whites.

POLITICAL MUSCLE

1. **Hispanics are concentrated** in the vital states that can control the presidential electoral vote. California, Texas, Florida, New York, and Illinois total 166 votes, over half of the 270 needed. Hispanic voter registration, though, is only 50 percent, and voter participation is 75 percent of registered voters.
2. **Election 2000,** in Roger Hernandez's analysis, was a pivotal event. Hispanics became a truly recognized political force in national politics. In the recent past, Hispanics were influential in elections but were taken for granted by Democrats and ignored by Republicans. But, in 2000, both Republicans and Democrats wooed Hispanics in their conventions and campaigns. Cynthia Orosco observes that Latinos tend to vote for Hispanic candidates regardless of party, but that tendency is so flexible that neither major party can rely on automatic Hispanic votes.
3. **Hispanics in Congress:** 19 in the House, 0 in Senate in 2000.
4. Major cities with **Hispanic mayors:** San José, El Paso, San Antonio, Miami. In the future watch New York City, Los Angeles, and Houston.
5. **Hispanics in state legislatures:** Still only 200 out of 7,400 seats. But 5,200 Hispanics are on school boards and in city halls, a level that leads to higher offices in the next decade.
6. **Historical footnote:** A first in Texas and possibly the nation was the debate in English and Spanish by two Democratic candidates for governor of Texas (March 1, 2002), and both candidates were Hispanic.
7. **Three major problems** in moving this muscle: the large number of Hispanics who are not yet citizens, the number of youth in the Hispanic population, and the large percentage that does not vote in elections.
8. **Political preferences:** Democrat 54.7 percent; 17.2 Republican; 11.2 independent. This pattern increasingly is less certain.
9. **Political philosophies:** conservative 34.8 percent; moderate 29.2 percent; liberal 24.9 percent.

What Are Some Miscellaneous Statistics in the Hispanic Picture?
1. Hispanic households with **cellular phones:** 10-15 percent.

2. Hispanic households having a **computer:** 42 to 49 percent.
3. Hispanic adults who have **never used a computer:** about one-third.
4. Hispanics who use the **Internet:** 43 percent.
5. *Salsa* now outsells catsup, and *tortillas* outsell bread. In 2000, sales of Mexican sauces and marinades totaled $960 million, only $515 million for catsup.
6. Hispanic men in **prisons** between ages 20-39: 1 in 25 (compare 1 in 65 Anglo men, 1 in 9 African-Americans). The highest prison number for all groups is California, then Texas. The most Hispanics on death row are in Texas (88) and California (79).
7. Hispanic views on a total **ban on handguns sales** in the U.S.: 45 percent in favor, 48 percent against, 7 percent undecided.
8. Hispanic ownership of **firearms:** 11 percent (but 16 percent of African-Americans, 27 percent of Whites). The U.S. gun industry is accused of targeting Hispanics and other minorities as a fruitful market.
9. Hispanic **homicide** rates from guns: 72 percent of victims (second only to Blacks, nearly four times that of Whites).
10. Hispanic non-fatal **gun-related injuries:** 41.3 of every 100,000 Latinos (but 8.7 among Whites, 87.5 among Blacks).
11. **Death penalty:** 42 percent favor it, 40 percent do not.
12. Hispanic views on **abortion:** 61 percent disapprove of making the abortion pill available in the first weeks of pregnancy, 25 percent approve, 14 percent undecided.
13. **Adoption:** 1 out of 5 Hispanics and African Americans would be willing to adopt a child with medical or behavioral problems, compared with only 1 out of 10 Anglos.
14. Only one out of every 50 characters on **prime time U.S. television** is a Latino.
15. **Fertility rate:** the average Hispanic woman has 2.9 children in a lifetime (versus 2.0 in the national average).
16. Use of **birth control pills:** 1 in 10 (the same for Blacks, but 1 in 3 among non-Hispanic women).
17. Hispanic **movie ticket buyers:** 80 percent of total purchases.
18. **Latino newspapers/magazines:** 1,389 (with a 90 percent circulation increase). Half of the 550 Hispanic newspapers are termed "very viable," according to Cynthia L. Orosco's report. Besides, around 2,000 Hispanics work in newsrooms of English-language newspapers.
19. **Bilingual TV:** Three out of four Latinos watch both English and Spanish television. Spanish-language TV draws audiences for news, situation comedies and sports. Ramon Renteria says Texas is

far ahead of the nation in having news shows with Hispanic news-casters or anchors.

20. **Discrimination:** Only 25 percent of persons in a poll had felt discrimination in 2000.
21. **School vouchers:** 49 percent were against, 41 percent in favor.
22. **Federal employees:** 1.7 million, or 6.6 percent.
23. **Hispanic judges:** 665 in 1990, 1,029 in 2000 on federal & state level (now 3.7 percent federal, 3.8 state). Thirty-seven states have no Hispanic federal judges. Texas has the most.
24. Confidence in **Social Security:** limited confidence 47.1 percent; belief in its total bankruptcy in 38 years 62.7 percent.
25. Confidence in **public schools:** fair or poor rating 57.7 percent; excellent or good 37.5 percent.

EDUCATION
Is Hispanic Education Adequate?
As described by Sergio Buston, only one in five Hispanic children under five attends early childhood education programs. Hispanic students generally score lower on SAT tests, as much as 150 points lower than Anglos or Asians, though above Blacks. In 1999, 63 percent of Hispanics finished high school (94 percent for Asians, 91 percent for non-Hispanic Whites, and 84 percent for African Americans). By 2000, the percentage of adults who finished high school was 57 percent. This means a Hispanic dropout rate of 40+ percent, twice that of Blacks, four times that of Anglos. Nine percent of Hispanics go to college (a majority to two-year junior college programs), and 5 percent among immigrants. Eleven percent of those students graduate. Four percent of graduate students are Hispanic. Just 10.6 percent of Hispanics hold a bachelor's degree (against 25.6 percent across the nation).

On a very specific level, Hispanic girls/young women present a "bleak" situation, described by Annette Fuentes. Whereas the number of Latinas is the fastest-growing group of young women in the country, they also are lowest in high school graduation rates. They often do not take the SAT for college, few are enrolled in gifted or advanced programs, and they have the lowest rate of getting a college bachelor's degree.

One more fact. Robert Gehrke reports that the Hispanic school-age population is the fastest growing school group in the nation, especially in the Midwest and the South. And one-third of these students fall behind in reading, math, and science by age 9. More than a third are at least a grade behind, and many are even further behind.

What Are the Reasons for the Latino Educational Crisis?

A very broad answer is that schools in poverty areas—where so many Hispanics are concentrated—are too often inadequate. Exceptions appear to offer some hope.

Mike Davis gives a more specific list of reasons.

1. **Family poverty:** Inner-city Hispanics attend schools already crippled by *barrio* poverty.

2. **Lack of political commitment:** With most inner-city school systems rated as "national scandals," in Davis's words, the power structures dodge adequate funding.

3. **Low teacher expertise and morale:** With too many inner-city teachers "dispirited, underqualified and increasingly temporary, [and who] are sent as cannon fodder into the district's massively overcrowded and under-equipped schools," better trained teachers move to higher-paying suburban public or elite private schools.

Mural "Discover the Secrets of the Universe Through Your Library," by Carlos Callejo, 1994, Armijo Branch Library, El Paso, Texas—Photo by Richard Campbell

4. **Low academic expectations:** Some administrators and teachers are negative and pessimistic about Hispanic abilities.

5. **Troubled children and youth:** School systems avoid this growing classroom crisis even in affluent areas—students with severe psychological or mental problems, child abuse (physical and emotional), family alcoholism, drug use, gang pressures, teen pregnancy, suicide, and delinquency. Those arriving at school with this baggage will not have motivation to learn. These are not the tradition-

al "problem kids" just chewing gum, cussing, running in hallways, or occasionally skipping school.

6. **Family limitations:** Parents often cannot read, write, or speak English and thus cannot help with homework. Parents might not understand the educational world and thus cannot give academic guidance. Homes may lack enrichment of high-quality books, music, art, and intellectual stimulation. In Norman Lockman's words: "U.S. education is not designed to help the least prepared to learn."

7. **Family patterns:** Families sometimes urge their female high school graduates to stay home for college even when they receive a quality scholarship to attend an out-of-state university. Families and friends pressure them to become wives and mothers. Families push their youth into the work force to help support the household.

8. **Adult obstacles:** Long work hours, parenting demands, lack of affordable child care, problems in finding English literacy classes or vocational training programs in Spanish—all become barriers.

9. **Rising tuition:** Further education becomes out of reach for many.

Reprinted by Permission of Mr. Jeff Dansiger

Do Most Hispanics Support the English-Only Movement?
In 1983 former Senator S.I. Hayakawa and Michigan ophthalmologist John H. Tanton initiated U.S. English (USE). The goal was to end multi-lingual ballots, restrict bilingual education, and pass a Constitutional amendment declaring English as the nation's official language. Proponents express a concern for national unity through a common, thriving language.

Opponents of the movement point out that the effort is unnecessary, that the money spent could be used to improve English education, and that an anti-Hispanic bias lies behind the camouflage. Multiple studies have shown that third generation Hispanics from immigrant families (or in any other language, for that matter), will speak English as their first language. Even first generation immigrants in many cases become fluent in English. And even if the parents cannot use English or if Spanish is the invariable language in the home, the children can still become fluent in English and without accent. A political crusade is unnecessary.

But beyond bilingualism, enlightened Hispanics and Anglos alike real-ize the value of multilingualism in our pluralistic world. One anonymous wit defines a person who speaks two languages as bilingual, three lan-guages make one trilingual, and one who speaks only one language is an American. Although English has been adopted as the official lan-guage by only 26 states, recent court rulings and local elections signal an opposite trend. Roger Hernandez states that the present state of the English Only Movement is dead. Exception: in early 2002, Iowa made English its official state language. Time will tell about this movement.

Do Most Hispanics Favor Bilingual Education?
Here is one topic in the U.S. that can turn even Caspar Milquetoast and his twin brother into screaming opponents! According to Ilan Stavans, bilingual education began in 1960 among Cuban refugees in Dade County, Florida. Expecting to return soon to Cuba, exiled parents want-ed their children to retain their Spanish while they learned English. The concept became a broader movement to teach English to all minorities, while still retaining their native languages. The movement became an argument and then turned political. In 1998 California passed its Proposition 227 that outlawed bilingual education in its public schools. English immersion was made the official method. Hispanics voted 2:1 against the proposal. Wherever this issue is discussed, however, the facts are usually missing.

Goal. The goal in bilingual education is (1) to teach English; (2) to maintain and develop the native language (even English Plus, adding other languages later); and (3) to teach not just conversational English but academic English for education past high school.

Process. Bilingual education is a concept: "It's beautiful to be bilingual." The approach is not remedial but enrichment. The process allows students to learn English gradually while maintaining and advancing in their native tongue. Obviously, bilingual education is also a program. For example, instruction will use 90 percent of class time in Spanish during kindergarten and first grade, 80 percent in second and third grade, and 50 percent in fifth grade. By the sixth grade the students will be functionally bilingual. An alternative approach is dual language process whereby students work in their own or in another language concurrently.

Negative Views. Many persons think bilingualism threatens the unifying force of English in our country. Some also think the bilingual industry has become a self-seeking, entrenched bureaucracy. And a fear exists that our children are not becoming functional in English.

Positive Reasons. Beyond the often-volatile discussions, a large body of research underlies the concept of bilingual education. See Virginia P. Collier on language acquisition studies.

1. **Learning English.** B. Margot Hornblower in a TIME article provides this excellent summary. "Serious research increasingly points toward a consensus: Children learn English faster and are more likely to excel academically if they are given several years of instruction in their native language first." The same article presents also the next two statements.

2. **Length of time.** Research supports taking five to seven years to achieve "academic" mastery in a new language. Heavy criticism comes at this very point. But Kathryn M. Cordova reemphasizes the goal of going beyond "playground English." Academic language level just takes more time.

3. **Test Results.** Testing shows that after six years in bilingual instruction, children do better on 11th grade English tests.

4. **Caveat.** Another quote from Kathryn Cordova: Either immersion or bilingual instruction will fail "...if classes are too crowded, taught by unqualified teachers, lacking in appropriate materials, or filled with the wrong combination of students." Hello! Nothing works if it is not done correctly, and usually that is what has happened where bilingual education has seemed to fail.

5. **Other supporting reasons.** Language ideas and concepts put into the brain are coded for any language and will transfer from native language to English. Therefore, time spent in Spanish contributes to English learning as well as to learning other languages.

Many, many youngsters entering "sink-or-swim" English programs just sink. Those who succeed would succeed in any program. The failures neither learn English nor maintain their native tongue. Students become illiterate in two languages.

Some studies indicate that learning two or more languages improves cognitive development in all academic learning. Diane Dismuke shares research showing that children in bilingual programs keep up academically with other students and do better than other at-risk students. The research shows also that children in bilingual programs are not at all slowed down in learning English.

What Changes Would Improve Hispanic (and All) Education?

Across America, many schools with Hispanics and other ethnic groups are turning out quality graduates who go on to excel in American life. But what about those many schools that lack excellence and where so many students are given so little? Certain measures would make a huge difference in schools everywhere.

1. Increased enrollment in **Head Start.**
2. More **Hispanic teachers,** especially principals.
3. Strong and correct **bilingual** and/or **dual-language** instruction.
4. **Culturally relevant** curriculum and class materials.
5. Stronger **remedial** programs and intensive **special** programs to bring some students up to normal grade level.
6. Strategies for incorporating **parents** into the process.
7. More well-run **alternative schools** and **time-out programs,** with automatic procedures for testing problem students, less cumbersome documentation, and quicker entry into such programs.
8. **Pinpointing** future academic and behavioral problems at the earliest ages, with prompt and thorough counseling, medication, and therapy.
9. **Reducing** bureaucracy and instead **hiring** psychiatrists, clinical psychologists, social workers, diagnosticians, and reading specialists.
10. **Increase** in federal and state funding for Child Protective Services, allowing more case workers and better tracking of abuse and neglect.
11. **Focus** on pre-kinder and kindergarten, followed by special focus on the crucial ninth grade.
12. **Family education** to teach parents how to read to children from birth, to build quality family life, to discipline children and adolescents, to structure homework, and to encourage future education.
13. Encouraging **Hispanic girls** to remain in high school and motivating some to enter college.
14. **Training teachers** to teach in the poorer *barrios* and making it a

speciality (with extra pay). Preparation would include effective English language learning, classroom management, special teaching techniques, *barrio* culture, and Spanish study (at least, enough to pronounce names correctly).

15. **Removing** total responsibility for student success on teachers (like test scores alone determining future salary and advancement), and giving responsibility also to students and parents.

16. And, **in all systems**, raise salaries, reduce long hours of endless paper work and administrative details, defend teachers against unwarranted parental and student abuse, forget mandated robot education that stifles fun and artistry and builds up anger and frustration, avoid making the daily teaching task so frantic, drop the use of fear tactics by nervous administrators to motivate teachers, and instead see administration as supporting and guiding the teachers. Too many teachers today are frazzled, and exodus from the profession is appalling.

FAMILY

How Stable Is the Hispanic Family?

Well over half of Hispanic households are single-parent families. Combined with other problems, social problems can result. On the other hand, the National Center of Health Statistics showed Hispanic infant mortality is almost equal to the Anglo rate and only half the African American rate. Also, Hispanic babies with late or no prenatal care seem to be healthier than those born to Anglo or black mothers with the same lack of medical care. The explanation could be the traditional Hispanic family's strength and support. Nevertheless, the formula for healthy Hispanic family life is the same as any other ethnic or racial group. Unhealthy family dynamics place huge obstacles in the paths of children and youth as they grow up. Families living in healthy environments have a much better chance (though not automatically) to have wholesome children and youth.

Jonathan Kozol writes about New York City's South Bronx, not at all different from the poorest Hispanic *barrios*.

Everything breaks down in a place like this. The pipes break down. The phone breaks down. The electricity and heat break down. The spirit breaks down. The body breaks down. The immune agents of the heart break down. Why wouldn't the family break down also?

Meanwhile, more affluent Hispanic families, like those in all ethnic groups, do not face the ground-level problems listed for many *barrio* families. But they still have to cope with the economy and jobs, guiding children and communicating with teenagers, managing busy schedules and splintered family life, maintaining cultural traditions or further assimilating, coping with our secular society and its often opposite values, finding balanced living, and growing in religious faith while religion goes through profound change.

Mural "Tribute to the Chicano Family," by Carlos Rosas and Felix Gallegos, 1990, Centro de Salud Familiar La Fe, El Paso, Texas—Photo by Richard Campbell.

HEALTH CARE
What Is the State of Health Care among Hispanics?
Regrettably, the problem of health care is actually a crisis. Here are some basic facts:

1. **Abortion.** Among Latinos ages 15–44, the rate is 42.6 percent per 1,000 (cf. 26.6 per 1,000 in the rest of the population).
2. **Alzheimer's.** Hispanics contract this disease twice as frequently as Whites (Blacks are four times higher).
3. **Auto accidents.** These tragedies often occur among immigrants, whose first desire is to own and drive a car but who have no driving instruction. Such classes are usually not available in Spanish.
4. **Cancer.** El Paso has the nation's highest rate of breast cancer, higher than lung cancer. Cervical cancer is twice as high along the border as among Anglo women; Hispanic women have the second-highest rate across the country. Stomach cancer among Hispanics is twice that of Whites. Hispanic men have the highest rate of prostate cancer. Hispanic farm workers in California, exposed to harmful pesticides, have unusually higher rates of brain, blood, skin, and stomach cancers than other Hispanics in the state.

5. **Cirrhosis of the liver.** Hispanics have the second-highest rate in the nation for cirrhosis of the liver, though the rate is decreasing. Hispanics have the highest rate of deaths from this disease.

6. **Depression.** Elderly Hispanic women are two times more likely to battle depression than in any other ethnic group.

7. **Diabetes.** For the Type 2 diabetes rate in the 45-74 age range, 26.1 percent of Puerto Rican Hispanics have the disease, Mexican Americans 23.9 percent, Cuban Americans 15.8 percent, 19.3 for non-Hispanic Blacks, and 12 percent for non-Hispanic Whites. Doctors call this problem an epidemic.

8. **Heart disease.** This is the leading cause of Hispanic deaths in the U.S. (25.4 percent among males, 34 percent among females). A specific gene has been located, and studies have shown evidence of future problems existing already in Hispanic children. Yet, para-doxically, Hispanic mortality rates from respiratory disease, cancer, and heart disease are 24-33 percent lower than rates for non-Hispanic white Americans.

9. **Obesity.** Eighteen percent of Hispanic boys and 14 percent of girls in the nation are obese (11 percent for Anglo boys and girls). Even worse, in El Paso, Texas, 20 percent of all boys and 16 percent of all girls are obese. Approximately 40 percent of men and 48 per-cent of women (Mexican, Puerto Ricans, Cubans) are overweight (42 and 50 percent among African Americans, and 32 and 34 per-cent among non-Hispanic Whites).

10. **Sexually-transmitted diseases.** Alarmingly, Texas ranks second in the nation for syphilis cases, much of this in the Hispanic community. With 8 percent of the U.S. population, Hispanics have an HIV rate of 16 percent and account for 32 percent of AIDS cases and 19 percent of new cases. HIV is the third-leading cause of Hispanic deaths.

11. **Suicide.** Hispanic teenage girls lead in this national problem.

12. **Tooth decay.** Karen Guilo quotes Dr. David Satcher, former U.S. Surgeon General. After a national survey, he finds American oral health better than ever, but not among the poor. Oral diseases from cavities to cancer represent a "silent epidemic." Fewer than two-thirds of Hispanic adults see a dentist in a year. Melissa Martínez says the poor cannot afford dental care, and they do not know about services. Many do not brush regularly or eat properly. Few have insurance. Nearly half of all Hispanics (and Blacks too) have untreated tooth decay (but one-third for other Americans). Tooth decay is the top chronic disease among Hispanic children (5 times more common than asthma) and more than twice that of

their affluent peers. About 25 percent of Hispanic poor children have not been to a dentist before kindergarten. Almost 25 percent of older Hispanic adults suffer severe gum disease, and about 30 percent over 65 have lost their teeth.

13. **Tuberculosis.** The World Health Organization calls tuberculosis a world emergency. Along the border the rapid rise connects with the same rise in AIDS—a co-infection, says Diana Washington-Valdez. The rate is four times higher than across the nation.

What Are Major Obstacles in Hispanic Health Care?

1. **Lack of health insurance.** Uninsured persons in the U.S. number 44.3 million (another figure is 38.9 million). Of these, one out of 5 adult Hispanics have no health insurance. One-third are children. Three-quarters of these uninsured Hispanics live in Texas, California, New York, and Florida. In Texas the uninsured rate is 45 percent.

2. **Reluctance to go to doctors and clinics.** One out of three Hispanics has no family doctor or health clinic registration. The reasons: insufficient money for even minimum costs, clinic locations too far away, lack of transportation, confusion over procedures to get care, and acute discomfort because caregivers so often are neither Hispanic nor bilingual. Furthermore, many Hispanics circulate among several doctors and then seek serious treatment when it is too late.

3. **A total life situation.** Guadalupe Silva describes low-income *barrio* women who are also single heads of households, women in their mid-thirties and with small children. They frequently live in substandard housing or in tiny apartments without water or heat. Their custom might be to take herbal medicines or, in the Borderlands, to buy medications across the Mexican border where no prescriptions are necessary. These women commonly do not know what health services are available and could not read a brochure if they had one.

4. **Cultural beliefs.** Women who have never touched their own breasts cringe at the thought of a doctor or nurse who touches their bodies to check for lumps or to take a Pap smear. Many fear that a Pap smear can cause an abortion. Among men, states Joe Olvera, Mexican males feel that a physical exam is an intrusion into their bodies; thus any medical attention is postponed until a crisis develops. This is *machismo* interfering with good health.

Antonia Novello lists another cultural attitude, fatalism: "You're born, you die. That's life."

What Is the Health Status of Hispanic Children?

In July, 2002, the *Journal of the American Medical Association* reported on the critical level of health care among Hispanic children. Those children have a higher rate of diabetes, asthma, and obesity than other children. Puerto Rican children have a rate of asthma 11 percent higher than Anglos or African Americans. Other high rates exist for behavioral and developmental problems. Their rate is 13 times higher for tuberculosis infection, much higher for dental cavities, at greater risk for hospitalization or dying from injuries. Dr. Jorge Magaña, director of the El Paso City-County Health and Environmental District, warns that exacerbated problems when children reach adulthood will result in a huge economic impact.

How Does Culture Affect Medical Care?

Dr. Elena Ríos states that our national health care system "...has little or no capacity to deal with populations of different cultural backgrounds."

1. **Language.** Many Hispanic sick do not speak enough English to get the help they need. And many Hispanic health care providers may speak academic or scientific Spanish but not *barrio* Spanish. An example is the Spanish word for tonsils, *amígdalas*. A Chicano would use *anginas* and then get treated for chest pains! One medical school refused to teach its students anything but peninsular Spanish, the idiom of Spain but not of the Americas.

2. **Touch.** Dr. Mitra Zehtab tells of a patient who felt better by going to her office for an appointment, but all the doctor had done was to put her arm around his shoulder while talking with him. The solitary touch of a cold, metal stethoscope just does not suffice.

3. **Warm personal approach.** Hispanics in particular (and others too) appreciate a doctor who is more than a scientifically precise diagnostic machine. They like someone who relates as person to person, with sincere expressions that show empathy.

4. **Feelings about death.** Hispanics (and Blacks) more often than Anglos prefer extensive use of life support for loved ones, according to David Sheppard.

What Are the Patterns in Hispanic Alcoholism?

Randolph E. Schmid refers to studies showing that average Hispanic men do not drink that much more than other men. But they drink heavily on weekends rather than stretching out their imbibing over an entire week. Other causes for alcoholism are the impact of poverty and the lack of knowledge about the availability and use of medical or counseling services. Perhaps culture contributes. Every celebration has its toasts, José Burciaga points out. Every infant baptism, for example, becomes an adult family gathering with food and lots of drink. Burciaga thinks that such occasions can bring out some of the "macho myth."

What Needs Inclusion in a National Health Plan for Hispanics?
Former U.S. Surgeon General Antonia Novello once proposed this plan:
1. Better access to community health care.
2. More statistical data on Hispanics and their health.
3. Training more Hispanic health care professionals.
4. More health care programs for migrants and undocumented workers ("viruses and bacteria don't ask for a green card").

What Is the Statistic We Would Not Expect in Hispanic Health?
Statistically, Hispanics live longer than others and will do so into 2050. Life expectancy looks like this:
- Hispanics: 79 years average and 87 in 2050.
- Asians: 82 years now, 86 in 2050.
- Whites: 77 years now, 84 in 2050.
- Native Americans: 76 now, 82 in 2050.
- African Americans: 69 now, 74 in 2050.

IMMIGRATION
Annual legal immigration numbers around a million, with Mexicans numbering 173,919, or 20.5 percent of the total. The next largest category is China, with only 5.4 percent. Then, around 2 to 4 million undocumented immigrants enter this country each year, around a thousand a day. Those from Mexico who cross the Río Grande are often called *mojados* (wetbacks). Immigration officers are called *La Migra*. The current estimate of undocumented immigrants is 8.7 million, an increase during the '90s of 5 million. Fifty-eight percent of undocumented immigrants are Mexicans. As for Puerto Ricans, they are already U.S. citizens and have automatic entry to the mainland.

What Are the Main Immigration Myths and the Truth?
1. **Myth:** Immigrants cost our government more than they pay out in taxes.

   Truth: One study found that immigrants annually give $1,800 more in taxes than they receive in local, state, and federal services combined, or over a lifetime an average of $80,000. Problem: States carry most of the services load and often are losers; the federal government gains.

2. **Myth:** Immigrants increase unemployment and reduce wages.
   Truth: True in some extra-high immigrant areas. But much research has shown that immigrants usually take jobs that citizens do not want. In that case, immigration actually mitigates inflation and maintains economic growth, according to Cato Institute and Alan Greenspan.

3. **Myth:** Immigrants bring diseases.
   Truth: False and true. Immigrants are generally healthier than U.S.-born population. Birth weight and infant mortality are better among babies born to immigrants than to U.S.-born mothers (Cato Institute). Immigrants become sick while living in the inner cities and the *colonias* and adopting American diets.

4. **Myth:** More immigrants come here now than in the past.
   Truth: False. The percent of immigration today is lower than during the 1900–1920s. In those days the percentage was 1 percent, now it is around one-third of 1 percent.

5. **Myth:** Anti-immigrant feelings are something new.
   Truth: False. Benjamin Franklin was irritated at the clannish new Germans settling in the colonies. In the middle of the 19th century the Irish were feared and reviled as drunken Catholic subversives. Subsequently, Italians and Jews went through the same ordeal of fear and rejection.

Why Do So Many Hispanics Want to Come to America?

Hispanic immigrants do not all come for the same reasons. Mexicans fled chaotic revolution in the early 1900s and ever since have fled poverty. Many Puerto Ricans and Dominicans face intolerable living conditions. Cubans have sought refuge from Castro's dictatorship and now from poverty. Central Americans have fled poverty, civil war, and bloody violence. In Latin America, poverty and the nagging internal economic problems constitute a future time bomb.

Mike Davis reports that in 1990 a mere 2 percent of the Mexican people received 78.55 percent of the national income. Between 1984 to 1996, poverty increased from 28.5 percent to 36 percent. Between 1982 and 1991, labor salaries declined in purchasing power by 36 percent. Minimum wage in 2000 was 4 dollars a day, which in the U.S. could be earned in an hour. Reverse those statistics and imagine the American flight to Canada—or Mexico!

According to Juan Flores, an influential event was the U.S. Immigration Act of 1965 that ended the national quota system favoring northern Europeans since the 1920s. Now the doors were opened for a wave of immigration from Asia and Latin America. New York City was changed forever.

Juan González thinks the flight northward correlates precisely with America's economic penetration of Latin America. American corporations set up their low-wage factories in the Caribbean or anywhere in Latin America. They recruited workers from the farms to the cities. Surplus workers then migrated to the U.S. as contract workers or as illegal immigrants.

Are Hispanic Immigrants Truly Assimilating into U.S. Society?

Mae Cheng comes out with a firm "yes." Examining four measurements (naturalization, homeownership, English-language acquisition, and intermarriage), a national report has found that (1) citizenship applications become more certain the longer an immigrant is in the U.S., (2) immigrants are owning their homes at an increasing rate (within 20 years from arrival, 6 out of 10), (3) in 1990, 58.2 percent of immigrants arriving in the previous five years said that they spoke Spanish adequately or better (by the second generation, only 1 in 10 relies only on Spanish, and fluent English is spoken by the third generation), and (4) intermarriage of Latinos with Anglos or others increases with each generation (one-third of third-generation Latinas marry non-Hispanics). This scene is nothing new but merely a repeat from earlier immigration waves.

The National Immigration Forum published results of a 2000 study showing today's immigrants from all countries go through the same slow progression into mainstream American life as immigrants have done since the mid-1800s. Nine out of ten recent Latino immigrants feel the importance of adapting to American society. Isis Artze refers to another prestigious report in 2000 presented in *Hispanic* magazine. It stated that almost nine-tenths of Hispanics aim both at becoming a normal part of American society and also at maintaining their own traditional culture.

What Is the Problematic Side of Immigration?

1. **Immigration is emotional.** Illegal undocumented immigrants are persons who despair over waiting for the bureaucratic process to obtain legal documents, who cannot afford the fees, who do not have family in the U.S., or who do not have a technical skill that this country needs. Ted Connover captures the feelings, in this case, of Mexican immigrants. They are:

...ambitious and strong Mexicans, gambling on getting through, facing danger, hardship, loneliness, separation, confusion, [even death]—but earning enough to pay debts and return to Mexico and families. If caught, they try again next year.

These immigrants, without a decent income at home, despair of taking care of their families and see no hope for better days. Some have come fleeing the terror of civil war, massacres, and disappearances at home. Human desperation usually trumps legal details.

2. **U.S. immigration policy is not always fair.** In the recent past, doors swung open for Cubans, not for Haitians. Doors opened for Nicaraguans, not for Salvadorans. In wartime the Mexican workers were welcomed; afterwards they were deported. Immigration policy frequently follows foreign policy.

3. **Immigration creates stresses.** In many urban areas, the states, counties, and cities bear most of the costs of education, law enforcement, court trials, and health care. Congressional legislation can force deportations that split families or uproot U.S. citizens. Poor immigrants settle in already poor urban areas and swell the unskilled and unusable labor pool (almost half of recent Mexican immigrants have less than a high school education.)

In Arizona, Arthur H. Rotstein describes how Border Patrol agents often have to ignore injured illegal immigrants because some hospitals refuse to give treatment or because some hospital services have closed down—not from heartlessness but because of uncompensated expenses for care.

At the same time, ranchers along the border have concerns. Rotstein tells how "water tank valves are left open, fences destroyed and property littered with trash and human feces."

4. **Immigration can be deadly.** Hundreds die trying to cross steaming or freezing deserts to enter this country. Oscar Martínez estimates that between 1993-1996 nearly 1,200 immigrants have died from "drownings, accidents, exposure, and homicide." But attempting to stop the human flow is like trying to turn off Niagara Falls. When the Border Patrol in El Paso built fences and posted patrolmen along the Río Grande, undocumented crossers simply detoured to the less-populated but more dangerous deserts of Arizona. An added danger comes from *coyotes* (immigration smugglers in countries of origin) who charge high fees and all too often abandon their charges in locked train cars or on the scorching desert.

5. **Immigration can be cruel.** Families on both sides of the border

often endure lengthy separation while the cumbersome application process goes through its motions. Undocumented immigrants apprehended by the Border Patrol endure uncomfortable warehousing. Appeals to stay here can meet arbitrary rejections, and denaturalizations can occur that are completely unfair. Deportation can mean getting dumped into Mexico with no money for food or for transportation home.

6. **Legalized entry requires jumping through endless hoops.** Backlogs from the enormous volume of applications cannot be expedited adequately by the bureaucracy. Expenses for attorneys and costs for application fees keep rising for people without much money.

7. **Immigration's huge, knotted tangle has just quadrupled in size.** Today's war on terrorism demands more stringent measures to monitor immigration. This means from Canada, not just Mexico and the rest of the world.

8. **Every nation has an obligation to control its borders.** The U.S. cannot absorb every poor citizen from other countries. This obligation makes quotas mandatory. In addition, the U.S. does not want every poor person who wants to come here—such as the mentally incompetent or diseased, and definitely not criminals or terrorists. Some favor militarizing the borders, but others fear confusing the task of the military. Others call for open borders. That concept is humanitarian but totally unrealistic, and now extremely perilous. Some persons advocate open borders between twin cities for economic reasons but controlled borders a certain distance outside of the cities; the idea may have merit. A fact of life is that the elegant lady in New York Harbor must today restrict her wide invitation to all the desperate people of the world. We just don't know how to word the invitation anymore.

What Is the Positive Side of Immigration?

1. **Immigration is the story of America.** The U.S. has received the largest immigration flow of any nation in history. Today one in four Americans is foreign born. Immigrants have made America what it is.

2. **Immigrants are needed.** Imagine our economy without immigrants to wash restaurant dishes, clean houses, dig ditches, pick fruit and vegetables, pluck chickens, and labor on ranches, in hotels, in body shops, and at car washes. Many of these immigrants are illegal. Eliminate them and inflation would go higher than a Fourth of July rocket.

3. **Immigrants enrich the nation.** Observe the Gómez Fushille family in El Paso, Texas. Mexican grandparents who fled the Mexican Revolution in 1913 have since given the community and nation 74 descendants. Their descendants have entered education, social work, medicine, architecture, nursing, art, linguistics, research, geology, and geophysics. Furthermore, over 30 percent of U.S. Nobel Prize winners since 1901 have been immigrants.

4. **Immigration challenges religious ethics.** U.S. Roman Catholic bishops, for example, urge giving asylum to persons fleeing persecution, freeing workers from exploitation, reuniting families, and addressing root causes of poverty that people are fleeing.

Will Latino Immigration Continue?

Yes, it will. The reasons are clear: (1) the economic crisis in Latin America, (2) modern travel and communication making movement and relocation so easy, (3) an aging U.S. population needing workers for unskilled jobs, and (4) the U.S. role as a safety valve to economic stress in Latin America. Workers here send precious dollars home to support their families and the economies of their nations.

When Is a *Coyote* Not an Animal?

Coyote, that fox– or wolf-like animal, comes from *Náhuatl coyotl,* or Spanish *agujerar,* meaning to dig a hole. Rafaela Castro explains that since World War I the word *coyote* has been used also for illegal immigrant smugglers. Smugglers are both appreciated (for providing a service in high demand) and despised (for charging high fees from poor people and often putting people in danger during the journey). Another use of the word is for *enganchistas* (labor contractors) who illegally recruit people to enter and work in the U.S.

At Ports of Entry, What Does *Migra* Mean?

The word *migra* (**mee**-grah) is the slang term for the Immigration and Naturalization Service (INS) and the Border Patrol. The common occasion to use the word comes in raids on homes or businesses or outdoor street sweeps with the cry, "Here come the *migra!*" Rafaela Castro also describes how Chicano children play a game where *la migra* chase the Mexicans, just as Anglo children used to play cowboys and Indians.

POLITICS
What Is the Hispanic Political Future?

With Hispanic concentration in New York, Texas, Florida, Illinois, and

California, those 157 electoral votes make up over half of the 270 needed to elect a President. It is not true, of course, that Hispanics vote as a
block. Nevertheless, both political parties recognize the growing importance of the Hispanic presence at the ballot box.

What then is holding back Hispanic political power? The stereotype
states that Hispanics are too lazy or apathetic to get involved in politics.
What are the real reasons? One reason is a certain fragmentation among
Hispanics. No one strong leader has emerged to unify the political
strength. Another reason is the low voter turnout, but there are explanations for this absence. Some Hispanics may feel the political system is
hypocritical and that their participation would be meaningless and futile.
Even though the law allows two hours off the job for voting, many
workers fear even that time off could jeopardize their jobs. Also, many
work at fatiguing, physical labor; after a long day, plain exhaustion
might keep a person from standing in line after work to vote. Or, workers might not be able to get to polls before closing, especially if they
lack transportation. Some are threatened by the long, confusing ballot.
Physical voter intimidation can still occur. Underneath much of this
whole pattern may be echoes of the experience in Latin America where
the individual feels very little power in touching public policy. Latino
leaders in the U.S., however, are very aware of this problem and are
working hard to increase citizenship classes, voter registration, and voter
participation.

Are Hispanics likely to be more conservative politically than Anglos?
A national survey discovered that Mexicans, Puerto Ricans, and Cubans
were more conservative in their politics than Anglos. The three groups
also tend to trust government more than Anglos. But Latinos react like
liberals as they support government funding for education, law and
order, and other national concerns. The three groups differ in how they
get involved politically. Cubans go to the polls and make campaign contributions. Puerto Ricans turn to school board elections. Mexican
Americans run their candidates in elections and also use boycotts.
Mexican Americans and Puerto Ricans tend to vote Democratic; Cuban
Americans tend to vote Republican.

POVERTY

What Is the Number One Hispanic Social Problem?

The answer in one word is poverty. Recent years have seen impressive
achievements of Hispanics in the professions, in business, and in every
possible career. Cynthia Orosco refers to this growth of a more affluent
Latino middle class but complains that the media overlook it and paint

the entire Latino community as a victimized collection of immigrants. For the true picture, later in this book read the section on "Hispanics Who Enrich America Today." The record is eye-opening and stereotype-smashing.

Oscar Martínez, though, puts this development into perspective by describing the difficulties in the climb, quoting one successful man:

> By jumping hoops, scaling walls, skirting barriers, embracing luck, seizing opportunity and working like devils, a good number of us penetrated the middle class, and achieved status and material comfort.

Still, this is the common American pattern. Many Hispanics would agree, but feel they have to jump higher.

Given this impressive sociological change, the other side of the coin must not be overlooked, with data from Cynthia Orozco's study of an AARP report.

1. One fourth of Hispanics live below the poverty line.
2. Only one in ten is college-educated.
3. Net worth of poor families earning under $10,000 has dropped around $1,000. But families with a net worth of $40,000 to $1 million saw their net worth jump by more than $25,000.
4. Finances, according to an AARP study, forced 65 percent of Hispanics to work past age 65, caused 26 percent of families to postpone having children, 39 percent to forgo health care, and 40 percent to abandon plans for college.

Where Is This Poverty the Worst?

Painful poverty exists in the *barrios* of the inner cities, but possibly the worst examples are located in the *colonias* or rural subdivisions that have sprung up within the 2,000-mile-long and 150-mile-wide strip of land comprising the U.S.-Mexico border. Steve DiMeglio reports on the 1,500 *colonias*, mostly in Texas, that are usually invisible to nearby city residents. More than 72,000 colonia residents crowd their communities in the El Paso area alone, 400,000 along the entire border. Nearly all residents are Hispanic.

Often illegal subdivisions, the areas are blessed with stray dogs, broken glass, trash, and graffiti. They lack adequate sewage treatment or garbage collection, convenient transportation, mail addresses, street names, sometimes electricity, street lights, or adequate medical services. Water hauled in on trucks has to cover drinking, bathing, cooking, and washing dishes. Among the residents, 26 percent lack adequate heating, 24 percent lack safe drinking water, 44 percent get flooded in rainy seasons for lack of paved streets and drainage systems, 43 percent live below the poverty line, 36 percent are children, 65 percent have no health care, and 40 percent have less than a ninth grade education.

Here, though, is the clincher: 85 percent of these residents are American citizens. These are Americans living in the Third World in the United States. EPISO (El Paso Interreligious Sponsoring Organization) has been a rather solitary voice calling for action while politicians dither and churches stay busy within their sanctuaries. The *colonias* are an abomination and an embarrassment to America.

Why Are Many Hispanics Poor?

Sociologists can study and publish their reports, but, as Oscar Martínez says, poor Hispanics know why they are poor. They face barriers. After the 1960s, the nation experienced major social changes. Farm workers and those in the inner cities saw corporate agriculture and globalization wipe out many jobs formerly available to blue-collar and unskilled workers. What remained was minimum wage (and sub-minimum) and unemployment. Other specific barriers continue:

1. The crisis in public education.
2. Reduction in government programs for the poor.
3. Continuing flow of immigration.
4. Continuing unemployment when impoverished immigrants enter already overloaded labor pools in the inner cities.
5. Racism that appears on many societal levels.
6. Dips in the national economy that make jobs hard to find.
7. Changes in the work world with a demand for technical skills rather than traditional entry-level jobs of manual labor.
8. Inadequate job training, English instruction, and child care.

Why Does Hispanic Economic Status Concern Economists?

Isis Artze reports that the future of the U.S. economy rests very much on the Hispanic population. If the country's largest ethnic minority has inadequate income opportunity, society as a whole will suffer. Continuing efforts are needed to enlarge job training, improve education, and provide ways for low-income Latinos to obtain health and dental care, pension coverage, and affordable child care. To use biblical imagery, when one part of the body suffers, the whole body suffers. The Hispanic Dream is quite simple. Mary Otto lists Hispanic concerns: a steady job with sufficient income to pay bills and to provide decent housing, basic health care, and then college or other education for the children. But that's the American Dream too. If the largest ethnic minority cannot share fully in that Dream, something is radically wrong with American society.

RACISM

Why Do Hispanics Think They Face Racism in the U.S.?

Racism against Mexicans and other Hispanics can be traced to English distaste for Spain in the 16th century and to England's own attitudes toward "whiteness" and all people of color. American antipathy to Mexico was fueled further during the tensions of the 19th and 20th centuries. Mexicans were viewed as people hopelessly backward and inferior. Thomas Nakayama and Judith Martin (1999) analyze contemporary American "whiteness" and social identity and show its reality in our nation's social structure. Whatever the analysis, a deep prejudice and often animosity exist toward Hispanics of any kind, certainly toward those with darker skin.

1. **Writers.** Walter Prescott Webb, distinguished Texas historian, in 1935 wrote that "there is a cruel streak in the Mexican nature." He described the Mexican warrior to be inferior to the Comanche and wholly unequal to the Texan. "In fact," he said, "Mexican blood, when compared with that of the Plains Indian, was as ditch water." In the 1800s American literature would commonly apply the label "greaser" to the Mexican or Mexican American. Willa Cather depicted a Mexican's hand as "greasy," meaning "dirty." O. Henry pictured Mexico as the land of "bull fights, fleas, and revolution," and its immigrants to this country have "greased us all, greased an entire nation with your tamales."

2. **Movies.** In early movies, George Hadley-García states that at first Hispanics appeared only as bandits or lovers, "scoundrels or sensualists." There were more women, usually with exotic accents. Latinas had love affairs with Caucasians but not with Latinos. The woman was won by a fair-skinned Anglo leading man against a dark-skinned Latin. Besides these stereotypes, the setting was almost always the *barrio*. Hardly ever was there a light-skinned, affluent, and educated Hispanic from the middle or upper class. Incredibly for us today, early western films had titles like *The Greaser's Gauntlet* (1911), *The Girl and the Greaser* (1913), *The Greaser's Revenge* (1914), *The Greaser* (1915), and *Guns and Greasers* (1918). Actually, President Wilson pleaded for fairer treatment of Mexicans. The Mexican government complained enough until these offending movies were barred; Americans didn't want

to lose the Mexican film market. Instead, Hollywood switched to Native Americans for their villains.

3. **New Mexico.** Maurilio Vigil chronicles the emergence of New Mexico as a state. Despite ten attempts to enter the Union, New Mexico had to wait sixty-two years. Why? Quoting Robert W. Larson, the cause in part was "Anglo prejudices against the culture and religion of New Mexico...." The *Chicago Tribune* portrayed New Mexicans as "not American but greaser persons" ignorant of our laws, manners, customs, language and institutions and grossly illiterate and superstitious." Soldiers fared no better. New Mexicans who served in the U.S. military during and after the Civil War, despite their brave performance, had to endure racial slurs and lack of respect from Anglo troops and officers. Jacqueline Meketa relates how the "Greaser Soldiers" displayed their stamina, good humor, and low sick rate in the worst kinds of weather, but nevertheless endured continuing prejudice.

4. **Orphan Abduction.** Then there was the Great Arizona Orphan Abduction. In 1904, with nuns to supervise, 40 orphans from ages 2 to 6 were taken by train to Arizona. They came from the New York Foundling Hospital to be put into Catholic homes ready to adopt them. Linda Gordon adds the sad part of the story. The receiving families were Mexican, most of them U.S. citizens. But Anglo townspeople thought that those children of Irish descent should not be given to Mexicans. Although the nuns and a local priest vigorously protested, the Anglos terrorized the Mexican families, threatened lynching, and forcibly took some of the children. Even the Arizona and the U.S. Supreme Courts supported the Anglo families. By 1904, no adoptions had been authorized for Mexican families.

5. **Los Angeles.** In the 1940s many Chicano youth began copying young Blacks in Harlem and dressing in bizarre zoot suits, walking in a certain swaggering style, and conversing in a street lingo called *caló*. Himilce Novas details how Anglos saw the youth as hoodlums and blamed rising crime on these Mexicans. In 1942, violence broke out, called the Sleepy Lagoon Riot. A Chicano gang, the 38th St. Club, had clashed one night with another gang. The next day a Chicano from the 38th St. Gang, José Díaz, was found dead near a reservoir named Sleepy Lagoon. The Los Angeles police threw the entire gang in jail. Tensions between Chicanos and Anglos began to heat up more than ever. The Chicano youth, admittedly, were not entirely innocent of provocation either. On June 3, 1943, hundreds of Navy sailors from ships

docked at Los Angeles and others on shore confronted Mexican American youth (whether or not they were in zoot suits) and beat them savagely. Days later anti-Mexican hysteria still flamed, reaching the Los Angeles suburbs and spreading as far east as Detroit, Philadelphia, and Harlem. The Los Angeles City Council passed a law forbidding any more zoot suits. Seventeen Chicano youth were found guilty. Hank Leyvas, their leader, received life in prison. All were later released through efforts by Hollywood stars, but legally were still considered guilty. Joseph Tovares's recent documentary on public television provides a dramatic view of this story.

6. **Texas. Sgt. Félix Longoria** was killed in the Philippines in World War II, and his body was shipped to Three Rivers, Texas, in 1948 for interment in the town's cemetery that had the Mexican section separated with barbed wire. A funeral home director denied service ("the whites wouldn't like it"). The family and the GI Forum appealed to Senator Lyndon Johnson. He promptly ordered the soldier's burial in Arlington National Cemetery, and the service was attended by Senator Johnson and President Truman. A subsequent local investigative committee found no discrimination had been involved!

   Oscar Martínez gives another prize example: One American town even ran a segregated pet cemetery, one for Anglos, the other for Latinos. Hilarious, if not so tragic.

   In 1999, a nationwide radio jockey commented on a situation in a Texas border town and told residents who didn't speak English to "get on their burros and go back to Mexico."

7. **Florida.** In more modern times, we keep hearing periodically a story from Clearwater, Florida, where years ago a sign allegedly read, "No Negroes, Latins, or Dogs Allowed." Whether actually true or not, many Hispanics would say that they have run into the equivalent experience. J. Edgar Hoover of the F.B.I warned on December 14, 1970: "You never have to bother about a president being shot by a Puerto Rican or Mexican. They don't shoot very straight. But if they come at you with a knife, beware."

8. **Religion.** A quasi-religious movement called Christian Identity attracts white extremists who believe that northern European people (mainly from Great Britain) are descendants of the Ten Lost Tribes of Israel in the Jewish Scriptures/Old Testament and therefore inherit God's covenant as God's chosen people. America becomes the new Promised Land. White Aryans come from Adam. People of color are "pre-Adamic." America's greatest danger is

mongrelization. Consult the Southern Poverty Law Center for detailed documentation of this extremism against Hispanics and all people of color.

9. **TV.** On television, racism is more subtle. Once popular *Dallas* failed to show even one Hispanic ranch hand. In television programming, Hispanics are known by their absence. From 1955 to 1992, states Oscar Martínez, Hispanic appearances declined from around 3 to 1 percent. But Black and women's representation increased. And Hispanic faces seldom appear in TV commercials.

10. **Business.** Hispanics allegedly find sellers reluctant to sell. Renters find higher rental prices or no vacancies. Banks hide information about mortgages. Silicon Valley itself has been fined or sued for failure to follow federal diversity guidelines. Three of the largest firms lack a single Latino official or manager.

11. **Education.** Another subtle form of racism appears in education. Textbook materials usually omit Don Juan de Oñate and the earlier Thanksgiving, the Mexican-American War and the concluding treaty, the Mexican Revolution, the Mexicans who fought on the Texan side at the Alamo or in all of America's wars, and the many contributions of Hispanics to America's life. Then we have the common disparity between funding for schools in Hispanic and Anglo areas.

12. **Names.** Beyond a doubt, Hispanics hear and resent names like wetbacks, green-carders, spics, greasers, or beaners. Nor do they appreciate the familiar Texan name, Meskins, which to Mexican Hispanics sounds too much like nigger, wop, or dago.

How Do Hispanics View African Americans?

Frequently, tensions arise between Hispanics and Blacks. Blacks fear Hispanics will take away available low-paying jobs. They also resent Hispanics who receive rights and privileges that the Blacks fought so hard to win; whereas Hispanics, they say, have not faced an equally painful political struggle. Hispanics charge that African Americans unfairly block government jobs for Hispanics and funding for adult education and job training. Still, there is hope that a common agenda and effort can be made to work on the common poverty that injures both communities so painfully.

WORK
What Is the World of Work Like for Hispanics?

A startling development in America has been the rocket-like rise of

Hispanics in every conceivable profession and their impressive entrance into leadership in business, politics, and every category of American life (see Appendix B). Among lower-income Hispanics, women commonly appear as clerical workers, store clerks, cashiers, dressmakers, assemblers, packers, and graders. Men usually get jobs as farm workers, mechanics, and construction workers. Increasing numbers are becoming technicians and even managers. Hispanics help America function.

A major employment category among Hispanics is agricultural labor. In too many cases, these jobs have some of the worst labor conditions in the country. Migrant and other crop workers: Face daily early recruiting call-ups (at one or four o'clock in the morning). Transportation away from the city in buses that might be unsafe or uninsured. Summer temperatures over 100 degrees. Backbreaking labor (laws had to be fought for in order to eliminate the torturous short-handled hoe). Exposure from pesticide-sprayed fields. Maybe no drinking water, restrooms, or showers. At times staying overnight but without sleeping quarters. Bathing in a nearby river. Washing dishes in a canal. Buying their own beer or soft drinks. Low wages. In some states no workers' compensation. And firing when they complain of poor work conditions.

A related workplace problem exists in sweatshops in the garment industries. In El Paso, Texas, *La Mujer Obrera* (The Worker Woman) effort has combatted concerns of low pay, long hours, broken toilets without toilet paper, poor lighting, dangerous machinery and lack of workers' compensation or health insurance, even plant closures with workers denied their earned paychecks.

One more concern about Hispanics (and others) at work are conditions in meat processing plants, reported by Karen Olsson. Workers complain about shortages of workers and excessive speed on the assembly lines. Serious injuries result. Meatpacking jobs have the highest reported injury rate in the country. Other complaints are personal abuse by supervisors, shortened breaks, delayed permission for restroom breaks, and physical damage from constantly repetitive work. Now duplicate this sad scene in chicken processing plants.

What Is the Hispanic Work Ethic?
The oft-quoted Protestant work ethic flourishes among Hispanic workers, whether Catholic or Protestant. No harder working persons can be found anywhere. This work ethic is visible with Hispanics in the professions and business. Likewise, the hard-working people who labor more invisibly to keep our society running—those who clean, cook, dig, lug, repair, build, pick, and assemble—their work ethic is unquestioned.

How Do Hispanics Feel about Affirmative Action?
Affirmative action became national policy out of the civil rights movement. People of color were given more opportunities to enter jobs and
colleges. Employers were required to make room for non-Whites. Many
Hispanics and other minorities today are in professions that otherwise
might have been closed to them.

On the other hand, author Richard Rodríguez represents Hispanics
who resent advantages given to them because of skin color and not for
talent and competence. Rodríguez wrote *Hunger of Memory* to assert his
ideas. Syndicated columnist Roger Hernandez likewise dislikes a practice that implies that Hispanics are not qualified to succeed without legal
advantages.

Many Anglos, to be sure, reject affirmative action as a form of reverse
racism. Increasingly, though, many persons of all ethnic backgrounds
urge that affirmative action be kept because racism has not at all disappeared, but they prefer openings to all disadvantaged citizens based on
economic status rather than on membership in an ethnic group.

YOUTH
Can Hispanic Youth Feel Any Hope?
Definitely, but there are barriers. One need is money. Cynthia Orosco
reports that 40 percent of Hispanics postpone or forego college for lack
of money. Scholarship aid must be provided for Latinos who fall into
the cracks of the financial aid system, and supplementary scholarships
must become available to cover extra expenses of books, transportation,
clothing, and meals on campus—expenses often beyond a family's ability to handle.

At the same time, Hispanic students need to familiarize themselves
with the many opportunities that do exist for U.S.-born or naturalized
citizens. The U.S. offers scholarships, loans, work-study programs, Job
Corps, vocational training, day care for student mothers, and GED classes for high school dropouts. Roger Hernandez encourages Hispanic
youth with this statement: "There is enough opportunity to provide any
individual Hispanic, who knows how to seize opportunities, with a
share of the American dream."

Who Are The Heroes Of Today's Hispanic Youth?
A decade ago at the University of Texas at El Paso, an ESL class with
Mexican students eighteen to thirty years of age came up with this list:
parents, Gandhi, Superman, and Mexican President **Salinas de Gotari.**
Others were Michael Jordan, **Benito Juárez,** *los Niños Héroes,* **Juan de la**

Cruz, God, Jesus, Leonardo da Vinci, Martin Luther King Jr., Mandela, Lincoln, **Villa,** and Mickey Mouse. Significantly, action on behalf of others is a common theme: Superman helps others, Mickey treats Minnie courteously, and most of the others obviously have impacted the world for good.

A decade ago among high school students at Lydia Patterson Institute in El Paso, the following list emerged: parents, God, and Jesus came out at the top. Next were King, **Villa, Juárez, Hidalgo,** Michael Jordan, the Pope, Mother Teresa, friends, family, Lincoln, *los Niños Héroes,* Abraham and Moses, Magic Johnson, Einstein, Madonna (she lives honestly), Schwarzenegger, **Julio César Chávez** (the boxer), **Zapata,** and John Lennon (he sang about peace). Among these Mexican and Mexican American youth, then, a pattern emerges—a respect for persons who in some way have paid attention to the needs of others.

Ana María Salazar writes about the need among Hispanic youth for Latino role models beyond the Latino "athletes, actors or singers." Models are needed to promote "education, strength and valor," especially education. The need is to recruit successful high school and college graduates, business persons, and all kinds of professionals to visit schools with large numbers of Latino kids and glamorize the educated Hispanic. In fact, the Hispanic athletes, actors, and singers themselves need to assume that task, Salazar insists.

THE BORDERLANDS
What Are the Borderlands?
The Borderlands comprise the lands of the old Spanish empire that follow the international border between Mexico and the United States. This wide strip of land originates at the Pacific Ocean at San Diego County, California, across from Tijuana, Mexico. The border crawls east across Arizona and New Mexico through desert and past mountains, punctuated by small twin cities on each side of the border. At El Paso/Cd. Juárez, the border meets the Río Grande (in Mexico the river is named Río Bravo del Norte). The border now meanders through Big Bend National Park, past other twin cities, and reaches the Lower Valley in Texas with its green fields, arriving finally at Brownsville, Matamoros, and the Gulf of Mexico. This U.S.-Mexico border, unlike anything anywhere else, in Carey McWilliam's description, is "an imaginary line, a barbed-wire fence, an easily forded river, and an undergrowth of mesquite or chaparral."

What Makes the Borderlands So Different?
Nancy Gibbs calls the area "its own country, 'Amexica,' neither Mexican

nor American." The area mingles Mexican and Anglo cultures so pervasively and yet maintains the identities of each so clearly that we can speak of the land as a state of mind as well as a border. Mike Davis calls *la frontera* (the frontier) "a transnational cultural system in its own right." TIME magazine uses the title "A World Apart" about

> ...a third very unsovereign nation, not wholly American and not quite Mexican either, with its own customs, mores, values, and even its own language, Spanglish. Family ties, religious roots, and economic interdependence knit the border region in both countries together.

Why Are the Borderlands Such a Problem?

This nearly two thousand mile line has more traffic crossings than any other international border anywhere. The vehicle and walk-over traffic each way numbers into the millions. The border is also the location of stubborn, pressing problems that affect not only Hispanics but also non-Hispanics. Here are some of those problems.

1. **Poverty.** Leon Metz quotes an article in the *Philadelphia Inquirer* (with an El Paso dateline) that if the 43 counties in the Texas border region (between I-10 and the border) were our 51st state, it would be (1) the poorest state in the Union, (2) with the nation's highest birth rate, (3) with the highest percentage of high school dropouts, (4) standing last in per capita income, (5) ranking 48th in death rate per 100,000 population, (6) 49th in percent of households with a telephone, and (7) an unemployment rate double the nation's average.

2. **Violence.** Persons who seek to enter the U.S. face danger of robbery, rape, and murder. The heat on desert crossings and the waters of the river claim more deaths than the many reported. In June, 2002, for example, Border Patrol Agents found 14 bodies of undocumented immigrant in the Sonoran desert south of Phoenix. Over 100 other dehydrated persons needed rescue in the triple-digit desert heat. Another kind of violence is the traffic in guns that moves from Texas into Mexico to arm criminals and drug cartels there. Anglo vigilante groups also hunt immigrants across Arizona border areas. And, ominously, Mexican Army units at times cross the border and fire on Border Patrol agents, possibly to aid drug runners.

3. **Drugs.** As much as 20 percent of heroin, 50 percent of cocaine, and 70 percent of the marijuana entering the U.S. come through Mexico across this border, despite massive efforts by both governments to interdict and destroy. Mike Davis calls the "drug barons...the invisible third government" along the border.

4. **Education.** Many border communities face overcrowded classrooms caused in part by students from Mexico who attend schools in the U.S. Border communities generally have low property values and tax base. The result is a severe budget crunch. The effects of families in poverty, constant immigration, *barrio* social problems, inadequate or nonexistent English skills, low tax base, and inadequate school funding in border schools leave many students at any given grade as much as two or even more years behind their peers elsewhere.

5. **Water.** Both the U.S. and Mexico depend on water sources from the snow melt in northern Colorado and the aquifers of New Mexico and Texas. A severe water crisis looms in the decades ahead as aquifers are depleted and river runoff is reduced.

6. **Pollution.** Both nations contribute to contamination of water, soil, and air. Smokestack emissions and toxic chemical wastes dumped into the ground are contributions of many *maquila* factories. Automobile exhaust from long lines at the border bridges fill the air with noxious chemicals. Some border cities like Tijuana and Cd. Juárez have no sewage treatment facilities, so raw sewage contaminates their rivers with human feces and industrial toxins. Other contributors are Colorado and New Mexico mining and pesticide runoff from agricultural fields between El Paso and Brownsville. The Río Grande for the fifth time since 1993 is on the list of the country's most endangered rivers, this time number 7. Mike Davis calls the border "North America's toxic sink." And Bill Moyers has documented how NAFTA regulations allow corporate lawsuits against governments whose environmental laws might conflict with an industry's investment.

7. **Health.** Exacerbated by poverty, the border region has received the American Medical Association's assessment of "a cesspool and breeding ground for infectious disease." Mosquitoes bred in sewage spread malaria. Borderland encephalitis, typhoid, hepatitis, cholera, tuberculosis, and dysentery rates are twice those of the nation and three times worse than the rest of Texas.

8. **Unemployment.** The unemployment rate is at least double the national average. Per capita income is far below the average.

9. *Maquilas.* The borderland *maquiladoras* (or *maquilas*) began in 1965. They are assembly plants owned by companies in the U.S. (over 2,000) or other nations. Materials cross the border for assembly without tariffs and return with tariffs only on value added. Taxes are extremely low. A positive effect is the employment found by thousands of Mexican workers along with other corpo-

rate benefits. The best *maquilas* will have cafeterias and even basic medical care. Workers are mostly young women from poverty-burdened interior Mexican cities, villages, and farms. Turnover is quite high. One concern in Cd. Juárez has been the continuing and still mysterious murders of young women workers. Another concern is the impact on the environment by industries that do not comply with Mexican regulations. A third concern is the trend of *maquilas* that move overseas to find even cheaper labor.

10. **Free trade.** The North American Free Trade Agreement (NAFTA) has opened up borders to trade and commerce. Impressive dollar figures in increased trade between the two nations demonstrate boosted gross national income. Economic interdependence is already a reality. Thousands of jobs have been created to implement free trade. The agreement fits the globalization of the new world economy. Still, critics point to jobs lost in the U.S., dismantling of small businesses and farms in Mexico, and the flow of big money to strong corporate interests rather than to the common people on either side of the border. And while border traffic increases, neither government has invested in the increasingly over-burdened infrastructures that tie together 14 twin cities with 16 million people. The border would need ten years and billions of dollars just to catch up to the requirements of this present moment..

11. **Immigration**. This complex issue has already been described.

PUERTO RICO AND CUBA
What Is the Puerto Rican Situation in New York City?
Himilce Novas analyzes the situation from three vantage points. One direction is the level of poverty among mainland Puerto Ricans. Their level is the highest among all Hispanics. The symptoms are unemployment, inferior educational performance, inadequate housing, and crime. More than a majority of Hispanic males in prison are Puerto Ricans. Likewise, cases of AIDS and drug addiction approach a disaster level.

This scenario, though, needs to have balance by counting the Puerto Ricans working in white-collar and professional positions. Significantly, Puerto Rican political power is rising. The Puerto Rican vote can affect New York City elections. Names that stand out are **Fernando Ferrer** (the long-time Bronx borough president and recently a strong but defeated candidate in the city's mayoral race), **José Serrano** and **Nydia Velásquez** (in Congress), **Dennis Rivera** (health care labor leader), **José Fernández** (former chair of the Board of Education), **Carlos Rivera** (former city fire commissioner), and **Hermán Baldillo** (in 1970 the first Puerto Rican elected to Congress and until recently an advisor to former New York Mayor Guiliani). Within this total Puerto Rican picture is the extensive contribution of that community to the nation's life, in academics, entertainment, sports, the arts, and the military (see "Hispanics Who Enrich America Today," Appendix B).

What Does Miami's Little Havana Look Like?
This name was given to downtown Miami after the Cuban influx following the Cuban Revolution in 1959. Eighth Street became *Calle Ocho.* Himilce Novas describes the Cuban sandwich stands, clothing stores, supermarkets, *botánicas,* Cuban restaurants, Cuban and American flags, Spanish guitars, Gloria Estefan music, signs in Spanish, men seated at card tables smoking cigars and playing dominos (a game from Spain in the 17th century and popular also in Puerto Rico and the Dominican Republic), and reminders to buy a ticket in the lottery.

HISPANICS IN THE AMERICAN SYSTEM
How Do Hispanics See Themselves in the American System?

1. Many Hispanics desire acculturation and a blending into Anglo society. They identify more with the United States than with their country of origin. Many (not all) professionals and business executives and those more affluent and college educated fit in this category.
2. Some Hispanics are hostile toward Anglo society. They value their rights and privileges as Americans but chafe under the feeling that they are looked upon as second-class citizens. This attitude used to be visible on a wall mural in South El Paso: *Yanki fuera de México ocupado!* (Yankee get out of occupied Mexico).
3. Many Hispanics are a bit confused about who they are, but they have no desire to be Anglos. They just want to be loyal Americans but also to retain their customs and language and blend them with some Anglo customs and English. They want equal opportunities for jobs and pay. They want the United States to be their country but see Mexico or Cuba or wherever as their cultural background. Consciously or not, these persons will assimilate American culture along the way.
4. Finally, some persons feel they are caught in-between the two cultures. Pat Mora wrote her poem "Legal Alien" and spoke of being a hyphenated American, viewed by Anglos as "exotic, perhaps inferior, definitely different,...a Mexican to Americans" [but also] "an American to Mexicans,...sliding back and forth between the fringes of both worlds...."

Why in the Past Have Some Chicanos Been Angry with America?

In 1970, Antonio S. Vigil published *The Coming of the Gringo* in which he laid out a history of the United States from a Hispanic perspective. He portrayed what Spain contributed to this nation: religion, language, roads, cities, agriculture, literature, education, and interracial relationships. Then he scathingly depicted the English record: pirate attacks against Spanish shipping, slaveholding (Washington, Jefferson, and Davy Crockett, even Lincoln's earlier attitude toward Blacks), character (James Bowie a land thief, Barrett Travis a murderer, also some of the English settlers in the colonies), cruelty to Indians and stealing their land, bloody English raids on Spanish settlements, religious intolerance, attitudes and actions toward Mexico and the infamous war followed by seizure of half of that nation's territory, economic policies, and military intervention in Latin America, WASP version of American history in school textbooks, the artificially contrived war with Spain, land grabs in the Southwest in violation of its own treaty—well, one gets the drift. Facts speak here. This record is undeniable. Unfortunately, Vigil missed the noble side of the American experience, thus a painful imbalance. But especially in today's confusing world, why cannot our youth study an American history with a balanced story, just to teach honesty in citizenship? But does that textbook exist?

And where is that textbook used among Hispanic youth across the land? In the late 1960s and early '70s, some very angry voices even spoke of political separatism. They were ready to burn. Chicanos spoke of belonging to *Aztlán*, (a mythical place of Aztec origins and a common Chicano symbol in their literature), but the dreamy details were quite vague. Many (definitely not all) Spanish-Americans in northern New Mexico and elsewhere, however, firmly rejected the Chicano Movement in its entirety because of its militancy and this talk of separation.

Today the word represents a concept more than a place, cultural pride more than rebellious anger, spiritual vision of justice without a call to arms. Frank Lechuga calls it "a longing for roots and identity, political and economic parity with mainstream American society, a humanistic, non-materialistic society based upon love and brotherhood" in Marcienne Rocard's phrasing.

So what about 2002? Some voices still remain on the fringe. As recently as 1984, the University of New Mexico Press published *The Lost Land: The Chicano Image of the Southwest* by John R. Chávez. The writer called *Aztlán* a myth that still stirred Chicano hopes for "the recovery of that territory in one form or another," "the vision of a new state for the Chicano." The Associated Press quoted a University of New Mexico

Chicano studies professor, Felipe Gonzales, who insists that a "Hispanic nation along the border is inevitable," not by war but through elections. Frank Lechuga quotes a Stanford University professor who predicts "a kind of Chicano Quebec" in the American Southwest within a generation or two. And a California group seeks reunion of lost territories with Mexico. Pat Buchanan and others react to such statements and call Mexican Americans a security threat.

Are Most Hispanics This Angry Today?
For most, no. Of course, anger simmers among some Hispanic poor, some Hispanic scholars who ponder history, and some Latino activists working in the *barrios*. Amitai Etzioni, author of *Monochrome Society,* makes this observation. In time, all ethnic groups find that hard work and education do allow them to climb the American ladder. "That makes a radicalization of Hispanics [and others] very unlikely."

To observe Hispanic commitment to the American vision, we only have to examine the number of Congressional Medal of Honor awards throughout our history (see Chapter X, "Hispanics in America's Story"). Likewise, in a letter to the editor of the *El Paso Times*, Eduardo Delgado wrote so eloquently about his feelings when viewing the enormous Mexican flag floating over Cd. Juárez in full view of El Paso.

> It [the flag] reminds me of my roots. I am still proud of them..., but I carry the biggest American flag in my heart, and in my actions [which] are louder than words on this side of the border, where it counts.

A young, first-generation Hispanic American who came from Mexico as a teenager, learned English, received his university education here, and soon will be a full citizen, wrote these lines after the September 11, 2001, terrorist attacks on the U.S.

> I had felt part of America, the U.S.A. before, but not as much as I do right now. This [terrorist tragedy] really hurt me and concerns me every day. [Once] I was there [at the wTC] watching the world from the top. Now it's gone with so many lives, so many stories, so much dust in the wind.

The typical Hispanic has no desire whatsoever to betray or leave the United States. Hispanics love this country as much as any other American citizen of whatever racial or ethnic background, including white northern Europeans and Anglos. Syndicated columnist Roger Hernandez shares his fervent pride in his Cuban heritage but assures any doubter that all Hispanics do not spend all their time thinking that they are Hispanics. They are "just regular folks," just "a human being who happens to be Hispanic." They are, to say it as simply as possible, Americans.

LOOKING AHEAD
What Issues Form the Hispanic National Agenda?
Cynthia Orosco and Surea Santana report results of the National Hispanic Leadership Agenda's 2000 Policy Summit held in Washington, DC.

1. **Affirmative action and civil rights:** Fund, enforce, and inform. Also, get Hispanics into government agencies.
2. **Child care:** Expand Head Start, CHIP, and dental programs.
3. **Education:** Headstart, teacher competency, curricula, equitable funding, school accountability, less emphasis on tests for higher education entry.
4. **Bilingual education:** A second language for all students, increased funding, accurate assessment.
5. **Health care:** Universal, affordable coverage. Expand CHIP to include parents and legal immigrants. Increase research funding.
6. **Social security:** Protection and monitoring of pension funds.
7. **Immigration:** Family reunification, faster naturalization process, and delay of a guest-worker program until farm workers are guaranteed better wages and working conditions. Legal safeguards in deportation cases.
8. **The courts:** Get Latinos in state and federal judgeships, on the Supreme Court, and into law schools.
9. **Hate crimes:** Expand federal prosecution.
10. **Racial profiling:** Eliminate it across the nation
11. **Minimum wage:** Raise it to a living wage.
12. **Economy:** Expand federal funds for business and job growth in depressed areas.
13. **Crime and violence:** Collect more data on Latinos, expand criminal background checks, publish federal survey results in Spanish, and create coalitions that include Latinos for designing programs to reduce violence. The gun industry is asked to stop targeting Hispanic youth in its advertising. A related issue at this point is ethnic inclusion on police and other law enforcement forces.
14. **Housing.** The National Council of La Raza lists one more objective—housing: Encourage savings, provide housing and home purchase counseling, and make loans more available for home ownership.

What Are Two Requirements for the Struggle Against Poverty?
One, America's attitude must eliminate the belief that most poor people suffer just because of their own irrational "behaviors." Life in poverty is much more complex than that. Not everyone has bootstraps.

Two, a new "War on Poverty" needs to be launched, but with more efficiency and fiscal responsibility than the program under LBJ. The nation that led the victory over Naziism and put a man on the moon could reduce poverty if the political will were present to set priorities. Hispanics who have become more affluent will need to catch the vision and lead in changing the public will. The barrier here is funding, and this problem will require the setting of national priorities. The nation must commit to capitalism "with a human face."

What Are the Specific Concerns of Mexican Americans?
In the Mexican election of 2000, Mexico experienced a history-changing surprise. After 71 years of one-party power ever since the Mexican Revolution, the PRI party lost the presidency to the PAN party under Vicente Fox. Mexico took a strong step toward genuine democracy. This dramatic change impacted Mexican-background Hispanics in the U.S. who now enjoy the privilege of dual citizenship, both Mexican and American.

So, with one cautious eye on their cultural homeland, Mexico, their concern here centers on this list of public issues as Americans.

1. **Borderland problems:** Attack crime, industrial and municipal pollution, unfiltered water supply, and contagious health conditions— all of the problems listed earlier.

2. **Drug traffic:** Reduce the flow of drugs into the U.S. and reduce the demand in the U.S. Overcome the collusion in Mexico between government, law enforcement, and the drug cartels.

3. **Immigration:** Encourage Mexican economic development to diminish the wave of emigrants fleeing poverty for opportunities in the U.S., and to reduce the flow of U.S. jobs into the low-paying Mexican economy. Speed up legal residency and citizenship procedures. Reform the U.S. Immigration & Naturalization deportation policy so that families are not unnecessarily separated.

4. **Mutual respect:** Accept all the nations of the hemisphere as partners and neighbors with different cultures but the same fundamental needs and hopes.

5. **Mexico itself:** Hope that Mexico will see solid progress toward true democracy and economic development. Also, change NAFTA to offer economic benefits to the Mexican middle class and the poor. Also, find ways to further Mexican economic development without overwhelming Mexican culture by American influence.

What Are the Specific Concerns of Puerto Rican Americans?

Puerto Rico, says Roger Hernandez, is culturally "more Americanized than any Latin American nation" but still is totally Latin American. Puerto Ricans are U.S. citizens, have many government benefits, pay no federal taxes, elect a non-voting delegate to the U.S. Congress, can travel freely to and from the U.S. mainland, and while in the U.S. can vote in elections. These three million islanders in the U.S. live mostly in the New York City area but also in New Jersey, Philadelphia, Ohio, Chicago, Wisconsin, Florida, and California.

Juan Flores points out that Puerto Ricans are second to Mexicans in the U.S. Hispanic population, are second to Mexicans in length of time lived here, and are the poorest among all the Hispanic groups. These Puerto Rican Americans have their own specific issues.

1. **Political status:** Decide among the three options: the present commonwealth status, statehood, or independence. A related concern is the removal of U.S. surveillance within the independence movement. Juan Flores calls this status issue "the unfinished business" of Puerto Rico.

2. **Culture:** Juan Flores sees the development of a subversive, post-colonial, "lite" colonialism, no longer based on military presence but on commercial, corporate, and media takeover of original cultural expressions.

3. **Poverty:** Confront the island's economy so that fewer islanders will feel forced to flee to the mainland. The goal is to be a healthy economy rather than a welfare dependent one. This problem includes unemployment, housing, education, drug abuse, alcoholism, and crime. By 1990, 70 percent of Puerto Ricans 25 years or younger lived at poverty level.

4. **Respect:** Encourage mainlanders to accept Puerto Rican islanders as Americans, and to realize that more Puerto Rican political power, Spanish language, and cultural differences are not a threat to American "purity." In 1993, when Madonna passed the Puerto Rican flag between her legs in one of her songs, Puerto Ricans called the act "sacrilegious." Fury arose also when a Seinfeld show had Kramer trashing the Puerto Rican flag in a traffic jam during a Puerto Rican Day parade. Puerto Ricans are sensitive to attitudes that put down who they are.

5. **Linkage:** Develop a joint strategy for confronting the economic and political needs of the island and the Puerto Rican communities on the mainland.

6. **English-only:** In Puerto Rico, both English and Spanish are official languages. Oppose any effort to push English-only.
7. **Viequez Island:** Oppose the U.S. Navy's use of this little island for bombing practice that endangers life, limb, and the environment.
8. **Recognition:** Mike Davis mentions the near-total ignoring of Puerto Rican life by the mainland media. Equally so, Juan Flores insists that the emigrant Puerto Ricans in the U.S. need to be included in any story and study of Puerto Rico. They also need to be included in the pan-ethnic reality of American Hispanics and not to be considered continually as an "exception."

What are the Specific Concerns of Cuban Americans?

Cuban Americans, centered mostly in South Florida, particularly in the Miami area, but also in New York City and elsewhere, intently focus on Cuba, their beloved homeland. Elderly Cubans think of Castro's dictatorship and communist oppression. Some of them dream of returning. They grieve over separated families. Meanwhile, younger Cubans go through deeper and deeper acculturation and assimilation and feel totally American. In general, here are their issues.

1. **U.S. embargo against Cuba:** Debate anew this question and decide to continue or remove it. Strive for free discussion and open minds.
2. **Family visits to Cuba:** Expedite the process.
3. **Dealing with Castro:** Work on some basic questions: Try to topple him, or just wait for the man to die? But then what? Let Cuba take care of its own future or get involved in that future? But how?
4. **Sanctuary:** Refine the policy toward Cubans who seek political refuge or relief from poverty. Or, from another angle, help the U.S. decide what to do with a future Elián González.
5. **Safety:** Provide more safety for those fleeing Cuba in rickety boats that often flounder in dangerous Gulf waters.
6. **Poverty:** Develop programs and enlist the Cuban community to reduce the poverty in Miami—thirty percent of whom are at or below the poverty line.

How Can We Summarize Hispanic Identity Now?

Guadalupe Silva expresses her self-identity as an acculturated Mexican American, and in doing so she can speak as well for most acculturated Puerto Ricans, Cubans, Dominicans, and Central and South Americans. Silva, from Mexican descent, sees herself as an American. But she has no need to look down on Mexico and Mexican people. She has absorbed American culture but does not ignore her roots. She speaks English without forgetting Spanish.

Still another dimension is more and more visible. A growing "collective identity" seems to be developing, in Mike Davis's expression. In New York City we see a "cultural syncretism" of Puerto Ricans, Mexicans, Cubans, Dominicans, Salvadorans, Panamanians, Colombians, Peruvians—indeed, from all over Latin America and the Caribbean. The different cultures "coalesce and interact in everyday life" to form "a variegated alternative to mainstream North American culture." To illustrate, half of the Spanish-surname marriages in New York are among these different Latino ethnic groups.

Ilan Stavans calls this development the fulfillment of the dream of **Simón Bolívar,** the great liberator for independence from Spain in South America. His dream was to see the United States of Latin America that would someday be the equal of the United States of North America. And to think that such a dream of Latino unity is taking place within the United States itself!

The further task, to be sure, is to weave that "collective identity" into the American mainstream in such a way that on one hand nothing Hispanic is lost and on the other hand that America is unified. Always it is *e pluribus unum*.

O. Ricardo Pimental offers a brisk summary of the Hispanic scene. In the '60s and '70s, Hispanics made enough noise to get noticed. The '80s were called the "Decade of the Hispanic," but the attempt fizzled. In the '90s, Hispanics in some places seemed a threat because of the constant flow of immigration.

Today, suggests Pimental, let the '00s "be the decade of Latinos-who-don't-forget-where-they-came-from-even-as-they're-well-on-their-way-to-wherever-they're-going." One question to close this chapter: How high do Hispanics aspire in their work towards full equality and influence in American life? Hispanics dream of the day when a Hispanic will become President of the United States. That's how high they aspire. The desire is not to see such an achievement for its own sake, for bragging rights, but rather to show that a Hispanic has the ability to stand at the top with any other American and run in an election with any other American in the strongest nation in the world.

History—
Hispanics in America's Story

THE 14TH THROUGH THE 18TH CENTURIES
When Does Hispanic History in America Start?

As a broad answer, Hispanic history begins in the misty past of early Spain and later in the centuries of Moorish conquest and the infusion of brilliant Moorish/Arabian culture into Spanish life. Hispanic history begins also in the centuries of rich Aztec and Mayan civilizations with cities surpassing any city in Europe at that time. These scenes dazzled the Spanish soldiers years later as they looked down from the mountain pass on gleaming Tenochtitlán.

In a stricter sense, however, Hispanic history begins with Christopher Columbus. Schoolchildren may not remember many dates or names in American history. But, if they know any dates at all, the date will likely be 1492. The name they will know is **Christopher Columbus.** Born probably in Genoa, this man, with the name of Cristóbal Colón and the title of Admiral of Spain, sailed across the forbidding Atlantic waters hoping to find a route to the wealth of India and Asia. Samuel Eliot Morison sums up what happened: Columbus landed in the Americas by accident while "...looking for something else ...and most of the exploration for the next fifty years was done in the hopes of getting through or around it."

But is that all there is to say about the enormous accomplishments of Columbus? He didn't really prove the earth is round, since others had believed that before him. But he did initiate a turning point in Western history, and certainly in world history. He turned Spain's history in a dramatically new direction and opened the door for a totally new culture on the continents of the so-called New World. Francisco López, an early Spanish church historian, called Columbus's feat "the greatest event since the creation of the world, excepting, of course, the incarnation and death of Jesus." Well, if not that great, Columbus certainly did something major in the human story.

How Did Columbus Impact Our Lives Here and Around the World?

His impact reaches our world even today. New World sweet potatoes added to the rice in China's diet, and New World dyes became as valuable as Asian spices. Chocolate entered Europe, and coffee came here. Middle East wheat made possible the fields of the Great Plains. Spanish cowboys from Moorish influence became the heroes of the West. Rice came this way, chiles went east. Indian medicinal plants filled Europe's pharmacies, and five hundred American herbs still find use in modern prescription drugs. Native Americans used wheels as toys; Europeans taught their use on carts, water wheels, and pottery wheels. Horses, donkeys, and oxen were introduced to pull loads, plow fields, and carry warriors. New techniques of weaving and dyeing refined cloth production here, and the finer strands of Mesoamerican cotton replaced the coarse materials used in Europe and around the world. European roses flourished here. European hogs, Castilian cattle, and Spanish fowl did well in this new hemisphere. But where would Africa and Asia be without the New World peanut? Or Italy's pasta without the tomato? Or India's curries and Hungary's stews without chile peppers? Or England without the Aztec turkey? Or northern Europe and Russia without the sunflower? Or northern Europe and especially Ireland without the potato? Or Africa without corn? Or Africa and India without pineapple? Sadly, the potent and lucrative tobacco plant also was shared with the world. All of this development was indeed "The Grand Exchange."

Why Is Columbus Controversial?
Historians have their questions: his nationality (Spanish or Italian, possibly born in Genoa, Italy), the date of the discovery (October 12 or 11), the site of his first landing (probably Guanahaní in the Bahamas, called San Salvador), and his physical appearance (at least 71 portraits, no two alike). But the most profound controversy concerns social ethics. At the 1992 Quincentenary celebration of Columbus's arrival, serious soul-searching by Hispanics and Anglos alike focused on the tragic side of that arrival. Some used words like national mourning, Spanish invasion, genocide, slavery, and exploitation. South Dakota even changed Columbus Day to Native American Day. John Elson had to confess to the pain of the Conquest, calling the events following Columbus an atrocity, a rape of persons and cultures, a moral embarrassment.

Bartolomé de las Casas, one who crossed the sea with Columbus, severely criticized the Admiral for taking back to Spain some specimens of his discoveries: fruits, flowers, birds—and six natives. De las Casas labeled this act "an offense towards God and humankind...." On a later trip, Columbus shipped five hundred Arawak men, women, and children as slaves to Spain; two hundred died during the voyage. Columbus actually boasted about the slave trade that he was initiating. But that was just the beginning. On the island of Hispaniola, all indigenous males over fourteen were compelled to present required amounts of gold every three months or have their hands cut off, which meant they bled to death. Two years after Columbus arrived at what is now Haiti, half of the Indians had died and by 1650 none were left. In Mexico, from war, atrocity, smallpox epidemics, overwork, malnutrition, and suicide, the native population fell from twenty-five million in 1519 to one million in 1620. In all of Latin America, between 1492 and 1650, the population dropped from around 54 million to five million, a net loss of ninety percent. Even though some Anglos insist that the word genocide here is a buzzword and mere propaganda, the statistics speak for themselves. The arrival of Columbus spelled disaster for Indoamericans. Jorge Lara-Braud goes so far as to insist that as the result of the Conquest and the genocide we can justly ask the question: "Can we believe in God after this?" The same question has attached itself in recent history to Armenia and Ukraine, Auschwitz and Treblinka, Cambodia and Rwanda.

Can Celebration and Reflection about Columbus Be Balanced?

Notwithstanding that horrible genocidal conquest, the positive side of Columbus still does not deserve the trash can, in the opinion of many historians. William C. Graham points out how others in his time only dreamed of routes across the unknown ocean, but Columbus found them. Mexican journalist Humberto López Torres feels also that we cannot minimize his feat. Yes, Columbus could be proud, distrustful, undiplomatic, greedy, miserly, and indifferent to slavery. Still, he was a shrewd geographer, observing the new lands with an inquiring Renaissance mind on top of his medieval philosophical, theological, and scientific views. He was not the first to touch the shores of the New World, but his accomplishment was to believe sincerely that land and not abyss lay beyond the ocean. He persevered against great odds, and sailed forth with a bravery that must be recognized.

John Elson insists that 1492 was a watershed in western history. To condemn it because of evil consequences is to condemn all history and to turn blind eyes to the good. Michael Hart put together brief biographies of 100 of his choices for the greatest persons in history. In his chapter on Columbus, his choice for number 9, he makes this statement:

> This is not, however, a list of the noblest characters in history, but rather of the most influential ones, and by that criterion Columbus deserves a place near the top of the list. Christopher Columbus is a "both...and." We celebrate, and we likewise reflect with agony. Such a

balance is mandatory for all who read history of any kind, not only for this man. That's one way we learn from history.

What *Taíno* Vocabulary Survives in Spanish Language Today?

A peaceful people called the *Taíno* (the name Columbus gave them, really Arawak) had flourished for a thousand years in modern-day Cuba, the Virgin Islands, Puerto Rico, and many other spots in the Lesser and Greater Antilles. Michael D. Lemonick then says that less than 30 years after Columbus, not one *Taíno* was left alive. They died from execution, hard labor, and European diseases. No pyramids or temples or other evidences of *Taíno* culture survived. One evidence that remains is some of their vocabulary lingering in modern Spanish and English. The first word learned by the Spanish was *canoa* (canoe), a boat made from a single trunk of the *ceiba* tree. Other words are barbecue (*barbacoa*), hammock (*hamaca*), hurricane (*huracán*), and tobacco (*tobaco*). Tantalizing discoveries, though, were made in 1998 on the northern coast of Cuba where a *Taíno* village was discovered. And in forests of the Dominican Republic, a *Taíno* ceremonial well for sacrificial offerings was unearthed. Future archaeological digs without doubt will reveal new discoveries about this long-forgotten people.

What Did Cortés Accomplish?

The conqueror of Mexico, **Hernán Cortés,** is usually remembered for his brilliant strategy in conquering the Aztec nation ruled by Emperor Moctezuma (Montezuma form is no longer in use), but remembered also for his bloody slaughter of Aztec warriors and rulers. In 1519 this adventurous leader marched from Veracruz on the Gulf, up the tortuous mountain road to the highlands, and on to Tenochtitlán, the capital. His army numbered only 553 soldiers, 200 Indians, 10 cannon and 4 lighter pieces, 16 horses, and some dogs. The Aztecs had thousands of warriors but only bows and arrows for battle.

But guided by his Aztec mistress, Doña **Marina** or **Malinche,** and warned by leaders from other tribes, Cortés avoided entrapment and imprisonment at Cholula by murdering three thousand men in two hours of battle. Subsequently, in the siege of Tenochtitlán and in the attack, military action, starvation, and dysentery resulted in forty thousand Aztec bodies stacked in buildings and floating in canals and lakes. An empire had died. By the tens of thousands, the conquered people were put to work as slaves to knock down the city's temples and clear the rubble by sheer muscle. They erected on the site of those temples the cathedral and government palace whose baroque architecture adorns Mexico City's *Zócalo* (Central Plaza) today.

In a positive assessment, William H. Prescott writes how Cortés, just before his death in Seville, Spain, in 1544, wrote final documents in which he expressed doubts about Indian slavery. Not many Spaniards would have said that. He also arranged for endowments that were to establish in Mexico City a hospital (Hospital of Jesus of Nazareth), a college to educate missionaries, and a convent for nuns. Prescott thinks that Cortés was not particularly cruel when comparing him to other military men of this age. He needs to be seen against the morality and religion of that time. But, says Prescott, he was also a brilliant general, skillful leader, knight for the Faith, generous provider, and beloved husband and father. José Cisneros laments that this man, who against all odds conquered a people and opened up a new culture, does not have even a street named for him or a simple marker "in the land he loved so much and where he wanted to die."

How Could Cortés Defeat the Mighty Aztecs?
It would seem that the thousands of Aztec warriors could have wiped out the Spanish expedition. Instead, the Spanish overwhelmingly conquered them. Himilce Novas lists five reasons: (1) Moctezuma's belief that the Spanish were gods and that Aztec defeat was preordained, (2) other tribes long-oppressed by the Aztecs and ready for revolt and revenge, (3) Spanish armor, horses, bows, and cannons, (4) "biological warfare," that is, intentionally or not, spreading smallpox and other European diseases that killed thousands, and (5) Malinche.

Who Was Malinche?
Born into a wealthy Aztec family, **Malinche** was sold into Mayan slavery. In 1519, when Cortés invaded Yucatán, the Maya offered her to Cortés. Her names were **Malintzín** to the indigenous tribes and Doña **Marina** or **la Malinche** to the Spanish. Knowing the Aztec and Mayan languages, and having learned Spanish in a few weeks, she was able to serve as interpreter, even as advisor, to Cortés. Her other important role was to be the man's mistress. The two had a son, **Martín.** She was present at the meeting between Moctezuma and Cortés and may have helped persuade the emperor to surrender.

To modern Mexicans, states Navas, Malinche is the symbol of Mexican betrayal and servitude. Octavio Paz sees Malinche reflected in the Mexican psyche: the extreme courtesy, fear of masters, suspicion of equals, resignation among the masses, abuse of power by politicians, and eruption into violence in fiestas and drinking, even killing. She is seen in Mexico's history of conquest, colonial domination, in U.S. and French invasion, and life in the shadow of its powerful northern neighbor. So, writes Paz, when Mexicans exclaim, *¡Viva México, hijos de la chingada!* (from *chingar*, to rape), they mean, "We were raped, but we repudiate that violation. We are neither Indian nor Spaniard. We are still in search of who we are."

How Did Cuba Become Part of Spain's Empire?

Columbus landed on Cuba in 1492 and was deeply impressed by the island's beauty. The native Arawak (*Taíno*, Siboney, and Mayarí) tribes numbered around 100,000. By the end of the century those inhabitants had disappeared. The *Taínos* showed how to raise tobacco and how to roll the leaves by hand. That's the origin of Cuban cigars, says Himilce Novas. **Diego Velásquez** occupied the island and prepared for future settlements and gold mining. Velásquez founded Havana in 1514. Some gold was found, but agriculture soon appeared to be the true wealth of the island. And, it was from Cuba that Spanish expeditions were launched to Central America, Yucatán in Mexico (including Cortés), and Florida (**Narváez** and **Cabeza de Vaca**).

What Is the Incredible Story of Cabeza de Vaca?

Alvar Nuñez Cabeza de Vaca in 1528 sailed with **Pánfilo de Narváez** on an exploratory expedition to Florida. There were 400 troops, 80 horses, 4 ships, and one warship. They landed and moved northward where natives, eager to get the Spaniards to leave, tantalized them with a story about golden cities. After the natives killed some of the group, the expedition returned to the coast but found their ships gone. So, they built five boats, set sail on the Gulf of Mexico, but then ran into a violent storm. Three boats sank. The survivors landed somewhere on the coast of Texas. In time the group dwindled to four: **Alonzo del Castillo, Andrés Dorantes, Estevanico (or Estevan),** and **Cabeza de Vaca.** Estevan was a Moor, perhaps an African black, and the slave of Dorantes. The four were enslaved by the natives, learned the language, and eventually escaped. De Vaca alone, or perhaps at times with the four, traveled from village to village, performing like a medicine man and salesman with trinkets.

After eight endless years and one thousand miles, often under blistering sun or in chilling cold, the men in 1536 crossed the Río Grande and finally ran into some Spanish soldiers who rescued the wild-looking wanderers. What a journey. Such an example of remarkable endurance, courage, and resourcefulness by four half-dead men. De Vaca's written record forced the revision of all existing maps and offered descriptions of the land, rivers, mountains, deserts, minerals, trees, flora, fauna, animals, and tribes in the vast land mass between Florida and Mexico.

What many do not know is that Vaca returned to Spain and later received appointment as governor of a province in present-day Paraguay. His goal was to establish a society where the native tribes would enjoy justice and decent treatment. Entrenched Spanish elite pressed false charges against de Vaca. He was returned to Spain in chains, was released, and died in poverty in 1557. He felt that he was a failure.

What Happened to Estevan?

Poor soul. Apparently, he repeated and enlarged on rumors about the seven cities of gold until he found himself on an expedition under the Franciscan, Fray **Marcos de Niza.** But no golden Seven Cities of Cíbola appeared, only adobe Zuñi villages. Nevertheless, Niza filed a positive report to the viceroy in Mexico City about glorious cities more dazzling than Mexico City itself. Such continuing rumors fueled **Coronado** and **Soto** and so many others in their later search for the unfindable in the Southwest. As for Estevan himself, probably somewhere in New Mexico, the natives killed him as he one day pushed ahead of the main group. His story is "the first great American folk myth," states William Loren Katz. A few persons have lamented that there is no memorial, monument, river, highway, or mountain peak named for Estevan.

He does, after all, represent a black Hispanic in the early American story. Fittingly, he will appear as one of the barely-begun Twelve Travelers sculptures envisioned for downtown El Paso.

Who Were the Earliest Explorers in the Southwest?

Francisco Vásquez Coronado was sent by the viceroy to search for the "Seven Cities of Cíbola." On this expedition north through today's New Mexico, a lieutenant went west and discovered the Grand Canyon. The main group marched across the Texas Panhandle. All that Coronado found were the same mud villages. Still, his report to the Spanish viceroy listed seven towns at Cíbola, or Zuñi. Archaeologists have found only six, but certainly no glitter of gold. The dream of yet another wealthy kingdom called Quivira led Coronado to probe as far as the plains of western Kansas where he planted a cross in the summer of 1542. It was, of course, a disappointed man who returned to Mexico City, but not before he strangled the devious Plains Indian named The Turk, who had apparently on purpose led the expedition on a wrong course. What the expedition did accomplish, in David J. Weber's words, was an example of

Spanish Explorer—José Cisneros
Reprinted with permission from *Riders Across the Centuries,* Texas Western
Press, The University of Texas at El Paso, 1984

courage, the introduction of horses and other domestic animals into the Southwest, and a unique literary record of events, people, and ecology that helps us understand this part of our history.

Francisco de Ulloa was sent by Cortés to explore the Gulf of California and discovered that the peninsula of Baja California (Lower California) was not an island.

Juan Rodríguez Cabrillo, a Portuguese serving under Spain, in 1542 sailed along the west coast of Mexico to find the rumored rich cities and a water passage between the Atlantic and Pacific. He did discover San Diego Bay. He died in 1543, but his crew under pilot **Bartolomé Ferrelo** continued north as far as Oregon. Later Francis Drake sailed along the coast and in 1579 claimed the land for England,

Sebastián Viscaino led an expedition along the California coast in 1602, named some landmarks, and afterwards urged the Spanish king to colonize California.

Gaspar Castaño de Sosa in 1590 led a small expedition (170 persons, supplies, cattle, and ten carts) to pacify New Mexico. The group visited the Tewa Pueblos between Santa Fe and San Juan as well as Picurís and Pecos. At Santo Domingo Pueblo, Castaño found two Indian interpreters (one was Don Tomás Cristóbal) whom some years later Oñate found and put to work. Castaño also was the one who selected the site at San Gabriel where Oñate later established his capital of New Spain in 1598. The expedition returned in 1591.

Who Were Some of the Earliest Missionaries?

We have looked so far only at the military adventurers. But, with every military advance, men of the church accompanied them, began missionary work, and sometimes suffered martyrdom. Fray **Juan Padilla** left Coronado's expedition on its return and went back to the Indians in Kansas. Things went sour, and the tribesmen stripped and stoned the missionary. Others on the expedition who had witnessed the event from a distance later returned to bury the body. Fray Juan, then, is the first European we know of who was martyred in the New World.

Fray **Agustín Rodríguez** with two other Franciscans, Fray **Francisco López** and Fray **Juan de Santa María**, along with escort **Francisco Sánchez Chamascado,** in 1581 headed for New Mexico possibly through present-day El Paso. He was the first Spaniard at the Pass of the North. Indians killed Fray Santa María that same year. Chamascado returned to report to his viceroy. Frays Rodríguez and López stayed. With concern for the two men left behind, a second expedition under **Antonio de Espejo** and Fray **Bernardino Beltrán** entered today's El Paso area in 1583 only to discover that the two priests had been killed near the Sandia Mountains far to the north. Espejo continued to San Felipe Pueblo and then west to Arizona but subsequently returned to his Mexican home base with the intention of leading another expedition into New Mexico.

At El Morro National Monument in western New Mexico, a Padre **Letrado-Luján** has his name knife-cut on the rock. A group had passed that way in August of 1629 in hopes of converting Zuñis and Hopis to the Catholic faith. The priest was murdered and scalped. A punitive expedition left Santa Fe and on March 23, 1632, passed El Morro, inscribing its intent to avenge the death of the padre.

But where do we also weave into our story the unknown brave and good Native American tribal leaders and followers who are mostly forgotten because they were on the losing side of a period of history? They too merit mention. In fact, many of such Native Americans made the explorations possible as they guided explorers to the trails, taught skills of hunting and agriculture, and, in fact, often provided food for the hungry travelers.

Who Were Some Early Explorers in Other Regions?

Vasco Nuñez de Balboa was the first European to see the Pacific Ocean, in 1513. **Juan Ponce de León** colonized Puerto Rico and in 1513 found Florida. **Alonso Alvarez de Piñeda** in 1519 mapped the north shore of the Gulf of Mexico and visited the mouths of the Mississippi River and the Río Grande. **Lucas Vázquez de Ayllón** in 1526 planted an unsuccessful colony in Georgia.

Who Brought Puerto Rico into This Story?

Although Columbus landed on the island in 1493 and named it *San Juan Bautista* (St. John the Baptist), **Juan Ponce de León,** following rumors of gold, took over the island in 1508, set up the first Spanish settlement at Caparra, and became the first governor that same year. When he first saw the island, he reportedly exclaimed, *"¡Ay, qué puerto rico!* (My, what a lovely port!). Puerto Rico ultimately became the island's name, and Ponce de León's landing spot became port and capital, with the name abbreviated to San Juan. The town of Ponce on the island's southern coast, Puerto Rico's third-largest city, bears the governor's name.

De León did something, though, that mars his record. In 1511 he executed 6,000 *Taíno* natives who had rebelled over outrageous working conditions. Others fled. Without his work force, León imported African slaves. European smallpox wiped out 4,000 more natives (forty thousand lived there before the arrival of Columbus). Since gold was conspicuous by its absence, the land was put to sugar cane, later coffee, tobacco, and ginger. The island's economy thrived in the sweat of *Taíno* and African workers. Most significantly, the interbreeding of Spanish, *Taíno* and Africans developed the present mix of Puerto Rican people. This diverse cultural mixture gets expressed in the island's art, music, literature, and religion.

When Did Florida Become Spanish?

Juan Ponce de León, after his Puerto Rican years, in 1508 moved to modern Florida and immediately became the first known European to land on the southern shores of mainland North America. He was following still another rumor, the exciting Fountain of Youth. Supposedly, this miraculous spring or fountain located on an island would rejuvenate mind and body. He thought Florida was that island. He marveled at the flowers everywhere and named the place *Florida* (full of flowers). Later, he was wounded by a Seminole Indian arrow and taken to Cuba where he died.

Hernando de Soto left Cuba and landed at Tampa Bay in 1539. He put natives to hard physical labor, and Spanish and Indians engaged in mutual killing. His force explored large areas of swamp and wilderness in modern Georgia, South Carolina, Alabama, Mississippi, Arkansas, and Louisiana He died of a fever in 1542, and his corpse was lowered into the waters of the Mississippi.

Why Was Puerto Rico's Famous El Morro Fort Built?

From the 1500s into the 1700s, English, French, and Dutch pirates and armies periodically attacked the island. England especially was drooling over the chance to own it. But Spain needed the island to protect its vessels loaded with the riches of their new empire. The governor, **Diego Menéndez de Valdez,** erected El Morro in 1533 and a few other forts as well. England's official scourge of the ocean, Sir Walter Drake, in 1595 tried to land on Puerto Rico, but furious Spanish artillery fire drove Drake out to sea. In 1597, the Earl of Cumberland led English and Dutch forces and captured the island, hoisting the English flag over El Morro. But, the Puerto Ricans harassed the invaders mercilessly and, together with a smallpox epidemic, forced them to leave two weeks later. In 1597 the English king signed a treaty that promised no more English raids on Spain's New World colonies.

Who Was the Father of New Mexico?

That is the title historian Marc Simmons gives Don **Juan de Oñate.** This man was a member of a wealthy, illustrious family from Spain. Born in

Mexico, the son of the founder of Guadalajara, he married the grand-daughter of Cortés. He ran a thriving silver mining business near Zacatecas and helped establish the city of San Luis Potosí. Then a dream captured him, the dream of leading an expedition into largely-uncharted New Mexico. Only Coronado and Castaño had led white men into that land. Espejo had wanted to try again and go further. But now Oñate's turn had come to fulfill his own dream.

But why pursue a dream that also had so much danger and risk? And why did the hundreds of recruits respond to that dream? Marc Simmons gives these answers:

To find wealth. Certainly the recruits had that goal. And perhaps Oñate thought of rich silver deposits like his mines at Zacatecas.

To obtain the title *hidalguía*. From the king, one could receive this lowest but still valuable rank in Spanish nobility. People addressed them as *don*, also *caballero*, or knight. *Don* before one's name was an acronym for *de origen noble* (of noble origin). Besides that ego stroking, recipients also no longer paid taxes and could not be arrested for debt.

For Oñate himself, beyond the dream of wealth, he invested his money, energy, and time for an even larger dream. He asked for three titles: governor, captain-general, and *adelantado* (an old title of honor). And he asked for the titles for life and then to his heirs. His dream was a frontier kingdom and an Oñate dynasty to rule it.

After interminable delays from the sluggish royal administrative machinery in Madrid and Mexico City, and after pledging a million dollars from his own fortune and from his relatives as well, Oñate finally recruited his expedition and was ready to head north. On January 26, 1598, the large aggregation lumbered forward on this journey of a thousand miles: over five hundred settlers and soldiers, some Franciscan missionaries, eighty-three ox-drawn carts, and over seven thousand cattle, oxen, horses, mules, donkeys, sheep, goats, hogs, and chickens. The colorful, noisy column stretched over two miles in length as it crawled along its endless trek through northern Mexico, forded the Río Grande at today's El Paso, crossed the desert of *Jornado del Muerto* (Journey of the Dead Man), received rest and food at Socorro (Succor) from the Pueblo people there, and on July 11, 1598, reached Yunque, renamed *San Gabriel de los Españoles* (Saint Gabriel of the Spanish), later shortened to Española, near the junction of the Chama River and the Río Grande. Spain's flag was unfurled over this first capital of New Mexico, a European settlement antedating Jamestown or Plymouth Rock by ten and twenty years. Some of the ruins of that colony have been unearthed by archaeologists at today's San Juan Pueblo. The story of that trek, the colony, and the years that followed were faithfully recorded by a member of the expedition, Capt. **Gaspar Pérez de Villagrá,** in his epic poem that ranks as the first history about any part of the American continent. *Historia de la Nueva México* is now available in an English translation.

The first days were busy. The Spaniards laid out the *acequias* (irrigation ditch network) still in use in the valley. On September 11 the people dedicated a church building with ceremonies that lasted several days.

Not all the action took place at San Gabriel. Oñate sent a group west to Arizona. He himself led troops east to the buffalo plains of south-central Kansas and in 1605 to the Colorado River and the Gulf of California. Returning from the Gulf, the expedition stopped to rest underneath the rocky form of El Morro, located today between Grants and Gallup, New Mexico. Either Oñate or one of his soldiers cut into the rock's surface the letters that can still be read by visitors to that National Monument in New Mexico: "*Pasó por aquí el adelantado don Juan de Oñate del descubrimiento de la mar del sur a 16 de abril de 1605.*" (Passed by here the *adelantado* Don Juan de Oñate after the discovery of the South Sea on the 16th of April 1605.)

Over these years, however, the strain of leadership left Oñate dispirited. The dream had vanished. In 1610 he wrote a letter of resignation. Ordered back to Mexico City, Oñate was relieved as governor by Don **Pedro de Peralta.** Oñate and his son Cristóbal returned to the capital. He repaired his ruined mines and ultimately rebuilt his fortune. In 1612 Oñate endured the death of Cristóbal, only twenty-two years old. Nobody knows the cause of the young man's death, according to Marc Simmons. This statement seems to void an earlier theory that the son had perished at Pueblo hands on the trip back to Mexico City and was buried in an unknown grave. After charges were brought against Oñate because of some cases of violence by his men against the Pueblos, he was arrested, convicted, and condemned to exile from New Mexico and Mexico City. He died in Spain.

Today Oñate is honored by an annual summer Oñate Fiesta in Española, New Mexico. A statue and a $3.3 million Don Juan de Oñate Hispanic Visitor and Culture Center stands at Alcalde, New Mexico, just north of San Gabriel. Oñate High School is a fairly recent new school in the Las Cruces, New Mexico, school district. El Paso, Texas, awaits the placement downtown of a controversial 28-foot, three-story high bronze equestrian statue of Oñate. Costing a half million dollars, the statue will be the largest equestrian statue in the U.S.

How Do We Evaluate Oñate Today?

Alfonso Ortiz, professor of anthropology at the University of New Mexico, calls Oñate both "brutal" and administratively "inept," a man who "doesn't deserve recognition." It is true that he was brutal. Some deserters were caught and beheaded. Also, bitter is the memory of the event at Acoma, a Pueblo village. Unexpectedly, a rebellious faction there had killed his nephew and ten of his soldiers. Oñate ordered the assault on the four hundred-foot mesa. Hundreds died in the struggle, but only one Spaniard. Pueblo male survivors over twenty-five had one foot cut off. Those males, as well as males twelve to twenty-five, plus women over twelve, were sentenced to twenty years of slavery. Some children under twelve were sent to Mexico City to live in convents and were never seen again.

Was Oñate vicious villain or valiant visionary? Perhaps both. Native Americans some years ago cut off one of the feet on the Oñate statue at Alcalde, New Mexico. Their historical memory still holds the barbarity enacted at Acoma. Rightly so. Historians remind people, though, that Oñate's actions were consistent with the standards of that time, as with Cortés. Michael Hart's observation about Columbus is valid here as well: Oñate is not honored for noble character but for far-reaching influence that continues until today. His impact benefits Whites, Hispanics, and Pueblos alike. Moreover, Randy Lee Eickhoff tells how the Pueblo medicine man, Popé, who led the 1680 revolt, had killed several missionaries before 1675, and in the capture of Santa Fe killed nearly 500 Spaniards. Most Anglos would think that Oñate's cruelty was still below that of Popé. Herman Agoyo, who has headed the Eight Northern Indian Pueblos Council, agrees with this assessment, expresses no hate for Oñate, and credits the man at least for his courage.

Some go beyond even that gracious appraisal. Despite flaws and mistakes, Oñate made a tremendous contribution to his world and ours. One, as already stated, he established one of the first European settlements in this country. Simmons calls him the last of the medieval-like conquistadors and the Father of New Mexico, the area which became the hub of Spain's northern empire. Two, he did all this while enduring fatigue, hunger, cold, drought, despair, betrayal, mutiny, desertion, and near-assassination. He exhausted his fortune and his health.

Marc Simmons completes this list. Oñate made possible the chain of Franciscan missions that later stretched the length of the border. He laid the basis for livestock, ranching, and mining in the Southwest. He was at least partially involved in the founding of Santa Fe. He laid out *el Camino Real* (the Royal Road) from Mexico City to Santa Fe, the first major road in today's United States. Oñate was both visionary and victim. He died never dreaming of the achievements that we list today.

How Was Oñate's Expedition Different from Earlier Ones?

Tony Hillerman explains that Oñate's expedition was not the fierce, ruthless invasion that demolished the Aztecs and Incas eight decades earlier. The Spanish Armada had been sunk by Queen Elizabeth's navy. As a consequence, the international power balance shifted and Spanish philosophy-theology softened. Catholic theologians had convinced the Spanish court that native populations were human beings after all, and as God's children they needed Christianity instead of slavery and extermination.

Those Native American tribes on Oñate's path are very much alive today. Where are the tribes in the path of English, Dutch, and French colonists in America's East? Calvinist and Puritan predestination allowed colonists to seize Indian land and to relocate or exterminate natives as a pure business proposition. They could not understand theological discussions over Indian humanity. Neither could they understand Oñate's failure to bring many wives along; the Spaniards planned to marry Indian women. Cortés in Mexico and Pizarro in Peru combined bravery and bloodshed. Native cultures shrank or vanished. But many of the Pueblos along Oñate's path live today with deep pride, political astuteness, and economic progress.

When and Where Was the First Thanksgiving?

It comes as a shock to some people when the rest of the nation hears the Texans boast that the real first Thanksgiving (often called *el Día de Acción de Gracias*) occurred not among the Pilgrims in 1620 on New England's rocky coast, with turkey and cranberries, but twenty-three years earlier, in 1598, near El Paso, Texas. In that year Don **Juan de Oñate's** expedition en route north from Mexico was just ending an exhausting and throat-drying trek across the hot Chihuahua desert when everyone wearily staggered to the south bank of the Río Grande near present-day San Elizario. It was April 20. W.H. Timmons records the chronicle of that moment by **Gaspar Pérez de Villagrá.** The men, their tongues swollen with thirst, desperately gulped water from the river, then flopped on the sandy shore. Later, after building a large bonfire, they cooked meat and fish and ate as they never had eaten in their lives. On April 30 High Mass with thanksgiving was celebrated, and in formal ceremony the land was claimed for King Philip II of Spain. Texans call that event The First Thanksgiving. Naturally, Massachusetts disputes all of this talk as Texan nonsense. The rivalry is friendly but intense—fueled even more by St. Augustine's claim that the first thanksgiving took place there on June 30, 1564, when French Huguenots celebrated Thanksgiving near today's Jacksonville, Florida. This tri-state rivalry is settled easily. In a letter to the editor of the *El Paso Times,* Jay W. Sharp calmly suggested giving the Texas event the title of "the first Thanksgiving celebrated by Europeans in America west of the Atlantic seaboard states." Less romantic, he says, but truer.

Hal Marcus painted *El Paso Gracias A Dios/El Paso Thanksgiving* in 1993 to represent this first Thanksgiving (See page 213 and page 214 for a companion painting, *El Mercado Juárez*). He provides the following statements about his paintings:

El Paso Gracias A Dios/ El Paso Thanksgiving 10' x 13' oil on canvas, ©1993

This painting is my imaginative scenario of El Paso's first Thanksgiving. I tried to convey the celebration of life that makes this theme the cultural banquet that it is. It is a poetic vision. In 1598, nearly 23 years before the Pilgrims landed at Plymouth Rock, a large group of Spanish colonists rested from their hard march northward and gave thanks along the banks of the Río Grande long before there were borders. They feasted with the Jumano Indians who greeted them. This scenario is my dream with all the spirits, archetypes and imagery of Mexico past, present and future in El Paso.

EL SOL is the gloriously golden Sun Carnival Host gazing at us with the eyes of perception and ageless beauty.

The main center panel is focused on the radiant sun. The sun has always been the central element in our cosmos. The Mayan, Aztec, Olmec and practically all indigenous cultures have revered the sun. Its top main ray encompasses the Virgin de Guadalupe—also known as the Aztec Mother Goddess, Tonantzín. Below her and traveling clockwise we have a Spanish monk, an Apache Indian, an American frontiersman, and a conquistador. The mouth of the sun is composed of a Mexican star-shaped *piñata*. To the left, we have an array of *mariachis* and other musicians along with skeleton characters celebrating the Day of the Dead. Above them and continuing in our circle, we have *El Diablo*—the devil—counterbalanced by the guardian angel hovering the balance of good and evil around the Virgin. Above her flames flickering into the Mt. Franklins, North American Indians dance as if carved into its cliffs. Birds' spirits fly and clouds move above downtown El Paso.

In the forefront of this same panel, fruits and vegetables of this region are being brought to the first Thanksgiving meal showing an abundance of watermelon, cantaloupe, pineapple, corn, pears, grapes, papayas, tomatoes, chilies, onions and peaches.

There are thirteen panels in all making up this dream. In the top left-hand panel, Quetzalcóatl, the god of stars and the cosmos—the plumbed serpent deity with his Quetzal bird. He controls the clouds and the lightening and the realm of the enlightened. Halley's Comet is approaching his forehead spurred on by El Paso's famous full moon.

Traveling clockwise and in the extreme right top, we have the European influence upon our culture being that of the Spanish Conquistador with his steel helmet and his long ax-like weapon. The conquistadors brought to this continent the knowledge of metal-craft and steel which was the main factor for their success in their pursuit to destroy the Indian culture.

Below is the corn field and the peasants. In the Middle of the corn field, we find Jesus in the garden contemplating the scenario. Christianity plays an overwhelming role in the culture, beliefs and religion. But what makes this Jesus different is that he is in a corn field—the corn, or *maize,* is the gift of the indigenous people to all civilizations. The corn is the main food source in today's world and believed to be sacred. Below Jesus is a Mayan male god holding the corn as if it were a weapon—blue and perfectly carved—looking towards the heavens. Just to the left, a mother and her son bring offerings to the Thanksgiving meal in the form of fruit, and the dove of peace flutters in the hands of the boy.

The middle-bottom panel is composed of the staple food group of this region: *frijoles, tortillas,* guacamole, garlic, *tamales, pico de gallo, buñuelos,* limes, chilies, and a fish from the Río Grande. This table in its entirety makes a bridge that connects both sides of the border. The Río Grande passes below the bridge. Indians wade in the river washing their clothes and living their life in the tranquility of long ago.

In the left-bottom corner is the blue female Mayan deity blowing life into the river. Above her proudly stands Cuahtémoc, the last Aztec prince who was tortured and killed by the conquistadors. His last prophesy stated that one day the NEW SUN would rise again after the five hundred years of darkness. He gazes over the landscape to the eagle and the snake symbolizing the founding of the Aztec Empire's capital city, Tenochtitlán. And bringing us back to the fulfillment of the prophecy which is the NEW SUN. The NEW SUN is the symbol for respect of the earth and the Great Spirit.

What Is Another Interpretation of *el Día de las Gracias?*

Joe Olvera writes a personal interpretation of *El Paso Gracias a Dios* in *Full Moon Joys/Full Moon Sorrow* ©1994:

Tizoc—the god of rain—thunders forth, snaps his finger and lightening streaks through the Aztec night in *el Día de las Gracias.*

The Aztec-Mexico world that inhabits the very mural of Hal Marcus meanders through centuries-old strife; the survival of a people is at the center as *la Virgin Morena* holds court amidst the flames of righteousness, as sacrifice, bloody sacrifice, becomes the Mexican illusion.

An Eagles Knight, the feathers of *quetzal* atop his resplendent form, gazes off into the distance—he is a distance gazer—he sees *la talaca* howl the last songs for mankind. Tonatiuh—the Fifth Sun—sports blue eyes as booming cannons greet the bloody red morning; *Conquistador* squares off against a down-hearted Jesus; He knows that soon death and destruction will cover the bloody fate and Eagle marks the spot with feathered serpent under-foot.

The night is jasmine-quiet, serene as *ebecatl,* the night wind, blows softly on the mirrored landscape.

The center is bright, full-moon lips grace the face of *señor Sol—el demonio* licks the flames of his heart. Demonized filters through Mexican folk as good becomes evil and evil joins the forces of revolution.

Bloody war forms the modern Mexico. Marcus' vision elaborates, enfolds, embraces *la raza cósmica,* continues its path through the *cosmos;* a creation of creation—a vision, a remembrance of Teotihuacan; *los tamales se ven bien ricos,* to say nothing of *la sandia...*

And the comedian once asked: If Jesus was a Jew, why does he have a Mexican name? Ahuuuuuaaaaaa!!!!!!!!!

Who Were Some Later Leaders in New Mexico?

Pedro de Peralta succeeded Oñate as governor and in 1610 officially established Santa Fe, the second oldest permanent settlement in continental United States (after St. Augustine) and the oldest state capital. Peralta built the well-known Palace of the Governors facing the downtown plaza, the oldest government building in the United States.

Diego de Vargas became governor of New Mexico after the bloody Pueblo Revolt of 1680 when surviving Spanish settlers had to flee south to El Paso del Norte (today's Cd. Juárez). In 1692, from El Paso, Vargas led his first *entrada* into Santa Fe to restore Spanish control over the city and area pueblos and was able to arrange baptisms for two thousand Indians. The expedition returned to El Paso. In 1693 Vargas led a colonizing expedition (800 persons, 900 cattle, 2000 horses, 1000 mules). But

El Paso Thanksgiving/*El Paso Gracias a Dios* ©Hal Marcus 1993

El Mercado Juarez ©Hal Marcus 1988

in this second *entrada* he had to fight resistance and spend two years to subjugate the entire region. But, without military help, information, food, and other supplies from the Pueblo Indians, the Spanish force would probably have met complete failure.

What Hispanic Names Stand Out in Early Texas History?

Capt. **Alonso de León** was dispatched to capture a French fort in East Texas but in 1689 found it already destroyed by Native Americans. In 1690 he returned to establish a mission at San Francisco de los Tejas, *tejas* being a Native American word for "friends."

Marques de San Miguel de Aguayo led the largest expedition into Texas, secured the territory against the French incursions, encouraged settlement of the land, and contributed to the spread of wild mustangs and cattle throughout Texas.

How Did Mexico and Peru Help Create Northern Europe's Wealth?

Spanish ships loaded with gold and silver from its colonies (especially Mexico and Peru) were attacked freely not only by pirates but also by the English Navy whose ships then transferred that wealth to England's coffers. Suffering from spiraling inflation and running short of money to finance its vast empire, Spain had to get enormous loans from English, Dutch, and Italian bankers. Those loans helped spur English industry and economic development.

Who Put His Mark on Arizona?

Italian by birth, educated in Bavaria, and consecrated to the priesthood in Spain, **Eusebio Francisco Kino** left an unforgettable imprint on Arizona. John Francis Bannon calls him "one of those occasional remarkable individuals who leave their indelible stamp on the history of a nation or an area." After unsuccessful missionary work in California, Fr. Kino was assigned in 1687 to the southwest part of today's state of Arizona and spent 24 years exploring and mapping territory as far north as Tucson—thus his title, "The Great Geographer of Northwestern New Spain." He discovered that California could be reached by land and wasn't an island. That discovery made Arizona a major route to the West Coast. He became known also as the Padre on Horseback. During those more than 50 trips across the nearly-empty land he founded a string of missions in today's southern Arizona. One of those missions was San Antonio de Bexar, today's city of San Antonio. Moreover, he organized cattle-ranching and livestock breeding at those mission stations as well as wheat-growing. He opposed use of Native Americans as slaves in the northern Mexican silver mines. In gratitude the tribes served as guardians of the northwestern frontier against Apaches and others. Fr. Kino died in 1711 at the age of 66. The State of Arizona declared him an outstanding son, and his statue stands in the National Statuary Hall in the Capitol in Washington, D.C.

18TH–19TH CENTURIES

How Did a Russian Threat Develop in California?

Ever since Danish Capt. Vitus Bering had been commissioned by Peter the Great to explore the waters to Alaska in 1728 and had reached as far south as California, the Russians could see the value of colonies along the California coast. Their strategy was to establish a post on the Columbia River and also one north of San Francisco. Besides gaining California, the Russians also wanted at least a trading station on Hawaii. A Russian-American Company was organized for trade. Spain's strategy in reply was to establish a chain of Franciscan missions and military *presidios* (forts), close her Pacific ports to all non-Spanish ships (leaving only Hawaii open), and send ships occasionally from Mexico to observe the Russian advance. In retrospect, as Martin Marty observes, this was Spain's last display of international power.

Nikolai Rezanov, who had founded the Russian-American Company, led a visit to San Francisco Bay in March, 1806. Rezanov knew some Spanish. He discussed trade with the Spanish governor and military commander. **María de la Concepción Arguello,** the fifteen year-old daughter of the commander, agreed to change her faith and ended up betrothed to Rezanov, who then had to return to Russia. This unexpected development, approved by the Vatican and St. Petersburg as a step for an international Russian-Spanish alliance, was prematurely halted by Rezanov's death on his return trip in Siberia. Maria eventually entered the first Dominican convent established in California and is buried there. It is interesting to note that in the 1820s the same fear of Russian advance from Alaska, plus Russia's aim to help Spain regain her lost Latin American colonies, and Britain's alliance with Russia over trade in the Northwest, all helped to encourage the declaration of the Monroe Doctrine by the United States.

Who Was an Influential Irish Puerto Rican Economic Reformer?

In 1765, with the Puerto Rican economy in trouble, the king of Spain sent **Marshall Alejandro O'Rilly** to the island. His eventual report to the king represented one of Spain's most enlightened insights into the needs of its colonies. O'Rilly, the social planner, initiated wiser economic policies, land reform, new schools, new cities and Spanish style architecture in new houses. Spain's awakened interest in its flourishing colony encouraged a developing cultural life as well.

What Developed with Mission Churches in California?

It was one thing to establish the chain of forts, but Mexico was too far away to supply them. Jack Weatherford explains that the solution was to send Franciscan missionaries to convert the Native Americans who in turn would become the workers to supply food, cloth, and leather for the forts. These workers became virtual slaves, with a high death rate from working conditions and Spanish diseases. At the beginning of the projects, there were around 70,000 natives; by 1835 only 15,000 remained.

Twenty-one stations were developed eventually, built along the coast of California on a road called *el Camino Real*, which in turn followed old Indian trails. Each mission was positioned one day's journey from the other. The missions stretched from San Diego to San Francisco.

What Did Junípero Serra Do in California?

Fray **Junípero Serra,** born in 1713 in Majorca, Spain, at 17 decided to follow St. Francis of Assisi and become a Franciscan. He was assigned at first to Mexico, then ordered to a mission in north Texas near San Saba. But a massacre in 1758 eliminated the mission. The Spanish viceroy, however, died before Serra could be sent to revive the work. The project was dropped. If all of these events had not happened, mentions Charles E. Chapman, Serra today might be a hero of Texas instead of California.

In 1765 King Carlos III assigned him to California. **José de Gálvez** planned the expedition. Fr. Serra served as religious leader, with Capt. **Gaspar de Portolá** as military leader. Although handicapped by a disabled leg, Serra managed to see a mission established at San Diego in 1769, with eight more later. Other Franciscans added still other sites until there were twenty-one in all. Serra has been described by Chapman as "an enthusiastic, battling, almost quarrelsome, fearless, keen-witted, fervidly devout, unselfish, single-minded missionary." He died in 1784 at 71, after thirty-four years of hard missionary labor. He carries the title of "Father of Catholic Missions in California" (nine, totaling 21 after his death). Considering the number of settlements that later became California's cities, the distinguished American borderlands historian Herbert Eugene Bolton honors Serra as "the outstanding Spanish pioneer of California."

In 1988 Pope John Paul II conferred beatification on Junípero Serra.

The next step would be canonization and sainthood. The problem is how Serra allegedly treated the Native Americans.

James Sandos says that in the missionary thinking of the day, converts were treated like children. Church rules were taught. Disobedience was punished by whipping, shackles, or stocks. Serra had no problem with this thinking, although he himself probably did no beating and tried to control excessive violence by other missionaries. A member of the historical commission investigating the Serra case, Herbert E. Bolton, former president of the American Historical Association, and a scholar in Spanish borderlands history, has looked at the criticisms and concludes that, "all in all, indeed, Serra was the outstanding Spanish pioneer of California." As for sainthood, there must still be proof of miracles.

Despite Pope John Paul II's praise of Serra at the beatification ceremony in Rome in 1988 (declaring that Sierra had brought the Catholic faith to thousands of California's Indians in the 18th century and had built many churches), some recent historians and many Native Americans disagree. They cite evidence of abuse of Indians, confiscation of lands, and forced labor in the fields or on construction projects. It seems that once again we judge an 18th century man by social and church practices of our century and need to balance negatives with positive contributions to get the complete picture.

Do the Early Missionaries Have a Negative Side?

Any fair observer of priests who braved danger and hardship to take Christianity to those they considered destitute of true faith must be struck by the passion and commitment such efforts demanded. Many of their incredible accomplishments remain to this day. The story is inspiring. On the other hand, Randy Lee Eickhoff states a contrary viewpoint. He says that the popular image of the humble, hard-working priest or fray, bringing Christianity to the Pueblo Indians, toiling with them in the fields, working hard to educate them, as shown in many history books, is simply not true. The first Spaniards were welcomed by the tribes. Immediately, though, the priests demanded food and blankets, and forced men to toil for the missionaries as well as on their own fields. Public whippings followed infractions of church rules. Church hatred of "idolatry" led to destruction of sacred objects and prohibition of sacred dances. Any resistance brought brutal killing by the military or sentencing to slavery. That treatment explains the native revolts that used identical killing as revenge. Noble deeds of faith, yes, but also the evil of human cruelty.

Do the Early Missionaries Have a Positive Side?

Fairness and accuracy would encourage a rereading of the lives of certain stalwart men of faith and justice, presented by Justo L. González: the Dominican **Antonio de Montesinos, St. Luis Beltrán** (the first Spanish missionary in the New World to be canonized), the Jesuit missionaries in Paraguay (depicted in the film *Mission*), and in Chile the Dominican **Gil González de San Nicolás.** A better-known missionary was **Bartolomé de las Casas.** He arrived with Columbus and in 1502 landed on Cuba as a slaveholding planter. After ordination as a priest in 1507 (perhaps the first ordination in the Americas), in 1514 he experienced a conversion from his own sermon on Ecclesiasticus 34. He suddenly realized before God the mockery of slavery. He freed his slaves, sold his estate, and spent the next 50 years fighting for justice for the slaves. Besides writing *Historia de las Indias* (*History of the Indies*), he fought for human rights right up to the throne of the king of Spain. He helped bring about the New Laws for the Indies that theoretically prohibited slavery and mistreatment of the natives (laws later revoked). He continued decade after decade to decry the resistance of slave-holding landowners. While bishop of Chiapas in southern Mexico, he had slaveholders who tried to lynch him! Sadly, Casas recommended importing Africans for slave labor as native laborers became scarce. Despite this horrible blind spot, the man fought for Indian rights. Thus his title: "Universal Procurator and Protector of All the Indians of the Indies." His statue stands in Mexico City's *Zócalo* near the cathedral.

Not as well-known is **San Pedro Claver** (1581-1654). This Jesuit missionary was sent to Cartagena in Colombia. There he observed blacks shackled on ships and in slave markets. Appalled, he determined to attack that evil and called himself "the slave of Negroes forever." With interpreters, he boarded every slave ship and visited the slave pens, carrying food and medicines, nursing the sick, and teaching religion. He died at age 38. He had baptized an estimated 300,000 slaves and was canonized by Pope Leo XIII in 1888. In 1896 he was named "Patron to all Roman Catholic missions to blacks." Commonly, his title is "Apostle of the Negroes."

Who Figured in the Stories of San Diego and Los Angeles?

In 1769, Capt. **Gaspar de Portolá,** Governor of Lower California, led an expedition that built the first fort at modern San Diego. That same year he was the first white man at the site of today's Los Angeles and named the river. Later, the name became the town's name. **Felipe de Neve,** Spanish governor of Upper California, founded today's Los Angeles in 1781. The original name was *El Pueblo de Nuestra Señora la Reina de los Angeles de Porciuncula* (The Town of Our Lady, Queen of the Angels of Porciuncula). In time the name was shortened (wisely—think of letterheads, signs, and maps!) to Los Angeles, now America's second-largest city.

In 1542, Portuguese explorer **Juan Rodríguez Cabrillo,** coping with a thick fog, concentrated on some northern islands off present-day San Francisco. In 1769, Capt. **Gaspar de Portolá** on the eventual site built a *presidio* (barracks) and mission. In 1775, **Juan Bautista de Anza** built a fort and mission there. England's Sir Francis Drake touched land a few miles north in 1579 and gave the name Nova Albion. Later, Capt. John Montgomery planted the American flag and gave the name *Yerba Buena*. In 1595, the Spanish explorer **Sebastián Rodríguez Cermeño,** finding de Anza's fort and mission, named the site *Puerto de San Francisco* (Port of St. Francis). San Francisco became the official name for the whole area in 1847.

How Is de Anza Connected with California and New Mexico?
Juan Bautista de Anza in 1774 received permission to find an overland route from Tubas in southern Arizona to California. On a second trip in 1775 he reached the site of San Francisco and established both a mission and a fort. Later he was appointed governor of New Mexico and defeated Comanche warriors under Cuerno Verdo. In 1785 he held peace talks with over 400 Comanches at Taos, reached agreement, and established the peace that allowed New Mexico to grow.

Who Explored Colorado and Utah?
Again, **Francisco Domínguez** and **Silvestre Vélez de Escalante,** both Franciscan friars, left Santa Fe on a five-month expedition that explored northern New Mexico, Colorado, Utah (as far north as Provo), and northern Arizona. Although their intention was to find a northern route to California, what they accomplished was to establish the later trade trails into northern Utah, known as the Old Spanish Trail. This increasingly valuable trade route ran from Santa Fe, New Mexico, through western Colorado and southern Utah to Las Vegas, Nevada, and on to Los Angeles in California.

Do We Affirm or Curse the 300-Year Spanish Heritage?
Many minds are genuinely troubled over Spanish cruelty in their conquest of the Americas: the wipe-out of the *Taína* and Arawak and other tribes, 24 million deaths in Mexico between 1519-1620, 50 million

throughout the continent. This was genocide! Nothing can mitigate the horror of that record.

To omit the other side of the coin is unrealistic and unbalanced. The same Spanish Conquest brought the beginnings of a new civilization called Latin American, something apparent in every conversation in Spanish and in every Spanish dance or every strum of guitar in the Americas. In Spain's aid to the colonies and thus America's victory over England. In modern highways laid down first by Spanish explorers. In every cowboy movie or novel. In gifts of adobe, mining, cities, schools, universities and churches. In dredged harbors, printing presses and books. In every wheel on vehicles or in machines. In imported cattle, sheep, goats, horses, pigs, chickens, hoes, plows, spades, shovels, oranges, peaches, apples, apricots, pears, olives, lemons, limes, plums, figs, strawberries, raspberries, cherries, pomegranates, grapes, raisins, fine cotton, wheat, almonds, walnuts, pistachios, and sugar cane. Moreover, gifts from the Americas traveled to the rest of the world: chile peppers, 500 medicinal herbs, regular and sweet potatoes, peanuts, tomatoes, the turkey, corn, and pineapple. The only negative gift was tobacco.

The *National Geographic* on its insert map with the February 1992 issue compiled this impressive two-way list and called the process "The Grand Exchange." Therefore, if we were to reject Spain's heritage because of its all-too-human cruelty, we would have to reject most of human and American history. So, let there be celebration of Spain's heritage today, but also let there be sorrow along with healing and justice for those who still suffer the burdens of that ancient conquest.

Who Was America's Secret Weapon in the Revolution?

Most Americans learn about France's Marquis de Lafayette, Poland's Kosciuszko, and Germany's de Kalba and von Steuben. But Spain's Gen. **Bernardo de Gálvez,** governor of Louisiana, has been almost forgotten in the story of the American Revolution. Lorenzo G. LaFarelle calls him "the hero" of that conflict and "America's Secret Weapon."

De Gálvez responded to American pleas and cleared the upper Mississippi to keep the British from encircling the colonies from the west. When Spain declared war on England in 1779, Gálvez gathered a militia of men drawn from Spanish volunteers in Texas as well as Cuban, Puerto Rican, and Mexican-Indian soldiers. Spanish cowboys drove Texas longhorn cattle as far as New Orleans to feed the army. Lorenzo LaFarelle tells how De Gálvez organized cattle drives from San Antonio to Nagadoches where the beef became beef jerky. The jerky was then sent up the Mississippi and Ohio Rivers to the eastern colonies to feed the colonial troops. Spain and her colonies sent money, including funds from Cuba.

Under Gálvez, the army captured Spanish forts on the lower Mississippi and cleared the waterway for American shipping. De Gálvez opened up a second front by capturing British forts across the Gulf Coast. In 1781 he took Pensacola, the capital of British West Indies and a major naval base. The Texan city of Galveston today bears the general's name. In fact, those Spanish victories tied down British troops in the south. That action and also Spain's millions of dollars, armaments, and supplies all contributed significantly to Washington's victory over Cornwallis at Yorktown and a quicker end to the Revolution.

What Are the Origins of the Cowboys of the American West?

These are mostly unnamed individuals, but they simply must be included. When Columbus made his second voyage to the Americas in 1493, he brought along domestic animals and *vaqueros* (*vaca* means cow, so herdsmen of cattle and horses, or cowboys). When Coronado marched north in 1540, he drove five hundred cows, calves, and bulls, a veritable food supply on the hoof. Any lame or tired animals were left behind. Years later other explorers found thousands of cattle running wild, and by 1600 there were tens of thousands of animals on the loose. In 1690 two hundred head of cattle were driven into eastern Texas near today's Louisiana border. A mission station there developed cattle raising and trained Native Americans as mounted herdsmen. The famous Texas longhorns of our time developed from these Spanish herds.

One of the most successful colonizers of the lower Río Grande in what is now Mexico was Don **José de Excandón.** In seven years he established twenty-three independent settlements and then recruited over four thousand ranchers with cattle, horses, mules, goats, and sheep to settle farther north. They became the cowboys of the huge King Ranch. So, from Columbus, Coronado, Oñate, Excandón and so many others, the contemporary western cattle industry had its beginning.

Most of these *vaqueros* of Mexico and Texas were *mulatos* or *mestizos,* not your movie or television Anglo. After Mexico's defeat in the war with the U.S. in 1848, Anglo Texas ranchers began to call themselves "cowboys." They copied the earlier *vaqueros.* Carey McWilliams describes the lariat, lasso, cinch, chaps (that protected against cactus and gave warmth in winter), chin straps on the hats, horse feedbags, rope halter, and ten-gallon hat. Hollywood's cowboy myth, in Juan González's phrase, does not at all give a true historic view of the cowboy.

When the first English speakers arrived in Texas in 1821, they found wild cattle everywhere. By the mid-century, Texans were driving cattle to New Orleans, Kansas City, St. Louis, and even Ohio. In 1854, fifty thousand Texas cattle arrived in northern markets, and later they reached California, too. By 1860 Texas held nearly four to five million head of cattle.

Following the Civil War, for twenty years over ten million cattle were sent over the Chisholm Trail from Texas to the North. Abilene, Kansas, became the first western cow town where cattle were sold and then sent East by railroad to the stockyards of Chicago and beyond. A later cow town was Dodge City, Kansas. This is the cowboy story that goes back to the earliest days of the Spanish explorers.

What Is the Genealogy of Horses in the Southwest?
Wild horses galloping across barren areas of the Southwest, in Melissa W. Sais's words, are "a walking history lesson." Spanish Barbs developed in Spain were mixtures of Moorish horses from Africa and breeds in Spain. Cortés landed in Mexico with those horses, and they multiplied over the years through many expeditions and Indian trading. Records tell of the winter of 1599 when in a vicious storm an Oñate expedition to Zuni lost 30 animals. Naturally, those lost animals multiplied and scattered and contributed to more mixtures. Eventually the mustang emerged. Native Americans stole mustangs from the Spanish and later from the American settlers. These Indian ponies carried men in tribal travel and a thousand raids in war. Later, the horses rushed mail across the continent on the Pony Express. Cowboys rode them in herding cattle and chasing horse thieves. Limited numbers of mustangs still survive on a few ranches in New Mexico, Arizona and Texas. DNA tests on herds in New Mexico have proved the historical genealogy of these animals.

Walter I. Lopez explains how on the eastern seaboard the English had introduced what much later became the Quarter Horse. These animals, bred with imported Moorish horses, became mixed again with Spanish Barbs that entered Florida under de Soto and obtained by the Indians farther north. Trade with the English resulted in mixed breeds that carried persons and trade goods westward along the Santa Fe Trail and reached New Mexico by 1848. That breed mixed with mustang mixtures in the Southwest. What a complicated story of mixture upon mixture. It's quite a genealogy.

What Irishman Found a Place in the Southwest Story?
In the late 1500s, Britain was persecuting the Irish, forcing many to flee to Spain. Some were recruited into the army and sent to New Spain.

One such recruit was red-headed **Hugh O'Conner** who changed his name to **Hugo Oconor.** He was stationed as a commander along the northern frontier and traveled its every inch. On August 20, 1775, he established the Royal Presidio of San Agustín de Tucson, today's Tucson, Arizona. Oconor at a later date served as governor of Texas.

Why Was Slavery Introduced into Cuba?

For ten years the English flag flew over Cuba until 1763 when Spain traded Florida to recover Havana again. During that time, the English encouraged the importation of African slaves whose cheap labor made possible the rapid growth of sugar cane, tobacco, and coffee plantations. As in Puerto Rico, those slaves brought their rich cultural traditions that are so obvious in the music, customs, and religion of Cuba. Cuba also witnessed numerous slave rebellions, some very bloody. **Antonio Aponte** in 1811 led one rebellion in Havana. Some intellectuals began to question slavery, but the slave owners lashed back with violent fury.

THE NINETEENTH CENTURY
Which Hispanic Fought in Two American Wars?

Born in 1755 on Minorca, an island near Spain but ruled by England, **Jorge Farragut** became a sea captain at 17, sailing the Caribbean, the Gulf of Mexico, and the Atlantic. When the American Revolution broke out, his dislike of England moved him to join South Carolina's navy. He fought the British at Savannah and was captured in Charleston. After gaining his freedom in a prisoner exchange, he joined the Continental Army and was wounded. Following the war he moved to Tennessee, married a young American woman, changed his name to George, moved on to New Orleans, and became captain of an armed ship. In the War of 1812 he used his ship to fight the British once again. From his marriage came a son, David, who gained fame and the title of admiral in the Civil War.

Who Are Important Persons in the Santa Fe Trail Story?

Eager to do business in New Mexico but prohibited by Spanish authorities, merchants from the East sneaked in from the north to Santa Fe to avoid Spanish troops. According to Himilce Novas, John Peyton in 1773 and Captain Zebulon Pike in 1806 had already laid out the original route. A further opening was made by a Missouri trader named William Becknell.

Hollis Walker relates how in 1821 Becknell headed west from St. Louis on an expedition toward New Mexico. At the same time, Mexican

Captain Don **Pedro Ignazcio Gallego** and a good-sized military contingent were on a hunt for raiding Comanches and also for an American who reportedly had entered Mexican territory. By accident, Gallego stumbled upon Becknell and his small group of six. We know this story from a few pages of the diary of Capt. Gallego discovered on microfiche in a Colorado library. The chance meeting of the two groups occurred just south of Las Vegas in New Mexico. Gallego sent Becknell to Santa Fe to meet the Mexican Governor, Don **Facundo Melgares.** From that meeting, the governor authorized trade between New Mexicans and the United States. Previously, New Mexicans were restricted to trade only with Mexico. That meeting is considered the official establishment of the Santa Fe Trail. Covering the years from 1821-1880, the annual trade reached $500,000 by the 1840s as large numbers of traders and merchants from east of the Mississippi followed Becknell's route into the Southwest.

A further detail corrects the common impression that only Anglo merchants traveled the famous trail. Hispano business persons visited eastern cities and even Europe to buy items for sale in the Southwest. Those merchants along with Anglos became wealthy in the growing trade.

What Cuban Priest Has Been Honored on a U.S. Postage Stamp?

A stamp issued in 1997 honored Padre **Félix Varela,** a Cuban-born priest, professor, philosopher, patriot, writer, newspaper publisher, and social reformer. Even in the early 1800s, he championed human rights (decrying slavery), equality before the law, and democracy aligned with Catholic Christianity. Cuba's first modern thinker served in the Spanish *Cortes* (parliament). His promotion of Cuban independence and slave emancipation, however, resulted in expulsion from Spain and the threat of death if caught. In 1823 he settled in New York City as a parish priest. There he published a philosophical, scientific, and literary newspaper, the first Catholic U.S. newspaper in Spanish. He spoke out for Cuban independence and against racism and slavery. He translated books and launched four other newspapers. As a pastor he ministered to Irish immigrants in the city, started a temperance movement, began two schools and an orphanage for children, and remodeled his church building. One cold winter he once gave his coat to a stranger on the street and regularly gave food to the hungry. He died in Florida in 1853.

What Was the Doctrine of Manifest Destiny?

This political doctrine has driven American foreign policy for almost two centuries. Its origins go back to the Puritans who, aboard ship crossing the Atlantic, heard John Winthrop challenge them to be "a city upon a hill." Their mission came from God. Himilce Novas pictures how, almost from colonial days, English colonists along the Eastern Seaboard began moving into Ohio, Indiana, and Kentucky. Actually, a dream was forming in the new nation, perhaps not yet clearly articulated, a dream of occupying the entire continent. Jefferson's purchase of Louisiana doubled the country's size. Only Mexican territory stood between America and the Pacific. The story moves along with the invasion and purchase of Florida and the purchase of Oregon; the beaver trapping trade into New Mexico; the blossoming mercantile traffic on the Santa Fe Trail; and the Anglo economic dominance that followed.

In the summer of 1845, the *United States Magazine* carried an article with the unvarnished statement that "our manifest destiny overspread the continent allotted by Providence." Both political parties began thinking the concept and mouthing the phrase. The vision was the United States as the chosen people led by God in its predestined task of spreading American sovereignty and Protestant Christianity to the benighted millions languishing in darkness. Follow the story: the Louisiana Purchase; the Monroe Doctrine that forbade Europeans from incursions into the hemisphere but gave an open door to this nation; the Anglo settlements in Texas, then the revolt, independence and annexation into the Union; the Mexican-American War of 1846 with the gain of half of Mexico's territory, with California an especially rich prize; disputes with England over Oregon; the purchase of Alaska—these were just the first fruits of a more radical dream that saw American hegemony reach from the Arctic Circle to the tip of South America. Continue viewing the story: economic penetration into the Caribbean and Central America during the later 1800s; military interventions on scores of occasions; discussion about annexing Cuba; the artificial Spanish-American War and a new empire emerging with American troops controlling Cuba, Puerto Rico, Guam, Wake Island, and the Philippines; the annexation of Hawaii; control over Pacific islands like Samoa and in the Caribbean the Virgin Islands; the Panama Canal—the story goes on.

Were the Defenders of the Alamo All Anglos?
In 1835 Texas declared itself independent from Mexico. Mexico's President Gen. **Antonio López de Santa Anna** marched an army of 1800 men northward and besieged a Texas force of 183 men in a fort at San Antonio, the Alamo. On March 6, 1836, the Mexican army attacked the Texans. A furious hour-and-a-half battle left hundreds dead and the fort in shambles. The names of Davy Crockett, James Bowie, and William Travis were afterwards inscribed in American history. Few know the

names of Mexicans on the Texan side who also died: **Juan Abamillo, Juan Badillo, Carlos Espalier, Gregorio Esparza, Antonio Fuentes, José Mária Guerrero, Toribio Losoya, Andrés Nava,** and others. **Juan Nepomuceno Seguín,** with his orderly **Antonio Cruz** and Bowie's horse, escaped the Alamo to reach Sam Houston with a plea for help.

What Mexican Became a Leader in Independent Texas?
Lorenzo de Zavala, born in southeastern Mexico in 1788, studied to be a priest, decided against it, then entered politics. He represented Mexico briefly in the Spanish Parliament and later helped write the Mexican Constitution of 1824. He served as senator, state governor, treasury minister, and representative to France. In 1829 Mexico provided him a land grant in Texas. Disliking Santa Anna, Zavala moved to his new property. This move put him in the center of action as Texas became independent. He signed the Texas Declaration of Independence, designed the first flag of the new republic, and was elected vice president in 1836. Poor health forced his resignation and his death that same year. His granddaughter, **Adina Amilia de Zavala,** struggled to save Texan historical sites and was instrumental in rescuing the Alamo from destruction.

Is It True that Texas Once Invaded New Mexico?
To be a Texan does not necessarily make one overly popular in New Mexico to this day. Texas won its independence from Mexico in 1836. Texas President Mirabeau Lamar envisioned a Republic of Texas stretching as far as the Pacific. Manifest Destiny did not ring only in Washington! Lamar thought New Mexico could be the first step in that dream. Besides, he thought Mexican control in New Mexico was weak. So, in 1841, 270 soldiers left Austin for the north. Heat, thirst, and inept leadership sapped their strength and weakened their ability to handle the unexpected Mexican resistance under Gov. **Manuel Armijo.** All 172 soldiers became prisoners and were force-marched 2,000 miles to Mexico City. While still en route through New Mexico, they were "manacled, tortured and starved." But in El Paso, compassionate care from Fray **Ramón Ortiz,** gave them a brief respite. After reaching Mexico City, some prisoners were released early, some escaped, and all were let go by Santa Anna in 1842. If other reasons today underlie some New Mexican ill will toward Texans, perhaps this "invasion" was the opener.

Did Hispanics Serve on the U.S. Side in the U.S.–Mexican War?
In 1846 American armies captured today's Southwest (New Mexico, Arizona, and California) and invaded Mexico below the Río Grande. The

American flag soon fluttered over Mexico City, and Mexico lay prostrate in defeat. That war is undoubtedly the least understood and the most embarrassing war in America's history. Even Abraham Lincoln, James Russell Lowell, and Henry Thoreau publicly opposed the conflict. In later years, Gen. U.S. Grant expressed his strong regret for the war. As in all wars, of course, men fought bravely on both sides. On the American side, Capt. **Refugio Benavides** commanded a Texas army company in action against Mexican raiders along the border. After capturing Mexico City, American Marines ever afterwards sang their song about the "Halls of Montezuma," and Mexico gained its martyred heroes in the boy cadets who died defending Chapultapec Castle against the attacking Americans (although Ilan Stavans refers to recent research that questions the historical authenticity of the story). For the U.S. Army, many officers such as Lee and Grant learned tactics utilized 14 years later on both sides of the Civil War.

What Treaty Ended a War and Still Affects the U.S. 150 Years Later?
The war ended in 1848 with the Treaty of Guadalupe Hidalgo. The Treaty recognized the border at the Río Grande. Mexico ceded half its territory, namely, Upper California, Nevada, Utah, one-third of modern Texas, New Mexico, Arizona, and parts of Oklahoma, Colorado, and Wyoming.

That treaty continues to affect the U.S. over 150 years later. In Articles VIII and IX of the Treaty, Mexicans living in the ceded territories were given the choice of American citizenship. Around 113,000 Mexicans chose to become citizens, while two or three thousand moved to Mexico. The Treaty specifically guaranteed that these new citizens would have their freedom of worship and the protection of their property titles (along with rights of sale and inheritance).

The ensuing story is documented history (see "Land Grabs" in New Mexico and California in the sections following). Two cultures, two systems of law, and two philosophies of property and rights collided. The Mexicans lost. One can trace the results in the contemporary life of the United States, which Benjamin Johnson presents succinctly: The Mexican defeat in 1848, he says, was "a watershed not because it helped catapult an Anglo-Saxon country to new heights of power, but because it eventually created a truly multi-racial nation."

How Did Hispanics React to the American Conquest in 1848?
They reacted in various ways, something perfectly normal. Manuel Gonzales tells this story. **Mariano Samaniego** practiced medicine in El

Paso, then moved to Arizona and served in city, county, and territorial governments for nearly thirty years, becoming quite an extensive land owner in the process. He helped maintain some of the power of the wealthier Hispanics in Arizona.

Donaciano Vigil was a former Mexican soldier and aide to Gov. Armijo in New Mexico. He helped repel the Texan invasion of 1841. Later he became governor of New Mexico and then a member of the territorial legislature. As a land speculator, he saw 80 percent of the Hispanics lose their land, and he may even have worked with the infamous Santa Fe Gang in land grabs against his own people.

Mariano Vallejo was a respected soldier who helped the Spanish gain control over northern California and the San Francisco area. He was given grants in the region and thus became owner of one of California's finest ranches. In subsequent political discussion, he favored U.S. annexation over that of England or France. Even though he lost much of his land after the Mexican War, his supportive feelings toward the Americans made him something like a traitor among his own people.

José Antonio Navarro was a representative to Congress from independent Texas. He participated in the failed Texan invasion of New Mexico and ended up in prison in Mexico City. After escaping, he later was elected as the only Hispanic representative to the Constitutional Convention of Texas in 1845 and voted for annexation by the United States. He supported Texan secession in the Civil War and saw four sons fight in the Confederate Army. In Reconstruction years his sympathies lay with the Ku Klux Klan.

Juan Nepomuceno Seguín was a wealthy landowner who sided with the rebellious Texans against Mexico and participated in the defense of the Alamo. He escaped just before the fateful battle, along with his orderly Antonio Cruz and Bowie's horse, to carry an appeal to Sam Houston for help. He later fought with the Texans to defeat Santa Anna at the Battle of San Jacinto. He served as mayor of San Antonio but was falsely accused of helping the Mexican Army capture the city. He fled to Mexico, was given a choice between the army and prison, and fought against the Americans in the Mexican American War. When the war ended, he returned to Texas, but harassment drove him once again back to Mexico where he died in 1890.

Pablo de la Guerra supported the Union during the Civil War. Later he served as mayor of Santa Barbara and as district judge.

Manuel Antonio Chaves helped repel the Texans in 1841, assisted in putting down the Taos rebellion, yet changed and gave his support to the

U.S. He fought in military action to pacify some of the Native American tribes and involved himself in land transactions and sheep raising.

Estevan Ochoa was mayor of Tucson and friend of the Anglo governor. He became a wealthy man through his freight business but lost much of this trade with the coming of the railroads.

These so-called Hispanic elites after Guadalupe Hidalgo were generally conservative in their desire to maintain their privileged positions, and most accommodated to the new American culture. None of this response is too surprising. It was a difficult period for these people, and some succeeded better than others. Also, it must be remembered that these men were elites who fared better than the average Mexican after the war.

How Did Hispanics Make California Gold Mining Such a Success?

Two weeks after the signing of the Treaty of Guadalupe Hidalgo in 1848, Anglos discovered gold in California's Sacramento Valley. The treaty transferred California to the U.S., so that in one year mostly Anglo hopefuls increased California's population from 20,000 to 100,000. Some 38,000 came by ship and 42,000 by land. The first to arrive, though, were Peruvian and Chilean miners, later Mexicans and Mexican Americans. The Anglos knew nothing about mining, explains Himilce Novas. So, the Latino immigrants shared their professional experience inherited from centuries past and taught those skills to the thousands of new prospectors. In other words, "the success of California mining was owed directly to the sweat of the Mexican and South American miners." Even more, because of the gold mining, California was able to gain admission to the Union faster than usual. Despite that Hispanic contribution, however, those Anglo miners turned on their teachers, claimed that all the gold was theirs, and stooped to lynchings and murder to dominate the gold business.

What Was the California Land Grab?

The San Diego area was populated by squatters, settlers, and Spanish-Mexican landowners. Then the Central Pacific Railroad came chugging in. The U.S. Congress in the Federal Land Grant Act of 1851 arbitrarily questioned all land titles (though guaranteed by the Treaty of Guadalupe Hidalgo in 1848) and even encouraged squatters to settle on the new "public lands." So Hispanic landowners had to pay taxes on their property occupied by squatters. Long-time wealth vanished in litigation costs. Squatters killed the cattle of landowners. Violence was in the air.

Next, Congress in its wisdom passed a law granting nine million acres of land to the Central Pacific Railroad monopolists. The monopoly quickly hired lobbyists and bought legislators to control California's rail routes. In 1880 even Anglo settlers and squatters lost out. The railroads told poor farmers to improve their land with orchards, vineyards and canals and to fear no higher taxes on the improvements. The farmers did so with hard work and high cost. Subsequently, the greedy railroad monopoly treacherously raised the price of the improved land and, predictably, the taxes. Farmers protested, police arrived to eject those people, and in the Mussel Slough Massacre some farmers died. Not surprisingly, those with power and money won.

What New Mexicans Participated in the Taos Indian Revolt?

During the Mexico-U.S. War in 1847, Col. Stephen Watts Kearny led the Union Army of the West and recaptured Santa Fe without one battle or even one shot. Mexican Gov. **Manuel Armijo** had dismissed his forces and fled to Chihuahua. Col. Kearny proclaimed New Mexico to be a part of the United States and all New Mexicans to be U.S. citizens. **Charles Bent** was appointed governor of the new territory. Some folks were happy for this sudden America citizenship. Others, to the contrary, resented being conquered without any fight. Also, Union garrison troops upset many people with their rowdy drinking and gambling. A plot began hatching in early 1848.

Two of the leaders were **Tomasito** from the Taos Pueblo and **Pablo Montoya.** Early in the morning of January 19, a hostile crowd of Taos Indians and native Mexicans stormed the jail and murdered the Anglo prefect. Moving to Gov. Bent's house, the mob was now after all Americans. Bent was killed and scalped. Next to die was the sheriff, the Mexican brother of the governor's wife, the district attorney, and some mill workers, traders, and trappers. The mob headed for Santa Fe, but Col. Sterling Price marched his force to meet them and overcame the rebels in a battle at Santa Cruz de la Cañada (today's Santa Cruz) and again at Embudo. Reaching the Taos Pueblo, at the San Geronimo church where the remnant had holed up for a last stand, Price's men blasted their way into the church. In the fierce fight, both sides spilled blood. Rebels fleeing were hunted down and shot. Montoya was later hanged. Tomasito was killed in his prison cell. All told, at least 17 executions took place. Sporadic rebel attacks continued under **Manuel Cortez** in eastern New Mexico and along the Santa Fe Trail, but the end of the war and the Treaty of 1848 finally ended this bloody violence.

Why Is Father Antonio José Martínez Famous?

Father **Antonio José Martínez** was a native-born New Mexican and a Catholic priest, scholar, and educator. When the territory became Mexican after independence from Spain, money for education dried up. So Fr. Martínez started a school. He was the faculty. He bought a printing press (in today's U.S. the first press west of the Mississippi) and printed his own textbooks, bibles, and pamphlets. He courageously sheltered terrified targets in the Taos Revolt and saved their lives. He served in the Mexican Assembly, the Legislative Assembly under the American military government, the Territorial Legislature, the Territorial Constitutional Convention, and presided over the first Legislative Assembly. After the American takeover in 1846, Gen. Stephen Kearny invited Fr. Martínez to become a U.S. citizen, which made him the first New Mexican American citizen.

Since the priest exercised nearly total authority in his parish, and resisted paying for the new St. Francis Cathedral in Santa Fe, Archbishop Lamy determined to bring ecclesiastical law and order to that parish (the story may be read in Willa Cather's *Death Comes for the Archbishop*). Lamy excommunicated the padre, but Martínez immediately founded his own independent church and carried on as the local priest.

Who Were Some Hispanic Women Across the Early Centuries?

The names of Mexican and Mexican American women are often overlooked. With Himilce Novas's assistance, here are some specifics. **Francisca de Hozas** accompanied Coronado. Her map skills kept him from getting hopelessly lost. She also helped him organize his effort more efficiently. Two other women in that journey were **María Maldonado** and Señora **Caballero.** Similarly, in the mining camps of California's gold rush, tough women took their place and generally more than held their own (see "Loretta Jane Velásquez" in the Civil War section below).

Which Hispanics Saw Civil War Action?

While historians debate the question, Joyce Valdez informs us that possibly 200,000 Hispanics wore the blue and gray. "Hispanics from Mexico, Spain, Cuba, Puerto Rico and other parts of Latin America...huddled in trenches with Johnny Reb or Billy Yank." Katherine Díaz reports that the Union recruited Mexican American Californians into the First Battalion of Native Cavalry, commanded by Maj. **Salvador Vallejo.** New Mexico Col. **Miguel E. Pino** commanded volunteer units and Gen. **Stanilus Montoya** commanded militia units. Another unit that served was the 55th New

York State Militia that carried the name The Garde Lafayette. Approximately 2,500 Hispanic Texans fought for the Confederacy, and 950 for the Union, including some Mexican nationals.

Loretta Jane Velásquez was born in Cuba. She enlisted in the Confederate Army by impersonating her dead soldier-husband and disguising herself as a man. She fought in the battles of Bull Run and Balls' Bluff in Virginia and at Fort Donelson in Tennessee. In 1862 her disguise was discovered, and she was promptly discharged. But she re-enlisted, fought at Shiloh in 1862, then was again discovered and discharged the second time. Never one to give up, her next job was spying for the South. Following the war she traveled to the West to look for a new husband. In Omaha she charmed old Gen. W. S. Harney into providing her with a buffalo robe, some blankets, and a revolver with which she moved into the Nevada mining camps. By the end of two days in Austin, Nevada, a sixty-year-old man proposed, but she found a younger fellow a few days later and lived many happy years of married life with him.

Federico Fernández Cavada, Cuban-born, became a captain and engineer in the Union forces and was put in charge of hot-air balloons used to spy on the Confederates. He participated in the battles of Antietam, Fredericksburg, and Gettysburg. Captured at Gettysburg, he was sent to the infamous Confederate Libby Prison in Richmond, Virginia. While in that terrible place he wrote and drew pictures on old newspapers and scrap paper, hid them in socks and shoes, and after his release in 1864 wrote *Libby Life* with vivid accounts of the horror that he had endured.

José Agustín Quintero in the Confederate Army took charge of Confederate supply routes from Europe via northern Mexico. Col. **Santos Benavides,** formerly a Texas Ranger, a rancher, and political figure in Laredo, Texas, commanded the Confederate Benavides Regiment. Made up of Mexican Americans, they defeated Union forces in the 1864 Battle of Laredo. Benavides also slew the Union guerrilla chief, Octaviano Zapata. Rising to the rank of Major, he was the highest-ranking Hispanic in the armies of the South. **Ambrosio José González** became artillery officer under Confederate Gen. P.G.T. Beauregard in Charleston and later became a leader in Cuba's struggle to gain independence from Spain. **Julio P. Garesch du Rocher,** a Cuban with French background, served the Union forces as strategist and chief of staff to Gen. William Rosecrans only to be decapitated by a cannon ball at the Battle of Stone's River. Lt. Col. **Manuel Chaves** fought for Mexico in the U.S. Mexican War, afterwards becoming a U.S. citizen in 1848. As a volunteer in the Civil War, he saw action at the Battle of Glorieta Pass. But, in that same battle, **José Francisco Chaves,** fought in the Union Army and helped recapture areas around Albuquerque and Santa Fe. Capt. **Refugio Benavides** commanded a Texas army company against Mexican raiders along the border.

David Farragut was the most famous Hispanic in that war. Son of **Jorge (George) Farragut** and an Anglo mother, he was born in Tennessee in 1801 and changed his original name of James to David to honor David Porter, the naval captain who adopted him and taught him naval tactics. He fought in the War of 1812, against pirates in the West Indies, and in an attack on Veracruz, Mexico, in 1822. As a naval officer on the Union side in the Civil War, he captured New Orleans in 1862 and later took Confederate forts along the Mississippi, thus cutting enemy supply and communication routes so that Gen. Grant could capture Vicksburg. In 1864 he captured Mobile, Alabama, using ironclad submarines and wooden ships. Leading the attack with one of those wooden vessels against Confederate torpedoes, he uttered his famous command: "Damn the torpedoes! Full speed ahead!" At the White House for a brief service just before taking the body of the assassinated President Lincoln to the Capitol, among the high and mighty of the land and from abroad who stood by the casket, next to Gen. Grant and his generals was Adm. Farragut in his much-decorated uniform. The United States Congress created the rank of Admiral of the Navy to honor him.

Which Hispanics Were Early Recipients of the Medal of Honor?

The nation's highest military award, the Congressional Medal of Honor, was established by Congress in 1861. Several Hispanic men were awarded the early Congressional Medals of Honor: Seaman **John Ortega** (USN) from Spain fought gallantly in two battles in 1864. Seaman **Philip Bazaar** (USN) from Chile carried dispatches in the face of heavy Confederate fire. Corp. **Joseph H. de Castro** was awarded the medal. Pvt. **France Silva** in 1900 received the award for action in the Boxer Rebellion in Peking, China.

What Was the New Mexico Land Grab?

At the time of the Treaty of Guadalupe Hidalgo in 1848, prosperous Mexican ranches dotted the New Mexico Territory. Article VIII of the Treaty promised that Mexicans who chose to remain rather than go to Mexico would become American citizens, and their land's security would be guaranteed—later deleted but reinstated the same year in the Protocol of Querétaro. Unfortunately, as Americans poured into the newly won territory, by means fair and foul, and within decades, once-prosperous land owners lost land that their families had held for over 200 years. They became the new poor, a process stated clearly by syndicated columnist Linda Chavez and by *Albuquerque Journal* journalist Frankie McCarty.

In 2001, the U.S. General Accounting Office released the first part of its study on old land grants. Their conclusion stated that since 1848 only 25 percent of 152 land grant claims have been validated by Congress and the courts. Senators Pete Domenici and Jeff Bingaman, who pushed for the study, vow to pursue justice for New Mexico land grant heirs. Marisa Trevio quotes one of those heirs who stated that so many of northern New Mexico's troubles stem from this unresolved issue, problems such as school dropouts, drug use, and disintegration of Spanish American culture.

How could this legal but unjust theft ever happen? Rodolfo Acuña makes clear that the Anglos simply used their own imported legal system that Mexicans did not understand, and at the same time malevolently distorted that system.

1. Land registration notices were posted but were not easy to find, and they were in English for people who could read only Spanish. Overdue deadlines meant loss of lands.
2. Taxes were higher for Mexican ranchers, lower for Americans. Non-payment of taxes meant loss of lands.
3. Anglos ran the banks and charged high interest. Non-payment on bank loans meant foreclosure and loss of lands.
4. Anglo land speculators overgrazed their lands and overcut their timber. Result: erosion and ruin for neighboring small farmers.
5. Government reclamation projects like dams charged farmers. If the farmers could not pay, they lost their lands.
6. Large corporations obtained huge farm areas and crowded out small farmers in the price competition. Those farmers had to sell and thus lost their lands.
7. Railroads gained land by government decree. Mexican farmers and ranchers lost their lands.
8. Village forest land taken over by the National Forest Service received better conservation of resources, but traditional common use of the forests and pastures outside of the towns was destroyed. Even from Aztec culture, land belonged to no one individual but rather to the community. The Forest Service reduced pasture areas and grazing times for sheep and goats. Fences cut across formerly open land, something considered almost sacrilegious. Village spinning and weaving in home industries began disappearing. Villagers complained that grazing permits were too expensive, and that most of them went to large stock owners. In Suzanne Forrest's

analysis, this conflict over forest land explains much of the decline and death of many villages in north central New Mexico. The issue also simmers in present-day hostility of villagers against the Forest Service.

How Did Hispanics Contribute to the Early Prosperity of the West?

The development of the cattle industry in South Texas has already been described. Oñate brought along sheep on his expedition, so sheep-raising became an industry for New Mexico, Colorado, and parts of California and created enormous wealth. Copper found in southern Arizona led to the huge copper mines. The sweaty toil of Mexican miners contributed billions of dollars to American and other investors. Mexicans were the teamsters moving the mule caravans with commerce from the East. They worked also as section hands and laborers maintaining the spreading railroad lines. Juan González lifts up this story of Hispanic contribution to the wealth of the West and decries its absence in popular frontier history. Instead, that story gets replaced by "the enduring myth of the lazy, shiftless Mexican."

Who Was the Outlaw Named Joaquín Murieta?

Three *bandidos* (outlaws) over the last half of the 19th century came to epitomize the Mexican-American frustration after the Treaty of Guadalupe Hidalgo in 1848. **Joaquín Murieta** (sometimes spelled Murrieta) lived in the early 1850s. As described by Himilce Novas, Murieta was an ordinary California gold miner. He exploded, however, when Anglos stole his rich land claim, murdered his brother and raped his wife. With a gang of four other Joaquins—**Venequela, Ocormorenia, Carillo, Botellier**—he began a wild revenge spree, killing, robbing, even setting a fire that destroyed the mining town of Stockton. In 1853 the gang stole gold and livestock from miners in the foothills of the Sierra Madre mountains.

Official reports at the time radically differ, according to Susan Lee Johnson. Therefore, it is difficult to know for sure if Murieta was "a crazed, dark-skinned, vicious outlaw who slaughtered unprotected miners, or a righteous avenger punishing Anglos...," a modern-day Robin Hood. Whatever, he was a true desperado (from the Spanish *desesperado*, meaning desperate one). Understandably, the California legislature demanded Murieta's capture. The State of California offered a $1,000,000 reward. A temporary Ranger force was assembled to chase after this gang. One day a shoot-out killed two Mexicans. Later a head and a hand, supposedly of Murieta, were displayed in jars of alcohol but with no real proof of identity.

In 1854 John Rolin Ridge wrote a book about Murieta's life. Subsequent paperbacks and poems helped create a legend that years later made its way to Hollywood and the Cisco Kid film. Like the Robin Hood tale in England, this legend remains one of the myths of our country.

How Did an Outlaw Get a War Named after Him?

Juan Nepomuceno Cortina was known as "the red robber of the Río Grande." Both Carey McWillimas and Américo Paredes detail how in 1859 Cortina shot a Brownsville city marshall because the fellow was trying to arrest a Mexican who had been a servant of Cortina's mother. Stimulated by such an experience, Cortina led an armed force into Brownsville, killed 5 Americans, emptied the jail, and looted stores. He virtually destroyed the 550-mile area between Brownsville and Río Grande City, and in the process killed 15 Americans and 80 Mexicans in his raids.

The Civil War erupted and the French invasion of Mexico occurred. As with most U.S. Mexicans, Cortina supported the Union cause on the Lower Border and the Liberal Party of Benito Juárez in Mexico. Union agents enlisted guerrillas like Cortina for raids both against Confederates on one side of the border and Maximilian's imperial forces on the other. All in all, for 15 years he eluded desperate attempts to capture him, defeating both Texas Rangers and Mexican troops as he scampered back and forth across the Mexican–U.S. border. As a bandit and cattle thief, his reputation among Mexicans was more like a hero, like another Mexican Robin Hood. But authorities both in the U.S. and Mexico were having fits of frustration over the wily outlaw. Finally, in 1873, Mexico's President **Porfirio Díaz** ended the Cortina War when his soldiers captured the desperado and kept him a prisoner for the rest of Cortina's life. And that is the story of the Cortina War.

Was Gregorio Cortez a Hero or an Outlaw?

Described by Américo Paredes, this story concerns **Gregorio Cortez** who had recently traded a mare (female) for a stallion (male). On the afternoon of June 12, 1901, he received a visit by several Texas Rangers on suspicion that he was a horse thief. Using inadequate Spanish, one officer asked Gregorio if he had traded a horse (*caballo,* stallion, male) to another man. Cortez answered, "No." This answer was correct, because he had traded a mare (*yegua,* female). The Rangers then attempted to arrest Gregorio. Innocent but in peril, Gregorio shot and killed the sheriff. Of course, he had to flee his home. Traveling for ten days, first north, then south, over rough terrain and barbed wire fences and even across rivers, Gregorio covered more than four hundred miles and wore out three mares. Weak from lack of food and sleep, then betrayed by a man he knew, the fugitive was finally caught and arrested. After a series of trials, he was sentenced to twelve years in prison, but in 1913 he was granted a pardon by the governor of Texas.

Somewhere during those years the ballad originated and took on many forms. History got mixed with legend, but each version celebrates this Mexican who was caught "with his pistol in his hand, ah, so many mounted Rangers just to take one Mexican." Paredes tells us that men still sing this ballad in stores and on ranches in the cool of the night as they recall the tales of days long gone.

Why Were Mexican Hispanics
Less Powerful Than Anglos in the Southwest?
Oscar Martínez explains how in the 1880s the American economy changed drastically. Large corporations in a capitalist structure crowded out small businesses. This effect was clearly evident in railroading, mining, ranching, and agriculture. Demographic change came as Anglo arrivals in the Southwest soon outnumbered the Mexican American population. Young and middle-aged Anglo entrepreneurs possessed financial resources and political connections that an aging Mexican population simply could not match.

Now we can understand why Arizona, when the Territory separated from the New Mexico Territory in 1863, moved its capital to Phoenix rather than to Tucson with its high Mexican population. Anglos feared Hispanic political domination from New Mexico and proceeded to use political muscle. A 1906 proposal to admit Arizona and New Mexico as one state into the Union was firmly rejected by Arizona. The two Territories became separate states in 1912.

In 1902 Texas instituted a poll tax and later added other ingenious tricks for disenfranchisement. In 1919, in Corpus Christi, Texas Rangers threatened imprisonment of anyone who couldn't speak English and tried to vote. The Ku Klux Klan in El Paso in 1922 used harassment against Mexican American voters. Workers feared being fired at their jobs if they got involved politically. For Mexican Americans, therefore, the field was in no way level.

What Was Happening in Puerto Rico?

Resistance to Spanish rule was spreading. Navas lists some of the patriots who led efforts toward freedom. **Ramón Power** in the early 1800s was one of the first to bring the Puerto Rican situation to Spain's attention and was able to negotiate a more liberal constitution for Puerto Rico. **José María Quiñones** urged independence from Spain, whereupon Spain sent a more despotic governor. **Ramón Emeterio Betances,** a physician, was exiled for expressing revolutionary ideas.

In 1868 he issued his Ten Commandments of Freedom, similar to our Bill of Rights, and called for an end to slavery. Thousands of Puerto Ricans joined him in the town of Lares in the western part of the island. With guns and machetes the crowd took control of the town, but soon they were overcome by Spanish troops. *El Grito de Lares* (the Cry of Lares) was a cry of revolt. On September 23 that event gets celebrated as a national holiday on the island and in the States.

Luis Muñoz Rivera forged a union of similar Puerto Rican political parties. The poet **José de Diego** and **Pedro Albizu Campos** wrote and organized for independence. Another patriot, **José Celso Barbosa,** led another party. Ironically, in 1897 Spain granted the islanders local government, control over taxes, budgets, and education. Muñoz won the election for governor. Seven days later the U.S. invaded and made the island a protectorate. Free for seven days! Afterwards, Muños Rivera, "the spiritual governor of Puerto Rico," worked to overcome the Foraker Act (restricting the island to a mere territorial status, with fewer rights than Spain had given earlier). Ever since that "freedom," in Juan Flores's explanation, the one-star flag (*la monoestrellada*), while always flying loyally along with the American flag, has become "the most venerated emblem of the Puerto Rican nationality." **Eugenio María de Hostos** in Puerto Rico and in the U.S. agitated for independence along with **Ruiz Belvis.**

What Was Happening in Cuba?

Cuba had long existed on the American radar screen as territory that logically ought to be American. John Quincy Adams when Secretary of State proposed the idea. Presidents James Polk and Franklin Pierce offered Spain a purchase price of millions of dollars. The reason was Cuba's existence in the path of Manifest Destiny. By the 1880s, trade with Cuba amounted to one-fourth of America's world commerce. The island was even then an American colony economically, as Juan González tells the story. Trouble, meanwhile, was rumbling between Spain and Cuba.

By the mid–1800s an African-Cuban led an uprising against Spain. He was **Antonio Maceo,** along with **Carlos Manuel de Céspedes, Máximo Gómez,** and **José Martí.** Spain simply tightened its authoritarian grip on the island while dissatisfaction simmered. On October 10, 1868, rebellion-minded Cubans gathered at a little town called Yara. They issued *el Grito de Yara* (the Cry of Yara, like Fr. Hidalgo in Mexico in 1810, and the Cry of Lares in Puerto Rico). They even proclaimed Cuba's independence. A murderous ten years of civil war ensued, with the Spanish destroying property and executing prisoners until the island lay desolate. Another patriot in the ten year struggle was **Ignacio Agramonte.** He signed the 1869 decree abolishing slavery, and he wrote and signed the first constitution of the Cuban nation. **Pedro "Perucho" Figueredo** wrote the hymn that became the national anthem. He was taken prisoner by the Spanish and executed in 1870. Into this devastation moved U.S. corporations who easily acquired the vast sugar plantations. Toward the end of the 1800s, Americans owned 80 percent of the island's sugar mills. Cuba had become a single-crop economy.

**Why at This Time Did Cuba
Expect to Achieve Independence from Spain?**
José Martí y Pérez was the Cuban equivalent of George Washington and Thomas Jefferson, in Himilce Novas's evaluation. Martí was a brilliant political leader. He was also a prolific poet, orator, writer (his complete works fill 32 volumes), critic, newspaperman, historian, teacher, diplomat, and economist. Lines from one of his poems were used in the song *Guantanamera.* Martí suffered arrest and exile more than once as he joined the struggle for Cuban independence. His views on a better Cuba were remarkably progressive for his time. He also warned against absorption by the U.S. Death came in battle against Spanish forces at Dos Ríos in 1895.

At this time also, Winston Churchill began his exceptional exploits as a 22–year–old war correspondent reporting on the revolt, and acquiring his life-long taste for Cuban cigars. Men like Gen. **Calixto García,** Gen. **Máximo Gómez** and revolutionary **Antonio Maceo** carried on where Martí left off and looked forward to victory by 1898. But the prospects of an independent Cuba only 90 miles from Florida made American leadership nervous. The battleship Maine blew up mysteriously in Havana harbor. Congress declared war. American troops invaded Cuba. Teddy Roosevelt had his military thrill with his Rough Riders. At the end, the U.S. found itself in charge of Puerto Rico, Cuba, the Philippines, and Guam and Wake Island in the mid Pacific. In 1906, through the Platt Amendment, the U.S. granted Cuba its sovereignty, but also kept the ideal site in eastern Cuba, Guantánamo Bay, as a naval base. Cuba's first elected president was **Ramón Grau San Martín.**

When Did Hispanics Fight Against Spain?

When the battleship Maine blew up in Havana harbor in 1898, the U.S. accused Spain of being responsible, probably incorrectly. American newspapers whipped American anger into a force that exploded into a 115-day war.

Marc Simmons relates how New Mexico's territorial governor, **Miguel Antonio Otero,** promptly called up the National Guard and offered them to the cause. The War Department requested three regiments of cowboys, many of them Hispanics. One of the first to receive a captain's commission was **Maximiliano Luna** from Los Lunas, New Mexico. The First U.S. Volunteer Cavalry Regiment formed under the command of Col. Theodore Roosevelt; Sgt. **George Washington Armijo** from Santa Fe was his aide. Others were Privates **G.W. Arringo, José M. Baca, Frank C. Brito, Abel B. Durán, Joseph L. Durán,** and **Joe T. Sandoval.** The cowboys called themselves the Rough Riders.

Dale Walker describes the total confusion at the final staging area in Tampa, Florida; a shortage of horses meant that only certain troops could sail for the invasion of Cuba. Thousands of volunteers muttered with bitter disappointment. But Capt. Maximiliano Luna confronted his general and boldly stated that as "the only pure-blooded Spaniard in the regiment," he needed to get into the action and prove that the loyalty of Mexican Americans was equal to any of the others. He was given command of Troop F. In the sometimes chaotic assault up San Juan Hill (actually Kettle Hill), Roosevelt took command of a squadron from New Mexico consisting of Troop E. Capt. Luna led Troop F. The furious charge on foot to the top remains one of America's most dramatic stories. Elsewhere, in the Battle of Guasimas, Roosevelt's aide, **George Armijo,** was wounded.

How Did the U.S. View
Latin America at the End of the 19th Century?

The U.S., since the early years of the 19th century, had promoted its vision of "Manifest Destiny," the vision of the U.S. as God's "City on a Hill" with a divine mandate to civilize and "Christianize" the unfortunate primitives of Latin America. On the other hand, Latin Americans (and Mexicans in particular) had watched Florida, Texas, and half of Mexico disappear into the North American shopping basket. They had witnessed William Walker's antics in Nicaragua. Mexicans had experienced arrogant treatment by U.S. diplomats, racist references in American newspapers, and "massive economic penetration" (Juan González's phrase) that had turned Mexico, the Dominican Republic, Central America, and Spain's colonies of Puerto Rico and Cuba into American "economic satellites"—necessitating at least 19 military interventions. Latin Americans admired the United States. Some nations wrote their constitutions on the American model. In wars for independence, nations pleaded for American military aid. After victory, they pursued friendship and requested more assistance. The reception was cold.

20TH CENTURY
Why Should We Include Here the Dominican Republic's Story?

This Caribbean country that shares an island with Haiti has a story so similar to that of other Latin American nations that it would not be necessary to add further illustrations. But the Dominican population in the U.S. has surged in the past forty years. In New York City by 1990, the Dominican population had risen to 300,000 and was the second-largest Hispanic group in the Northeast.

Juan González relates the Dominican story. Independent in 1844, by 1882 half of all Dominican trade was with the U.S. The U.S. extended debt relief but in effect took over the country's finances. In 1916 President Wilson sent in Marines who established martial law and occupied the nation for eight years. Guerrilla warfare and atrocities on both sides followed. By the 1920s, Americans owned more than 80 percent of the island's arable land. The U.S. built a police force that kept dictator **Rafael Trujillo** in power for thirty years. His "psychotic cruelty" appears in Gabriel Márquez's novel *The Autumn of the Patriarch*. In 1961 the CIA helped arrange Trujillo's assassination. Mario Vargas Llosa has recently written another novel about the Trujillo era, *The Feast of the Goat*. A TIME book review called the book "harrowing." Trujillo's death, according to Juan Flores, removed the prevailing barriers for migration. According to Ilan Stavans, the economy declined severely.

Those facts, plus civil war and American military invasion, pushed many Dominicans to emigrate to the U.S. In 1966 the people, in their first democratic election, chose **Juan Bosch** as president, but President Lyndon Johnson sent in marines and placed **Joaquín Balaguer** in office. That turmoil sparked more of the massive flight of Dominicans to the U.S. Political violence along with insufferable poverty in the next thirty years had the same effect. One immigrant lamented that her people were "in love with their island but unable to live there." If more U.S. visas were available, the immigrant continued, no one would be left in her homeland. But Dominicans were not political refugees, said the U.S. Government, and therefore were not entitled to any governmental benefits as the Cubans received. These immigrants, however, were better educated and very politically active. In the U.S. they began successful businesses by the thousands. Unfortunately, their black skin color caused more racial discrimination than most other Hispanics experienced.

**Who Were New Mexico's
Influential Politicians in the New Century?**
One such person was **Maximiliano Luna.** Dale Walker says that after Luna's military service in the Spanish American War, he returned to New Mexico, helped draft the state Constitution in 1910, and later became speaker of the state House. During the insurrection in the Philippines, he re-enlisted to serve under Gen. Leonard Wood, and died there by drowning.

Another gentleman was **Miguel Antonio Otero** who served as governor of the New Mexico Territory between 1897 and 1906. During that time he worked hard toward statehood. That goal was realized in 1912. While in office, he began the custom of pardoning a deserving convict on Christmas, New Year's Day, Fourth of July, and Thanksgiving Day.

A third outstanding individual was **Octaviano A. Larrazolo,** who was born in Mexico and later resided in Texas, Arizona, and New Mexico. As a Democrat he tried and failed three times to win a seat in the U.S. House of Representatives. So he switched to the Republican Party and won the office of governor. In 1928 he became the first Hispanic member of the U.S. Senate. It is said that colleagues were surprised that "this Mexican could speak English so fluently." Illness kept him from serving more than two years, and he died soon after leaving Washington.

How Did the Mexican Revolution Impact the U.S.?
Benito Juárez was undoubtedly Mexico's greatest president, often called Mexico's Lincoln. That would make Lincoln Mexico's Juárez. Juárez's unfortunate death in 1872 allowed **Porfirio Díaz** to climb to power and rule as dictator for 35 years (*el porfiriato*). He dismantled most of the reforms instituted by Juárez, imposed strict law and order, handed the country to foreign investors, strengthened the power of rich Mexican landowners, reduced the amount of land for the peasants, built a railroad system from Mexican mines to U.S. rail lines, and sold much of Mexico's mineral rights to millionaires in the U.S. and other countries. The gap between the rich and the poor widened. Food shortages, rising prices, unemployment, labor unrest, mounting national debt, all were confront-

ed with the usual governmental lethargy. Profits fled Mexico to New York, London, and Paris. At some point, also, Mexican liberals began resenting their exclusion from the President's restricted power circle.

This mounting social debris awaited only a spark to set off a national conflagration. That spark was the Mexican Revolution. From 1910 into the 1920s, Mexico became convulsed in violent and bloody chaos. To put it mildly, the story is extremely complex. Names rise and fall: **Madero, Huerta, Zapata, Villa, Carranza,** Woodrow Wilson, Gen. John J. Pershing, and **Obregón.** When the turmoil finally subsided, Mexico was devastated (one in ten Mexicans had died, buildings and infrastructure lay in ruins). The nation witnessed some land distribution and a new Constitution. The political power of the Roman Catholic Church was diminished, and one political party (PRI) gained control that lasted for 71 years (PRI finally lost the presidential election in 2001).

A positive result was a political stability that our southern neighbor maintained over the following decades, a feat unsurpassed anywhere else in Latin America. The Mexican Revolution impacted the U.S. Thousands of refugees fled across the border and settled here, and many became U.S. citizens. This influx had already begun before the Revolution as desperate poverty drove *campesinos* (peasants) from the Central Plateau to the American companies along the northern border and eventually to the even higher wages across that border. From 1850 to 1900, according to Oscar Martínez, Mexican immigration rose from 13,317 to 103,393. Then, during the violent turbulence of the Revolution, this flood of refugees expanded. As a result, a half-century of immigration became the base of today's Mexican American, Chicano, Latino, and Hispanic community in the U.S. From 1940 to mid-1960, 400,000 Mexicans entered legally. No figures are available for the number of undocumented entries. Let us realize, then, that the Hispanic experience in the southwestern U.S. can be comprehended only in the light of the Treaty of Guadalupe Hidalgo in 1848 and the repercussions of the Mexican Revolution of 1910. American society was forever changed.

Which Hispanics Fought in World War I?
Records are incomplete on how many Hispanics served during World War I. We do know that nearly 20,000 Puerto Ricans served in the various U.S. military forces, and the Puerto Rican people bought over $10 million worth of war bonds. Around 65 percent of New Mexico's volunteers and draftees were Hispanos. The 129 homes (the 1910 count) in tiny Chimayó, New Mexico, gave 41 of its youth to the American cause in the Great War. Certain individuals stand out. **Nicolás Lucero** was pre-

sented the French Croix de Guerre for valor in action against enemy fire. Pvt. **David Barkley** won the Medal of Honor. **Marcos B. Armijo** received the Distinguished Service Cross for valor in France in 1918 but was killed in combat 4 days later.

Then there is the heroism of Pvt. **Marcelino Serna.** As described by Joe Olvera, this Mexican youth living in the U.S. found himself in Europe fighting the Germans. By the end of the war he had killed 32 Germans and had captured 30 others. Italy and France awarded him their highest military honors, the Italian Cross of Merit and the French Croix de Guerre with Palm. The U.S. gave him its Distinguished Service Cross, as well as the Purple Heart with Cluster.

He became a citizen in 1924. Now in his '90s, he resides in El Paso. The Veterans of Foreign Wars have made strong efforts to get Serna a belated Congressional Medal of Honor. The reason given in 1919 for not awarding him this honor was that he was a mere buck private, spoke poor English, and was not a U.S. citizen, none of which were requirements. Efforts continue to move the government to correct this injustice.

Which New Mexico Woman Enabled Others in the Early 1900s?

Nina Otero Warren became a part of women's efforts to enter political campaigns and public office. She participated in the women's suffrage movement of 1916–1917, served as superintendent of the Santa Fe school system, and helped New Mexico become the 32nd state to ratify the Constitutional Amendment of 1920 that gave women the right to vote. In later years she worked in various public agencies and federal programs.

Who Was a Distinguished New Mexican Soldier and Legislator Almost Unknown Today?

Profiled by Jacqueline Meketa, **Rafael Chacón** (1833–1925) was a 13–year-old Mexican military cadet who served under Armijo when Gen. Stephen Kearny's forces marched toward Santa Fe. He served in American military operations against raiding Indian groups, commanded Union volunteer companies at the Battle of Valverde in the Civil War, commanded Fort Stanton, and achieved the rank of Army major. He was a territorial legislator for several terms and later homesteaded at Trinidad, Colorado. His memoirs, written when he was 70, give invaluable documentation of western history from the Mexican period into the America of modern times.

Which Hispanics Fought in World War II?

Perhaps as many as 500,000 Hispanics served in World War II. The first draftee in the war was **Pete Aguilar Despart,** a Mexican American from Los Angeles. Latinos were an important part of action in all theaters of action around the world and often were among the first casualties. No other ethnic group provided as many men in overseas combat.

Chicanos received more Congressional Medals of Honor than any other ethnic group. Among these men was **José López** from Brownsville, Texas. In the invasion of Normandy in 1944, he held off a German counterattack practically by himself. This machine gunner killed over 100 enemy troops in this engagement, more than any other American during the war.

Sgt. **Lorenzo Gonzales** was captured by the Germans after the crossing of the Remagen Bridge and was severely wounded by beatings from German captors. After escaping, Gonzales was treated by British medics, then was wounded again in the Battle of the Bulge. He never received his Purple Heart. When he inquired, he was told that because American medics did not treat him, army records had been destroyed. The time limit had passed. Nothing could be done. To this day, not even his Congressman's advocacy has budged the Pentagon to give Gonzales his medal and 20 months of delayed combat pay.

Raúl Morín lists other Hispanics in that war. At the war's outbreak in 1941, 43 out of 107 men had Hispanic names in the 200th Coast Artillery in the Philippines. Many were from New Mexico and with their comrades fought in the retreat down the Bataan Peninsula to Corregidor Island. They suffered and some died on the dreadful Bataan Death march to Japanese prison camps.

Not at all to be forgotten are the thousands of Hispanic women who served in all the wars. Cuban women gave financial aid in the American Revolution. Cuban-born **Loretta Janet Velásquez** fought in the Civil War. Katharine A. Díaz tells how in World WAr II about 200 Puerto Rican women served in the Women's Army Corps. Hispanic civilians like "Rosita the Riveter" did welding, electrical work and plane and ship building or took jobs in government offices.

These men received the Congressional Medal of Honor in World War II: Pvt. **José P. Martínez** (Posthumously), killed on Attu in the Aleutians and first in the Pacific Theater to get this award; Staff Sgt. **Luciano Adams** (European Theater); Staff Sgt. **Macario García** (European Theater); Pfc. **Harold Gonsales** (S. Pacific Theater); Pfc. **David Gonzales** (Posthumously, S. Pacific Theater); Pfc. **Silvestre Herrera** (European Theater); Pfc. **Manuel Pérez Jr.** (Posthumously, S. Pacific Theater); Tech. Sgt. **Cleto Rodríguez** (S. Pacific Theater); Sgt. **Alejandro Ruiz** (South Pacific Theater); Pfc. **José F. Valdez** (Posthumously, European Theater);

Staff Sgt. **Ysmael R. Villegas** (South Pacific Theater); Sgt. Maj. **Roy P. Benavídez;** Lance Cpl. **Emilio de la Garza** (USMC); Sgt. **Alfredo González** (USMC); Lance Cpl. **José Francisco Jiménez** (USMC); Lance Cpl. **Miguel Keith** (USMC); Pfc. **Carlos J. Lozada;** Pfc. **Alejandro R. Rentería;** Sgt. **Louis R. Rocco;** Capt. **Eurípedes Rubio;** Spec. 4th Cl. **Héctor Santiago Colón;** Maj. **Jay R. Vargas Jr.** (USMC); Sgt. **Máximo Yabes.**

Hispanics received other military honors. The All-Chicano Infantry Company E, 141st Regiment, 36th (TX) Division, fought bravely at Salerno and at the Rapido River in Italy. Sgt. **Manuel S. Gonzales** received the Distinguished Service Cross. Capt. **Gabriel Navarrete** was awarded the Distinguished Service Cross, Bronze Star, two Silver Stars, and was recommended for the Congressional Medal of Honor but denied it because he stood up just as bravely to Army brass. Here are some others: Staff Sgt. **Augustín Lucio:** Silver Star, Bronze Star, Purple Heart, French Croix de Guerre (European Theater); Marine Pfc. **Guy L. Gabaldón:** Silver Star (South Pacific Theater) for capturing over 1000 Japanese prisoners; Navy Pharmacist's Mate Third Class **Carlos V. Porras Jr.:** Silver Star (South Pacific Theater) for capturing over 1,000 Japanese prisoners; Air Force Lt. Col. **José Holguín:** Distinguished Flying Cross and Oak Leaf Cluster (South Pacific).

How Did Mexico Support the U.S. in World War II?
Gordon Dickson and Archie Waters tell this story. At first, Mexico was neutral in World War II. After German subs sank several Mexican ships in the Gulf of Mexico, the nation declared war "to save its honor." Though it had perhaps 60,000 men in its Army and Navy, in 1942 it decided instead to send a token volunteer force, the 201st Mexican Fighter Squadron with its 35 officers and 300 enlisted men. In 1945 the squadron deployed to the Philippines and attached to the 58th Fighter Group. The relatively inexperienced men flew 50 combat missions, dropped 180 tons of bombs, and lost seven pilots in aerial combat. Add 293 sorties to the count. This record compares favorably with that of the American veteran 58th Fighter Group. The men returned to Mexico as heroes. U.S. Gen. George C. Kenney went to Mexico to pin medals on the men, one of whom was **Carlos Garduño** who lives now in El Paso. **Carlos Faustinos** flew 25 missions and shot down six Japanese Zeros. Mexico awarded him *La Cruz de Honor* (the Cross of Honor), Mexico's equivalent of the U.S. Medal of Honor.

What Else Did Mexico Contribute to the War and Afterwards?
Thousands of Mexican nationals were recruited during World War II in

an effort called the Bracero Program (from *brazo*, meaning arm, thus typically a farm worker). With so many American men gone into military service, around 250,000 Mexican workers between 1942–1947 provided invaluable farm and factory labor. A second phase of the program, under Public Law 78, functioned from 1945–1964. Over 4.5 million Mexican nationals came to work on farms, in trucking, and on the railroads. Despite laws that gave the workers the minimum wage and basic labor rights, many unscrupulous and prejudiced employers purposely provided poor food and inadequate housing, deducted wages illegally, inflicted physical punishment, and exposed workers to dangerous pesticides. The program was cancelled in 1964, but the program did provide considerable benefits both during and after the War to the states of Texas, California, Arizona, New Mexico, Colorado, and Michigan.

After the mid-'60s, Mexicans spread beyond the Southwest. Oscar Martínez depicts the Mexicans who came to cultivate mushrooms in Pennsylvania, build offices in Atlanta, milk cows in Idaho, harvest tobacco in North Carolina, slaughter pigs in Iowa, manicure lawns in New Jersey, wash dishes in Michigan, clean fish in Maryland, and bale hay in South Dakota.

What Is Luis Muños Marín's Importance in Puerto Rico?
Luis Muñoz Marín, son of the patriot leader **Luis Muñoz Rivera,** became the first Puerto Rican to be elected governor of the territory and was re-elected overwhelmingly three more times. He created the idea of tax-free status for new industries and promoted Operation Bootstrap that stimulated industrial growth. His other efforts moved the U.S. Congress in 1950 to change the island's status to a commonwealth linked to the U.S. Two other achievements were to create the Puerto Rican flag and to lead in the composition of a new constitution in 1952. Constitution Day on July 25 is a Puerto Rican holiday.

Did Puerto Ricans Try to Assassinate President Truman?
Regrettably, that is true. In 1952, **Rafael Miranda, Andrés Cordero,** and **Lolita Lebrón,** members of a Puerto Rican independence group, fired guns at President Truman from the balcony of the U.S. House of Representatives. Truman was not injured, but several congressmen were wounded. The three served time in prison and were released in 1979. Gov. Muñoz apologized for the embarrassing act.

How Did Hispanic Copper Miners in Arizona Affect Politics?
This story had never before been told until PBS presented a documen-

tary on national television in 1991. Around the turn of the century, Mexican workers came north into Arizona to work in the copper mines and lived at Clifton and Morenci. They toiled for twelve hours a day, four thousand feet deep into the earth, in one hundred miles of winding tunnels supported by less-than-solid wooden beams and illumined only by candles. In the summer they sweated in those cramped quarters in one hundred degree heat. The mines were dangerous. Tunnels collapsed. Motor carts hit workers in the darkness and killed them. Only a handkerchief over the face kept out the dangerous dust. One out of three miners came down with silicosis of the lungs, from which some died. For all this they earned half an Anglo's wage. Phelps Dodge Corporation ran its company town and marked up prices 200 percent at its store. Mexicans lived on the hillsides without electricity or water, in houses made of scrap wood and with powder boxes for chairs.

When Anglo miners tried to drive Mexicans out of the mines, the Mexicans called a strike and took control with guns. The governor called on three hundred Arizona Rangers to confront the two thousand strikers. Federal troops arrived as well. Violence erupted. Fifty Mexicans died. The rest were disarmed. Martial law was declared, and ten leaders spent three years in prison.

During World War I, the U.S. needed copper. Prices rose from thirteen to twenty-seven cents a pound, but profits did not go to the workers. Another strike was called. The company called the miners German spies and arrested two thousand. Those who would not pledge company loyalty were packed into cattle cars, taken two hundred miles to Columbus, New Mexico, without food or water, and dumped into the desert.

In 1931 the Depression closed the mines. Unemployment hit the entire country. Thousands of Mexicans, many of them now naturalized citizens, were deported. In 1936 as the economy brightened, the mines were reopened. Mexicans were hired for the worst and lowest-paid jobs.

Then came World War II. In the company towns the Mexicans supported the war. Some were drafted and left willingly. Some of those were killed, especially in savage fighting on Okinawa. Back in the mining towns, the workers struggled for a union, and after eleven months they finally won, the first Mexican American union in Arizona's history.

At the war's end, Hispanic veterans returned to find the same old racism in jobs, recreation, restaurants, schools, and theaters. But the veterans were not the same! They wore more medals of honor than any other group in the nation. The company would not negotiate with the union. In 1946 there was another strike. It lasted 104 days and spread throughout the Southwest. At last the company surrendered, recognized the union, abolished the dual-wage system, and promised hospital bene-fits and pensions. A fifty-year struggle was won. From this struggle Mexican Americans entered Arizona politics. In 1975 they helped to elect the first Hispanic governor in that state, **Raúl Castro.**

Which Hispanics Fought in the Korean Conflict?

Thousands of Hispanics served in Korea. The Puerto Rican 65th Infantry Regiment engaged in nine campaigns and received the Presidential Unit Citation. Col. **Manuel J. Fernández** flew 125 combat missions and shot down nine North Korean MIGS.

Staff Sgt. **Ambrosio Guillén** from El Paso was in a Marine platoon defending Sanguch-on, well ahead of the main fighting line. In a night-time battle on July 25, 1953, enemy mortar and artillery fire pinned down the platoon as two battalions attacked. The American platoon repulsed the enemy in hand-to-hand combat. Mortally wounded, Guillén refused medical aid, continued to direct the attack, and died several hours later, only two days before the Korean cease fire and just short of his 24th birthday. He is buried in El Paso's Fort Bliss Cemetery.

Roy Tachias from New Mexico joined the Army in the early 1940s at age 16. In 1950, the eighteen-year-old soldier was in the first American combat unit to join with the South Korean army. Wounded five times, he received the Purple Heart, the Silver Star and the Bronze Star. Years later he enlisted again and served two tours in Vietnam.

These are other Hispanics who received the Medal of Honor for their service in Korea: Capt. **Reginald B. Desiderio;** Pfc. **Ferrando Luis García** (Puerto Rico); Pfc. **Edwardo Gómez;** Cpl. **Rodolfo P. Hernández;** Pvt. **Baldomero López;** Cpl. **Benito Martínez;** Pfc. **Eugene A. Obregón;** Staff Sgt. **Joseph C. Rodríguez.**

Which Two Hispanic U.S. Senators from New Mexico Together Spanned Nearly a Half-Century of Service?

Dennis Chávez was elected to the U.S. House of Representatives as a Democrat in 1930 when the state was strongly Republican. He worked hard to get New Deal projects functioning in the state and did so well that Hispanics struggling with poverty began switching to the Democratic Party. Somehow he knew how to get votes also from ex-Texans living on the state's eastern plains. He won re-election. But when Sen. Bronson Cutting died in a plane crash in 1935, the governor appointed Chávez to the U.S. Senate seat. He won successive re-elections until his death in 1962. In Washington he pushed fair employment, western resources development, Latin American relations, and social needs of his Hispanic

constituents. When New Mexico was asked to select a citizen to represent the state in the Capitol's Statuary Hall in Washington, D.C., the New
Mexico Historical Society chose Senator Chávez.

Sen. **Joseph Montoya** served in the U.S. Senate from 1964 to 1977.
Those two men not only represented their state but also were a Hispanic
presence in the Senate that ran from 1935 to 1977, a total of 42 years.

When Did Hispanics First Affect a Presidential Election?

In John F. Kennedy's election, the Hispanic vote for the first time was
extremely significant. Vigorous efforts to register voters in Texas likely
gave those electoral votes to the Democrats.

Who Was the First Hispanic Large-City Mayor
and the First Hispanic U.S. Ambassador?

Raymond L. Telles in 1957 won the election for mayor of El Paso, Texas,
and became the first Hispanic to win the mayor's office in a large
American city. As mayor he initiated many long-overdue reforms.
Reelected by a clear majority without opposition and headed for a third
term, Telles instead accepted the appointment by President John F.
Kennedy and became Ambassador to Costa Rica, the first Hispanic to
serve as an ambassador from the U.S. As ambassador he aided Costa
Rica during the devastating eruption of the volcano Irazú in 1963. After
six years in that post, and after working in several federal agencies, in
1978 Telles accepted President Carter's appointment to head the Inter-
American Development Bank in El Salvador (during that difficult time
when Archbishop Oscar Romero and the four American religious workers were murdered). He served his country earlier in World War II and
the Korean War and altogether worked for six American Presidents rang-
ing from Kennedy to Carter.

Which Chicano Journalist, Killed in 1970, Still Inspires?

Rubén Salazar was born in Mexico but grew up in El Paso. He attended
Texas Western College, now the University of Texas at El Paso. He
became a reporter for the *El Paso Herald-Post* and developed a reputa-
tion for investigative reporting. Later he joined the staff of the *Los
Angeles Times*. He covered Vietnam and became bureau chief in Mexico
City. As Chicano militancy erupted in the early 1970s, he was assigned
to write a new column to explain Chicano life to the people of Los
Angeles. He also became news director of Spanish-language television
station KMEX where he produced essays on racism and injustice toward
Mexican Americans.

In late August, 1970, as a part of the Chicano Moratorium, a rally was held in East Los Angeles, with participants from across the country preparing to march in an anti-war protest. On August 29, after going to Laguna Park to cover the story, Salazar found himself caught in a cafe while a riot exploded in the neighborhood. Amid the looting and burning, police fired high-velocity tear gas projectiles through the door of that cafe. Salazar, hit by one of the projectiles, died immediately. Still unresolved today is the Los Angeles Sheriff's Department's use of excessive force, poor riot control skills and alleged coverup. In 1995, the National Association of Hispanic Journalists asked for a new investigation into Salazar's untimely death.

In time a park was named in his honor, a *corrido* was composed about his life, and ten years later his wife dedicated the Rubén Salazar Library in Santa Rosa, California. The National Chicano Moratorium Committee also continues Salazar's struggle in its programs with school dropouts, police relations, housing, and jobs.

Who Was the Latina Rosa Parks?

Rosa Parks was the African American woman who refused to give up her seat in Montgomery, Alabama, and thus ignited the bus boycott that led to civil rights progress in the '50s. **Virginia Chacón** has been called the "Latina Rosa Parks."

On October 17, 1950, over 100 workers, mostly Mexican, went on strike against the powerful Empire Zinc Mine near Silver City, New Mexico. Virginia Chacón's husband was the main leader. All the strikers wanted was equal pay with white miners and an end to segregationist arrangements like separate restrooms, showers, and even paycheck windows. The company unleashed goons to attack and scabs to replace the strikers. A judge ended their picketing with a Taft-Hartley injunction. But the law didn't forbid over 150 wives from the Ladies Auxiliary and their children as they took over the picket lines from the men. Tear gassing and jail followed, but the miners eventually won their 15–month strike. In the midst of those McCarthy years, the strike inspired the film *Salt of the Earth* (that had to be produced secretly).

This struggle of the miners 20 years later inspired **César** and **Helen Chávez,** along with **Dolores Huerta,** to form the United Farm Workers union to protect mostly Hispanic workers in the vegetable fields and fruit orchards of California.

Which Hispanic Won the Nobel Prize in Physiology in 1959?

In 1959 Dr. **Severo Ochoa** was honored for his success in making RNA in a test tube. RNA in cells transmits the instructions of DNA. Dr. Ochoa found the enzyme that produces RNA. He shared the prize with fellow American Arthur Kornberg who discovered how also to make DNA in a test tube.

Why Is 1959 Pivotal for Cuba?

In the late 1920s and early 1930s, President **Gerardo Machado** ruled Cuba with cruelty and corruption. In 1933 he was ousted by an army officer, **Fulgencio Batista,** who either as president or as the power behind the scenes controlled Cuba until 1959. Cuba boasted a flourishing economy, its per capita income second only to Venezuela in Latin America. It enjoyed a standard of living that made television, telephones, cars, newspapers, and trains commonplace. At the same time, however, Batista's dictatorship smelled with corruption. Sugar prices dropped. The chasm between rich and poor became ridiculous. U.S. sugar corporations that held 25 percent of the productive land siphoned off huge profits. Wages and social services declined. Health care sagged as illiteracy increased. Gambling casinos (organized by the U.S. Mafia) and drug usage expanded. Pornography and prostitution thrived, and juvenile delinquency and suicide escalated. Cuba could not much longer tolerate such deterioration.

In the island's western mountains, a revolutionary named **Fidel Castro** gathered an army. As Castro's triumphant caravan rode across Cuba and into Havana, Batista fled, and the Cuban Revolution took over. Castro's inner circle included **Ernesto "Che" Guevara, Raúl Castro** and **Camilo Cienfuegos.** But Castro's early broad-based support disappeared as the government established a Marxist philosophy, trampled on human rights, set up concentration camps, executed opponents, made culture and sports political, and aligned the country with the Soviet Union.

Beginning with the early 1960s, hundreds of thousands of Cubans of all classes fled the country; most settled in Miami as political refugees. With so many of the refugees from the educated and business class, Cubans quickly transformed Miami's economic and social life. Most Cubans talked of returning to their homeland, but later generations have lost much of that passion. They have become Americans in more than name.

Himilce Novas records this Cuban upheaval but still notes how Castro improved Cuban life, mainly in education and health care. On the negative side, beyond the cruel violation of human rights was the economic debacle. He failed to change Cuba's sugar-industry dependency. His decision to exist with Soviet support became a disaster when that support ended in 1989. And his U.S. foreign policy caused the embargo that exists to the present time. Families remained separated. Persons fleeing Cuba for freedom in rickety boats have drowned in the Gulf. He gloried in the Bay of Pigs fiasco in 1962 (not really America's finest hour) and almost saw nuclear war in the 1963 Cuban missile crisis between President John F. Kennedy and Soviet Prime Minister Nikita Khrushchev.

In 1980, when Jimmy Carter was President, Castro released thousands from his jails and mental institutions. He dumped 125,000 of these mentally ill and criminal citizens, as well as some good citizens, on the U.S. That wave of Cubans received the name of the *Marielitos* (or, the Mariel boatlift). Ironically, the Mariel exodus from Cuba brought to the U.S. some of Cuba's outstanding writers, such as **Reinaldo Arenas, Juan Abreu, Carlos Alfonzo, Víctor Gómez** and **Andrés Valerio.** The feelings of many Cuban Americans toward their island homeland flow very deeply. **Olga Caturla de la Maza** writes her *Dirge for Cuba.*

Island of mine, palm grove in chains,
from the liquid forests of the Caribbean,
how it pains me to see you bowed
with your song of foam in decline!
. . . .
Cuba, Cuba, palm grove enchained,
I long to see you rise free in a tomorrow pierced
by libertarian bells!

Which Hispanics Fought in The Vietnam War?

Hispanics were at the heart of the struggle in Vietnam. Proportionately, more Chicanos died there than those of any other ethnic group. They made up more than a quarter of all casualties. Charley Trujillo described the nineteen migrant workers from California's San Joaquin Valley who represented so many Hispanics in that war. Those men were not headed for college. Some were high school dropouts because they had to support their families. Though some were drafted, some volunteered, either to escape the drudgery of migrant labor or in genuine gratitude for living in the U.S. In Vietnam, besides enduring fearful battle and bombardment, these Chicanos also faced discrimination and prejudice. They complained that minorities filled the infantry, but whites had jobs at the rear. Nevertheless, those Chicanos performed brilliantly in their extremely difficult assignment for their country.

In all branches of the military, many Hispanics fought in Vietnam. **Everett Alvarez Jr**. was a navy pilot shot down in 1964. The first American prisoner in North Vietnam, he was held for over eight years until his release in 1973. Later he became Deputy Administrator of the

Veterans Administration. Sgt. First Class **Isaac Camacho** was captured in action at Hiep Hoa in February, 1963. Twenty months later he escaped and sneaked through miles of enemy territory to reach his own forces. He was awarded the Silver Star and Bronze Star for his courage.

Daniel Fernández from Los Lunas, New Mexico, died in Vietnam on February 18, 1966, while fighting the Viet Cong near the village of Cu Chi in South Vietnam. A Viet Cong grenade hit Fernández on the foot and rolled toward four other U.S. troops. Fernández yelled, "Move out!" and fell on the grenade just before it exploded. He saved the lives of those buddies. He was mortally wounded and died while being evacuated by helicopter. Two years later President Johnson awarded him the Medal of Honor posthumously

Col. **Al Zapanta,** Airborne Ranger commander in the Mekong Delta fighting, received a Silver Star, five Bronze Stars for valor, a Purple Heart and 30 other awards and decorations.

Sgt. **Alfredo (Freddie) González** from Edinburg, Texas, received his Medal of Honor posthumously from President Nixon for running through fire to rescue and carry to safety a wounded comrade. Though badly wounded, he refused medical treatment and kept directing his men. In 1995 the Navy commissioned the high-tech destroyer USS Gonzalez in his honor.

Army Sgt. Major **Isaac Camacho** from El Paso was captured at the Battle of Hiep-Hoa in Vietnam and held captive for two years. In July 1965 he became the first U.S. soldier to escape prison in North Vietnam. He was awarded the Silver Star and Bronze Star and recommended for the Medal of Honor.

Staff Sgt. **Roy Benavídez,** a 33–year-old Mexican American from Texas, was awarded the Medal of Honor for bravery in battle on a secret mission inside Cambodia. Victor Landa, Jim Conley and Richard Estrada give us the remarkable story. On May 2, 1968, jumping from a helicopter, Benavídez rescued four wounded Green Berets under severe enemy fire. One at a time he dragged each man to the rescuing helicopter 80 yards away. Then he ran alongside the moving helicopter and picked up the other four, as well as recovering the team leader's body. When the helicopter was shot down and the pilot killed, Benavídez aided the wounded and directed tactical air strikes. An enemy clubbed him from behind; Benavídez killed the man in hand-to-hand combat. He killed two more before allowing himself to board another helicopter that had arrived. Through this terrible ordeal, he suffered 37 wounds in the right leg, face, head, back, and stomach and became weakened by obvious loss of blood. It took 13 years before he received his Medal of Honor from President Reagan in 1981.

Alfred Rascón was born in Chihuahua, Mexico. In the U.S., his parents were immigrant laborers. Though not an American citizen, Rascón at age 17 joined the Army and became a medic with the 173rd Airborne Brigade. While in battle in a Vietnamese jungle, he twice threw his body on wounded soldiers to protect them from machine gun fire and shrapnel. Later, wounded and bleeding from a grenade hit on his face, he fearlessly kept firing a machine gun that enabled his platoon to fight off the enemy. Despite his wounds, he rejoined the Army and served another hitch in Vietnam. After discharge, the Silver Star arrived one day by mail. He put aside the fact that he probably deserved the Medal of Honor. Years later, with patient, plodding efforts by his platoon buddies and a Congressman, the Pentagon gave up its bureaucratic "we've lost his papers" plea, and President Clinton presented the deserved award to Rascón in the year 2000, just 34 years years later.

Master Sgt. **Juan J. Valdez** was in charge of the Marine Security guard in Saigon and was on that last helicopter to lift off the embassy roof.

Others receiving Medals of Honor were Lance Corporal **Emilio A. de la Garza Jr.**, Pfc. **Ralph E. Díaz,** Lance Corp. **José Francisco Jiménez** (from Mexico City), Lance Corp. **Miguel Keith,** Pfc. **Carlos James Lozada** (Puerto Rico), Sgt. First Class **Louis R. Rocco,** Capt. **Eurípides Rubio,** Specialist Fourth Class **Héctor Santiago-Colón** (Puerto Rico), Capt. **Jay R. Vargas,** and First Sgt. **Máximo Yabes.**

One more example, from Archie Waters, is "Hero Street" in Silvis, Illinois, west of Chicago. On a one-and-a-half block dirt street once named Second Street, a monument honors Mexican-American men from 22 families living on that street. Eighty-four served, and 8 died in World War II, Korea, and Vietnam, a contribution above "any other place of comparable size in the United States."

What Was the Chicano Movement?

The struggle of Mexican Americans to gain their civil rights as citizens and to feel a part of the American society goes back to 1929 with the formation of LULAC (League of Latin American Citizens). After World War II, to get G.I. Bill and job benefits to often-rejected Mexican Americans, Dr. **Héctor Pérez García** organized the American G.I. Forum and used Hispanic veterans to give muscle to the movement. In Three Rivers, Texas, the Forum pushed hard to overcome the refusal by a funeral home to bury veteran **Félix Longoria** who had been killed on Okinawa. Forum chapters were organized across the nation. Together with LULAC and NAACP, the Forum dealt with discrimination issues, educational reform, the Bracero Program, police brutality, judicial problems, segregation, and employment difficulties for Latinos. Dennis J. Bixler-Marquez details how in the '70s the Forum gained some corporate support and set up programs for assistance and employment of veterans. In the 1980s Decade of the Hispanic, progress was clear in Hispanic appointments to federal positions and influence on political awareness.

An earlier split in the movement allowed more confrontational Chicanos to organize a school walkout in Crystal City, Texas. They took political power in Zavala County and launched the Raza Unida Party. **José Angel Gutiérrez** gave the leadership, but the political power did not last. By 1978 its voting strength had nearly collapsed, and a brief Chicano victory had ended. Gutiérrez went on to promote bilingual and bicultural education. In the late 1940s, led by Saul Alinsky, Community Service Organizations appeared and created mass political participation, voter registration, and recruitment of Mexican Americans for political office. One success was **Edward J. Roybal** from East Los Angeles who won a seat on the City Council and then went on to Congress.

Imitating the Black Panther group, Chicano youth in East Los Angeles in 1967 formed the Brown Berets, a paramilitary group called Young Citizens for Community Action. Similar groups formed in other major cities, like El Paso. In New York City, the Puerto Rican Young Lords was organized. These youth were angry, aggressive, confrontational, and revolutionary. They were tired of racism and injustice and societal resistance. They were loud voices in the Chicano Movement.

Raúl Yzaguirre ever since 1968 has led the Washington, D.C.–based National Council for La Raza, dedicated to advocacy in national politics, the federal government, and the private sector. Also in 1968, another effort was launched, the Mexican American Legal Defense and Educational Fund (MALDEF). It litigated cases involving "immigration rights, educational segregation…, employment discrimination and political representation." Oscar Martínez adds how in the 1970s MALDEF got Hispanics included in the Voting Rights Act and provided bilingual voting materials. In parts of Texas, the group forced many communities to choose district elections over at-large voting.

César Chávez and his United Farm Workers were another voice. They pushed efforts in California's fields and made people learn the meaning of *la huelga* (strike). **Rodolfo "Corky" González** launched his Crusade for Justice in Denver and still inspires Chicano youth with his poem, *I Am Joaquín*. The name of **Reyes Tijerina** deserves attention. During the 1960s he became nationally known for his leadership of *La Alianza*

Federal de Mercedes, an activist land grant group in New Mexico. He accused Anglos of robbing Mexican property-owners in direct violation of American laws: (1) Ordinance 99 of the Laws of the Indies, (2) Article IX of the Constitution of the U.S., and (3) the Treaty of Guadalupe Hidalgo in 1848.

In 1967 the group made world headlines when they drove to Tierra Amarilla in northern New Mexico to arrest the district attorney (who was not there) and in the process wounded a state policeman and a jailer as well as riddling some police cars and the courthouse windows with bullet holes. For good measure they took hostages. Every law enforcement agency in the state was called into action, along with the National Guard and two antiaircraft weapon carriers. Tijerina and his group were found in Echo Amphitheater and arrested. Tijerina served time in the state penitentiary. His contribution, despite the failure at Tierra Amarilla, was to focus national attention on the poverty of northern New Mexico.

Which Hispanic Women
Distinguished Themselves as Hispanic Activists?
Himilce Novas presents some examples. In the 1930s, **Ema Tenayuca** led the first pecan-shellers strike in San Antonio, a precursor of César Chávez years later. In the 1940s, **Josefina Sierro** organized an underground railway to bring back to the U.S. many Mexican American citizens deported in earlier mass removals and also helped stop the zoot suit riots in Los Angeles. Leaders in the Chicano labor movement in the '60s and '70s were **Marcela Lucero Trujillo** (with Corky González's Crusade for Justice), **Virginia Musquiz** (an organizer of the Raza Unida Party), and **Dolores Huerta** (with the United Farm Workers). Born into a family of farm workers, Huerta left university studies to work as a close aide to César Chávez. She became vice president of the union, spoke to nationally-known groups, and was present at the signing of the grape contracts. Since Chávez's death, she continues her leadership and labor for *la causa.*

What Chilean Poet
Supported Chicanos and Puerto Ricans in the U.S.?
Ilan Stavans mentions the Chilean poet, **Pablo Neruda.** Neruda received the Nobel Prize for Literature but also felt concern for *la Raza's* struggle in the U.S. He wrote a play about **Joaquín Murieta** and poems about Hispanics who died in their struggle for justice. One poem featured **Juan de la Cruz,** a 60-year-old field worker killed in the 1973 strike by the United Farm Workers in California.

How Can We Assess the Chicano Movement Today?

Decades later, the Chicano Movement can be assessed more clearly. Its strident approach upset many Mexican Americans and Anglos, but it got the nation's attention. Mexican American study programs were organized on university campuses, and Mexican Americans won election to hundreds of school boards and civic organizations. Sewage and water services were installed in needy areas. Books by Mexican and Mexican American authors appeared in public libraries. Medical clinics were established, also credit unions and legal aid services for migrants. Mexican Chambers of Commerce became common. And now the nation celebrates an annual Hispanic Heritage Month. Who says change cannot happen?

Which New Mexico Woman Became a Progressive Legislator and Received a National Appointment?

Concha Ortiz y Pino de Kleven was elected to the New Mexico State Legislature and was the first woman to be elected as Majority Whip. She sponsored major legislation such as permitting the teaching of Spanish in the seventh and eighth grades and establishing the School of Inter-American Affairs at the University of New Mexico (UNM). In the 1960s she pushed legislation for access for the disabled to public buildings. She received appointment by President Ford to the National Council of the Humanities. In 1977 UNM awarded her the doctor of humanities degree.

Which Hispanics Have Held High Appointive Office?

Ramona A. Bañuelos was President Nixon's choice for the first Hispanic Treasurer of the United States. President Jimmy Carter appointed Dr. **Julián Nava** as the first Mexican American Ambassador to Mexico. President Reagan appointed **Katherine Dávalos Ortega** as the second woman U.S. Treasurer. President George H.W. Bush placed the former Florida Gov. **Bob Martínez** as czar of the drug war effort, **Manuel Luján** as Secretary of the Interior, and for a time **Lauro Cavasos** as Secretary of Education. President Clinton appointed **Federico Peña** as Secretary of Transportation and **Henry Cisneros** as Secretary of Housing and Urban Development; **Bill Richardson,** former U.S. Representative, as U.S. Secretary of Energy; and **Louis Caldera,** as Secretary of the Army.

Which Hispanics Have Been Elected to City, State, and Federal Offices?

Following in the path of Mayor **Raymond L. Telles** in El Paso, **Ray Salazar** won the office in 1975. In the 1970s **Jerry Apodaca** and **Toney Anaya** were governors of New Mexico, and **Raúl Castro** became governor of Arizona. In the 1980s **Henry Cisneros** served as mayor of San

Antonio, **Federico Peña** in Denver, and **Xavier Suárez** in Miami. In the 1980s **Bob Martínez** was elected the first Hispanic governor of Florida and later a U.S. Senator. **Bill Richardson** was elected in 2002 as Governor of New Mexico.

Who Was the First Hispanic Congressman Elected from Texas?

Henry Gonzales served on the San Antonio City Council where he fought to desegregate public swimming pools. Elected to the Texas Senate, in 1957 he performed a 22–hour filibuster to oppose bills aimed at reinforcing segregation. On that floor he heard himself referred to as a "lousy Mexican." In 1963 he won election to the U.S. House of Representatives where he served for 37 years. He rose to become chairman of the powerful House Banking Committee. In his long tenure he defended the poor, fought for changes in the American banking system, opposed the ever-increasing power of the largest banks and deregulating the S&Ls, and championed public housing. Now for some tidbits: A former boxer (who spoke four languages), in 1986 he punched a man in a San Antonio restaurant for calling him a communist. He rode in the motorcade in Dallas the day President Kennedy was shot in 1963. And in 1994 he received the Kennedy Profile in Courage Award. He died in 2000.

Who Was the First Hispanic in Space?

Born and raised in Costa Rica until 18 years of age and without knowing any English, **Franklin Chang-Díaz** came to the U.S., eventually enrolled in MIT (Massachusetts Institute of Technology), and graduated in 1977 with a doctorate in applied plasma physics. After carrying out complex responsibilities with NASA in various major projects, he flew his first mission in 1985. In 1986 he flew on the shuttle Columbia and spoke from outer space in Spanish to television audiences in the United States and Latin America.

Who Has Been Called the Most
Under-Appreciated Chicano Leader in the Twentieth Century?

Bert Corona was born in El Paso and became known as a man with a passion for *la lucha*, the struggle over seven decades to get economic and social justice for Latinos. Corona has been ranked with César Chávez among the Chicano giants. He fought civil rights challenges, signed up Latinos to vote, organized workers, formed a coalition with African Americans, lobbied against unjust laws, and spoke up for voiceless undocumented workers.

Who Is New Mexico's World-Renowned Author, Poet, and Scholar?

Sabine R. Ulibarri was born in Tierra Amarilla in northern New Mexico and flew 35 combat missions over Europe in World War II as a gunner. A graduate of the University of New Mexico, Ulibarri earned a doctorate in California but returned to teach at Albuquerque. His writings have been entirely in Spanish and are recognized in all of Latin America and Spain. He has published poems, stories of New Mexico, and a dissertation on Spanish poet **Ramón Jiménez.** Besides his writing, he taught at the University, held language institutes, did research throughout Latin America and Spain, acted as a spokesperson for the Chicano movement, and promoted the Spanish language and bilingual education. In 1978 he was appointed to the Royal Academy of the Spanish language, a high honor from Spain, and from 1973 to 1982 worked as chairperson of the Modern and Classical Languages Department at UNM.

Who Is the Much-Honored Hispanic Illustrator from El Paso?

The name is **José Cisneros,** known across the nation as a consummate artist and warm human being. Born in a small Mexican village as the Mexican Revolution was beginning, Cisneros began drawing by age 6 but had to mark his colored pencils because he was color-blind. He studied English in El Paso, delivered early-morning newspapers, dropped out of school to support his family, and devoured books at the public library. Using meticulous research, he produced pen-and-ink illustrations of horses and riders from the Spanish colonial period to the early 20th century (see illustration page 202). Over 100 books and articles contain his illustrations, and a hundred drawings are on permanent display at the library of the University of Texas at El Paso. His exhibits have been shown across the country and in Mexico. He also produced maps, logos, sculptures, wood working, murals, and stained glass. He has received honors from LULAC, the DAR, and UTEP; the cities of San Antonio, Austin, and El Paso; the Western Writers of America; the State of New Mexico; the University of Chihuahua, Mexico, and the University of Alcalá, Spain; the King of Spain and the President of Mexico. In 2002 he received from President George W. Bush the National Humanities Medal. Cisneros still lives in El Paso and his legacy now spans nine decades.

Who Was Named Outstanding Hispanic Woman in the 20th Century?

At the end of the year 2000, *VISTA* newspaper magazine named **Gloria Estefan** the outstanding Hispanic Woman of the Century. The "Queen of Latin Pop" has sold over 45 million albums. Born **Gloria María Fajardo** in Cuba, she came to Miami with her family after Castro took power. In

1975 she began singing with a male musical group. This group's leader, **Emilio Estefan,** guided her performance, changed the name of the band to the Miami Sound Machine, and became Gloria's husband. Twenty years later they stand at the top of the entertainment world. She is admired as a Grammy winner, actress, composer, and singer—also wife and mother of two. Her musical accomplishment is quite clear: Using pop music with Latin rhythms, she gained respect for all Latin music. Her single *Reach* was the theme song for the Atlanta Olympics. From English words at first, she has turned in crossover fashion to songs in Spanish.

She is even more respected for her Gloria Estefan Foundation, set up in 1997 to help disadvantaged children through community projects and educational scholarships. She raised millions of dollars for hurricane relief. Through another foundation, she provides funding for cancer, leukemia and AIDS research. She makes possible Camillus House that gives shelter for the homeless in Miami. In 1990 she was almost killed in a vehicle crash. A broken and dislocated vertebra in her back required surgery and eight-inch iron implant bars for spinal stability. Following a year of physical therapy, she returned to her performing career, and through her foundation began giving funding for spinal cord injuries and pediatric AIDS. Christopher John Farley feels that her accident deepened her inner life, part of which was seen in her return to songs in Spanish. These words from one of her songs tell so much about her:

> ...I'll face whatever comes my way, Savor each moment of the day, Love as many people as I can along the way, Help someone who's given up if it's just to raise my eyes and pray.

Who Was Named the Outstanding Hispanic Man in the 20th Century?

César Chávez has that honor, again from *VISTA,* at the close of the year 2000. Carmen Teresa Roiz chronicles his life. Born in Arizona in 1927, Chávez grew up knowing the constant sweat, aching back, and dust-parched throat of pickers in the fields. Inspired by Gandhi and Martin Luther King Jr. with their philosophy of nonviolent social action, in 1962 Chávez founded the United Farm Workers (UFW) to protest below-minimum wages, unjust labor policies, and unsafe working conditions in the pesticide-saturated fields of California—the first union ever organized for farm workers. Leading a veritable revolution in labor rights, Chávez used nationwide boycotts, strikes, fasting, civil rights marches, and California legislative pressure. In 1965 he led a strike against grape growers in Delano, California. In 1966 a 340 mile march or pilgrimage of 10,000 people from Delano to the state capital in Sacramento gave the movement national recognition. In 1967 he led a nationwide boycott against buying grapes not picked by union workers.

In 1968 he demonstrated *la Causa* (the cause) with a 36–day fast on behalf of suffering farm workers and their children, many of whom had died of cancer. Senator Robert F. Kennedy was one of many visitors when this fast stopped. In 1970 the growers offered the first-ever contracts to farm workers. California politicians later watered down that progress, but Chávez never gave up. In 1978 the grape boycott officially ended, but a second boycott was called in 1984 to protest pesticide residues in fruit. Its official end came in 2000. Chávez, his body certainly weakened by hunger strikes and the strain of his life-long efforts, died in 1993 at 66.

César Chávez—
Gabriel Sánchez

Chávez has not gone unnoticed. He was the first Chicano whose face appeared on the cover of TIME. In 1990 he received the *Águila,* Mexico's highest civilian award. In 1994 President Clinton presented to Chávez's wife the United States Medal of Freedom, this country's highest civilian award. César Chávez Day has become an optional state holiday in many parts of the country, and his name identifies many a street in cities across the nation. It was no surprise, therefore, when the *VISTA* newspaper magazine named Chávez as the Hispanic Man of the Century. At the end of one hunger strike, Chávez prepared these words which echo the very words of Jesus himself as well as St. Francis of Assisi.

...We must admit that our lives are all that really belong to us. So it is how we use our lives that determines what kind of men (sic) we are.

It is my deepest belief that only by giving our lives do we find life.

THE TWENTY-FIRST CENTURY
What Is One Continuing Hispanic Task in Our Society?

Edna Acosta-Belén sighs over the typically shallow American awareness of Hispanic contributions to our society. Most people, she says, know the cliches about state, city and geographical names, and Hispanics in movies, on television, and in sports. They know about *tacos* and *burritos*. They have seen John Wayne murdered by the *bandidos* at the Alamo, and have heard the Puerto Rican gang sing about America in *West Side Story*. But, the continuing Hispanic task, Acosta-Belén says, in a culture fixated on "images rather than substance," is to construct new images that are not stereotyped, images that show colorful Hispanic threads in the tapestry of America.

Epilogue–
Two Eagles in the Sun

TWO EAGLES

In the English language, another tongue of the angels, we use an idiom about "having a place in the sun," meaning a right to exist and flourish. Anglo/European Americans have had no trouble seeing themselves in the American sunlight but certainly have fussed about seeing certain others there. Still, certain others *are* there. Perhaps the illustration of two eagles will make the picture clearer.

The American Eagle. The main eagle in the American sunlight is the one chosen by Congress on June 20, 1782, for the Great Seal of the United States. The eagle's beak holds a scroll with the Latin words *E Pluribus Unum,* "From the many, one." In 1782, those words reflected thirteen colonies forming one nation. But that one nation encompassed not only thirteen different colonies but also many national and ethnic groups. Richard Shenkman states that in 1790, three out of five Americans were of non-English origin, and two out of five did not come from English speaking backgrounds. Not only did America have English, Scotch, Irish, French, Dutch, German, and Swedish citizens, but it also had Native Americans and Africans. Correctly, Congressional adoption of the Seal's design proclaimed one nation that was also multicultural and multi-ethnic, as far back as the 1780s. Most European Americans, however, saw only northern European Whites.

The Mexican Eagle. In that American sunlight, however, we can see a second eagle representing an ethnic group not really apparent in early America. The second eagle is the eagle of Mexico, taken from ancient Aztec myth and placed in the coat of arms on the Mexican national flag. In Aztec legend, the god Huitzilopochtli, explaining to the people how to find a site for the new Aztec capital, instructed them to look for an eagle sitting on a cactus and holding a serpent in its beak. The legend says the people found that eagle and thus determined where to locate Tenochtitlán, today's Mexico City. This eagle, too, stands in America's sunlight. Hispanics have contributed so much to America's story from the very beginning (described in Chapter 10), and today across our land

Hispanics have become the country's largest ethnic group. Hispanics certainly belong (see Appendix B).

Hispanics in the American community who have come from other Latin American countries present their own symbol, for example, the star of Puerto Rico, Cuba, and the Dominican Republic. To simplify the symbolism, we will let these symbols and others gather around Mexico's eagle and fill space in America's sunlight.

So, what's the point? The point is that, for a couple of hundred years, Americans have usually seen only one eagle in the American sun, and saw only one color, white. Today we know other colors were there, too. But now another eagle seeks a place in that sun, the eagle of Mexico and all America's Hispanics. That eagle, too, has a place in America's sun, the right to exist and flourish.

SOME IDEAS TO THINK ABOUT

The melting pot is out-of-date. The image of the melting pot has dominated this nation since the concept appeared in a play by Israel Zangwill as recently as 1908. The concept meant diversity boiled down to homogeneous uniformity. The uniformity was white Anglo-Saxon and Protestant, or WASP. This image has long been taken for granted, but no longer. Sabine R. Ulibarri bluntly says that "It is one thing to homogenize milk; it is quite another thing to homogenize the citizenry." Therefore, new images have appeared, like stew, mosaic, quilt, tossed salad, tapestry, or mosaic. The many parts enhance the whole. No consensus exists yet on the new image, only the sense that the nation needs some other image to reflect today's reality.

Diversity has problems. Look at Yugoslavia, Cyprus, Czechoslovakia, Spain, India, Sri Lanka, Rwanda, even Canada. Do we want another Quebec? Jim Castelli uses the word "Balkanization." Arthur Schlesinger voices his fear of a radical multiculturalism, a growing "cult of ethnicity" that will stress *pluribus* over *unum*.

Diversity can mean enrichment, too. Back in 1883, quintessential American poet Walt Whitman wrote to the city fathers of Santa Fe, New Mexico. He had been invited to write a poem and read it personally to help the city celebrate its founding. Whitman declined with regrets but penned a letter in which he pointed out America's almost exclusive focus on British and German roots. But he saw a counterbalance from Spain and the Southwest—"religiousness and loyalty, ... patriotism, courage, decorum, gravity and honor." These virtues could "emerge like an underground river" now flowing beautifully in a new day.

America's true vision is its unity with diversity. The vision of America is one nation with liberty and justice for all, because everyone is equal under God, equal before the law, equal in the voting booth, and equal in opportunity for a better life. The vision lifts up the individual rights of freedom from fear and hunger, freedom of vote and voice, freedom of assembly and worship. The vision is a people who are Creator-endowed with certain inalienable rights, like life, liberty, and the pursuit of happiness. This vision calls us especially where its reality is dim.

Whatever the image, it must hold together both **diversity** and **unity.** A half century ago, anthropologist Clyde Kluckhohn in his *Mirror for Man* wrote about pursuing two national goals at the same time. He wrote about pride in and loyalty to the totality of America as well as enrichment from our diversity. The man was ahead of his time.

TWO MORE ESSENTIAL POINTS

Unity and diversity must include justice. In this new paradigm of America, we must include justice. Too many Hispanics (and too many in all ethnic groups, including Anglos) are left behind and live on the edge of the American dream. As Mexico's Benito Juárez stated the matter over 150 years ago, *"Respeto al derecho ajeno es la paz"* (respect for the rights of others is peace). Peace requires respect, and respect needs to issue in justice. And justice means fairness in action: in jobs, education, housing, health care, safety, political access, and freedom from racism. We lift up the common good, the good for all cultures and races.

The real issue is not diversity but attitudes. Diversity is already here. The crucial issue is our attitude toward diversity. All cultures are rich, but no one culture possesses all the richness of the human spirit. All have strengths to share and weaknesses to overcome. There is a place for cultural pride, but also for humility. The danger is ethnocentrism. The goal is, in some sense, for cultures to hold hands as Americans together. Six-year-old Fabian from Brooklyn expressed the idea on a poster: "If we all hold hands, we can't fight."

An enormous additional issue exists. In America's war on terrorism (with no end in sight), the stimulation of a balanced patriotism underlines the vision of unity with diversity. The issue is no longer the hobby of an enlightened elite. Patriotism is fed by the passion for unity. At the same time, America is strengthened by the affirmation of diversity, where the vitality of the many enhances the sturdiness of the whole. Enduring terrorist threats and actions demand, **demand**, the implementation of this vision.

GETTING FROM HERE TO THERE: INDIVIDUALS

Finally, we come to the most important question: Where can I go from here? What can *we* do? For individuals, the challenge is bicultural or multicultural growth.

Learn Spanish (or whatever the language). Language is the primary route into a culture. One need not aim at the fluency of a native speaker. Learn just enough to hear and speak and read with some degree of competence. Spanish (or other) language learning can take place at home by using tapes or videos. Or hire a private tutor. Or enroll in a class at a local college or community college, or at a local language school. Best of all, naturally, is total immersion by attending a language training program outside of the U.S. Some could try a sabbatical.

Travel. Travel can give the feel of a people and a culture. Eyes get opened. Monocultural narrowness gets splintered. Better than tourism are visits to friends in another country. More convenient, perhaps, is travel within the United States. This travel can be an eye-opener. Consider the California missions; Albuquerque, Santa Fe, and all of northern New Mexico; San Antonio and El Paso in Texas; Miami's "Little Havana"; and New York City. And what about a *barrio* in one's own city?

Invite an exchange student. Inviting a young person from another country to live in the family for a year will give the host family a taste of vocabulary and idioms in another language. Daily conversations will educate the family about the student's country and culture. Eventually, after the student returns home, the host family will often receive an invitation to visit the student's family and country.

Read and watch. The public library or your favorite book store offers more opportunities for cultural sensitivity than can be handled in one lifetime. Magazine and newspaper articles appear continually. Keep articles in a file folder or notebook and re-read them from time to time. Also, see movies and rent videos with Hispanic or other themes to combine entertainment and education. And the Internet is a gold mine.

Study. Get into a study group in the community. Encourage the forming of such a group in your church or organization. *Two Eagles* and similar books could be your guide.

Serve. Find an institution, agency, or program working with Hispanics (or another culture). Get to know people's needs and situations first-hand. See if any program needs a volunteer and get involved. Rub elbows in very down-to-earth activities. In dealing with Hispanics as individuals and sharing universal human experience, people will find benefits flowing in both directions.

GETTING FROM HERE TO THERE: SOCIETY

Beyond individuals, the nation and every community can lift up this double vision of unity and diversity, minus jingoism and artificial revisionism. We have already begun a few steps with Hispanic Heritage Month, Black History Month, Hanukkah, and Kwaanza. Surely, there is room for others as well. But the moment demands an intense and continuing effort beyond anything we have yet tried. From the highest federal, state and local levels, the nation needs to marshal educators, philosophers, anthropologists, community agency directors, social workers, legislators, historians, psychiatrists and psychologists (especially experts in group psychology), marketing agencies, physicians, political leaders, clergy, the media, and other leaders. Leadership must be found, a mission ignited, funds obtained, and strategies designed to reach our youth and children as well as to recall our adults to this national vision of unity, diversity, the common good, and justice.

To have a national community with "common references" (in Paul Gray's phrase), this effort will encourage authors to write, and publishers and schools to adopt new history texts. Students need to know a broader range of heroes without abandoning traditional heroes of the past. Even more, schools will emphasize civics and show what democracy and citizenship mean. Schools will be more creative in social studies and go beyond mere dates and facts to present America's great themes and values—and America's failures too.

To affirm diversity and build unity, the country will want to foster multicultural arts of every kind in the schools and in the community. The human heart is stirred by story, poetry, film, theater, music, art, and dance more than by logical argument.

This effort, urges Lance Morrow, will go beyond exclusive "homage to every cultural variation" but instead will "encourage universally accepted ideals of behavior: self-discipline, compassion, responsibility, friendship, work, courage, perseverance, honesty, loyalty and faith." Unity will be strengthened by encouraging "the virtue of virtue," a vital point from Lance Morrow, and William J. Bennett in *The Book of Virtues*.

If Isaac Newton's first law of motion is true, that nothing moves until propelled by a sufficient force, then in the same way these ideas toward a vision will need powerful action. But the well-known thousand-mile journey begins with a single step.

A FINAL WORD

In Harper Lee's *To Kill a Mockingbird*, Atticus passes on some sage advice to young Scout on how to get along with "all kinds of folks." His advice was that "you never really understand a person until you consider things from his point of view, … until you climb into his skin and walk around in it." Native Americans would talk about walking in someone else's moccasins.

As for *Two Eagles in the Sun*, this has been an invitation to walk for a while in some Hispanic shoes, to get inside the door of Hispanic minds, even to see and hear and smell and taste and feel just a little bit with Hispanic senses, and then to begin to walk together toward a common vision for this great nation.

Appendix–
Resources for Going Deeper

BOOKS

So many of the following books focus on the Southwest and the Mexican/Chicano experience. Many also cover Hispanic culture in general. For Puerto Rican, Cuban, Dominican, other Caribbean, or Central and South American experience in the U.S., some books are on the list. Many others are available at major bookstores and public libraries. For complete bibliographic information, please check "Bibliographic References."

Americanos: Latino Life in the U.S./La Vida Latina en los Estados Unidos. Preface by Edward James Olmos. Introduction by Carlos Fuentes. Photographs and bilingual text.

Anaya, Rodolfo. *Bless Me, Ultima.* A small boy's life in a remote New Mexican village.

Arreola, Daniel D., and James R. Curtis. *The Mexican Border Cities.* A study of complexity and diversity of cities along the border. A social guide.

Balido, Giselle. *Cuban Time, A Celebration of Cuban Life in America.* A look at features of the American Cuban experience.

Carrasco, David, Editor in Chief. *The Oxford Encyclopedia of Mesoamerican Cultures: The Civilizations of Mexico and Central America.* Exhaustive scholarship on the ancient indigenous civilizations.

Castro, Rafaela G., *Chicano Folklore: A Guide to the Folktales, Traditions, Rituals and Religious Practices of Mexican Americans.* A collection from A-Z with stories, myths, writings, customs, beliefs, and arts.

Cisneros, José, *Riders across the Centuries: Horsemen of the Spanish Borderlands.* Biography by John O.West. Over 100 matchless drawings by this nationally-known artist along with text.

—. *Borderlands: The Heritage of the Lower Río Grande through the Art of José Cisneros.* More drawings and descriptions of southwestern history and life.

—. *Cisneros 2000: Faces of the Borderlands.* One never gets enough of the artistry of Cisneros.

Davis, Mike. *Magical Realism: Latinos Reinvent the U.S. City.* A look at

Hispanics in the large cities and how the introduction of new culture brings new spark to jaded city life.

Elizondo, Virgilio. *Christianity and Culture*, also his *Galilean Journey* and *La Morenita*. An American Catholic priest, scholar, and educator looking at Mexican and American cultures from the standpoint of the Roman Catholic faith and heritage.

Fontana, Bernard L. *Entrada: The Legacy of Spain and Mexico in the United States*. Three centuries of Spanish and Mexican contributions to U.S. culture.

García, Mario T. *The Making of a Mexican American Mayor, Raymond Telles*. The account of a man who rises from a humble *barrio* background in El Paso to serve in World War II, to become the city's first Hispanic mayor, and to be appointed the nation's first Hispanic ambassador.

González, Juan, *Harvest of Empire: A History of Latinos in America*. An analysis of American economic policies in the Caribbean and their effect on Hispanics from Puerto Rico, Cuba, and the Dominican Republic in particular.

González, Justo L. *Mañana*. Protestant theological reflection on the Hispanic experience.

Griswold del Castillo, Richard, Teresa McKenna, and Yvonne Yarbro-Bejarano, eds. *Chicano Art: Resistance and Affirmation, 1965-1985*. Art exhibits, chronology, Chicano glossary, bibliography, and nine essays.

Kras, Eva. *Modernizing Mexican Management Style: With Insights for U.S. Companies Working in Mexico*. Discusses the cultural foundations that affect how Mexican companies view management.

Lewis, Oscar. *Five Families*, also *The Children of Sánchez*. A classic sociological examination of Mexican social strata and "the culture of poverty." In *La Vida* he analyzes a Puerto Rican family in San Juan and New York City. An up-to-date sequel is Judith A. Hellman, *Mexican Lives*. This sociologist examines contemporary Mexicans amidst the economic, social, and political changes of the past decade.

Marriott, Alice. *The Valley Below*. An out-of-print but priceless portrayal of Spanish Americans and Pueblo Indians in northern New Mexico.

Martínez, Oscar J. *Border People: Life and Society in the U.S.-Mexico Borderlands*. Analysis of the border scene and border people, including some oral histories.

—. *Mexican-Origin People in the United States: A Topical History*. A study of the Mexican American immigration experience, racism, employment, and politics.

Metz, Leon. *Border. The U.S.-Mexican Line*. A thorough study of the border's unique story, especially on problems between the two nations.

Martin, Judith N., and Thomas K. Nakayama. *Intercultural Communication in Contexts.* The influence of cultural communication patterns and their effects.

—. *Whiteness: The Communication of Social Identity.* A look at the sense of identity among Whites in America.

Nichols, John. *The Milagro Beanfield War.* The humorous and tender picture of Spanish Americans and Anglos in the area of Taos, New Mexico.

Novas, Himilce. *Everything You Need to Know about Latino History.* A popular guide to people and events in the Spanish conquest, the various ethnic roots among Hispanics, and historical details about Mexicans, Puerto Ricans, Cubans, Dominicans, and Central Americans.

Ortego, Philip D., Ed. *We Are Chicanos: An Anthology of Mexican-American Literature.* Old but still valuable.

Paz, Octavio. *The Labyrinth of Solitude.* A Mexican writer's analysis of his country's soul.

Pillsbury, Dorothy L. *No High Adobe and Adobe Doorways.* Quaint essays about life in Santa Fe half a century ago.

Sonnichsen, C.L. *Pass of the North.* The story of El Paso from Native American times to the present.

Stavans, Ilan. *Latino U.S.A.: A Cartoon History.* Illustrated by Lalo Alcaraz. A bit radical but helpful.

Timmons, W. H. *El Paso. A Borderlands History.* The account of two cultures and two cities across the centuries.

Urrea, Luis Alberto. *Vatos.* Poem by Luis Alberto Urrea, photographs by José Galvea.

Vigil, Angel *Una Linda Raza: Cultural and Artistic Traditions of the Hispanic Southwest.* A beautifully illustrated depiction of customs among Southwest Hispanics: arts, healing arts, history, family celebrations, religious celebrations, plays, music, riddles, crafts, and recipes.

Villaseñor, Victor. *Rain of Gold.* The story of a Mexican family, its roots in Mexico, and its American experience. Accomplishes what Alex Haley's *Roots* did for African Americans.

CALENDARS

Quiñones, Luis "Nacho," Ph.D. *2002 Raza Peace & Historical Calendar,* is also a bilingual collection of history and *dichos* (wise sayings) for every day in the year. 2091 Fran Drive, Las Cruces, NM 88005, (505) 524-2846. $11 each.

CULTURAL CENTER

The Hispanic Cultural Center is operated by the state of New Mexico. Spain's Prince Felipe spoke at the grand opening in 2000. On 22 acres, the centerpiece is a building with a Visual Arts Complex full of vivid photographs of villages in New Mexico and northern Mexico. A smaller section portrays the history and life of the nearby *barrio* named Barelas, with over 800 photographs. Future plans call for three specialized theaters (one an outdoor amphitheater), educational and workshop spaces, a bosque trail, and a state-of-the-art Research and Literary Arts Program for study of genealogy, ethnology, oral history, folklore, music, and other arts. The Center is located at 1701 4th St. SW, Albuquerque, NM 87102. (505) 246-2261.

INTERNET

www.TodoLatino.com; www.HispanicOnline.com; www.AOL Latino.com; www.mexgrocer.com; www.thenewsmexico.com; www.mexicodaily.com; www.mexconnect.com; www.pewhispanic.org; welcome.topuertorico.org; cubanculture.com

MOVIES

The Ballad of Gregorio Cortés. A Mexican American's ordeal with Anglo law and justice, complicated by a misunderstanding over a Spanish word for horse.

El Norte. A gripping depiction of a Guatemalan refugee from terror in his country and the excitement and pain in trying to find a new life in the "paradise" of the North.

Based on *Mi Familia/My Family.* Story about the Sánchez family in East Los Angeles, starring Edward James Olmos and Jennifer López.

The Old Gringo. Based on the novel by Carlos Fuentes about Mexico's Revolution with its volatile passions and politics.

The Milagro Beanfield War. Robert Redford's adaptation of John Nichol's novel about northern New Mexico.

The Price of Glory. Stars Jimmy Smits in a story of young sons, pushed into boxing, rebelling.

Selena. Story about the life of the murdered Tejana singing star, directed by Gregory Nava.

Stand and Deliver. A Los Angeles high school calculus teacher, Jaime Escalante, inspires his *barrio* teens to strive for excellence. A true story.

Tortilla Soup. Comedy and romance in a modern Mexican American family.

NEWSPAPERS

VISTA. Monthly insert in many Sunday newspapers.

PERIODICALS

Apuntes. Quarterly. $15.00 a year for a forum on theological issues from the Protestant Hispanic outlook. Mexican American Program, Perkins School of Theology, Southern Methodist University, Dallas, TX 75275.

La Herencia del Norte. Published quarterly. In English. Annual subscription $19.99. La Herencia del Norte, P.O. Box 22576, Santa Fe, NM 87502. www.herencia.com

Latina, a magazine for Hispanic women.

Hispanic. Monthly. $18.00 a year. The Hispanic Publicity Corp. 111 Massachusetts Ave., N.W., Suite 410, Washington, D.C. 20001.

New Mexico Magazine, a monthly publication with frequent articles and wonderful photos, including Hispanic themes. 1-800-711-9525.

POSTERS

460 Years of Chicano History. Dramatic, multi-colored collage of dozens of famous Hispanics. Also, posters on the *The Mexican Revolution of 1910*, and *Latinos in Hollywood*. By Gonzalo J. Plascencia, 8844 Dulce Cir., El Paso, TX 79907, (915) 858-6055.

400 Years of Chicano History. Multi-colored figures of famous Hispanics. Social Studies Service. 10200 Jefferson Blvd., Room R01. P.O. Box 802. Culver City, CA 90232-0802.

Hispanic American Hall of Fame, portraying dozens of Hispanic Americans across society. Also with teacher's guide. Same address.

Hispanic Culture, a poster series including *Mexican People and Culture, Puerto Rico: History and Culture, La Conquista: The Spanish Conquest of America, Bilingual Americans*, and *People of the Caribbean*. Same address.

Hispanic Heritage, 12 posters featuring Simón Bolívar, Pablo Casals, César Chávez, Roberto Clemente, Jaime Escalante, Gloria Estefan, Nancy López, Gabriel García Márquez, Rita Moreno, Antonia Novello, Pablo Picasso, and Juan Ponce de León. Knowledge Unlimited Inc., P.O. Box 52, Madison, WI 53701-0052

RADIO

Latino USA, a weekly program on Hispanic topics. PBS.

REFERENCES

The following are offered by Gale Research, Inc., 835 Penobscot Bldg., Detroit, MI 48226-4094.

The Hispanic American Almanac. Culture, civilization, language, bibliographies.

Hispanic Market Handbook. Background, demographics, characteristics, market research, case studies in Hispanic markets.

Hispanic Americans Information Directory. Organizations, agencies, programs, publications.

Hispanic Writers. Sketches from contemporary authors.

Who's Who Among Hispanic Americans. Over 11,000 entries.

Notable Hispanic American Women. Over 300 entries.

TELEVISION

American Family. Superb depiction of the González family in East Los Angeles, starring Edward James Olmos, Raquel Welch, Esai Morales, Constance Marie, A.J. Lamas, and Sonia Braga. Directed by Gregory Nava. On PBS.

The Brothers García on Nickelodeon.

Resurrection Blvd. on Showtime.

Taína on Nickelodean.

Dora the Explorer on CBS, a Saturday morning cartoon.

VIDEOS

Tapestry II, A Story of Rosa Guerrero. A nearly 50-minute presentation on Hispanic dance by a nationally-recognized *folklorico* and Latino music specialist in El Paso, Texas.

Appendix—
Hispanics Who Enrich America Today

This book's first edition, written in 1995, offered an impressive list of Hispanics in the public eye, but the list was not that difficult to compose. By contrast, this second edition faces such a multiplicity of examples that the following choices can be only representative. A few details before we begin: (1) Since accents are used inconsistently in contemporary Hispanic names, no accents will be used in this section, (2) details keep changing constantly, (3) errors are inevitable, and (4) selections will also require omissions. Apologies to all.

ARCHITECTURE

BERNARDO FORT-BRESCIA is head of Architectonia, one of the top architectural firms in the world, and SANTIAGO CALATRAVA is Spanish designer of the Milwaukee Museum of Art addition.

ART

John and Jane Livingston Beardsley listed and displayed these prominent Hispanic artists in the United States: CARLOS ALFONZO, CARLOS ALMARAZ, FELIPE ARCHULETA, LUIS CRUZ AZACETA, ROLANDO BRISENO, LIDYA BUZIO, IBSEN ESPADA, RUDY FERNANDEZ, ISMAEL FRIGERIO, CARMEN LOMAS GARZA, ROBERTO GIL DE MONTES, PATRICIA GONZALEZ, ROBERT GRAHAM, GRONK, LUIS JIMENEZ, ROBERTO JUAREZ, FELIX A. LOPEZ, GILBERT LUJAN, CESAR MARTINEZ, JESUS BAUTISTA MORELES, MANUEL NERI, PEDRO PEREZ, PARTIN RAMIREZ, ARNALDO ROCHE, FRANK ROMERO, PAUL SIERRA, LUIS STAND, LUIS TAPIA, and JOHN VALADEZ.

BEAUTY/FASHION

OSCAR DE LA RENTA, PALOMA PICASSO, CELIA TEJADA, ADOLFO AND CAROLINA HERRERA, WILLIAM TRAVILLA, ISABEL AND RUBEN TOLEDO, FERNANDO PENA, CARLOTS ALFARO, SUZANA MONACEALLA, ALFREDO CARAL, ROBERTO ROBLEDO, DINORAH DAO, MARIA RODRIGUEZ, MRIAMO ESPAILLAT, LUIS ARCHER, DOREEN RIVERA, HORTENSIA CISNERO, GISELLE BÜNDCHEN, NICK CHAVEZ, and ESTEVAN RAMOS. DENISE QUIÑONES (Puerto Rico) won the 2001 Miss Universe contest.

BUSINESS

HECTOR RUIZ is CEO of Advanced Micro Devices, world's second-largest chip maker; JOVITA CARRANZA is UPS regional president; MIRIAM LOPEZ is CEO of Transatlantic Bank in Miami; HENRY CISNEROS founded America City Vista which builds homes in inner cities in California and the Southwest; DAVID FUENTE is former CEO of Office Depot; ARTHUR C. MARTINEZ is former CEO of Sears, Roebuck and Co.; CARMEN BERMUDEZ founded and owns Tucson's Mission Management & Trust Co.; JOSEPH UNANUE founded Goya Foods, and ANDREW UNANUE is the CEO; FERNANDO FIGUEREDO is vice president of Lucent Technologies; CARLOS GUTIERREZ is CEO of the Kellogg Cereal Company; and ROSA SUGRAÑES is CEO of Iberia Tiles, largest independent distributor of ceramic tile, marble and stone in the Southwest.

CARTOONS

HECTOR CANTU and CARLOS CASTELLANO draw *Baldo* (Universal Press Syndicate); LALO ALCARAZ draws *La Cucaracha* (Universal Press Syndicate); PETER RAMIREZ draws *Raising Hector* (not yet syndicated but in over 20 newspapers); JOHN RIVAS draws *Bonzzo* (in Puerto Rico) and also draws for NASA); JAIME and GILBERT HERNANDEZ produced *Love and Rockets* (former comic book series), and now do the *Luba, Measles* and *Penny Century* series; PHIL ROMAN: worked with Disney on *Sleeping Beauty*, and now is animating for *Garfield, The Simpsons* and *King of the Hill.*; and *Speedy Gonzales* is on Cartoon Network.

CIRCUS

The ESPANA family is the heart of the Ringling Bros. and Barnum and Bailey flying trapeze show.

COMEDY

PAUL RODRIGUEZ is the best-known Hispanic comic, and he appears in stand-up club comedy, on television, and in film; JOHN LEGUIZAMO does stand-up routines off-Broadway and on Broadway, acts in several films, and is preparing a TV drama; PABLO FRANCISCO has appeared on Comedy Central; ADRIAN VILLEGAS performs a one-man show on national tour called Six Mexicans Named González; MIKE ROBLES hosts and co-produces the ¡Que Locos! Comedy Tour featuring the best Hispanic comics in the nation; and GEORGE LOPEZ is a screen writer and actor.

DANCE

AMALIA HERNANDEZ founded the Ballet Folklórico de México (d.1999); LYDIA DIAZ CRUZ founded the Ballet Concerto in Miami and is the main dancer with the National Ballet in Washington; EVELYN CISNEROS is the main dancer with the San Francisco Ballet; FERNANDO BUJONES is the principal dancer with the Boston Ballet; LOURDES LOPEZ is the principal dancer with the New York City Ballet; and JIMMY GAMONET DE LOS HEROS choreographes with the Miami City Ballet. See also Chapter 8 under "Dance."

DIPLOMACY

Out of 8,000 in the Foreign Service, only 340 Hispanics were listed a year or so ago. In the Department of State, out of 13,571 American employees, Hispanics number only 537. Hispanics make up 25 out of 685 among ambassadors and consuls general, 4 out of 99 Civil Service personnel. In the first edition of this book, only one Hispanic ambassador could be listed, CRECENCIO AREOS in Honduras. Today we find PETER F. ROMERO, Assistant Secretary of State for Western Hemisphere Affairs and former U.S. Ambassador to Ecuador; FRANK ALMAGUER, Honduras; STANLEY ESCUDERO, Azerbaijan; O.P. GARZA, Nicaragua; JAMES LEDESMA, Gabon, Sao Tome, and Príncipe; SIMON FERRO, Panama; PAUL CEJAS, Belgium; CAROLYN CURIEL, Belize; EDWARD L. ROMERO, Spain/Andorra; and ANTONIO GARZA JR., Mexico.

EDUCATION

JAIME ESCALANTE was depicted in the movie *Stand and Deliver* and was named The Best Teacher in America a decade ago; WILLIAM R. ANTON is the first Hispanic Superintendent of the Los Angeles Public School system; JOSEPH FERNANDEZ is former Chancellor of the New York City public school system; SABINE R. ULIBARRI was appointed a member of Spain's Royal Academy of the Spanish Language and is a professor at the University of New Mexico; AMERICO PAREDES is a Hispanic folklore scholar at the University of Texas at Austin; MIGUEL NEVAREZ is President of the University of Texas–Pan American; MARTA ISTOMIN is President of Manhattan School of Music and former Director of John F. Kennedy Center in Washington, D.C.; Rev. DAVID MALDONADO is the first Hispanic to be president of a United Methodist seminary, Iliff School of Theology in Denver; MARC CISNEROS is President of Texas A & M University; MARIO VARGAS LLOSA is Ibero-American Literature and Culture Chair in the Spanish and Portuguese Department, Georgetown University; and FELIPE ALANIS is the first Hispanic Commissioner of Education in Texas.

ENGINEERING

MARGARITA COMENARES is the first Latina elected to the Society of Hispanic Professional Engineers.

FINANCE

ALBERTO VILAR is a billionaire Wall Street invester in technology stocks; JULIE STAV is a stockbroker, financial planner, television speaker, and author; and ABEL GARCIA is head of United Service and Technology Fund.

FILM & THEATER

In the early silent films Hispanic stars were RAMON NAVARRO, ANTONIO MORENO, DOLORES DEL RIO, LUPE VELEZ and JOSE CRESPO.

In the decades after the twenties Hispanic stars were LUPITA TOVAR, ROSITA BALLESTEROS, CESAR ROMERO, ARTURO DE CORDOVA, PAUL MINI, DUNCAN RENALDO, PEARL CHAVEZ, CARLOS RAMIREZ, JOSE ITURBI, CARMEN MIRANDA, XAVIER CUGAT, MARIA CANDELARIA, MARIA MONTEZ, MARIA FELIX, FERNANDO LAMAS, PERRY LOPEZ, THOMAS GOMEZ, SARITA MONTIEL, RITA HAYWORTH (née CANSINO), KATY JURADO, LORENZO LAMAS, MIGUEL MATEO MAGUIELIN, PEDRO ARMENDARIZ, RAQUEL WELCH (née TEJADA), JAIME HERNANDEZ, ISELA VEGA, BARBARA CARRERA, HECTOR ELIZONDO, FERNANDO REY, EDDIE VELEZ, ROBERT BELTRAN, ANA ALICIA, DAPHNE ZUNIA, STEVEN BAUER, TRINA ALVARADO, ROSANA DE SOTO, ELIZABETH PENA, MAGALI ALVARADO, ROBBY ROSA, CHEECH MARIN and RACHEL TICOTIN.

In more recent times Hispanic stars were GILBERT ROWLANDS, JOSE FERRER, RITA MORENO, ANTHONY QUINN, RICARDO MONTALBAN, and IMOGENE COCA. Today Hispanic film stars are EDWARD JAMES OLMOS, MARTIN SHEEN (born RAMON ESTEVEZ), RAUL JULIA, LOU DIAMOND PHILLIPS, JIMMY SMITS, ANDY GARCIA, ESAI MORALES, CHARLIE SHEEN, EMILIO ESTEVEA, JESSE BOREGO, MARIA CONCHITA ALONSO, BENICIO DEL TORRO, JENNIFER LOPEZ, PENELOPE CRUZ, LANA PARILLA, MARISOL NICHOLS, CAMERON DIAZ, FREDDIE PRINZE JR., JON SEDA, MARIA DEL MAR, RITA MORENO, SALMA HAYEK, BENJAMIN BRATT, MARIA RIPOLI, ANTONIO BANDERAS, JOHN LEGUIZAMO, JAY HERNANDEZ, and LAURA ELENA HARRING.

Hispanic playwrights, screen writers, directors, and producers are LUIS BUNUEL, RAUL ESPARZA, EDUARDO MACHADO, OLIVIER MARTINEZ CARLOS MORTON, REINALDO PAVOD, MILCHA SANCHEZ-SCOTT, JOSE RIVERA, LYNNE ALVAREZ, REUBEN GONZALEZ, ROMOLO ARELLANO, TONY PLANA, JIMMY SANTIAGO BACA, GREGORY NAVA, HECTOR GALAN, MOCTESUMA ESPARZA, JOSE LUIS VALENZUELA, LUIS VALDEZ, CESAR ALEJANDRO, PEDRO ALMODOVAR, ROBERT RODRIGUEZ, ENRIQUE IGLESIAS, RODRIGO GARCIA, JOSEFINA LOPEZ, EMILIO ESTEVEZ, and PAUL ESPINOSA. See also Chapter 8, "Film" and "Theater."

GOVERNMENT/POLITICS

Hispanic members of the U.S. House of Representatives are Democrats SILVESTRE REYES, CIRO RODRIGUEZ, GRACE NAPOLITANO, JOE BACA, SOLOMON ORTIZ, JOSE SERRANO, ED PASTOR, JAVIER BECERRA, LUIS GUTIERREZ, ROBERT MENDENDEZ, LUCILLE ROYBAL-ALLARD, ROBERT UNDERWOOD, NYDIA VELASQUEZ, RUBEN HINOJOSA, LORETTA SANCHEZ, CHARLES GONZALEZ, CHARLES GONAZALEZ, ANIBAL ACEVEDO-VILA, and HILDA SOLIS. Republicans HENRY BONILLA, ILEANA ROS-LEHTINEN, and LINCOLN DIAZ-BALART.

Other Hispanics in government are ALBERTO R. GONZALES, White House counsel; ROSARIO MARIN, 41st U.S. Treasurer; JOSEFINA CARBONELL, leader in the Department of Health and Human Services; CARI DOMINGUEZ, head of the Equal Employment Opportunity Commission; HECTOR BARRETO, head of the Small Business Administration; MEL R. MARTINEZ, Secretary of Housing and Urban Development; SILA MARIA CALDERON, Governor of Puerto Rico; EDDIE PEREZ, first Hispanic mayor of Hartford, Connecticut.; GUSTAVO GARCIA, first Hispanic Mayor of Austin, TX; MANNY DIAZ, Mayor of Miami; ED GARZA, Mayor of San Antonio; GUADALUPE C. QUINTANILLA, first Hispanic named to the U.N.; FERNANDO FERRER, Bronx Borough President in New York City, defeated in race for mayor of the city; CARLOS RAMIREZ, former mayor of El Paso, currently Commissioner of the U.S. Section of the International Boundary and Water Commission; and in El Paso, Texas, Mayor RAY CABALLERO, four city representatives, County Judge DOLORES BRIONES, and two commissioners.

LABOR

LINDA CHAVEZ-THOMPSON, Executive Vice President of AFL-CIO, and DENNIS RIVERA, President of the Hospital Workers Union in New York.

LAW

MARGARITA ESQUIROZ, circuit court judge in Miami; MICHAEL OLIVAS, law professor and Associate Dean at University of Houston; JOSE CABRANES, Chief Judge of the U.S. District Court in Connecticut; RICHARD PAEZ, a judge of the Ninth U.S. Court of Appeals; JULIO FUENTES, judge of the Third Circuit of the U.S. Court of Appeals; NELSON A. DIAZ, first Puerto Rican admitted to Pennsylvania Bar and first Latino judge in Philadephia Court of Common Pleas; CESAR ALVAREZ: head of the 25th-largest law firm, named one of the 100 most influential lawyers in the country by the *National Law Journal,* and Lawyer of the Year by the Hispanic Bar Association.

LAW ENFORCEMENT

MARIA FERNANDEZ is an agent with the FBI; CARLOS LEON is Chief of Police in El Paso, Texas; LEO SAMANIEGO is Sheriff in El Paso County, with the department ranked among the best in the country; DANIEL RODRIGUEZ is a New York City police officer and popular singer of God Bless America after 9/11/01.

LITERATURE

Hispanic authors, among many, are RICARDO SANCHEZ, JIMMY SANTIAGO BACA, RUDOLFO ANAYA, OSCAR HIJUELOS, VICTOR VILLASEÑOR, RICHARD RODRIGUEZ, SANDRA CISNEROS, DENISE CHAVEZ, GUSTAVO PEREZ FIRMAT, ISABEL ALLENDE, PAT MORA, JUDITH ORTIZ COFER, and NICHOLASA MOHR. See also Chapter 8, "Literature."

MAGAZINES

RAMIRO FERNANDEZ is Associate Photo Editor at *People Magazine;* ANNA MARIA ARIAS owns *Latina Style,* first English-language magazine and only totally Hispanic-owned national magazine; CARLOS VERDECIA is an editor of *Hispanic* magazine; CHRISTY HAUBEGGER publishes *Latina* magazine; and CRISTINA SARALEGUI produces *Cristina la Revista.*

MATHEMATICS

JUAN MALDACENA, in theoretical physics, has united quantum mechanics with Einstein's general theory of relativity.

MEDICINE

ANTONIA NOVELLO, M.D., is former U.S. Surgeon General, now Health Commissioner of New York State; RICHARD CARMONA, M.D., is U.S. Surgeon General; CARMEN VAZQUEZ, M.D., is a New York psychiatrist; FRANKLIN GARCIA-GODAY, M.D., is editor of two dental journals and director of biomaterials research at Tufts University; RENE RODRIGUEZ, M.D., is an orthopedic surgeon and President of the Interamerican College of Physicians & Surgeons.

MILITARY

HORACIO RIVERO is former Vice-Chief of Naval Operations, Commander-in-Chief of allied forces in southern Europe, and then Ambassador to Spain; Maj. Gen. RICARDO SANCHEZ is Deputy Chief of Staff for U.S. Army in Europe; Maj. Gen. ALFRED VALENZUELA is the highest-ranking Hispanic Commander of U.S. Army Southern Command; Brig. Gen. MICHAEL J. AGUILAR is Deputy Commander, U.S. Marine Corps and Commanding

General of Fleet Marine Forces Southern Command; Brig. Gen. **BERNAR-DO NEGRETE,** is Assistant Division Commander (Support) for 82nd Airborne Division; and Pfc. **DOMINGO ARROY,** a 21-year-old Marine, was the first American killed in Somalia. Also see Congressional Medal of Honor awards in Chapter 10.

MODELING

CHRISTINE E. LEIVA, THERESA MARIE HARDY, TOM JAVIER GUAJARDO JR.; DOREEN RIVIRA: fashion fitter and booker for a New York modeling agency; **ELSA BENITEZ:** Mexican model and cover girl for 2001 swimsuit issue of *Sports Illustrated;* **YAMILA DIAZ-RAHI:** has appeared on the covers of *Elle, Glamour, Marie Claire* and *Harper's Bazaar,* in the 1999 Bathing Suit Edition of *Sports Illustrated,* and among the most beautiful persons in the June 1999 issue of *People Magazine.*

MUSIC

Hispanics in several fields of music are **LINDA MARIA RONSTADT, VIKKI CARR, JOAN BAEZ, GLORIA ESTEFAN, JOSE FELICIANO, BEN TAVERA KING, JON SECADA, CHRIS-TIAN AGUILERA, RICKY MARTIN, MARC ANTHONY, JENNIFER LOPEZ, ENRIQUE IGLESIAS, SHAKIRA, ALEJANDRO SANZ, LUIS MIGUEL, CELIA CRUZ, TITO PUENTE, EDDIE PALMIERI, CARLOS SANTANA, VICENTE FERNANDEZ, ELVIS CRESPO, THALIA, CHICO O'FARRILL, RUBEN BLADES, ATERCIOPELADOS** electric-rock duo, **EDUARDO "LALO" GUERRERO, EDNITA NAZARIO, CHEYANNE, SHALIM** and **PAULINE RUBIO.**

Those in classical music are **PEPE ROMERO** (classical guitarist), **EDUARDO MATA** (music director/conductor of the Dallas Symphony Orchestra), **ABRAHAM CHAVEZ** (former conductor of the El Paso Symphony Orchestra), and **SONIA MARIE DE LEON DE VEGA** (conductor of the St. Cecilia Orchestra in Los Angeles). See also Chapter 8, "Music."

NEWSPAPERS

LIZ BALMASEDA is a columnist for the *Miami Herald;* **LINDA CHAVEZ** is a syndicated columnist; **LIZETTE ALVAREZ** is congressional correspondent in the Washington bureau of the *New York Times;* **ROSSANA ROSADO** publishes *El Diario/La Prensa,* oldest Spanish language newspaper in the Northeast; **LIZA GROSS** is executive managing editor of *El Nuevo Dia* in Puerto Rico; and **MARIO GARCIA** is a top designer in the newspaper industry.

SCIENCE

LUIS ALVAREZ is a physicist who helped develop radar and the atomic bomb, receiving the Nobel Prize in 1968; **WALTER ALVAREZ,** with his father, **LUIS,** devised the asteroid impact theory on the extinction of dinosaurs;

SEVERO OCHOA is the biochemist who, in 1959, was the first Hispanic to win a Nobel Prize in Medicine for discovering the enzymes in nucleic acids and thus to synthesize RNA and DNA; NORBERTO ALVAREZ ROMO is an expert on artificial intelligence and director of a private cybernetic program for outer space; and PAUL SERENO, University of Chicago paleontologist, discovered one of the oldest dinosaurs, *hererasaurus*.

SPACE SCIENCE

FRANKLIN CHANG-DIAZ, first Hispanic astronaut, flew on the shuttle Columbia in 1986; ELLEN OCHOA, first Latina astronaut, flew on the Discovery space shuttle, and recently on the Atlantis space shuttle; SIDNEY GUTIERREZ flew on the Columbia Flight in '90 and Endeavor in '94; RAFAEL GARCIA is a top space researcher with NASA; HUMBERTO SANCHEZ is a specialist in space draft disaster rescue; and HECTOR DELGADO is lead engineer in the Systems Assurance office at John F. Kennedy Space Center in Florida.

SPORTS
Baseball:

In the past a proud, but lonely Hispanic made his presence felt in professional baseball—ROBERTO CLEMENTE, tragically killed in a plane crash in 1969. Other former Hispanic professional baseball players were ADOLFO LUQUE, MARTIN DIHIGO, LUIS APARICIO, ORESTES MIÑOSO, BETO AVILA, BERT CAMPANERIS, TONY OLIVA, LUIS TIANT, FELIPE ALOU, ORLANDO CEPEDA, ROD CAREW, WILLIE HERNANDEZ, AL LOPEZ, JUAN MARISHAL, AURELIO RODRIGUEZ, TONY PEREZ, LOU PINIELLA, JOE TORRE, ORLANDA CEPEDA, FERNANDO VALENZUELA, TONY PEREZ, RAFAEL "FELO" RAMIREZ, FELIPE ALOU, and BOBBY BONILLA.

Today in baseball we see, in Carlos Cortes's phrase, "the increasing Latinization of major league baseball." Hispanics have 40 percent of all players in the U.S., and three of the four highest-paid players are Hispanics. Twenty percent of all players come from Latin America. Two of the three highest paid athletes in baseball history are ALEX RODRIGUEZ and MANNY RAMIREZ. Other players are ROBERTO ALOMAR, MOISES ALOU, ROGER CEDEÑO, ERIC CHAVEZ, CARLOS DELGADO, ERUBIEL DURAZO, RAFAEL FURCAL, JUAN GONZALEZ, LUIS GONZALEZ, VLADIMIR GUERRERO, JUAN GUZMAN, LIVAN HERNANDEZ, JAVY LOPEZ, DENNIS MARTINEZ, IVAN MARTINEZ, PEDRO MARTINEZ, TINO MARTINEZ, MAGGLIO ORDOÑEZ, CARLOS PEÑA, SAMMY SOSA, OMAR VIZQUEL—and there are still more. The team with the highest number of Hispanics: New York Yankees (nearly half): ORLANDO "DUQUE" HERNANDEZ, LUIS POLONIA, MARIANO RIVERA, LUIS SOJO, ALFONSO SORIANO, JOSE VIZCAINO, BERNIE WILLIAMS and others.

Umpires are LAZARO DIAZ, ANGEL HERNANDEZ, and ALGONSO MARQUEZ.

Basketball:

Current Hispanic players are CEDRIC CEBALLOS, FELIP LOPEZ, and DANIEL SANTIAGO. A Hispanic referee is TOMMY NUÑEZ.

Boxing:

Former Hispanic boxers, among many others, are ALEXIS ARGÜELLO, WILFREDO BENITEZ, HECTOR "MACHO" CAMACHO, MICHAEL CARBAJAL, JULIO CESAR CHAVEZ, ROBERTO DURAN, CARLOS MONZON, ERIK MORALES, CARLOS ORTIZ, GABRIEL RUELAS and RAFAEL RUELAS, and SALVADOR SANCHEZ.

Current prominent Hispanic boxers are HECTOR "MACHO" CAMACHO JR., OSCAR DE LA HOYA (titles in five divisions), JOHN RUIZ, and FELIX TRINIDAD.

Football:

In the past Hispanics who excelled in professional football were LYLE ALZADO, TONY CASILLAS, MANDY FERNANDEZ, RAYMOND FLORES, TEDDY GARCIA, CARLOS HUERTA, ANTHONY MUÑOZ, JIM PLUNKETT, FUAD REVEIZ, RON RIVERA, and TONY, LUIS and MAX ZENDEJAS.

Today Hispanic players active in the NFL are ADAM ARCHULETA, STALIN COLINET, DAVID DIAZ-INFANTE, DONNIE EDWARDS, FRANK GARCIA, JEFF GARCIA, ROBERTO GARCIA, TONY GONZALEZ, MARTIN and BILL GRAMMATICA, JACQUEZ GREEN, MARCO RIVERA, MARIO RIVERA, O.J. SANTIAGO, and CHRIS VILLARRIAL.

Golf:

Professional Hispanic golfers are DAVID BERGANIO, ALICIA DIBOS, NANCY LOPEZ, JOSE MARIA OLAZABAL, ANTHONY RODRIGUEZ, JUAN "CHI CHI" RODRIGUEZ, and LEE TREVINO (no ñ in name).

Tennis

In the past Hispanic professional tennis players were RICHARD "PANCHO" GONZALES, RAFAEL OSUNA, MANUEL SANTANA, PANCHO SEGURA, and GUILLERMO VILAS.

Today Hispanic professional tennis players are ROSEMARY CASALS, MARY JOE FERNANDEZ, ROBERT GOMEZ, FLORENCIA LABAT, CONCHITA MARTINEZ, GABRIELA SABATINI. Those from other nations who play in the U.S. are SERGI BRUGUERA, ALBERTO COSTA, GUSTAVO KUERTEN, CONCHITA MARTINEZ, CARLOS MOYA, MARCELO RIOS, and ARANTXA SANCHEZ VICARIO.

Other Professional Sports:

Other Hispanics who have received recognition in professional sports are:

Gymnastics: TRENT DIMAS; **Hockey:** SCOTT GOMEZ and BILL GUERIN;

Martial Arts: MALIA BERNAL, GRACIELA CASILLAS, LILLY URQUIDEZ RODRIGUEZ, and BENNY URQUIDEZ; **Racing (car):** ADRIAN FERNANDEZ, ROBERTO GUERRERO, and JUAN MONTOYA; **Racing (horse):** JORGE CHAVEZ, ANGEL CORDERO, LAFFITT PINCAY JR., ALEX SOLIS, PAT VALENZUELA, and JORGE VELASQUEZ; **Racing (motorcycle):** ERNESTO FONSECA; **Skating:** RUDY GALINDO; **Soccer:** MARCELO BALBOA, MONICA GERARDO, HUGO PEREZ, TED RAMOS, and CLAUDIO REYNA; **Swimming:** WENDY LUCERO and PABLO MORALES.

TELEVISION:

The pioneers in TV had Latino lead roles in *The Cisco Kid, High Chaparral, Zorro,* and *I Love Lucy.* Stars were LINDA DARNEL, ERIC ESTRADA, CHEECH MARIN, RICARDO MONTALBAN, CESAR ROMERO, and ELENA VERDUGO. DESI ARNAZ invented the three-camera technique that changed TV programing.

Today Latinos starring in highly rated television shows are ESAI MORALES *(NYPD Blue),* FRANKIE MUÑIZ *(Malcolm in the Middle),* ANTHONY RUIVIVAR *(Third Watch),* CHARLIE SHEEN *(Spin City),* MARTIN SHEEN *(The West Wing),* and WILMER VALDERRAMA *(That '70s Show).* TV shows with Latino casts are: *The Sopranos, Resurrection Blvd., Dora the Explorer, Dark Angel* (JESSICA ALBA), *Taína, The Brothers Garcia, American Family* (EDWARD JAMES OLMOS, RAQUEL WELCH, SONIA BRAGA, CONSTANCE MARIE, ESAI MORALES, and A.J. LAMAS, directed by GREGORY NAVA), and *The George Lopez Show* (GEORGE LOPEZ).

Other TV personalities are HECTOR ELIZONDO, NELY GALAN, ANTONIO MORA *(Good Morning America* newsman), RITA MORENO, MARISOL NICHOLS, ANA MARIA OROZCO *(Betty La Fea),* JOHN QUIÑONES and GERALDO RIVERA (news correspondents), CRISTINA SARALEGUI (#1 talk show on Spanish TV), JIMMY SMITS, and RAY SUAREZ (PBS interviewer).

ZOOS

MANUEL MOLLINEDO is Director of the Los Angeles Zoo.

Bibliographic References

"Abortion, Pill, Handguns, Death Penalty: The Hispanic View." *Vista*. November 2000: 28.

Acosta-Belén, Edna. "From Settlers to Newcomers: The Hispanic Legacy in the United States." *The Hispanic Experience in the United States. Contemporary Issues and Perspectives*. Ed. Edna Acosta-Belén and Barbara R. Sjostrom. New York: Praeger, 1988.

Acuña, Rodolfo. *Occupied America. The Chicano's Struggle Toward Liberation*. San Francisco: Canfield Press, 1972.

Adauto, Alina, Jerome Ballard, Victor Manuel Correa and Linda Tarín. "A Hispanic Girl's Coming of Age." *Borderlands. Border Customs and Crafts*. Students of El Paso Community College. Spring 1992: 14-15. Supplement to the *El Paso Times*.

Alfaro, Juan. *La Semana Santa*. San Antonio: Mexican American Cultural Center, 1977.

Allen, John L. Jr. "Maybe He Isn't Real but He's Almost a Saint." *National Catholic Reporter*. 25 January 2002: 3.

Allis, Sam et al. "Whose America?" *Time*. 8 July 1991: 12-17.

Allsup, Dan. "Saluting Hispanics in Uniform." *Vista*. October 2000: 24-25.

Alvarado, Jesús. "The Magic of Mariachis." *Borderlands. Border Customs and Crafts*. Students of El Paso Community College. Spring 1992: 8-9. Supplement to the *El Paso Times*.

Americanos: Latino Life in the U.S./La Vida Latina en los Estados Unidos. Boston: Little Brown & Co., 1999.

"America's Secret Weapon: Gen. Bernardo de Gálvez." Editorial in *El Paso Times*. 22 July 1992: B 5.

Anaya, Rodolfo. *Bless Me, Ultima: A Novel*. Berkeley, CA: Tonatiuh International, Inc., 1972.

Anders, Gigi. "Top 10 Cities for Hispanics." *Hispanic*. August 2002: 20-30.

Apostolides, Alex. Personal conversation and materials from the Western Epigraphic Society, 1984 meeting in Albuquerque, NM.

Aranda, Charles. *Dichos: Proverbs and Sayings from the Spanish*. Santa Fe: Sunstone Press, 1977.

Arreola, Daniel D., and James R. Curtis. *Mexican Border Cities: Landscape Anatomy and Place Personality. Tucson: University of Arizona Press, 1994*

Artze, Isis. "To Be and Not to Be." *Hispanic*. October 2000: 32-34.

Associated Press. "Hispanic Nation along Border Is Inevitable, Professor Says." *El Paso Times*. 1 February 2000: B 4.

Atwater, Henry F. "Adobe: Still Going Strong." *Vista*. 9 July 1991: 8. Supplement in the *El Paso Times*.

Axtell, Roger E. *Gestures: Do's and Taboos of Body Language around the World*. New York: John Wiley and Sons, Inc., 1991.

Balido, Giselle. *Cubantime, A Celebration of Cuban Life in America*. New York: Silver Lining Books, 2001.

Bannon, John Francis. *The Spanish Borderlands Frontier, 1513–1821*. Albuquerque, NM: University of New Mexico Press, 1963, 1974.

The Barnhart Dictionary of Etymology. Ed. Robert K. Barnhart. New York: H.W. Wilson, 1988.

Barnouw, Victor. *An Introduction to Anthropology. Vol.1. Physical Anthropology and Archaeology*. Homewood, IL: The Dorsey Press, 1971.

Beardsley, John and Jan Livingston. *Hispanic Art in the United States*. New York: Abbeville Press, 1987.

Belejack, Barbara. "Looking for America." *The Texas Observer*. 21 August 1991: 17-18.

Bennati, Mary. "Curandierismo. Herbs, Folk Healers Still Meet Health Care Needs." *El Paso Times*. 23 September 1984: E 1.

_____. "Chicano Struggle Depicted in Artwork." *El Paso Times*. Insert "El Tiempo": 21 August 1992: 8-9.

Bentley, Harold W. *A Dictionary of Spanish Terms in English*. New York: Columbia University Press, 1932.

Bernardo, Stephanie. *The Ethnic Almanac*. Garden City, NJ: Doubleday and Col, Inc., 1981.

Bezick, Denise. "Day of the Dead Reaches Back to Aztec Roots." *El Paso Times*. 1 November 1992: B 1.

Bixler-Márquez, Dennis J. "Communication and Education Trends along the U.S.-Mexico Border." *Mexican-American Spanish in Its Societal and Cultural Contexts*. Ed. Dennis J. Bixler Márquez, Jacob L. Ornstein-Galicia, and George K. Green. Brownsville, TX: The University of Texas-Pan American at Brownsville, in cooperation with the University of Texas at El Paso, 1989: 205-208.

Borelli, Janet. "Flamenco: Festival Features Fiery Footwork." *New Mexico Magazine*. June 1999: 30-35.

Borrero, Antonia Marta. "Honor Our African Roots." *Hispanic*. April 2000.

Borunda, Daniel. "Selena: Documentary Details Slain Singer's Impact on Hispanics." *El Paso Times*. 6 July 1996: D 1,4.

Brame, Florence. "Day of the Dead Celebrates Spiritual Tradition," *Borderlands: Border Customs and Crafts*. Produced by students at El Paso Community College. Spring 1991: 1-16. Supplement in the *El Paso Times*.

Briggs, Kenneth. "Hispanics' Role in Tomorrow's Church Unclear." *National Catholic Reporter*. 14 July 1989: 19-21.

Brioso, César. "Latinos Swing into the Majors." *Hispanic*. April 2001: 45-50.

Brookhiser, Richard. "The Melting Pot Is Still Simmering." *Time*. 1 March 1993: 72.

Brown, Dee. *The Gentle Tamers. Women of the Old Wild West*. New York: Bantam Books, 1958: 111-112, 200.

Brown, Nancy. "The Price of Freedom." *Vista*. 7 July 1992: 22-25. Adapted and abridged from *Spanish Aid to American Independence*, Spanish History Museum, Albuquerque. Supplement in the *El Paso Times*.

Burciaga, José Antonio. *Weedee Peepo. A Collection of Essays/Una colección de ensayos*. Edinburg, TX: Pan American University Press, 1988.

Butler, Ron. "The Latin Charlie Chaplin, Cantínflas." *El Paso Times*. 11 February 1991: C 1,3.

_____. "Viva Tequila." *El Paso Times*. 6 January 1991: F 1-2.

Cabeza de Vaca, Alvar Núñez. *Relation of Nuñez Cabeza de Vaca*. Ann Arbor: University Microfilm, Inc., 1966.

Cabeza de Vaca, A.N. *Náufragos y comentarios*. Madrid: Taurus, 1969 Eng. trans.: *Adventures in the Unknown Interior of America*. New York: Collier Books, 1961.

Camacho, María. "Vietnam Hero Gets Overdue Recognition." *Hispanic*. April 2000: 48.

Campa, Arthur L. *Hispanic Culture in the Southwest*. Norman, OK: University of Oklahoma Press, 1979, 1993.

Campbell, Joseph. *The Power of Myth*. Ed. Betty Sue Flowers. New York: Doubleday, 1988.

Campos, Anthony John, trans. and ed. *Mexican Folk Tales*. Tucson, AZ: The University of Arizona Press, 1989.

Camposantos. A photographic essay by Dorothy Enrimo, commentary by Rebecca Salsbury James, and historical notes by E. Boyd. Fort Worth: Amon Carter Museum of Western Art, 1966.

Cantú, Hector D. "With Selena, Mainstream Latino Culture Came to Light." *El Paso Times*. 28 March 1999: F 1.

Caraway, Nancy. "Holes in the Melting Pot." *In These Times*. September 1992: 18.

Carrasco, David, Editor in Chief. *The Oxford Encyclopedia of Mesoamerican Cultures: The Civilizations of Mexico and Central America*. New York: Oxford: University Press, 2001.

Carrol, Nicole. "Chilehead Heaven." *El Paso Times*. 26 April 1992: F 1-2.

_____. "For Many, It's Culture vs. Health Care." *El Paso Times*. 18 October 1992: F 6.

_____. "Underware, Outer Wear Chiles." *El Paso Times*. 26 April 1992: F 1-2.

Caturla de la Maza, Olga. *Todo el mar para mis sueños/All the Sea for My Dreams: Colección de poesía/Poetry Collection*. Las Cruces, NM: Two Eagles Press International, 2001.

Castañeda, Laura. "Witches Thrive in Mexico." *El Paso Times*. 22 June 1991: D 1.

Castelli, Jim. "Lessons from the '60s, '70s on the New Multiculturalism." *National Catholic Reporter*. 18 October 1991:3.

Castillo, Ana, ed. *Goddess of the Americas: Writings on the Virgin of Guadalupe*. New York: Riverhead Books, 1996.

Castro, Janice. "Spanglish Spoken Here." *Time*. 11 July 1988: 53.

_____. "Latino Voices: What Are They Saying?" *Vista*. 9 February 1993: 10-11.

Castro, Rafaela G. *Chicano Folklore: A Guide to the Folktales, Traditions, Rituals and Religious Practices of Mexican Americans*. Oxford: Oxford University Press, 2001.

Catalano, Julia. *The Mexican Americans*. New York: Chelsea House Publishers, 1988.

Cervantes Saavedra, Miguel. *Don Quixote of La Mancha*. Trans. and ed. Walter Starkie. New York: Mentor Book/New American Library, 1957: Part II, chap.2, page 213.

Chan, Linda S. et al. *Maternal and Child Health on the U.S. Mexico Border. Special Project Report*. Lyndon B. Johnson School of Public Affairs, The University of Texas at Austin, 1987.

Chapman, Charles E. *A History of California*. New York: Macmillan Co., 1939.

Chávez, César. Speech Chávez had prepared to present to farm workers and supporters in Delano, California, on March 10, 1968 after his three-week fast. From Ed. Senator Robert Torricelli and Andrew Carroll, *In Our Own Words: Extraordinary Speeches of the American Century*. Ed. New York: Washington Square Press/Pocket Books, 1999: 272.

Chávez, Joh. *The Lost Land: The Chicano Image of the Southwest*. Albuquerque: University of New Mexico Press, 1984.

Chavez Leyva, Yolanda. "Honor Political Activism This Month." *El Paso Times*. 8 October 2000: A 11.

Chevigny, Hector. *Russian America. The Great Alaskan Adventure. 1741-1867*. Portland, OR: Binford and Mort Publishing, 1965: 48-124, 1890-185.

Christian, Chester C. "Sociocultural Contexts of Texas Spanish: Personal Encounters." *Mexican-American Spanish in Its Societal and Cultural Contexts*. Ed. Dennis J. Bixler Márquez, Jacob L. Ornstein-Galicia, and

George K. Green. Brownsville, TX: The University of Texas-Pan American at Brownsville, in cooperation with the University of Texas at El Paso, 1989: 124-129.

Cinisomo, Vincent. "Los Yanquis: Latino Players Are at the Heart of America's Team." *Hispanic*. October 2000: 45, 48.

Cisneros, José. *Borderlands: The Heritage of the Lower Rio Grande through the Art of José Cisneros*. Co-author Felix D. Almaráz and others. Edinburgh, TX: Hidalgo County Historical Museum, 1998.

_____. Cisneros 2000: Faces of the Borderlands. Foreword by Tom Lea, Leon Metz, John Hauser and John West. Co-author Felix D. Almaráz. El Paso: Sundance Press, 1999.

_____. *Riders across the Centuries. Horsemen of the Spanish Borderlands*. El Paso: Texas Western Press, University of Texas at El Paso, 1984. 2nd Printing 1988.

Clark, Kenneth. *Civilisation: A Personal View*. New York: Harper & Row, Publishers, 1969.

Cocks, Jay. "Of Ghosts and Magic." *Time*. 2

Collier, Virginia P. *Promoting Academic Success for ESL Students*. Jersey City, NJ: New Jersey Teachers of English to Speakers of Other Languages-Bilingual Educators, 1995.

Condon, John C. *Good Neighbors: Communicating with the Mexicans*. Intercultural Press, Inc., 1985.

Connover, Ted. *Coyotes: A Journey through the Secret World of America's Illegal Aliens*. New York: Vintage Books, 1987: 257.

Conway, Jim. "Wounded Benavidez Saved Eight Lives." *El Paso Times*. 4 December 1988: A 1.

Conway, William. "Mexican Spirituality: Flesh and Bone." *National Catholic Reporter*. 29 October 1982: 11,14.

Cordova, Kathryn M. "Buenos Días, Ahem, Good Morning! Bilingual Education Is Under Attack throughout the Country." *Hispanic*. May 2001: 34-35.

_____. "Righting a Wrong for Padre Martínez." *La Herencia*. Spring 2002: 20-21.

Córdova, Lynn, et al. "Tempting Sweet Breads, Pan de Dulce." *Borderlands: Border Customs and Crafts*. Produced by students at El Paso Community College. Spring 1991: 16. Supplement in the *El Paso Times*.

Cortés, María. "Ballet. Folklórico de México" in "El Tiempo." Supplement in *El Paso Times*. 23 August 1991: 1, 6-7.

Courant, Harford. "Get a Grip on Hugging." *El Paso Times*. 18 July 1991: D 1.

Craven, Margaret. *I Heard the Owl Call My Name*. New York: Dell Publishing Co., 1973.

Crenshaw, John. "Chile--New Mexico's Fiery Soul." *The Best from New Mexico's Kitchens*. Ed. Sheila Mac Niven Cameron. Santa Fe: *New Mexico Magazine*, 1987.

Crowell, Pers. *Cavalcade of American Horses*. New York: Bonanza Books, 1951.

Cummings, Margo. "Hispanic Heritage Month, September 15-October 15." *Hispanic*. September 1990: 10-11.

Dallas, Paloma. "The Big Apple's Mexican Face." *Hispanic*. July/August, 2001: 30-34.

Daniggells, Paul Dean. *Rodant Pel Mon with Urbici Soler, Sculptor 1890-1953*. El Paso: International Association for the Visual Arts, 1995.

D'Antonio, William V. "Latino Catholics: How Different?" *National Catholic Reporter*. 29 October 1999: 19.

Davis, Cary, Carl Haub, and Jo Anne Willette. "U.S. Hispanics: Changing the Face of America." *The Hispanic Experience in the United States. Contemporary Issues and Perspectives*. Eds. Edna Acosta-Belén and Barbara R. Sjostrom. New York: Praeger, 1988.

Davis, Mike. *Magical Urbanism: Latinos Reinvent the U.S. City.* London: Verso, 2000.

Deagan, Kathleen A. "La Isabela, Europe's First Foothold in the New World." *National Geographic.* January 1992: 40, 53.

Delgado, Eduardo."U.S. Flag in Heart." Letter to the Editor. *El Paso Times.* 29 August 1997.

Della Cava, Marco R. "Columbus, the Controversy." *El Paso Times.* 4 February 1991: C 1,3.

DellaFlora, Anthony. "Artistic Dance." *Albuquerque Journal.* 28 May 2000: F 1.

Dias, César. "To Mend Rift, U.S. Church Needs to Embrace Gifts of Latinos." *National Catholic Reporter.* 22 March 2002:30-33.

Díaz, Katharine. "In Service to Their Nation: Latinos Give Their All." *Vista.* November 1996: 18, 22.

Díaz, Rose and Jan Dodson Barnhart, eds. "The Domínguez-Escalante Expedition, 1776: Precursor of the Old Spanish Trail." *Hispanic Heroes. Portraits of New Mexicans Who Have Made a Difference.* Albuquerque: Starlight Publishing Co., 1992: 5.

DiMeglio, Steve. "El Paso Kids Tell Congress of Colonias." *El Paso Times.* 17 March 2000: A 1-2.

Dismuke, Kiane. "It's Beautiful to Be Bilingual." *NEA Today.* April 1991: 10-11.

Drabanski, Emily, ed. "Chile! Fiery Lore! Hot Trends! Spicy Recipes!" *New Mexico Magazine.* Special issue on chile. February/March 1996.

Duarte, Patricia. "Latinas of Influence." *Vista.* January/February 2000: 14, 28-30.

_____. "In the Eyes of the Beholder?" *Vista.* January/February 2001: 6,8.

Ehrenreich, Barbara. "Teach Diversity—with a Smile." *Time.* 8 April 1991: 84.

Eickhoff, Randy Lee. *Exiled: The Tigua Indians of Ysleta del Sur.* Plano, TX: Republic of Texas Press/Wordware Publishing, Inc., 1996.

Elliott, Michael. "From Davos to New York." *Time.* 4 February 2002: 72.

Elizondo, Virgilio. *Christianity and Culture.* San Antonio: Mexican American Cultural Center, 1975, 1983.

_____. *Galilean Journey.* Maryknoll: Orbis Books, 1985.

_____. *La Morenita.* San Antonio: Mexican American Cultural Center, 1980.

Estrada, Mary Betts. "Arroz con Pollo." *Hispanic.* September 1989: 62.

Estrada, Richard. "Benavidez Personified Patriotism." *El Paso Times.* 7 December 1998: A 11.

Etzioni, Amitai. "Inventing Hispanics: A Diverse Minority Resists Being Labeled." *Brookings Review.* The Brookings Institution, Washington, DC., 10-13.

Evans, Tom and Mary Anne. *Guitars. Music, History, Construction and Players from the Renaissance to Rock.* New York: Facts on File, 1949, 1977.

Fabian. "One World." *Teaching Tolerance.* Poster by a six year-old boy from Brooklyn, NY. Fall 2001: 65.

Fagan, Brian M. *The Aztecs.* New York: W.H.Freeman and Co., 1984.

Farley, Christopher John. "Latin Music Pops." *Time.* 24 May 1999: 74-79.

_____, ed. "Music Goes Global." *Time.* Special issue. Fall 2001.

Fauntleroy, Gussie. "Los Matachines." *New Mexico Magazine.* December 1998:44-51.

_____. "Family Chapels." *New Mexico Magazine.* 69-75. December 1999.

"The First Explorers: Father Junípero Serra." *Hispanic.* April 1991: 50.

Flores, Juan. *From Bomba to Hip-Hop: Puerto Rican Culture and Latino Identity.* New York: Columbia University Press, 2000.

Flynn, Ken. "Genuine Guayaberas." *El Paso Herald-Post.* 8 September 1974: A 3.

Fontana, Bernard L. *Entrada: The Legacy of Spain and Mexico in the United States.* Tucson: Southwest Parks and Monuments Press, 1994.

Forrest, James A. "Census 2000: The Plus and Minus for Hispanics." *Vista.* May 2001: 23.

Forrest, Suzanne. *The Preservation of the Village: New Mexico's Hispanics and the New Deal.* Ed. John R. Van Ness. *New Mexico Land Grant Series.* Albuquerque: University of New Mexico Press, 1989.

Fuentes, Annette. "Latinas Deserve More from Schools." *El Paso Times.* 6 February 2001: A 7.

Fugate, Francis. *Spanish Heritage in the Southwest.* El Paso: Texas Western Press, 1952.

Gann, L.H. and Peter J. Duignan. *The Hispanics in the United States. A History.* Boulder, Co: Westview Press, 1986.

García, Guy. "Food That Bites Back." *Time.* 16 November 1992: 11.

García, Mario T. *The Making of a Mexican American Mayor, Raymond L. Telles of El Paso.* El Paso: Texas Western Press, The University of Texas at El Paso, 1998.

Gardner, Mark L. "Tragedy in Taos: Bloody Rebellion of 1847 Haunts New Mexico's History." *New Mexico Magazine.* October 2000: 30 37.

Garza-Falcom-Sánchez, Leticia. "Railroaded in California: Reclaiming a Heritage." *The Texas Observer.* July 16, 1993: 19-20.

Gehrke, Robert. "Hispanic School-age Population Fastest-growing, Report Says." *El Paso Times.* 20 June 2002: A 4.

Geijerstam, Claesaf. *Popular Music in Mexico.* Albuquerque: University of New Mexico Press, 1976.

Gibbs, Nancy. "Welcome to Amexica." *Time.* Special issue on the U.S.-Mexico Border. 11 June 2001.

Gómez Fushille, Isabel. "Letter to the Editor." *El Paso Times.* 23 September 2001: A 10.

Gómez, Marisa. "Tortillas—Border Staff of Life." *Borderlands: Border Customs and Crafts.* Produced by students at El Paso Community College. Supplement in the *El Paso Times.* Spring 1991, 1-16.

Gómez, Roberto L. "Mestizo Spirituality: Motifs of Sacrifice, Transformation, Thanksgiving, and Family in Four Mexican American Rituals." *Apuntes.* Winter 1991: 86.

González, Juan. *Harvest of Empire: A History of Latinos in America.* New York: Viking Press, 2000.

González, Justo. *Mañana: Christian Theology from a Hispanic Perspective.* Nashville: Abinddon Press, 1990: 58-74.

González, Manuel G. *The Hispanic Elite of the Southwest.* Southwestern Studies Series No. 86: El Paso: Texas Western Press, 1989.

González, María Cortés. "Conflicts and Quinceañeras." *El Paso Times.* 16 June 1995: E 1-2.

Gordon, Linda. *The Great Arizona Orphan Abduction.* Boston: Harvard University Press, 1999.

Graedon, Joe and Dr. Teresa Graedon. "Review of Research Finds No Chile-Cancer Connection." *El Paso Times.* 5 September 1994: D 4.

Graham, William C. "Old World Gain Was New World's Mixed Blessing Author Says." *National Catholic Reporter.* Newspaper interview with author Newton Frohlich. 9 November 1990: 1.

Granados, Christine. "A New Poll Finds That the Term 'Hispanic' Is Preferred." *Hispanic.* December 2000: 39-41.

Green, George K. and Lino García Jr. "Domain-Related Lexical Borrowing in the English and Spanish of South Texas." *Mexican-American Spanish in Its Societal and Cultural Contexts.* Eds. Dennis J. Bixler-Márquez, Jacob L. Ornstein Galicia, and George K. Green. Brownsville, TX: The University of Texas-Pan American at Brownsville, in cooperation with The University of Texas at El Paso, 1989: 77-85.

Grisham, John. *The Testament.* New York: Dell Publishing/Random House, Inc., 1999: 110-101, 111.

Guadalupe Hidalgo: Treaty of Peace and the Gadsden Treaty with Mexico, 1853.

Reprinted from New Mexico Statutes 1963. Annotated Vol.1. Truchas, NM: Tate Gallery and Rio Grande Sun Press, Española, NM, 1967.

Guerro, Andrés. *A Chicano Theology*. Maryknoll: Orbis Books, 1987.

Guerrero, Rosa. *Tapestry*. Film produced by the El Paso Public Schools, 1972.

Gutiérrez, José Angel. "The Making of a Chicano Militant: Lessons from Cristal." Review by Dick J. Reavis. *The Texas Observer*. 10 December 1999:27, 29.

Hadley-García, George. *Hispanic Hollywood. The Latins in Motion Pictures*. New York: Carol Publishing Co., 1990.

Haddox, John. "Los Chicanos. An Awakening People." Southwestern Studies. Monograph No.28. El Paso: Texas Western Press, 1970.

Hamm, Elizabeth Catanach. "Roy Tachias: Life in Cabezón: A Character Builder." *New Mexico Magazine*. December 2001: 22.

Havel, O'Dette. "Day of the Dead." *El Paso Times*. 21 October 1988: D 1.

_____. "Zarzuelas Still Sizzle with Ageless Passions." *El Paso Times*. 7 October 1990: F 1-2.

Hazen-Hammond, Susan. "Make a Ristra: Decor That's Good Enough to Eat." *New Mexico Magazine*. September 1995: 48-53.

Judith A. Hellman. *Mexican Lives*. New York: The New Press, 1994.

Hernández, Frances. "The Secret Legacy of Christopher Columbus in the Southwest." *Password*. The El Paso Historical Society, Summer 1990: 55-70.

Hernández, Molly and Martha Becher. "Cockfights Legal in Surrounding Areas." *Borderlands: Border Customs and Crafts*. Produced by students at El Paso Community College. Supplement in *El Paso Times*. Spring 1993: 4.

Hernández Russi, Roberto. "Por Acción Meritoria." *Vista*. 5 November 1991: 12. Supplement in *El Paso Times*.

Hernandez, Roger. "Americanization Takes Toll on Traditional Hispanic Family Values." *El Paso Times*. 24 February 1991: G 2.

_____. "Just How, Exactly, Does a Hispanic Look? That's Hard to Say." *El Paso Times*. 12 August 1991: B 2.

_____. "Hispanic, Latino Debate Rooted in Political Correctness." *El Paso Times*. 24 January 1995: A 4.

_____. "Culture Clash: Latino Dads and Teens." *Vista*. June 1995: 6, 8.

_____. "U.S. Can Accept Puerto Rico." *El Paso Times*. 6 March 1998: A 1.

_____. "The Celtic Side of Hispanics." *El Paso Times*. 19 March 1999: A 11.

_____. "Hispanic Covers More Than Latino." *El Paso Times*. 25 June 1999: A 15.

_____. "Spanglish Threatens Spanish." *El Paso Times*. 8 September 2000: A 9.

_____. "Wrong: Hispanics Not a Race." *El Paso Times*. 22 September 2000: A 11.

Hevrdejs, Judy. "Tortillas Are on a Roll." *El Paso Times*. 6 March 2002: D3.

"Hispanic Heritage Month." *Hispanic*. September 1989: 74-80.

Hispanics in American History through 1865. Vols 1 and 2. Englewood Cliffs, NJ: Globe Book Co., 1989.

"Housing Market Mistreats Minorities." *El Paso Times*. 31 August 1991: A 1.

Hughes, Robert. "Heritage of Rich Imagery." *Time*. 11 July 1988: 62-64.

_____. "Onward from Olmec." *Time*. 15 October 1990.

"The Immigrants: Myths and Reality." *Intelligence Report, Blood on the Border: The Anti-immigration Movement Heats Up*. The Southern Poverty Law Center Special Annual Report. Spring 2001.

Hyman, Eric. "Metaphor, Language, Games, Cultures." *Reflections on Multiculturalism*. Ed. Robert Eddy. Yarmouth, MA: Intercultural Press, Inc., n.d., 47–62.

Isaacson, Philip M. *The American Eagle*. Boston: New York Graphic Society, 1975.

Ivins, Molly. "So Long to Henry B." *The Texas Observer*. 8 December 2000: 4.

Jacquez-Ortiz, Michele. "Salud de la Gente." *La Herencia del Norte*. Winter 1995: 43.

Jamail, Milton H. *Full Count: Inside Cuban Baseball*. Carbondale and Edwardsville, IL: Southern Illinois University Press, 2000.

Jasso, Heidi. "Santo Niño de Atocha Called Miracle Worker." *Borderlands: Border Customs and Crafts*. Produced by students at El Paso Community College. Spring 1993: 10. Supplement in *El Paso Times*.

Juan Nepomuceno Seguin (1806-1890). The Seguin Family Historical Society link. The West Film Project and WETA by Lifetime Learning Systems. *http://www.alamo-de-parras.welkin.org/history/bios/seguin.html*.

Johnson, Susan Lee. "Roaring Camp: The Social World of the California Gold Rush." Book review by Cathy Corman. In *The Texas Observer*. 28 September 2001: 16-17, 21.

Jones, Arthur. "Clinic Reports Relate Stories, Facts, Figures." *National Catholic Reporter*. 29 September 2000: 4.

Jones, E. Stanley. *A Song of Ascents*. Nashville: Abingdon Press, 1968: 128-129.

The Journal of Alvar Núñez Cabeza de Vaca. Trans. Fanny Bandelier. Chicago: The Rio Grande Press, Inc., 1905, 1965.

The Journal of the American Medical Association, July 2002. Quoted in Melissa Martínez, "Care Fails Hispanics, Study Says." *El Paso Times*. 4 July 2002: A-1-2.

Kay, Margarita. "Research Needs in Chicano Spanish for Health Care." *Mexican-American Spanish in Its Societal and Cultural Contexts*. Eds. Dennis J. Bixler-Márquez, Jacob L. Ornstein Galicia, and George K. Green. Brownsville, TX.: The University of Texas-Pan American at Brownsville, in cooperation with the University of Texas at El Paso. 1989: 61-67.

Keck, Benjamin. "Rio Grande Labeled a 'Cesspool.'" *El Paso Times*. 21 April 1993: A 1-2.

Kluckhohn, Clyde. *Mirror for Man. A Survey of Human Behavior and Social Attitudes*. New York: Fawcett World Library, 1944, 1967.

Kong, Deborah. "Study Shows Reliance on Undocumented Workers." *El Paso Times*. 22 March 2002: A 4.

_____. "For Some Hispanics, Islam Offers Answers." *El Paso Times*. 17 June, 2002: A 4.

Kozol, Jonathan. *Amazing Grace: The Lives of Children and the Conscience of a Nation*. New York: Crown Publishers, Inc., 1995: 180-181.

Kramer, Mark. "U.S.-Mexican Border, Life on the Line." *National Geographic*. June 1985: 720-749.

Kras, Eva. *Modernizing Mexican Management Style: With Insights for U.S. Companies Working in Mexico*. Las Cruces, NM: Editts...Publishing, 1994.

Krythe, Maymie R. *What So Proudly We Hailed: All About American Flag, Monuments and Symbols*. New York: Harper & Row, 1968.

Kusel. "Tamales: They're Hot No Matter How You Wrap Them." *New Mexico Magazine*. December 1999: 40-45.

LaFarelle, Lorenzo G. "Contributions of the Spanish in Our History." *El Paso Times*. 28 December 1992: B 1.

_____. *Bernardo de Gálvez: Hero of the American Revolution*. Austin, TX: Eakin Press, 1992.

_____. "El 5 de Mayo de 1862." Unpublished manuscript.

_____. "El 5 de Mayo—the 5th of May." Unpublished manuscript.

"La Llorona." *Dictionary of Folklore, Mythology and Legend*. 2 vols. Ed. Maria Leach, New York: Funk & Wagnalls Co., 1950.

Landa, Victor. "Benavídez Becomes Action Hero." *El Paso Times*. 4 September 2001: A 7.

Lara-Braud, Jorge. "Podemos creer en Dios después de esto?" *Apuntes*. Spring 1993: 73-85.

Larson, Vicki. "The Flight of the Faithful." *Hispanic*. November 1990: 18-24.

Lauber, Patricia. *Cowboys and Cattle Ranching Yesterday and Today*. New York: Thomas Y. Crowell, Co., 1973.

Lechuga, Frank S. "Mexican American 'Conspiracy' Incites Citizens Group." *Albuquerque Journal*. 12 July 1997: A 11.

Lee, Harper. *To Kill a Mockingbird*. Philadelphia: J.B. Lippincott Co., 1960.

Lemonick, Michael D. "Before Columbus." *Time*. 19 October 1998: 76 78.

Levy, Bernard. *Present-Day Spanish*. 3rd ed. New York: Holt, Rinehart and Winston, 1940, 1970.

Lewis, Oscar. *The Children of Sánchez: The Autobiography of a Mexican Family*. New York: Vintage Books/Random House, 1961.

_____. *Five Families: Mexican Case Studies in the Culture of Poverty*. New York: The New American Library/A Mentor Book, 1959.

_____. *La Vida: A Puerto Rican Family in the Culture of Poverty—San Juan and New York*. New York: Vintage Books/Random House, 1965, 1966.

Liddell, Marlane A. "Roots of Rhythm." *Smithsonian*. November 2001.

Lira, Solange de Azambuja, and Arnold Gordenstein. "The 'Other' before Me: A Bicultural Dialogue." *Reflections on Multiculturalism*. Ed. Robert Eddy. Yarmouth, MA: Intercultural Press, Inc., n.d., 177-190.

López Torres, Humberto. "Christopher Columbus, Self-Taught Geographer." *Voices of Mexico*. October-December 1992: 19-26.

"Los Mineros." *The American Experience #312*. Narr. David McCullough. Written and directed by Héctor Galán. Public Broadcasting System. KCOS-TV, El Paso, Texas. 28 January 1991.

Lowenberg, Denise. "Cutting Out Fat? Don't Throw Out Mexican Recipes." *El Paso Times*. 28 April 1993: D 1.

Lucas, Isidro. *The Browning of America*. Chicago: Fideo Claretian, *1981*.

Lyon, Eugene. "Search for Columbus." *National Geographic*. January 1992: 2-39.

Machamer, Gene. *Hispanic American Profiles*. New York: One World/Ballantine Books, 1993, 1996.

Maldonado, David. "Hispanic Protestantism: Historical Reflections." *Apuntes*. Spring 1991: 3-16.

Manchester, Ann and Albert. "Huachas Spin Out." *New Mexico Magazine*. August 1995.: 20.

Mares, E.A."Tony." "Duende and the Divine Comedy." *New Mexico Magazine*. February/March 1996: 38-41.

Marriott, Alice. *The Valley Below*. Norman: University of Oklahoma Press, 1949.

Martin, Judith and Thomas K. Nakayama. *Intercultural Communication in Contexts*. Mountain View, CA: Mayfield Publishing Co., 1997.

_____. *Whiteness: The Communication of Social Identity*. Thousand Oaks, CA: Sage Publications:1999.

Martínez, Arlene. "Poll Raises Questions about Hispanics." *El Paso Times*. 9 August 2001: A 7.

Martínez, Demetria. "Hispanics and the Church: A Minority No More." *National Catholic Reporter*. 2 November 1990: 1, 12-14.

_____. "Sánchez Renames Ancient 'La Conquistadora' Statue." *National Catholic Reporter*. 14 August 1992: 3.

Martinez, Melissa. "Crazy over Chiles." *El Paso Times*. 30 August 1998: F 1,8.

_____. "The Root of the Problem." *El Paso Times*. 26 June 2000: D 1, 6.

Martínez, Oscar J. *Border People: Life and Society in the U.S.-Mexico Borderlands*. Tucson: The University of Arizona Press, 1994, 1998.

_____. *Mexican-Origin People in the U.S.: A Topical History*. Tucson: The University of Arizona Press, 2000.

Martínez, Rubén. "The Undocumented Virgin." *Goddess of the Americas. Writings on the Virgin of Guadalupe*. Ed. Ana Castillo. New York: Riverhead Books, 1996.

Martinez, Victor R. "Zoot Suit Revolution." *El Paso Times*. 5 February 2002: D 1-2.

_____. "Sweet Words." *El Paso Scene*. 20 March 2002: D 1.

Martínez, Willie. "Guayabera-Embroidered Shirt Has Many Names." *El Paso Herald-Post.* 18 October 1983: A 8.

Marty, Martin E. *Pilgrims in Their Own Land: 500 Years of Religion in America.* Boston: Little, Brown & Co., 1984: 18-99.

Maya, Sr. Teresa. "The Powerful Influence of 'the Guadalupe Event' Endures." *National Catholic Reporter.* 26 October 2001: 34-35.

McCarty, Frankie. *Land Grant Problems in New Mexico.* Albuquerque Journal, 1969.

McCullough, L.E. "The Tejano Sound." *Vista.* Supplement in *El Paso Times.* 10 September 1988: 16-17.

McPhilomy, Janis and José Luís Guzman. "Looking Back at the Chile Pepper." *Borderlands: Border Customs and Crafts.* Produced by students at El Paso Community College. Spring 1991: 9. Supplement in *El Paso Times.*

McWilliams, Carey. *North from Mexico.* New York: Greenwood Press, Publishers, 1968.

Meir, Matt S. *Mexican American Biographies. A Historical Dictionary, 1836-1987.* New York: Greenwood Press, 1988.

Meketa, Jacqueline Dorgan. *Legacy of Honor: The Life of Rafael Chacón, Nineteenth-Century New Mexican.* Albuquerque: Yucca Tree Press, 2000.

Menard, Valerie. "Top Ten Cities for Hispanics." *Hispanic.* July/August, 2000: 28-35.

Merced, Monica. "Faithful Make Cristo Rey Trek." *El Paso Times.* 1 November 1999: B 1.

Metz, Leon. *Border. The U.S.-Mexican Line.* El Paso, TX: Mangan Books, 1989.

_____. "Treaty's Imperfections Can't Hide Promise of Equal Rights." *El Paso Times.* 11 February 1998: D 3.

_____. "Does El Paso Not See Big Picture?" *El Paso Times.* 17 October 1998: A 13.

"Mexican Machismo Coming upon Rough Times, Experts Find." *El Paso Times.* 6 October 1991: A 1.

Mihalik, Maria. "Fiery Goods Cremate Calories." *Everyday Health Tips. 2000 Practical Hints for Better Health and Happiness.* Ed. Debora Tkac. Emmaus, PA: Rodale Press, 1988.

Miller, Mark Charles. *Coyote Cafe: Foods from the Great Southwest.* Berkeley, CA: Ten Speed Press, 1989.

Miller, Tom. *On the Border. Portraits of America's Southwestern Frontier.* New York: Harper & Row, 1981.

Monárez Díaz, Paula. "Red Hot Relief." *El Paso Times.* 21 January 1995: C 1.

Montoya, Joe. "Santos Norteños." *La Herencia del Norte.* Fall 2000:59.

Moore, S. Derrickson. "The Saints Go Marching." *New Mexico Magazine.* December 1999: 83-85.

Morales, Ed. "All That Latin Jazz." *Vista.* 20 May 1989: 68. Supplement in the *El Paso Times.*

Morganthau, Tom. "America: Still a Melting Pot?" *Time.* 9 August 1993: 16-23.

Morín, Raúl. *Among the Valiant Mexican Americans in World War Two and Korea.* Alhambra, CA: Borden Publishing Co., 1966.

Morison, Samuel Eliot. *The Oxford History of the American People.* New York: Oxford University Press, 1965.

Morris, John Miller. *From Coronado to Escalante: The Explorers of the Spanish Southwest.* New York: Chelsea House, 1992.

Morrow, Lance. "The Search for Virtues." *Time.* 7 March 1994: 78.

Moyers, Bill. "Trading Democracy." *Bill Moyers Reports.* Public Broadcasting System. KCOS, cable channel 12, 5 February 2002.

Munar, Barbara. "Holy Hot Mole!" *Borderlands: Border Customs and Crafts.* Produced by students at El Paso Community College. Spring 1991: 8. Supplement in *El Paso Times.*

Muñoz, Agustín Mateos. *Etimologías latinas del español*. México, D.F.: Editorial Esfine, S.A., 1980.

Nakayama, Thomas K. and Judith N. Martin. *Whiteness: The Communication of Social Identity*. Thousand Oaks, CA: Sage Publications, 1999.

National Immigration Forum. "Unity in Diversity," Rev. by Rob Paral. Washington, D.C., 1999.

Navarro, Tomás. *Studies in Spanish Phonology*. Miami Linguistic Series No. 4. Trans. Richard D. Abraham. Coral Gables, FL: University of Miami Press, 1969.

Nelhaus, Arlynn. "Spotlight on New Mexico's Secret Jews." *San Francisco Chronicle* from the *Jerusalem Post*. 7 November 1991: A 7.

Nelson, Robert. "Religious Treasures." *El Paso Times*. 12 October 1991: D 1.

_____. "Artist Sculpts New Life into Oñate." *El Paso Times*. 29 December 1991: F 1,7.

_____. "Latino, Chicano Exhibit: A Parallel Heritage." *El Paso Times*. 14 February 1992: 2-3.

_____. "El Paso Festival Comparable to Shakespeare." *El Paso Times*. 6 March 1991. El *Tiempo: 3*. Supplement in *El Paso Times*.

Nichols, John. *The Milagro Beanfield War*. New York: Holt, Rineholt and Winston, 1974

Novas, Himilce. *Everything You Need to Know about Latino History*. New York: Penguin Books/Plume, 1994.

Novello, Antonia. "Surgeon General Urges Action on Hispanic Issues." Interview in *El Paso Times*. 24 April 1993: A 10.

Nuestra Señora de Guadalupe. Mother of God. Mother of the Americas. Exhibition marking the 500th anniversary of the encounter of two cultures. Curated by Dr. Edwin E. Sylvest Jr. Elizabeth Perkins Prothro Galleries, Bridwell Library, Perkins School of Theology, Southern Methodist University, Dallas, Texas. 25 July-September, 1991.

Olsson, Karen. "The View from Outside." *The Texas Observer*. 9 November 2001: 8-9, 13.

Olvera, Joe. "Veteran Feels Cheated out of Medal of Honor." *El Paso Times*. 8 August 1988: A 1-2.

_____. "Carlos Rosas' Mural Brings Pride to South Side." *El Paso Times*. 14 May 1989: F 4.

_____. "Children Are the Ones Who Suffer in Families Plagued by Macho." *El Paso Times*. 5 April 1992: G 4.

_____. Choosing a Life in the Chile Fields." *El Paso Times*. 20 September 1992: B 1.

_____. "Machismo Is Deadly, Clinic Says." *El Paso Times*. 10 August 1993: A 1.

_____. "Martyred Journalist Blazed Trail for Other Chicanos." *El Paso Times*. 25 August 1991: G 4.

_____. "Ancient Contest of Huachas Finds New El Paso Fans." *El Paso Times*. 23 July 1993: A 1-2.

Ornstein-Galicia, Jacob L. "The Sociolinguistic Status of a U.S. Mexico Border Caló." *Mexican-American Spanish in Its Societal and Cultural Contexts*. Eds. Dennis Bixler-Márquez, Jacob L. Ornstein-Galicia, and George K. Green. Brownsville, TX: The University of Texas-Pan American at Brownsville, in cooperation with the University of Texas at El Paso.

Orosco, Cynthia, and Suriá Santana. "How the Hispanic Agenda Shapes Up." *El Paso Times*. 30 November, 2000: A 11.

Ortega. "Latin Music Isn't New, but Now It Sells." *El Paso Times*. 12 July 2000.

Ortega, Peter Ribera. *Christmas in Old Santa Fe*. Santa Fe: Ancient City Book Shop, 1961.

Ortego, Philip D., ed. "Folklore." *We Are Chicanos: An Anthology of Mexican-American Literature*. New York: Washington Square Press/Pocket Books, 1973: 32-35.

Otto, May. "Surveys: Hispanic Voters' Concerns Same As Everyone Else's." *El Paso Times.* 17 September 1999: A 5.

Pacheco, Ana, ed. *La Herencia del Norte.* Issue on the National Cultural Center of New Mexico. Fall 2000.

Padilla, Maria T. "Spanish Surnames Increase in Popularity." *El Paso Times.* 1 January 2000: D 1.

Pantoja, Segundo. "Church, Community and Identity: Latinos' Experiences with Religious New York." *Apuntes.* Summer 2002: 64-79.

Paredes, Américo. *With His Pistol in His Hand.* Austin: University of Texas Press, 1958.

Pavia, Audrey. "An American Icon." *Horse Illustrated.* April 1998: 56-62.

_____. "Pure Spanish Horse." *Horse Illustrated.* August 1998: 48 54.

Paz, Octavio. Essay in John Beardsley and Jan Livingstone. *Hispanic Art in the United States.* New York: Abbeville Press, 1987: p.13.

_____. *The Labyrinth of Solitude. Life and Thought in Mexico.* Trans. Lysander Kemp. New York: Grove Press, Inc. 1961

Pedraja, Luis G. "A New Vision: Ministry through Hispanic Eyes." *Apuntes.* Summer 1996: 51-58.

Perez, Miguel. "Anniversaries Mark Latino History." *El Paso Times.* 5 August 1998: A 7.

_____. "Assimilation Is Not Cultural Surrender." *El Paso Times.* 29 July 1999: A 9.

Perrigo, Lynn I. *Hispanos: Historic Leaders in New Mexico.* Santa Fe, NM: Sunstone Press, 1985.

Peterson, Houston, ed. *A Treasury of the World's Great Speeches.* New York: Simon & Schuster, 1954.

Pierce, Ellise. "Chile Rush." *Southwest Airlines Spirit.* September 1997: 54-59, 146-151.

Pillsbury, Dorothy. *No High Adobe and Adobe Doorways.* Albuquerque: University of New Mexico Press, 1950, 1952, 1971.

Pimentel, O. Ricardo. "Census Shows Changing America." *El Paso Times.* 19 March 2001: A 7.

Poudevida, Antonio Raluy. *Historia de la lengua castellana.* 2nd ed. Mexico, D.F.: Editorial Patria, 1951, 1966.

Prescott, William H. *History of the Conquest of Mexico and History of the Conquest of Peru.* New York: Random House/The Modern Library, n.d.

Quiñones-Ortiz, Javier. "The Mestizo Journey: Challenge for Hispanic Theology." *Apuntes.* Fall 1991: 62-72.

Quintanilla, Michael. "Border Nourishes Distinctive Types of Religious Rites." *El Paso Herald-Post.* 4 August 1983: A 7.

Rafael, Hermes. *Orígen historia del mariachi.* Mexico: Editorial Katun, 1982.

Ramírez, Arnulfo G. "Spanish in the United States." *The Hispanic Experience in the United States. Contemporary Issues and Perspectives.* Eds. Edna Acosta-Belén and Barbara R. Sjostrom. New York: Praeger, 1988.

Ramos, Henry A.J. *The American G.I. Forum: In Pursuit of the Dream, 1947-1983.* Houston: Arte Público Press, University of Houston, 1998.

Raphael, Kathleen. "Herbal Essence: The Roots of Natural Healing Extend Deep in New Mexico." *New Mexico Magazine.* May 1996: 28-31.

Reid, T.R. "The New Europe." *National Geographic.* January 2002: 32-47.

Reith, John W. Ed. *California and the West.* Grand Rapids, MI: The Fideler Co., 1963.

Remas, Theodora A. "Keeping Guayabera Cool." *Americas.* January-February 1987: 37-39.

Renteria, Ramon. "No Hablo Español! Hispanics Fight Stereotypes Based on Skin Color, Surnames." *El Paso Times.* 11 November 1997: D 1,4.

_____. "Crypto-Judaism; 'Secret Jews' Try to Find Their Roots, New Place in Society." *El Paso Times.* 8 May 1998: D 1,4.

_____. "Bert Corona Left Legacy of Struggle." *El Paso Times*. 21 January 2001: A 11.

Rice, John. "Objection Raised to Juan Diego's Canonization." *El Paso Times*. 5 December 1999: A 18.

Rios, Elena. "Hispanic Health Needs Are Critical." *El Paso Times*. 6 September 2000: A 9.

Rittman, Dan, Lisa M. Carrascoi, and Roxanne J. Salazar. "Wedding Traditions on the Border." *Borderlands Border Customs and Crafts*. Students of El Paso Community College. Spring 1992: 16. Supplement in *El Paso Times*.

Rivera-Pagán, Luis N. "Discovery and Conquest of America: Myth and Reality." *Apuntes*. Winter 1989: 82.

Rizzo, Holly Ocasio. "Greeting the Real Millennium: Year-End Celebrations Highlight Hispanic Culture." *Hispanic*. December 2000:30-32.

Robinson, Linton H. *Mexican Slang, A Guide*. Campo, CA: Bueno Books, 1992, 1994, 1996.

Rocard, Marcienne. *The Children of the Sun: Mexican Americans in the Literature of the United States*. Trans. Edward G. Brown Jr.. Tucson: University of Arizona Press, 1989.

Rodríguez, Armando M. "Who Is La Raza?" *A Documentary History of the Mexican Americans*. Ed. Wayne Moquin with Charles Van Doren. New York: Praeger Publishers, Inc., 1971, 1972: 494 498.

Rodríguez, Raymond. "Catholic Church Ignores Its Latinos." *El Paso Times*. 3 January 1999: A 9.

Rodríguez, Roberto and Patrisia Gonzales. "Little Recognition for Latina Heroine of NM Labor Battle." *El Paso Times*. 16 October 1994: G 2.

_____. "Mexico's Rich African Legacy Still Flourishes Today." *El Paso Times*. 5 March 1996: A 4.

Roiz, Carmen Teresa. "Hispanic Woman and Man of the Century." *Vista*. January/February 2000: 6, 7, 12.

Romero, Mary Ann and Carlos. *Los Bilingos*. Santa Fe: Sunstone Press, 1976.

Rosins, Olga, Belinda Mendoza, and Christine Castro. "Piñatas." *Borderlands. Border Customs and Crafts*. Students of El Paso Community College. Spring 1992: 4. Supplement in *El Paso Times*.

Rotstein, Arthur H. "Arizona Sees Illegal Immigration, Drug Woes." *The Albuquerque Tribune*. 23 February 2002: A 4.

Said, Sally E. "Restandardization of Spanish in the Hispanic Press." *Mexican-American Spanish in Its Societal and Cultural Contexts*. Eds. Dennis J. Bixler-Márquez, Jacob L. Ornstein Galicia, and George K. Green. Brownsville, TX: The University of Texas-Pan American at Brownsville, in cooperation with the University of Texas at El Paso, 1989. 87-94.

Sais, Melissa W. "Spanish Barbs." *New Mexico Magazine*. June 2001:39-41.

Salazar, Ana María. "Wanted: Latino Role Models. Educated Hispanic Professionals Need to Step Up." *Hispanic*. September 2000:118.

Salopek, Paul. "Curandismo." *El Paso Times*. 9 March 1989: D 1.

_____. "Soup of Toxins Simmers in Rio Grande." *El Paso Times*. 15 May 1991: A 1, 4.

Samora, Julian, and Patricia Vandel Simon. *A History of the Mexican-American People*. Rev. ed. Notre Dame: University of Notre Dame Press, 1977, 1993.

Sandos, James A. "Junípero Serra's Canonization and the Historical Record." *American Historical Review*. December 1988: 1253 1257.

Sandoval, Frederick. "Compadrazgo Extends the Family Unit." *La Herencia del Norte*. Summer 1995: 38-39.

_____. "Jacal: An Earlier Form of Architecture." *La Herencia del Norte*. Spring 1995: 42.

Sandoval, Ricardo. "'Machismo' May Rule, but Female Vote Can Slap Back." *El Paso Times*. 26 March 2000:A 10.

Sands, Kathleen Mullen. *Charrería Mexicana*. Tucson: The University of Arizona Press, 1994.

Sanoff, Alvin P. "The Myths of Columbus." *U.S. News and World Report*. 8 October 1990: 74.

Schlesinger Jr., Arthur. "The Cult of Ethnicity, Good and Bad." *Time*. 8 July 1991: 21.

Schrambling, Regina. "Say Sí to Salsa." *Vista*. 9 June 1992: 6-9. Supplement in *El Paso Times*.

Sedeno, David, and Laurence Iliff. "Church Makes Juan Diego a Little Less Indian." *El Paso Times*. 9 March 2002: A 2.

Self, Beradette. "Statue Will Remind Us of the Cruelties." *El Paso Times*. 31 August 2001: A 12.

Sentinel, Orlando. "Doctors Call Peppers Potent Pain Relievers." *El Paso Times*. 13 February 1995: D 4.

Sexton, R.W. *Spanish Influence on American Architecture and Decoration*. New York: Brentano's, 1927.

Shenkman, Richard. *Legends, Lies, and Cherished Myths of American History*. New York: Harper & Row, 1988.

Shepherd, William R. "The Spanish Heritage in America." *A Documentary History of the Mexican Americans*. Ed. Wayne Moquin with Charles Van Doren. New York: Praeger Publishers, Inc., 1971-1972: 349-353.

Sheppard, David. "Culture Can Influence Care in Terminal Cases." *El Paso Times*. 23 August 1996: B 1.

Shirley, Carl R. and Paula W. Shirley. *Understanding Chicano Literature*. Columbia, SC: University of South Carolina Press, 1988.

Siefried, Stephen. "El Morro National Monument." *New Mexico Magazine*. August 1990: 14-15.

Silva, Guadalupe. "Bolillos." *El Paso Times*. 31 July 1985: C 1.

_____. "Posadas, Piñatas and Pageants." *El Paso Times*. 18 December 1993: D 1-2.

_____. "Cultural Influences Affect Holidays." *El Paso Times*. 6 January 1998: A 6.

_____. "Rosh Hashana Signals Renewal." *El Paso Times*. 10 September 1997: D 1.

_____. "Mexican-Americans Celebrate Legacy." *El Paso Times*. 5 October 1999: A 6.

Simmons, Marc. *The Last Conquistador: Juan de Oñate and the Settling of the Far Southwest*. Norman, OK: University of Oklahoma Press, 1991.

_____. "Quincentenary Celebration Is No Time for Undeserved Slander of Columbus." *El Paso Times*. 9 December 1990: B 8.

_____. "NM Played Integral Part in War with Spain." *El Paso Times*. 20 January 1991: B 6.

_____. "NM Governor Hoped to Fight over Mesilla." *El Paso Times*. 19 March 1991: B 3.

_____. "Territorial Governor Wrestled with Pardons." *El Paso Times*. 2 June 1991: B 6.

Sinkovec, Jerry. "Mystery Dance." *Hispanic*. September 1991: 58, 60.

Slonimsky, Nicolas. *Music of Latin America*. New York: Thomas Y. Cromwell Co., 1945.

Smith Jr., Griffin. "The Mexican Americans, A People on the Move." *National Geographic*. June 1980: 780-809.

Smith, Michael E. *The Aztecs. The People of America Series*. Cambridge, Mass.: Blackwell Publishers, 1996: 260-302.

Sonnichsen, C.O. *Pass of the North: Four Centuries on the Rio Grande*. El Paso: Texas Western Press, 1968.

"Spain in the Americas" and "The Great Exchange." Map insert for *National Geographic*. Ed. Willima Graves. February 1992.

The Spanish Land Grant Question Examined. The Alianza Federal de Mercedes. Albuquerque, 1966: 19.

Stamm, James R. *A Short History of Spanish Literature*. Garden City, NY: Doubleday & Co., Inc., 1967.

Stavans Ilan. "Coming to Terms with 'Latino' and 'Hispanic.'" In *These Times*. 8-21 July 1992: 6.

_____. *Latino USA: A Cartoon History*. Illustrated by Lalo Alcaraz. New York: Basic Books, 2000.

Steiner, Stan. "Jewish Conquistadores, America's First Cowboys." *America West*. September/October, 1983: 31-35.

Stevens-Arroyo, Anthony. "Juan Mateo Guaticabanú: The First to Be Baptized in America." *Apuntes*. Fall 1996: 67-77.

Sylvest, Edwin E. Jr. "Rethinking the Discovery of the Americas: A Provisional Historico-Theological Reflection." *Simposio I. Redescubrimiento: Five Centuries of Hispanic American Christianity. 1492-1992*. Hispanic Instructor Program, Mexican American Program, Perkins School of Theology, Southern Methodist University. Dallas: 16-18 January 1987.

Talbert, Frank X. *A Bowl of Red*. Dallas: Taylor Publishing Co., 1953, 1962, 1966, 1972, 1988: 20-21, 34-35.

Tate, Bill. *The Penitentes of the Sangre de Cristos: An American Tragedy*. Española, NM: Rio Grande Sun, 1966.

Tatum, Charles ed. *Mexican American Literature*. Orlando, FL: Harcourt Brace Jovanovich, 1990.

Teltsch, Kathleen. "Scholars and Descendants Uncover Hidden Legacy of Jews in Southwest." *New York Times*. 11 November 1990: Y 16.

Timmons, W.H. *El Paso. A Borderlands History*. El Paso: Texas Western Press, 1990.

Toor, Frances. *A Treasury of Mexican Folkways*. New York: Crown Publishers, 1947.

Torres, Eliseo. *The Folk Healer. The Mexican-American Tradition of Curanderismo*. Kingsville, TX: Nieves Press, n.d.

_____. *Green Medicine, Traditional Mexican-American Herbal*. Kingsville, TX: Nieves Press, n.d.

Trejos, Gonzalo Chacón. *Costa Rica es distinta en Hispano América*. San José: Imprenta Trejos Hnos., 1969.

Treib, Marc. *Sanctuaries of Spanish New Mexico*. Berkeley: University of California Press, 1993.

Tseng, Timothy, and David Yoo. "The Changing Face of America." *Sojourners*. March/April 1998: 26-29.

Ulibarri, Sabine R. "Cultural Heritage of the Southwest." *We Are Chicanos*. New York: Pocket Books/Simon & Schuster, Inc., 1973: 114-20.

Unamuno, Miguel de. *The Spanish Christ. Essays and Soliloquies*. New York: Alfred A. Knopf, 1925: 81.

_____. *The Tragic Sense of Life*. Trans J.E. Crawford Flitch. London: Dover Publications, 1954: 310.

Urrea, Luis Alberto. *Vatos. A Poem*. Photographs by José Galvez. El Paso: Cinco Puntos Press, 2000.

U.S.-Mexico Border: Issues and Challenges Confronting the United States and Mexico. United States General Accounting Office, Report to Congressional Requesters. July 1999.

Valdez, Diana A., Terry-Azíos, and Ana Radelat. "Leading Ladies." *Hispanic*. June 2000.

Valdez, Joyce. "Hispanic Soldiers Played a Notable Role in the Civil War." *Hispanic*. May 2001: 84.

Vasconcelos, José. *La raza cósmica: misión de la raza ibero americana*. Madrid: Aguilar, S.A. Di ediciones, 1961. Trans. Edward E. Barber. Original manuscript. June 26, 1972.

Valdez, Diana Washington. "Group Asks Inquiry into Newsman's Death." *El Paso Times*. 8 June 1995: B 1,4.

_____. "Three Kings Day Ends Holidays Sweetly." *El Paso Times*. 6 January 2000: B 1.

Vigil, Antonio. *Una Linda Raza: Cultural and Artistic Traditions of the Hispanic Southwest*. Golden, CO: Fulcrum Publishing, 1998.

Vigil, Antonio S. *The Coming of the Gringo and the Mexican American Revolt*. New York: Vantage Press, 1970.

Villanueva, Victor. "Literacy, Culture, and the Colonial Legacy." *Reflections on Multiculturalism*. Ed.Robert Eddy. Yarmouth, MA: Intercultural Press, Inc., n.d., 79-96.

Villaseñor, Victor. *Rain of Gold*. New York: Dell Publishing/ Bantam Doubleday Dell Publishing Group, Inc., 1991.

Walker, Dale L. *The Boys of '98: Theodore Roosevelt and the Rough Riders*. New York: A Forge Book/Tom Doherty Associates, Inc., 1998.

Walker, Hollis. "Diary Opens Another Page in History of Santa Fe Trail." *New Mexico Magazine*. May 1994: 44-51.

Walker, Theresa. "Piñatas Hit U.S. Heartland." *El Paso Times*. 19 January 1999: D 3.

Wall, Dennis. "Chimayó Weavers: Hispanic Tradition Flourishes in Valley." *New Mexico Magazine*. November 1995: 40-47.

Walters, Keith. "Chinks and Woolies." *The Western Horseman*. May 1986: 102-103.

Watson, Julie. "Border Saint: Mexico's Migrants Seek Saint's Protection." *El Paso Times*. 14 December 2001: D 1,5.

Weber, David J. *Myth and the History of the Hispanic Southwest*. Albuquerque: University of New Mexico, 1988.

Weil, Andrew. *Natural Health, Natural Medicine*. Boston: Houghton Mifflin Co., 1990.

West, John O. *Mexican-American Folklore, Legends, Songs, Festivals, Proverbs, Crafts, Tales of Saints, of Revolutionaries, and More*. Little Rock: August House, 1988.

"What Do the Bishops Say about Immigration?" *Annunciation House Newsletter*. Spring 1998: 5

"What's Hot?" *Santa Fe Visitors Guide, 1999*. Santa Fe foods glossary, 1999: 80.

Whitman, Walt. "Walt Whitman's View of the Spanish Element in the American Nationality." *A Documentary History of the Mexican Americans*. Ed.Wayne Moquin with Charles Van Doren. New York: Praeger Publisher, Inc. 1971: 296-298.

Will, George. "Education Reform Taking Hold." *El Paso Times*. 31 January 2001: A 7.

Williams, Stanley T. *The Spanish Background of American Literature*. New Haven: Yale University Press, 1955.

Wirpsa, Leslie. "Hispanic Trends Create Pastoral Puzzles." *National Catholic Reporter*. 2 December 1998: 6-7.

Yared, Roberta. "Cool Down Heartburn with Red Hot Jalapeños." *AARP Bulletin*. June 2000: 19.

Zehtab, Mitra. "Keeping Hispanics Healthy the Latino Way." *Vista*. November 1995: 18.

"Zoot Suit Riots." *American Experience*. Public Broadcasting System. KCOS, cable channel 12, 10 February 2002.

Index

N

Author & Contributors

Richard C. Campbell has served as a United Methodist pastor in Michigan and northern New Mexico, chaplain at church-related Lydia Patterson Institute, and in retirement as a teacher and community volunteer in El Paso, Texas. He writes monthly articles for *El Paso Scene*, anticipates writing other books, and doing more community service. His wife, Patricia, has recently retired as bilingual teacher in the El Paso Independent School District. *Two Eagles in the Sun* is his first major publication.

Joe Olvera is a free-lance journalist and creative writer whose columns currently appear in 60 newspapers across the country. He is also a published writer of poetry, fiction, and drama. Born and reared in an El Paso barrio, he was the first Chicano reporter on El Paso TV (Channel 4, CBS) in 1971. In 1985 he ran third in a race for mayor of El Paso. He has worked with Quinto Sol Publications and for 10 years was a newspaper columnist, six of those years with the *El Paso Times*. He works now with the Aliviane drug program.

Adair Margo is a fourth generation El Pasoan who founded Adair Margo Gallery in 1985. She recorded the oral history of famed Texas artist Tom Lea and edited *Tom Lea, An Oral History,* published by Texas Western Press. Adair Margo served as Chairman of the Texas Commission on the Arts and in 2001 was appointed by President George W. Bush as Chairman of the President's Committee on the Arts and Humanities. She also serves on the board of the U.S./Mexico Fund for Culture.

Hal Marcus is an El Paso artist with Arabic and Judaic multicultural heritage. His murals hang in the El Paso Chamizal National Memorial, the El Paso Library, the El Paso Public Library, and Temple Mt. Sinai in El Paso. His Hal Marcus Gallery in downtown El Paso is a center for displaying his own art and also that of other local artists needing a venue for their works.

José Cisneros is an El Paso artist well-known for his detailed, authentic pen-and-ink drawings of Spanish conquerors, commoners, and horses. He has illustrated over 100 books, articles, maps, and seals. Born in Mexico, he became a refugee in the U.S. during the Mexican Revolution. He briefly attended Lydia Patterson Institute. One hundred of his works are on permanent display at the University of Texas at El Paso Library. His works are reproduced in *Riders Across the Centuries: Horsemen of the Spanish Borderlands,* which has received national and regional awards. His life has been portrayed in *Cisneros: An Artist's Journey,* by Dr. John O. West, a life-long friend. He has been honored with awards from Spain and across the United States, most recently receiving the National Humanities Award from President Bush.

Gabriel Sánchez is a resident of Cd. Juárez, Mexico, and a graduate of Lydia Patterson Institute in 1987. He graduated from the University of Texas at El Paso with a Bachelor of Science in Civil Engineering (with honors) and an M.S. in Business Administration. He runs a successful building supply business in Cd. Juárez.